PEARL HARBOR: FINAL JUDGEMENT

PEARL HARBOR: FINAL JUDGEMENT

**HENRY C. CLAUSEN
AND
BRUCE LEE**

DA CAPO PRESS

Cataloging-in-Publication data is available from the Library of Congress.

This Da Capo paperback edition of *Pearl Harbor: Final Judgement* is an unabridged republication of the edition first published in 1992. It is reprinted by arrangement with the authors.

First Da Capo Press edition 2001
ISBN 0–306–81035–2

Published by Da Capo Press
A Member of the Perseus Books Group
http://www.dacapopress.com

1 2 3 4 5 6 7 8 9—05 04 03 02 01

A wit once said:

> *"Behind every successful man stands
> a surprised mother-in-law."*

*But it was no surprise that Virginia was my devoted
wife and loyal companion in my endeavors.*

To her I lovingly dedicate this volume.

‖ CONTENTS

PREFACE: PEARL HARBOR GHOSTS

It is believed by many that the most revealing investigation into the proximate causes of Pearl Harbor was conducted by the late Henry C. Clausen, the special investigator appointed by Secretary of War Henry Stimson and co-author of this book. Clausen's original report became volume 35 of the Pearl Harbor hearings. His report had no conclusion, however, for reasons of national security. This book is that missing conclusion in which Clausen found that on at least eleven occasions Admiral Husband E. Kimmel withheld from General Walter S. Short vital intelligence information that, if it had been passed along properly, might have caused Short to go on a full war alert prior to the Japanese attack.

Clausen also discovered that the Naval command at Pearl Harbor had withheld vital intelligence from Washington.

Clausen discovered that the 14th part of the Japanese message sent from Tokyo to Washington on December 6, 1941, about a break in diplomatic relations, was available nine hours before the attack but was not delivered to key decision makers in Washington until the following morning.

Clausen listed fifty-six specific communications on record from Washington to Pearl Harbor advising Kimmel and Short to be alert against a surprise air attack by the Japanese. These advisories began on January 24, 1941, with letters sent to the Hawaiian commanders by both Navy Secretary Frank Knox and Secretary of War Henry Stimson. Almost twenty-five percent of these warnings were sent to Pearl Harbor between December 1 and December 7, 1947.

Thus, with the dispatch of war warnings from Washington to the joint command at Pearl Harbor on November 27, plus additional warnings sent to Pearl Harbor on December 3, containing the news provided by London that Japanese embassies around the world were destroying their codes and *code machines*, both Kimmel and Short knew that somewhere in the Pacific a Japanese attack *could* occur within a day or a week.

The Congress never questioned the sworn affidavits that Clausen prepared during the course of his investigation, nor have they ever been challenged by any official investigative body. The final report of the congressional Pearl Harbor hearings accepts the Clausen affidavits as being true. This is a legal point that historians have misunderstood, because it is not convenient to their way of thinking.

Perhaps this explains why, until Henry asked me to be his coauthor, no historian ever asked Henry to explain his investigation. If they had done so, I know that Henry would have answered their questions fully and completely. But the fact is they did not. And that is the primary reason why Henry wanted to write this book: to firmly but politely correct the many errors made by these historians, who had written about Pearl Harbor but had never had access to the people or the classified documents that Henry did.

It was not until three years after the first publication of this book that Clausen's findings were confirmed by the National Security Agency (NSA). In a report released in 1995, and titled *Pearl Harbor Revisited: United States Navy Communications Intelligence 1924–1941*, Frederick D. Parker, of the center for Cryptologic History, listed in his Appendix B the basic texts of intercepted decrypts of Japanese diplomatic messages (MAGIC/ULTRA) interspersed in chronological order with the OPNAV warnings sent by Washington to Kimmel. Parker summarizes the importance of these messages saying: "[These messages] are so revealing that it is easy to lose sight of the fact that U.S. officials were often reading these messages at about the same time as the Japanese diplomats."

The key question remains: Did Kimmel ever believe the Japanese would attack Pearl Harbor?

Apparently not. But why?

After World War 1, it was generally believed throughout the Navy that war with Japan would come sooner or later. For the next two decades the Navy made its war plans and conducted exercises in the Pacific accordingly. But, as Fred Parker of the NSA pointed out in his thoughtful report, as regards the events of 1940 and 1941, the teachings of the Naval War College "produced planners whose perceptions of Japanese naval capabilities and national intentions may have been seriously flawed by war planning doctrines which ruled out enemy intentions all together as unreliable and subject to rapid change. Under these circumstances, COMINT [communications intelligence] producers who provided strategic warnings beginning in September 1941 that Japan was preparing for war should not have been surprised that their warnings were ignored until the eleventh hour." To put it more bluntly: Kimmel, Short and others badly underestimated the capabilities of Japan's armed forces and ignored evidence of its government's intentions until the disaster of Pearl Harbor had taken place.

Parker's report also cited Kimmel's testimony at the congressional hearings on Pearl Harbor when Kimmel said that he had no reason to suspect that the six Japanese carriers which had gone missing from the Japanese radio network had, in reality, been converted into a "lost fleet" during November. Parker refutes Kimmel, writing: "In fact, before the November 17 procedure change it was clear that these carriers had been assigned to a separate organization, the 1st Air Fleet. However, neither COM–16 [Corregidor] nor Layton [Kimmel's chief of intelligence] picked this up though it was reported by COM–14 [in Hawaii] on 6 November."

Kimmel's failure to appreciate the possible existence of a new Japanese carrier fleet is put into its proper context by Gordon Prange in his best-selling *At Dawn We Slept*, which I edited (see page 400), when Prange quotes a conversation between Kimmel and his Fleet war plans officer, Captain Charles E. "Soc" McMorris, a week before the Japanese attack. (The conversation can also be found in the Pearl Harbor Hearings.)

During a general discussion about American strategy in the Pacific, Kimmel had just been advised by one of his officers that the Japanese had the capability to attack Pearl Harbor by air.

"Capability, yes," conceded Kimmel, "but possibility?"

Kimmel turned to his Fleet war plans officer. "What do you think about the prospects of a Japanese air attack?" he asked McMorris.

"None, absolutely none," replied McMorris.

But the ultimate confirmation that Kimmel was wrong about Japan's intentions towards Pearl Harbor came to light a year after this book was first published. Joseph C. Harsch, a correspondent for the *Christian Science Monitor*, revealed for the *first* time in his memoirs that, at a special briefing on 0800 hours on December 6, 1941, Kimmel was confident when speaking in front of his staff and telling him that Japan would not attack in the Pacific.

With everyone dressed in white uniforms, and with Kimmel appearing so relaxed that he put his white shoes up on the low coffee table in front of him, Harsch recalls telling the Admiral about his recent experiences as a journalist in wartime Germany. Harsch wrote: "I remarked that I was totally new to the Pacific area and the general situation there. So would [Kimmel] please tell me whether there was going to be a war in the Pacific. Without a pause, immediately, almost casually, he [Kimmel] replied, no. His explanation (which I think I remember almost word for word) was the following:

"'Since you have been traveling you probably don't know that as of six days ago the German high command announced that the German armies in Russia had gone into winter quarters. That means that Moscow is not going to fall to the Germans this year. That means that the Japanese cannot attack us in the Pacific without running the risk of a two-front war. The Japanese are too intelligent to run the risk of a two-front war unnecessarily. They will want to wait until the Russians have been defeated.'"

Harsch confirmed his recollections to me in a letter dated May 21, 1996, saying: "Of course I have no way of knowing what he [Kimmel] believed in his own mind. I only know what he said within hearing of his staff. All I can say with certainty is that he seemed comfortable, relaxed, under no visible sense of strain or anxiety."

The irony of Harsch's account is that he never filed his Saturday exclusive. The *Monitor* doesn't publish on Sundays. And that Sunday morning Harsch witnessed the bombing of Pearl Harbor. When he tried to file his story, the phone and telegraph lines to America had been preempted by the military. His report never got through, and Harsch remained silent on the matter until 1993.

It is now generally acknowledged that Kimmel and Short were not the only ones making errors of judgement about a possible Japanese attack on Pearl Harbor. This book names the fourteen men Henry Clausen believed to be most responsible for Pearl Harbor. Even more important, however, Clausen determined that the entire pre-war system of gathering and sharing intelligence was fatally flawed. Later, the findings of the Joint Committee of Congress agreed with Clausen's analysis. And the Congress also agreed that as co-commanders at Pearl Harbor, both Kimmel and Short made improper command decisions and failed in their primary duty to protect the Pacific fleet from surprise attack. Thus, they were properly relieved of command and reduced to their permanent rank.

Ever since, Kimmel's supporters have tried unsuccessfully to have this judgement reversed. In April 1995, Sen. Strom Thurmond, Chairman of the Senate Committee on the Armed Services and a longtime Kimmel supporter, asked the Defense Department to review the case against Kimmel and Short so that they could be rehabilitated and advanced on the retirement list to their highest temporary grades (Admiral and Lieutenant General, respectively).

The Defense Department denied this request. The departmental reply was written by Under Secretary Edwin Dorn, who declared: "As a practical matter, Admiral Kimmel effectively placed total faith—and the security of the forces in Pearl Harbor against air attack—in Washington's ability to obtain and provide to him timely and unambiguous warning from the Magic and other intercepts alone. This faith was not justified, nor was it consistent with his assessment of other technological developments of the time. Even with today's satellite intelligence and instantaneous world-wide communication, it is still not prudent to depend exclusively on Washington for timely and unambiguous information."

Under Secretary Dorn was saying that neither Admiral Kimmel nor General Short used common sense. They refused to prepare their commands for a surprise attack which they had been warned might occur at any time. As Henry Clausen had viewed the situation, if Kimmel and Short had conferred and agreed that the warnings they had received merited having patrol planes flying at dawn, plus having the Army's radar operational and all their anti-aircraft guns ready to immediately answer an enemy air attack, the two co-commanders at Pearl Harbor would have been heroes. By being ready to defend the ramparts of Pearl Harbor, Kimmel and Short would have done everything in their power to save the Pacific fleet. They failed in this regard, however, and they became two of the first unsuspecting victims of the new technologies unleashed by World War II.

For any Congress, the historical trap involved with exonerating Short and Kimmel is this: Short acknowledged his failures in sworn testimony, but the Admiral has always charged that it was the mutual failures of the War and Navy Departments to warn him about an impending Japanese attack which led to the disaster at Pearl Harbor. Kimmel declared that these failures "must have been in accordance with high political direction . . . [as] these two agencies were responsible only to the President of the United States."

In other words, Kimmel and his supporters have always claimed that President Roosevelt withheld intelligence information from the Hawaiian Command so the Japanese could successfully attack Pearl Harbor and thereby force America into World War II.

Kimmel's allegations have been refuted by ten official investigations. The Dorn report also stated: ". . . To say that responsibility [for Pearl Harbor] is broadly shared is not to absolve Admiral Kimmel and General Short of accountability. . . . Military command is unique. A commander has plenary responsibility for the welfare of the people under his or her command, and is directly accountable for everything the unit does or fails to do. . . . It was appropriate that Admiral Kimmel and General Short be relieved of command. . . . Their relief was occasioned by the need to restore confidence in the Navy and Army's leadership. . . . Subsequently, investigations concluded that both commanders made errors in judgment. I have seen no evidence that leads me to contradict that conclusion."

The Dorn report also confirmed Henry Clausen's original findings that Kimmel and Short had enjoyed adequate intelligence, saying: "[They] made errors of judgment in the use of information and the employment of forces available to them." Dorn also denied that Kimmel and Short had been held to a higher standard than had their superiors. Dorn also denied other claims of Kimmel's supporters by saying that all the Pearl Harbor investigations were conducted fairly and properly, in accordance with military law.

Despite the Dorn report, the long-time supporters of Kimmel and Short kept working in their behalf. They managed to have the Senate pass a resolution on May 25, 2000, by a vote of 52 to 47, declaring that both commanders had performed their duties at Pearl Harbor "competently and professionally." The Senate resolution urged that President Clinton posthumously reverse their demotion in rank and the measure was included in the omnibus defense spending bill. As of mid-January 2001, as this edition of *Pearl Harbor: Final Judgement* was being readied for press, President Clinton had not taken the separate action necessary in his role as commander-in-chief to begin the process of restoring Kimmel and Short to their pre-war ranks.

After fifty years of investigations into Pearl Harbor, what many younger members of Congress do not comprehend is that neither Kimmel nor Short performed their duties "competently and professionally" at Pearl Harbor. Nor does the current Congress understand the horrific breach of national security that occurred on November 15, 1945, when Kimmel supporters and the Republicans fired their first salvo at the opening of the Pearl Harbor Hearings. By forcing the public hearings, the Republicans were seeking to prove Kimmel right, to discredit President Franklin D. Roosevelt and then remove President Harry S. Truman from office.

What those in Congress at that time did not know, however, was that after World War II ended the U.S. Army had convinced the Japanese that we had never broken the Japanese codes. Thus, the Japanese continued using the same war-time codes, which allowed the occupation government of General MacArthur to secretly monitor the frantic maneuvers of the new Japanese government to avoid American oversight as provided for in the surrender agreement. The decrypts of these messages as they crossed General Marshall's desk every day are riveting reading.

The Pearl Harbor hearings started with the Republicans forcing the Truman Administration to admit that America had broken the Japanese codes. Overnight, General MacArthur was cut off from the most valuable intelligence available to his command. This setback did more damage to the MacArthur government than any other act.

The lessons, then, are clear. First, it is unwise to seek historical exoneration when the facts do not warrant same. Secondly, the costly lessons America learned in World War II about national security and code breaking must be learned again by a Congress that is too young to remember the past.

As a former senior staff member of the National Security Agency wrote to me recently: "I have had sad experience in trying to get modern-day customers to accept today's ULTRA as a significant factor in decision making, and I believe that military people are less inclined to accept SIGINT today than one would naturally suppose."

These warning words are all important given the lessons we should have learned from Henry Clausen's investigation into Pearl Harbor. As Henry summed it up, "the trick will be to ensure that intelligence operations work properly in the future."

BRUCE LEE
NEW YORK CITY
FEBRUARY 2001

‖ ACKNOWLEDGMENTS

Serendipity must be acknowledged first and foremost in that the coauthors of this work met, worked and wrote this book in a genuine spirit of mutual admiration and affection.

In achieving our goals a number of people gave selflessly of their time, some of whom cannot be named by their own request, and the authors wish to thank them for their guidance. Among those we can single out, Sher Giannini typed the draft revisions, did research and kept the law office on an even keel. Jacqueline A. Jouret typed the final manuscript, making cogent comments, before returning to graduate school in journalism. Florian Clausen Elliot typed the original draft and kept a watchful eye on the coverage of the fiftieth anniversary of Pearl Harbor. Charlotte and Donald Clausen, also Pauline Crosse, provided warm, caring aid and assistance over the years. Maynard Garrison, a prominent San Francisco attorney and a member of the San Francisco Golf Club, was a perfect partner either on the course or in dominoes. Arch Monson, Jr., a political and business adviser, gave freely of his time, nautical expertise and background in the dramatic arts. And H. Douglas Lemons, the Sovereign Grand Inspector General of California, Member of the Supreme Council Scottish Rite, was a good friend.

Back in New York, Janetta M. Lee waded through reams of research in ninety-degree heat and daily made solid editorial suggestions as to how to keep the narrative moving. Meanwhile, the primary choreographer for the book was our intrepid and knowledgeable editor, James O'Shea Wade, who pursuaded his professional confreres at Crown that ours was a viable project. Authors are blessed when they have been supported by their publisher as we have been. Victoria Heacock fielded our queries; Dore Hollander performed an artful job of accurate, quick copyediting; Lucia Tarbox proved to be a delight as production editor; and when the crunch came, managing editor Laurie Stark handled the difficulties of scheduling with élan. Our publicist, Penney Simon, and Andrew K. Martin, the head of Crown's publicity department, put the icing on the cake. Last but not least, we want to thank Robert D. Loomis and Carl A. Kroch for their expert readings, and the sales reps, without whose support our book wouldn't have legs.

We were also blessed in that our agent, Lila Karpf, proved herself a publishing professional again and again, offering solid advice and enduring friendship.

If inspiration and a new transition were ever needed, the Hayes Street Grill in San Francisco proved that fish when lovingly cooked does indeed nourish the creative spirit. And finally there is Heidi, Henry's seven-year-old Alsation, who kept us all focused on reality. Not satisfied by a doggy bag of sand dabs meunière that was brought back to her at the office from the Hayes Grill, she ate the first draft of the manuscript, too.

FOREWORD: WHY I WROTE THIS BOOK

What caused the disaster of Pearl Harbor on December 7, 1941, has been one of the most contentious debates in American history—as well it should.

More than half a century after the surprise Japanese attack, historians are still making charges that include a number of conspiracy theories that are wildly inaccurate. They contain the following concepts:

■ President Franklin D. Roosevelt knew the attack was coming, but refrained from warning his Army and Navy commanders in Hawaii.

■ Prime Minister Winston Churchill so badly wanted America to join England in fighting Hitler that he conspired to keep warnings that the Japanese were going to attack Pearl Harbor from President Roosevelt.

■ The Soviet Union knew that the Japanese fleet was on its way to attack Pearl Harbor, but kept the information to itself because Russia, too, wanted America to join the war.

Adding fuel to the fire from the American point of view, the commanders of our Army and Naval forces at Hawaii claimed, during the many investigations that followed in the wake of disaster, that Washington had withheld from them vital information that prevented them from being alert against a surprise attack.

In its turn, the Army Pearl Harbor Board went so far as to charge that the Army's Chief of Staff, Gen. George C. Marshall, had failed to warn adequately his Hawaiian command about Japanese intentions; that Secretary of State Cordell Hull had forced the Japanese to make their attack by virtue of the impossible conditions he had set during last-minute negotiations with Tokyo; and that, as a result, President Roosevelt was also responsible for the attack, since Hull was carrying out the President's policies.

Now I know, from my own experience, as I will explain later, that these conspiracy theories are untrue, as are the charges made by the Army Pearl Harbor Board. One merely has to employ common sense and remember that Roosevelt was a Navy man through and through. He loved his ships; he loved the men who sailed them. Never, never would he allow his battleships to be sunk and his sailors drowned. Nor would the admirals and generals who advised Roosevelt allow a conspiracy that would destroy so much of our naval strength at a time when the nation needed it so badly.

Common sense, however, has no authority when books and television shows can make money by promoting conspiracy theories. But I was totally shocked by the outpouring of misinformation that surrounded the fiftieth anniversary of Pearl Harbor. It began for me with a letter published in the *New York Times* on September 24, 1991, which said in part: "The body of evidence [proves] that the United States had broken the Japanese code, knew of the attack in advance and permitted it to happen without alerting its commanding officers at Pearl Harbor or sending ships and planes to head off, or at least challenge, the Japanese ships and planes. . . ."

During the next ninety days, this letter was followed by a tidal wave of books, TV shows, cover stories in the weekly news magazines and Sunday papers, all commemorating in their own way what they believed happened at Pearl Harbor. The public, nearly two-thirds of whom were not alive when World War II started, was overwhelmed by a mass of contradictory stories. For example, the *New York Times* of November 30, 1991, reported that as of that date there were eleven books, either new or newly reprinted, on sale and all had conflicting views. Next, the *Wall Street Journal* of December 2 summarized four major TV shows about the Japanese attack. Aside from the inaccurate conspiracy theories I mentioned earlier, the article pointed out that one of the shows dealt in "crude revisionism" in which "the Japanese are portrayed as victims." In another show, the narrator sought the easy way out. Rather than make a sound conclusion based on fact, he said only that it might "be easier to search for conspiracies than to accept the fact that no one was to blame."

Meanwhile, the question of who was to blame for Pearl Harbor was being addressed by the *Washington Post*. On December 1, 1991, it reported at length on the efforts of the family of the late Adm. Husband E. Kimmel, the commander-in-chief of the U.S. and Pacific fleets at Pearl Harbor, to rescue his name from the dustbin of history following his relief from command only nine days after the Japanese attack. (The Army commander at Hawaii, Lt. Gen. Walter C. Short, was also relieved of command a few weeks after the attack.) But for the Kimmel family, and certain elements of the Navy, the relief of Kimmel is still a highly emotional issue. According to the *Post,* the controversy has been fanned recently by the following events:

- In October 1990, the officers and trustees of the U.S. Naval Academy Alumni Association at Annapolis unanimously adopted a resolution calling for the Navy to restore Kimmel posthumously to the four-star rank he held before the Japanese attack. (He lost this rank when he was relieved of command.)
- In December 1990, the Pearl Harbor Survivors Association adopted a resolution restoring the full wartime rank of both Admiral Kimmel and General Short.
- In October 1991, according to the *Post,* "36 retired flag rank officers—all but a few of them four-star admirals—wrote to President Bush urging him to take remedial action on his own authority." (It should be pointed out that this so-called "remedial action" was asked only for Kimmel.)

But then the *Post,* in a somewhat unusually partisan statement, heartily endorsed the admirals' petition, saying: "No day could be more favorable for restoring him [Kimmel] to the formal and public respect of his country than December 7, 1991."

All of which proves that America still does not understand the facts behind the disaster of Pearl Harbor.

I believe it unfortunate that so many fatal historical errors are being propounded about *why* the Japanese attack succeeded in catching our military forces at Pearl Harbor by surprise. The spreading of false information cannot go unchallenged. The history of Pearl Harbor needs correcting; a final judgement must be made.

And so, after fifty years of silence, but with official notice that my investigation into the causes of Pearl Harbor is now declassified, it is time for me to speak.

My story is impartial. I represent neither the Army nor the Navy. I am a civilian at heart, a lawyer and a civil litigator. But what gives me the authority to speak now is the fact that I was the independent prosecutor appointed by Secretary of War Henry L. Stimson to investigate the root causes of Pearl Harbor after it had been determined that the reports of the Army Pearl Harbor Board were inaccurate, because they were based on tainted or perjured testimony.

My report to Secretary Stimson was released as volume 35 of the Pearl Harbor Hearings. However, my report had no conclusion, because when I turned it in my work was considered Top Secret, and I was not empowered as the independent prosecutor to speak for the Secretary of War and show how the Navy was as guilty as the Army for what happened at Pearl Harbor. Thus, I could not say then what I believed about the failure of leadership by our President that contributed to the disaster.

It is important to remember that my involvement in the subject of Pearl Harbor came *after* it was determined that the two reports of the Army Pearl Harbor Board were fatally flawed because the Board made its two reports based on perjured and incomplete testimony. Too many historians have based their writings on the Board's incorrect reports, because they have wished to bolster their own views of what went wrong at Pearl Harbor. Thus, the various conspiracy theories of what went wrong at Pearl Harbor have gotten the upper hand in the debate, which is bad for history, bad for the public and bad for the military.

I have read all the books published to date on the subject of Pearl Harbor. These include the works of such notable authors as Walter Lord, John Toland, Gordon W. Prange and the late Rear Adm. Edwing T. Layton. All their books were best-sellers. Yet all of them contain errors, or omissions, or improper theories, or, in one book, outright lies.

I don't wish to denigrate these authors. But the truth is that none of them had access to the files that I had access to, which included Top Secret material that was unavailable to many of those in the high commands of either the Army or the Navy. Nor did they have access to the range of people with whom I dealt in both services on a formal and informal basis. And none of them had the extraordinary power that I possessed to make people tell me their stories *under oath*.

This means, of course, that in writing the behind-the-scenes story of my investigation of Pearl Harbor, I do so not as a historian but as an insider. I also do so as a lawyer, which means it was more important for me to determine the fact that something had been done, or not done, rather than an individual's motive. No matter that this might upset the historian, the fact of the matter was the most important thing for me to establish. Facts are the nails that the prosecutor uses to seal his case for the jury. So my investigation focused on what happened, how it happened and if it happened. From these facts, the reader can determine *why* Pearl Harbor happened.

This also means that I approach the subject from a different perspective than does the usual author, and I must stipulate that what has been published to date misses two crucial avenues of inquiry about Pearl Harbor.

The first is that the Joint Congressional Resolution of June 13, 1944, which directed the Secretary of War and the Secretary of the Navy to conduct investigations into the causes of Pearl Harbor, and to punish the guilty parties by courts-martial, failed to pose a fundamental question. Congress was seeking individual scapegoats. Possibly scapegoats who could lead to political charges being made against the White House. But I asked myself whether or not the military systems, or practices of the time, were more fatally flawed than the misconduct of any individual.

Other authors have not asked this question properly. Yet I always kept the thought in the back of my mind during the course of my investigation, because I believed it would be wrong to crush the military careers of brilliant, experienced and dedicated officers without making a thorough search as to whether an established system, or practice, prompted the alleged misconduct of an individual.

The second avenue historians have not queried is what was in my report to the Secretary of War that was *withheld* from the public. (I hasten to point out that only one historian, Gordon W. Prange, ever interviewed me, and he didn't ask.) Although the Secretary of War used my investigation as the basis for his statement to the American public and Congress about what had gone wrong at Pearl Harbor, the Secretary, for reasons of national security *and* interservice harmony, censored both his and my reports about the real causes for Pearl Harbor.

All of this means, of course, that no matter how hard previous historians thought they had tried to winkle out the true story, they were denied it.

My investigation for Secretary Stimson took place during seven months of 1944 and 1945. I traveled more than fifty-five thousand miles by air and interviewed ninety-two Army, Navy and civilian personnel (some of them British) at twenty locations in the U.S., the Far East and European theaters of war. From these individuals I took forty-three affidavits of sworn testimony, plus another seven statements. As Gordon Prange pointed out in his excellent work,[1] thirty of the people I questioned are not on record before any other investigation.

To ensure that the men and women I interviewed told me the truth, I carried a special letter from the Secretary of War that ordered them to cooperate with me, even to "volunteer" information. To prove to certain people who had taken the special cryptological oath, which was above Top Secret, that I knew all about our breaking of certain Japanese codes before Pearl Harbor, I strapped to my chest some forty Top Secret cryptological documents in a bomb pouch that was guaranteed to destroy the papers—and me—if it looked as though I might fall into enemy hands in the course of my extensive travel all over the world.

Upon concluding my investigation, happily without having to pull the trigger of the bomb pouch, I reported to Secretary Stimson. This led to a ruling by the Judge Advocate General that the earlier findings of the Army Pearl Harbor Board in its two reports, one Secret and one Top Secret, should be reversed. My own report was classified Top Secret. I did not include in it any specific findings, conclusions or recommendations. But now I can reveal what these would have been, plus what Secretary Stimson and I discussed in private.

I doubt that any historian has read my report from start to finish, which is a shame. If they had done so, they would have asked the questions that my conscientious coauthor, Bruce Lee, asked during the course of writing this book. It was serendipitous for me that Bruce was the editor for Gordon W. Prange's phenomenal best-seller, *At Dawn We Slept*, as well as editing Admiral Layton's best-selling *And I Was There*. When I first approached Bruce about writing my book, he demurred. He had already gone to the well twice, as he put it, and he

---

[1] Gordon W. Prange, *At Dawn We Slept*. New York: McGraw-Hill, 1981. Prange did not draw any conclusions in his book. This was partially rectified in the 1991 anniversary reprint by his collaborators, Donald M. Goldstein and Katherine V. Dillon.

was under contract to write another work. But I persuaded him to visit me in San Francisco, and he went through my files with me (I have a copy of my original report and a mass of other documents) and asked many questions. Finally, he said that he believed I really did have important new material on Pearl Harbor, and he'd be willing to do my book if his publisher would extend his first contract.

Bruce had been surprised by the Navy's reaction to Admiral Layton's book, which had won posthumously for Cmdr. Joseph J. Rochefort the Distinguished Service Medal for his role in breaking the codes that led to our winning the battle of Midway. But Layton's book, although it had defended Kimmel vigorously, had not won for Kimmel the restoration of the rank he had lost after being relieved of command following the Japanese attack.

"Henry," Bruce said, "I spoke with two Secretaries of the Navy about the matter, Lehman and Webb. From my conversations with them, I thought the Navy would be able to restore Kimmel's rank and exonerate him from blame. But it never happened, and I couldn't understand why until I talked to you. I believe your investigation, and your comments about what you could not say in your report, explains why Pearl Harbor went down the way it did. I must agree with you that there was no valid reason for our forces to have been surprised, no matter what Layton might have said. We have to publish your story, because I think you've made the final judgement."

"Thank you for your kind words," I replied. "More important to me at this time, I believe that if we can do the story of my investigation, I have finally fulfilled my duties to Secretary of War Stimson."

But let us go back to the climate of 1945, the time when I submitted my report to Stimson. In using my work to make his own report to the Congress and the public, Stimson censored himself, because, as he put it: "It is still not in the public interest to disclose sources of information. I have directed that all reports of the Army Pearl Harbor Board be made public *except that part which would reveal sources of secret information.*"

In other words, Stimson believed—as did others back in 1945 (including myself)—that the news about our having broken the Japanese codes before Pearl Harbor, and throughout the war, was so important that it was not in the national interest to reveal the information. How and why the story of our breaking the Japanese codes was made public is explained in detail in my narrative, but the news was not broken until a considerable time after I reported to Stimson and he, in turn, reported to the public. Now I can open doors to secrets that were hidden in my investigation. And as you, the reader, study the information my investigation reveals, I believe you will see why the writing of this book was necessary.

For example, long before Pearl Harbor, there were malpractices and malfunctions involved in the way Naval intelligence operated. In turn, these failures led Admiral Kimmel to withhold from General Short, the Army commander whose responsibility it was to protect Pearl Harbor from attack, the vital intelligence that would have forced Short to order a full war alert before the surprise Japanese attack.

Until I conducted my investigation, the Navy was successful in keeping Kimmel's failure secret.

I also explain the fatal flaws in the Army's intelligence system (in both services it was more important to know something than do anything about it). There were also fatal deficiencies in Short's command, plus horrendous errors of omission and commission in the high commands of both the Army and the Navy in Washington, all of which contributed mightily to the debacle at Pearl Harbor.

As I explain the background of the testimony that I took during the course of my investigation, I am hopeful that readers will be able to make their own judgements on the questions I pose in making my case. The questions are:

■ What were the proximate and contributory causes of the disaster at Pearl Harbor?

■ Did these causes involve military systems that were more fatally flawed than the misconduct of any of the individuals involved?

■ Did the reliance on established systems, or practices, excuse individual misbehavior?

■ Was appropriate disciplinary action meted out to those who were guilty?

■ Did the disaster at Pearl Harbor demonstrate that reforms were needed in the American military command structure?

■ Were these reforms undertaken? If so, what were they? And were they effective?

■ What can be learned from Pearl Harbor that is applicable today?

Remember, what occurred during the attack on Pearl Harbor is not as important as *why* it happened. But even today, it is difficult to comprehend the enormity of our defeat, or the damage America suffered that tragic Sunday morning.

The surprise Japanese attack began at 7:55 that morning and ran in five phases of activity until 9:45, when all enemy planes retired.[2] Three of the largest, most powerful battleships in our fleet sank on the bottom; a fourth capsized. Four more battleships were so badly damaged they were out of action for months (two of them had to be returned to the mainland for repairs). The target battleship, *Utah*, which had been used to train our own dive bombers, also sank. Also damaged beyond repair were three light cruisers, three destroyers and four auxiliary vessels. At a time when our Navy was frantically preparing to fight a two-ocean war, it lost eighteen of its more important and combat-ready warships (not including the *Utah*).

The Navy and Marines endured 2,086 fatalities to their officers and men; the Army lost 194. The Navy and Marines suffered 749 wounded; the Army, 360.

In summarizing the disaster, our Congress concluded that America suffered 3,435 casualties, the Japanese less than 100. We lost outright 188 fighter planes, bombers and patrol aircraft, out of a total of 402 Army and Navy aircraft. The Japanese brought to bear 360 planes during the attack, and they lost only 29. (Most of our planes were lined up on the ground, parked wing tip to wing tip, and nose to tail.) We lost 18 fighting ships; Japan lost five midget submarines. It was, said Congress, "the greatest military and naval disaster in our nation's history."

Investigations subsequent to the Japanese attack disclosed that when the first Japanese bombers appeared, roughly twenty-five percent of the Navy's antiaircraft batteries, consisting of 780 guns, were manned and firing. Within seven to ten minutes, all the Navy's antiaircraft guns were manned and firing.

The same could not be said for the Army. Of the thirty-one antiaircraft batteries under Army command, twenty-seven of them (or eighty-seven percent of them) were not in position, or supplied with ammunition and ready to fire, until after the attack ended.

Why did all this happen? Especially when one considers the power and responsibility, the capability for devastating retaliation, and the experience and training of our brilliant military commanders of the time. It is an awesome question.

I respectfully submit my answer in the pages that follow.

HENRY C. CLAUSEN

---

[2] Report of the Joint Committee on the Investigation of the Pearl Harbor Attack, pp. 58–62.

TOP SECRET

WAR DEPARTMENT

WASHINGTON

14 September 1945

MEMORANDUM FOR THE SECRETARY OF WAR:

SUBJECT: Report of investigation by Lt. Colonel Henry C. Clausen, JAGD, for the Secretary of War, supplementary to proceedings of the Army Pearl Harbor Board.

Pursuant to orders of the Secretary of War, I have conducted the investigation supplementary to the proceedings of the Army Pearl Harbor Board, mentioned in the public statements of the Secretary of War on 1 December 1944 and 29 August 1945. Copies of these statements and of my orders and some related documents are attached as Exhibit "A."

In the course of this investigation, I travelled over 55,000 miles by air and interviewed 92 Army, Navy and civilian personnel at the following places:

Berlin, Germany	London, England
Bletchley Park, England	Luzon, P.I.
Boston, Massachusetts	Manila, P.I.
Cannes, France	Neuenahr, Germany
Casserta, Italy	New York, New York
Frankfurt on Main, Germany	Paris, France
Guam	Potsdam, Germany
Honolulu, T.H.	Saipan
Langley Field, Virginia	Versailles, France
Leyte, P.I.	Washington, D.C.

Some of these persons were interviewed where they were engaged in combat in active theaters of operation, as the Secretary of War stated in his public statement of 1 December 1944 would be necessary.

Of those interviewed, the following persons testified before me. I recorded their testimony in the form of affidavits, copies of which are attached as Exhibit "B":

General George C. Marshall	Lt. General Leonard T. Gerow
General Douglas MacArthur	Lt. General Walter B. Smith
Lt. General Richard K. Sutherland	Colonel Otis K. Sadtler

Major General John R. Deane   Colonel Rex W. Minckler
Major General Charles D. Herron   Colonel Harold Doud
Major General Sherman Miles   Captain Joseph J. Rochefort, USN

TOP SECRET

Major General C.A. Willoughby   Captain Edwin T. Layton, USN
Major General Ralph C. Smith   Captain Wilfred J. Holmes, USN
Brig. General Thomas J. Betts   Captain Thomas A. Huckins, USN
Brig. General Kendall J. Fielder   Lt. Colonel Frank B. Rowlett
Brig. General Morrill W. Marston   Major Edward B. Anderson
Brig. General Robert H. Dunlop   Captain Howard W. Martin
Brig. General Charles K. Gailey   Chief Warrant Officer L. R. Lane
Colonel Rufus S. Bratton   Chief Ships Clerk Theodore
                                       Emanuel, USN
Colonel Robert E. Schukraft   Miss Mary J. Dunning
Colonel George W. Bicknell   Miss Margaret McKenney
Colonel Clarence G. Jensen   Miss Louise Prather
Colonel Carlisle Clyde Dusenbury   Miss Mary L. Ross
Colonel Moses W. Pettigrew   Mr. George W. Renchard
Colonel Joseph K. Evans   Mr. Robert L. Shivers
Colonel Edward F. French   Mr. John F. Stone
Colonel Edward W. Raley

The following persons gave me signed statements which, with some records of my interviews, are also included in Exhibit "B":

Brigadier General C. A. Powell   Lt. Donald Woodrum, Jr., USN
Colonel O. H. Thompson   Mr. Harry L. Dawson
Lt. Colonel Byron M. Muerlott   Mr. John E. Russell
Commander J. S. Holtwick, Jr., USN

I also obtained a great deal of additional documentary evidence. A list of this is attached as Exhibit "C" and the documents are presented herewith.

Periodic oral and written reports were heretofore made. The written reports are attached as Exhibit "D."

There are attached as Exhibits "E" and "F" memoranda of The Judge Advocate General giving his comments upon the Top Secret Reports of the Army Pearl Harbor Board, and supplementing and commenting upon certain aspects of his previous memorandum to the Secretary of War dated 25 November 1944, in the light of my investigation.

HENRY C. CLAUSEN
Lt. Colonel, JAGD

6 Incls
  1. Ex. "A"
  2. Ex. "B"
  3. Ex. "C"
  4. Ex. "D"
  5. Ex. "E"
  6. Ex. "F"

NAMES AND POSITIONS OF PRINCIPAL ARMY AND NAVY OFFICIALS IN WASHINGTON AND AT HAWAII AT THE TIME OF THE ATTACK ALONG WITH THE LEADING WITNESSES IN THE VARIOUS PROCEEDINGS PRIOR TO THE JOINT COMMITTEE

(NOTE: THE STYLE IN WHICH PERSONNEL ARE IDENTIFIED MAY SEEM INCONSISTENT, BUT THE AUTHORS HAVE FOLLOWED OFFICIAL DESIGNATIONS IN SUCH CASES.)

Organization and Personnel, War Department, Dec. 7, 1941

Secretary of War, Henry L. Stimson.
Chief of Staff, Gen. George C. Marshall.
Deputy Chiefs of Staff:
  General Administration and Ground Forces, Maj. Gen. William Bryden.
  Armed Forces and Supply, Maj. Gen. Richard C. Moore.
  Air, Maj. Gen. Henry H. Arnold.
  Secretary, General Staff, Col. Walter Bedell Smith.
  Assistant Secretary, General Staff, Col. John R. Deane.
G-1 (Personnel Division), Brig. Gen. Wade H. Haislip.
G-2 (Intelligence Division), Brig. Gen. Sherman Miles.
  Administrative Branch, Col. Ralph C. Smith.
  Counterintelligence Branch, Lt. Col. John T. Bissell.
  Intelligence Branch, Col. Hayes A. Kroner.
  Administrative Section, Lt. Col. Moses W. Pettigrew.
  Situation Section, Lt. Col. Thomas J. Betts.
  Far Eastern Section, Col. Rufus S. Bratton.
    Assistant, Col. Carlisle Clyde Dusenbury.
G-3 (Operations and Training Division), Brig. Gen. Harry L. Twaddle.
G-4 (Supply Division), Brig. Gen. Brehon B. Somervell.

War Plans Division, Brig. Gen. Leonard T. Gerow.
  Executive Officer, Maj. Charles K. Gailey, Jr.
    Plans Group, Col. Charles W. Bundy.
    Projects Group, Col. Robert W. Crawford.
Chief Signal Officer, Maj. Gen. Dawson Olmstead.
  Operations Branch, Col. Otis K. Sadtler.
    Traffic Division and Signal Center, Col. Edward T. French.
    Signal Intelligence Service, Col. Rex W. Minckler.
      Principal Cryptoanalyst, William F. Friedman.
    Communication Liaison Division, Lt. Col. W. T. Guest.

Army Air Forces

(Under overall command of General Marshall)

Commanding General, Maj. Gen. Henry H. Arnold.
Chief of Air Staff, Brig. Gen. Martin F. Scanlon.
Air Forces Combat Command, Lt. Gen. Delos C. Emmons.
Air Corps, Maj. Gen. George Brett.

Organization and Personnel, Navy Department, Dec. 7, 1941

Secretary of the Navy, Frank Knox.
Chief of Naval Operations, Adm. Harold R. Stark.
  Administrative aide and flag secretary, Capt. Charles Wellborn, Jr.
  Aide, Capt. John L. McCrea.
Assistant Chief of Naval Operations, Rear Adm. Royal E. Ingersoll.
War Plans Division, Rear Adm. Richmond K. Turner.
  Pacific Ocean and Asiatic Areas Section, Capt. Robert O. Glover.
Central Division (State Department liaison), Capt. R. E. Schuirmann.
Ship Movements Division, Vice Adm. Roland M. Brainard.
  War Information Room, Rear Adm. F. T. Leighton.
Intelligence Division, Rear Adm. Theodore S. Wilkinson.
  Domestic Branch and Assistant, Rear Adm. Howard F. Kingman.
  Foreign Branch, Capt. William A. Heard.
    Far Eastern Section, Capt. Arthur H. McCollum.
Communications Division, Rear Adm. Leigh Noyes.
  Assistant, Capt. Joseph R. Redman.
  Security (Intelligence) Section, Capt. L. F. Safford.
  Translation Section, Lt. Comdr. A. D. Kramer (on loan from Far Eastern
    Section, Intelligence Division).

Cryptographic Research:
(Decrypting) Section:
Senior watch officer, Lt. (jg) George W. Lynn.
Watch Officers, Lt. (jg) Alfred V. Pering, Lt. (jg) F. M. Brotherhood,
Lt. (jg) Allan A. Murray.
Correlating and Dissemination Section, Lt. Fredrick L. Freeman.

Organization and Personnel, Hawaiian Department, Dec. 7, 1941

Commanding General, Lt. Gen. Walter C. Short.
Chief of Staff, Col. Walter C. Phillips.
G-1 (Personnel), Lt. Col. Russell C. Throckmorton.
G-2 (Intelligence), Lt. Col. Kendall J. Fielder.
    Assistant G-2, Lt. Col. George W. Bicknell.
G-3 (Operations and Training), Lt. Col. William E. Donegan.
G-4 (Supply), Col. Morrill W. Marston.
    Assistant G-4, Maj. Robert J. Fleming.
Adjutant General, Col. Robert H. Dunlop.
Chemical Warfare, Lt. Col. G. F. Unmacht.
Ordnance, Col. W. A. Capron.
Judge Advocate General, Col. T. H. Green.
Provost Marshal, Lt. Col. Melvin L. Craig.
Engineer, Col. A. K. B. Lyman.
Quartermaster, Col. William R. White.
Finance, Col. E. S. Ely.
Signal Corps, Lt. Col. Carrol A. Powell.
Inspector General, Col. Lathe B. Row.
Surgeon General, Col. Edgar King.
Twenty-fourth Infantry Division, Brig. Gen. Durward S. Wilson.
Twenty-fifth Infantry Division, Maj. Gen. Maxwell Murray.
Coast Artillery Command, Maj. Gen. Henry T. Burgin.

Hawaiian Air Force

(Under overall command of General Short)

Commanding General, Maj. Gen. Frederick L. Martin.
Chief of Staff, Col. James A. Mollison.
Intelligence, Col. Edward W. Raley.
Signal Officer, Lt. Col. Clay I. Hoppough.
Eighteenth Bombardment Wing, Brig. Gen. Jacob H. Rudolph.

Fourteenth Pursuit Wing, Brig. Gen. Howard C. Davidson.
Hickam Field, Col. W. E. Farthing.
Wheeler Field, Col. William J. Flood.
Bellows Field, Lt. Col. Leonard D. Weddington.

Staff of Commander in Chief, U.S. Fleet and U.S. Pacific Fleet, Dec. 7, 1941

Commander in Chief, Adm. Husband E. Kimmel.
Chief of Staff and personal aide, Capt. W. W. Smith.
Flag Secretary and personal aide, Lt. Comdr. P. C. Crosley.
Operations Officer and Assistant Chief of Staff, Capt. W. S. DeLany.
  First assistant operations officer, Comdr. R. F. Good.
  Second assistant operations officer, Lt. Comdr. H. L. Collins.
War Plans Officer, Capt. Charles H. McMorris.
  Assistants, Commander V. R. Murphy, Comdr. L. D. McCormick, Lt. F. R. DuBorg.
  Assistant War Plans and Marine Officer, Col. O. T. Pheifer, United States Marine Corps.
Communications officer, Comdr. M. E. Curtis.
  Assistant, Lt. (jg) W. J. East, Jr.
Security officer, Lt. Allan Reed.
Radio officer, Lt. Comdr. D. C. Beard.
Public Relations officer, Lt. Comdr. W. W. Drake.
  Assistant, Lt. (jg) J. E. Bassett.
Maintenance officer, Comdr. H. D. Clark.
Medical officer, Capt. E. A. M. Genreau, United States Marine Corps.
Gunnery officer, Comdr. W. A. Kitts III.
Aviation officer, Comdr. Howard C. Davis
Aerologist and personnel officer, Lt. Comdr. R. B. Black.

Commander, Navy Pacific Fleet Air Wing, Rear Adm. P. N. L. Bellinger.
  Also commander Hawaiian Based Patrol Wings 1 and 2; commander, Fleet Air Detachment, Ford Island, Pearl Harbor; commander, Naval Base Defense Air Force (under commandant, Fourteenth Naval District as naval base defense officer, Pacific Fleet).
Operations officer, Capt. Logan C. Ramsey.

Commander Battle Force (Task Force 1), Vice Adm. W. S. Pye.
Commander Aircraft, Battle Force (Task Force 2), Vice Adm. William F. Halsey.
Commander Scouting Force (Task Force 3), Vice Adm. Wilson Brown.

Commander Task Force 4, Rear Adm. Claude C. Bloch.
Commander Submarines Scouting Force (Task Force 7), Rear Adm. Thomas
   Withers.
Commander Task Force 9, Rear Adm. P. N. L. Bellinger.
Commander Base Force (Task Force 15), Rear Adm. W. L. Calhoun.

Organization and Personnel, Fourteenth Naval District, Dec. 7, 1941

Commandant (also commander, Hawaiian Naval Coastal Sea Frontier; com-
   mandant, Pearl Harbor Navy Yard; commander of local defense forces and,
   as an officer of Pacific Fleet, the naval base defense officer; commander
   Task Force 4, United States Pacific Fleet), Rear Adm. Claude C. Bloch.
Chief of Staff, Capt. J. B. Earle.
Intelligence officer, Captain Irving H. Mayfield.
   Counterespionage Section, Lt. William B. Stephensen.
Communications Security (Intelligence) Unit, Comdr. Joseph J. Rochefort.
   Translator, Col. Alva B. Lasswell, United States Marine Corps.
   Cryptoanalyst, Lt. (jg) F. C. Woodward, Comdr. Wesley A. Wright (on
   loan from staff of Admiral Kimmel, where he was assistant communi-
   cations officer).

LIST OF WITNESSES APPEARING BEFORE THE JOINT COMMITTEE AND THEIR ASSIGNMENTS AS OF DEC. 7, 1941

Beardall, John R., rear admiral; naval aide to President Roosevelt.
Beatty, Frank E., rear admiral; aide to Secretary of the Navy Frank Knox.
Bellinger, P. N. L., vice admiral, commander Hawaiian Naval Base Air
   Force (commander Patrol Wing 2).
Bicknell, George W., colonel, assistant chief, Military Intelligence Service,
   Hawaiian Department.
Bratton, Rufus S., colonel, chief, Far Eastern Section, Military Intelligence
   Service, War Department.
Clausen, Henry C., lieutenant colonel,[1] Judge Advocate General's Office,
   assisting Army Pearl Harbor Board and conducting supplemental investi-
   gation for Secretary of War.
Creighton, John M., captain, U.S.N., naval observer, Singapore.
Dillon, John H., major, U.S.M.C., aide to Secretary Knox.
Elliott, George E., sergeant, A.U.S., operator at Opan radar detector station,
   Oahu, T.H.

[1] Denotes witness whose connection with this investigation relates to his assignment after December 7, 1941.

Gerow, Leonard T., major general, Chief, War Plans Division, Army General Staff, War Department.

Grew, Joseph C., United States Ambassador to Japan.

Hart, Thomas C., admiral, commander in chief, Asiatic Fleet.

Hull, Cordell, Secretary of State.

Ingersoll, Royal E., admiral, Assistant Chief of Naval Operations, Navy Department.

Inglis, R. B., rear admiral,[1] presented to committee Navy summary of Pearl Harbor attack.

Kimmel, Husband E., rear admiral, commander in chief, United States Fleet; commander in chief, Pacific Fleet.

Kramer, A. D., commander, Section Chief, Division of Naval Communications, handling translations and recovery of intercepted Japanese codes.

Krick, Harold D., captain, U.S.N., former flag secretary to Admiral Stark.

Leahy, William D., admiral, Chief of Staff to the President.

Layton, Edwin T., captain, U.S.N., fleet intelligence officer, Pacific Fleet.

Marshall, George C., general, Chief of Staff, United States Army, War Department.

McCollum, Arthur N., captain, U.S.N., Chief, Far Eastern Section, Office of Naval Intelligence, Navy Department.

Miles, Sherman, major general, Chief, Military Intelligence Service, Army General Staff, War Department.

Noyes, Leigh, rear admiral, Chief, Office of Naval Communications, Navy Department.

Phillips, Walter C., colonel, Chief of Staff to General Short.

Richardson, J. O., admiral, former commander in chief, United States Fleet and Pacific Fleet.

Roberts, Owen J., Mr. Justice,[1] Chairman, Roberts Commission.

Rochefort, Joseph John, captain, U.S.N., communications intelligence officer, Pacific Fleet.

Sadtler, Otis K., colonel, Chief, Military Branch, Army Signal Corps, War Department.

Safford, L. F., captain, U.S.N., Chief, Radio Intelligence Unit, Office of Naval Communications, Navy Department.

Schukraft, Robert E., colonel, Chief, Radio Intelligence Unit, Army Signal Corps, War Department.

Schulz, Lester Robert, commander, assistant to Admiral Beardall.

Short, Walter C., major general, commanding general, Hawaiian Department.

Smith, William W., rear admiral, Chief of Staff to Admiral Kimmel.

Sonnett, John F., lieutenant commander,[1] Special Assistant to the Secretary of the Navy, and assistant to Admiral H. K. Hewitt in his inquiry.

Stark, Harold R., admiral, Chief of Naval Operations, Navy Department.

Stimson, Henry L., Secretary of War (sworn statement and sworn replies to interrogatories only).

Thielen, Bernard, colonel,[1] presented to committee Army summary of Pearl Harbor attack.

Turner, Richmond K., rear admiral, Chief, War Plans Division, Navy Department.

Welles, Sumner, Under Secretary of State.

Wilkinson, T. S., rear admiral, Chief, Office of Naval Intelligence, Navy Department.

Zacharias, Ellis M., captain, United States Navy, commanding officer, U.S.S. *Salt Lake City*, Pacific Fleet.

LIST OF LEADING WITNESSES IN PRIOR PROCEEDINGS WHO DID *NOT* TESTIFY BEFORE THE JOINT COMMITTEE, AND THEIR ASSIGNMENTS AS OF DEC. 7, 1941

Arnold, H. H., general, commanding general, Army Air Forces, War Department.

Bissell, John T., colonel, executive officer, Counter Intelligence Group, Military Intelligence Division, War Department.

Bloch, Claude C., admiral, commandant, Fourteenth Naval District; commander, Hawaiian Sea Frontier; Pearl Harbor Naval Base defense officer.

Brotherhood, Francis M., lieutenant (jg), watch officer, Security Section, Office of Naval Communications, Navy Department.

Brown, Wilson, rear admiral, commander, Scouting Force, (Task Force 3), Pacific Fleet.

Calhoun, W. L., vice admiral, commander, Base Force, Pacific Fleet.

Crosley, Paul C., commander; flag secretary to Admiral Kimmel.

Curts, M. E., captain, U.S.N., communication officer, Pacific Fleet, and liaison officer, Radio and Sound Division.

Davidson, Howard C., major general, commanding general, Fourteenth Pursuit Wing, Hawaiian Air Force.

Davis, Howard C., rear admiral, fleet aviation officer, Pacific Fleet.

DeLany, Walter S., rear admiral, Chief of Staff for Operations, staff of commander in chief, Pacific Fleet.

Dusenbury, Carlisle Clyde, colonel, assistant to Col. R. S. Bratton, Far Eastern Section, Military Intelligence Division, War Department.

Fielder, Kendall J., colonel, Chief, Military Intelligence Division, Hawaiian Department.

French, Edward F., colonel, officer in charge, Traffic Division and Signal Center, Signal Corps, War Department.

Friedman, William F., principal cryptoanalyst, Signal Intelligence Service, Signal Corps, War Department.

Halsey, William F., admiral, commander, Aircraft Battle Force (Task Force 2), Pacific Fleet.

Hamilton, Maxwell M., Chief, Division of Far Eastern Affairs, State Department.

Heard, William A., captain, U.S.N., Chief, Foreign Branch, Office of Naval Intelligence, Navy Department.

Herron, Charles D., major general, former commanding general, Hawaiian Department.

Hornbeck, Stanley K., adviser on foreign relations, State Department.

Kitts, Willard A. III, rear admiral, fleet gunnery officer, staff of commander in chief, Pacific Fleet.

Kroner, Hayes A., brigadier general, Chief, Intelligence Branch, Military Intelligence Division, War Department.

Lockard, Joseph L., lieutenant A.U.S., operator OPAN radar detector station, Oahu, T.H.

Lynn, George W., lieutenant commander, senior watch officer, Security Section, Office of Naval Communications, Navy Department.

MacArthur, Douglas, general, commanding general, United States Armed Forces in the Far East.

Martin, F. L., major general, commanding general, Hawaiian Air Force.

Mayfield, Irving H., captain, U.S.N., Chief, Office of Naval Intelligence, Fourteenth Naval District.

McDonald, Joseph P., sergeant, 580th Aircraft Warning Company, assigned as telephone switchboard operator, operations center, Aircraft Warning Service, Hawaiian Department.

McMorris, C. H., rear admiral, war plans officer, staff of commander in chief, Pacific Fleet.

Murray, Allan A., lieutenant commander, watch officer, Cryptographic (Decrypting) Unit, Security Section, Office of Naval Communications, Navy Department.

Newton, J. H., vice admiral, commander, Cruisers Scouting Force, Pacific Fleet.

Nimitz, C. W., admiral, Chief, Bureau of Navigation (now Personnel), Navy Department.

O'Dell, Robert H., lieutenant A.U.S., assistant military attaché, American Legation, Melbourne, Australia, under Col. Van S. Merle-Smith, military attaché.

Pering, Alfred V., lieutenant commander, watch officer, Security Section, Office of Naval Communications, Navy Department.

Pettigrew, Moses W., colonel, executive officer, Intelligence Group, Military Intelligence Division, War Department.

Poindexter, Joseph B., governor, Governor of the Territory of Hawaii.

Powell, C. A., colonel, chief signal officer, Hawaiian Department.

Pye, William S., vice admiral, commander, Battle Force (Task Force 1), Pacific Fleet.

Ramsey, Logan C., captain, U.S.N., operations officer, Commander Patrol Wing 2 (Admiral Bellinger), Pacific Fleet, and Commander Patrol Wings, Hawaiian Area.

Redman, Joseph R., rear admiral, Assistant Director, Office of Naval Communications, Navy Department.

Schuirmann, R. E., rear admiral, Director, Central Division, Office of Chief of Naval Operations, Navy Department.

Shivers, Robert L., special agent in charge, Federal Bureau of Investigation, Department of Justice, Honolulu, T.H.

Smith-Hutton, H. H., captain, U.S.N., naval attaché, United States Embassy, Tokyo, Japan.

Stimson, Henry L., Secretary of War.

Sutherland, Richard K., lieutenant general, Chief of Staff to General MacArthur.

Taylor, William E. G., commander, temporary duty with Army Interceptor Command, Hawaiian Air Force, as adviser for establishment of aircraft warning service.

Tyler, Kermit A., lieutenant colonel, executive officer, Eighth Pursuit Squadron, Hawaiian Air Force, on duty December 7, 1941, at information center, Aircraft Warning Service, Hawaiian Department.

Willoughby, C. A., major general, Chief, Military Intelligence Division, staff of General MacArthur.

Wilson, Durward S., major general, commanding general, Twenty-fourth Division, Hawaiian Department.

Withers, Thomas, rear admiral, commander submarines, Pacific Fleet.

1 "LEAVE NO STONE UNTURNED"

I was born to survive calamitous events.

At least, that's what my mother always claimed.

Whenever she recalled the great earthquake and fire that destroyed San Francisco in 1906, she would tell everyone how I was only a few months old at the time and was snoozing on a Murphy bed when the quake hit. Instead of its usual reluctance to spring upright and tuck itself into the wall, with the first tremor the bed snapped itself back and held me securely against the strongest interior support while the exterior of the house crumbled away.

After the quake, when my parents finally managed to reach the bed and pull it down, there I was, looking somewhat startled, but otherwise happy and content. By another stroke of luck, I had even been turned right side up.

Such recollections were far from my mind in late November 1944, however, when as usual I rose with the sun. The war in Europe was going well. Our Allied forces were moving steadily forward on a broad front across Europe. The Canadians had secured the Beveland Peninsula and the entrance to the vital port of Antwerp; the British

Second Army was mopping up the Geilenkirchen salient after heavy fighting; and the American Third Army, under General Patton, was about to penetrate the Maginot Line. In Italy, the British and the Americans were driving steadily north along the Mediterranean coast, while on the Adriatic side of the peninsula, the Canadians, Poles and British were advancing on the city of Ravenna. Meanwhile, the Russians were moving toward Budapest after having driven the Germans out of Romania. In the Pacific, the American Navy was celebrating its victory in the Battle of Leyte Gulf, in which it had sunk the last of Japan's aircraft carriers.

I cannot recall the exact date, but that morning in Washington, D.C., the sun was bright. The city's foliage was at its best: a rich green-gold, yellow and burnished bronze, electrifying in its beauty. I looked longingly at the golf clubs standing in the corner of my bedroom, especially at the new putter with which I had been practicing with great success, and I thought of a number of schemes I might employ to escape from my office at the Pentagon and hit the golf course.

I could almost hear my ball drop into the cup of the eighteenth hole, and I could feel the crisp dollar bills that I would win when I remembered that I was supposed to meet that morning with Brig. Gen. Carter Clarke, the Assistant Chief of Staff, G-2 (Army Intelligence). My heart sank. I didn't realize it, but I was about to be dropped into some truly calamitous events.

As a Major in the Army's Judge Advocate General's Corps, I had recently served as the Assistant Recorder to the Army Pearl Harbor Board's investigation, during the period July 24 to October 19, 1944, into the greatest military defeat in American history. Some unusual things had occurred during this investigation, and after the Board submitted its final reports, it became apparent that information had been withheld from the investigating officers. I also suspected that the Board had been given tainted testimony. I didn't know exactly what information had been withheld, nor did I know the extent of the questionable testimony given to the Board. But I had been asked to investigate.

My mission this day on behalf of the Army's Judge Advocate General was to gain access to and review the Japanese radio messages the Americans had intercepted and which had been given to the Army Board as evidence. I was a relative newcomer to this code breaking, and I needed the messages to supplement a study that Col. William

Hughes and I were writing on the findings and recommendations of the Army Pearl Harbor Board for a report that the Judge Advocate General would submit to the Secretary of War, Henry L. Stimson. Although I sat on the Army Board as a Recorder, I had never seen the intercepts and I needed to know what they said. In turn, Stimson would make his report to Congress and the nation about what had gone wrong at Pearl Harbor.

The man who held the key to the decrypted messages I needed to review was General Clarke. I suspected that he had been involved in whatever hanky-panky had taken place with the Army Board, and I knew he was going to be a hard nut to crack. His office was famous for never giving out any information, even the time of day.

In those days, only a tiny number of people knew about our having broken the Japanese codes before Pearl Harbor. Nor did the public know that General Clarke, as Commander of the Army's Communications Intelligence Operations, had been the courier between the Army's Chief of Staff, George C. Marshall, and the Republican presidential candidate, Thomas E. Dewey, in the election of 1944. Somehow, I am not sure how exactly, Dewey had learned that the United States had broken the Japanese codes before Pearl Harbor. His campaign strategy was obvious: to charge that the administration of President Franklin D. Roosevelt had been aware of the Japanese intentions to attack Pearl Harbor but had done nothing to prevent it. In turn, this brought America into the war against the Axis powers, which Roosevelt had wanted and the Republicans had been trying to prevent. Needless to say, if Dewey followed this strategy, he would probably win the election.

However, General Marshall feared that a presidential campaign revealing the greatest secret of the war, that we had broken the enemy's codes (those of both Japan and Germany), would endanger the Allied war effort, to say nothing of starting a bitter political struggle between Republicans and Democrats. It might needlessly cost thousands upon thousands of Allied soldiers' lives, plus prolong the war, if not make our goal of unconditional surrender by the Axis impossible.

So Clarke had carried a special message from Marshall to Dewey, in which Marshall asked Dewey *not* to discuss the issue of breaking the Japanese codes during the campaign. A true patriot, Dewey acquiesced to the Chief of Staff's request. It cost him the election. Roosevelt won an unprecedented fourth term in office that November 1944. (The nation had no idea how ill Roosevelt was at the time.)

I knew that Clarke had an explosive temper. Although quite a decent person, he laced his language with frequent bursts of profanity. He was tall, with a great shock of black hair that sometimes streamed like rivulets over his ears and forehead. From experience in dealing with him, I expected that if I was going to get the documents I needed, I'd have to slug it out, toe to toe.

I was pleasantly surprised when I entered Clarke's office and he said, "Clausen, how the hell are you? Take a seat."

I sat, and then reminded him about our earlier phone conversation, that Colonel Hughes and I were reviewing the Army Pearl Harbor Board's findings and that I needed to check the decrypts.

"Ordinarily, I'd tell you to go to hell," Clarke replied with cheerful good humor that amazed me. "If the Japs ever learned we'd broken their Purple codes, it could cost us the damn war. But I'll level with you. Before you came, I checked with a higher authority. I was told to give you whatever you wanted and to cooperate fully. I don't understand why. I think it's dead wrong."

"Well, maybe it'll keep me from going off half-cocked like the Army Pearl Harbor Board seems to have done," I said. "We don't need another fiasco."

"You're damned right about that," said Clarke. He ordered a portable desk set up alongside his own and handed me one file folder after another filled with decrypts of Japanese messages. It took several hours to go through the lot and be briefed on their meaning, but I finally got all the messages that the Army Board had seen. Clarke had true copies made while I waited. He then bound them together in a special folder. As he handed them over, he said, "Clausen, guard these documents as though they are vials of nitroglycerin. If you lose a single one, may God have mercy on your soul."

I put the file folder in my special briefcase, locked it, put it under my arm and hurried to my office.

Mine wasn't an ordinary office. The outer door was made of steel and had a big combination lock for a doorknob. It looked like a bank vault. No one could enter without the permission of Colonel Hughes or myself, and access was so tightly restricted that only we had the combination for the door. Inside, there were no desks with drawers, only flat-topped tables plus row upon row of armored file cabinets, each with its special combination lock, containing all the records of the Army Pearl Harbor Board and related papers.

It was nearing noon, and I found it difficult to work the combination of the outer door with my briefcase under my arm. Suddenly, I heard my telephone inside start to ring, so I put the case down, spun the dial frantically and got to the phone before the calling party hung up. I immediately recognized the voice as that of the secretary for Gen. Myron Cramer, the Judge Advocate General.

"Major Clausen?"

"Hi, Bernice."

"Major, I've been trying to reach you all morning. The General wants you to join him in a meeting with Secretary of War Stimson at two P.M. today."

"Please tell the General I'll be there. What's up?"

"The Secretary of War is worried about how the public will react to the report of the Army Pearl Harbor Board. He has asked General Cramer to brief him and make recommendations."

"Okay. I think I can help, and thanks for the tip. I bet you thought I'd snuck off to play golf this morning. Actually, I was with General Clarke."

"I know," Bernice said.

The way she said "I know" made me nervous. Something was up.

Although it was getting on toward lunchtime, this wasn't a day to go to the cafeteria for coffee. I made a cup of tea and sat at my table eating the sandwich I'd brought from home, trying to figure out what was going on.

The memoranda about potential errors in the Army Board's two reports I had prepared with Colonel Hughes had obviously struck home with someone. But with whom? And why?

The problems with the Board's report (in reality there were two reports, one Secret and one Top Secret, the latter dealing with the issue of the breaking of the Japanese codes) were myriad. The Board members had reached mistaken assumptions about when the Japanese had actually set sail on their way to attack. They preferred to believe that the Japanese had dispatched their attacking force toward Pearl Harbor as a result of Secretary of State Cordell Hull's proposals of November 26, when in fact the Japanese fleet had gone to sea before that date. (The report said that Hull had to bear some responsibility for Pearl Harbor because his message to Tokyo of November 26 "was used by the Japanese as a signal to begin war by the attack on Pearl Harbor.") There also were errors about spying in Hawaii, and claims that the Japanese had their submarines inside Pearl Harbor before the attack.

The Board found that the Army commander on the spot, Lt. Gen. Walter C. Short, had failed to alert his command adequately for war. But then the Board had gone on to fault the War Department for not ordering Short to prepare "an adequate alert," and for not keeping Short properly informed about the ongoing diplomatic negotiations between Japan and America.

The Board had also been extremely critical of the actions of Chief of Staff Marshall. He was accused of failing to keep his immediate staff properly informed about developments, of failing to brief General Short adequately and of failing to send Short "important information" on December 6 and 7 that would have warned Short that an attack was coming. Lastly, the Board said that Marshall was responsible for not knowing that Short's command was not prepared for war. In brief, the Army Board was saying that, like Short, Marshall should be relieved of command.

There were other criticisms, but the primary ones were aimed at the Secretary of State and the Chief of Staff. I didn't know it at the time, but Marshall had been so devastated by the report that he had told Secretary Stimson he believed the report had destroyed his usefulness to the Army. This estimate wasn't completely true, but as I will show later, the Army Board's reports severely wounded Marshall's reputation.

So, as I sat munching my sandwich, it seemed to me that two issues were most likely to come up for discussion that afternoon: (1) How should Secretary Stimson tell the public that the Army Board had found, erroneously I suspected, that the Secretary of State and Chief of Staff were largely responsible for Pearl Harbor? (2) How could he say that the findings of the Army Board were not really true? As I said earlier, I already knew that many so-called facts found in the Board's report were false. But proving that the Board was wrong about Marshall and Hull was another matter. I could foresee a real legal challenge in the offing. My guess was that either the Army Board would have to be reconvened or yet another one would have to be appointed to review the findings of the first. This inquiry into Pearl Harbor was becoming a major scandal, if not a miscarriage of justice. The meeting with Secretary Stimson was going to be interesting.

Thus, I was in the Secretary's waiting room well before the appointed hour. The Judge Advocate General arrived next. Cramer was a short, squat man, with a chin like a bulldog's. He was a great paper pusher, a delegator who liked to claim that he ran the biggest law firm in the world. The claim was true. There were more lawyers in the Army than anywhere else in the country. But he could spare me the "law firm" bit. I don't believe Cramer ever tried a major case in a civilian court.

Just before two P.M., we were joined by Harvey Bundy, Special Assistant to the Secretary of War. Tall, slim, with thick eyeglasses and a ready smile, Bundy had been a prominent Boston lawyer before joining forces with Stimson. Bundy's genealogical roots ran deep in American history, and he was the best aide a Secretary of War could have asked for: smart, loyal, with trustworthy judgement.

When we entered Stimson's office, I was struck yet again by his magnetic personality. He was a tall, distinguished-looking man with a heavy, imposing presence. He had a short mustache and a rather stern face that lit up with an attractive smile. I would have hated to have him angry at me, because he was tough as nails. He had served as Secretary of War under President Calvin Coolidge and as Secretary of State under President Herbert Hoover. He was proudest of his title of Colonel, however, which he had earned in combat as an artilleryman in the First World War. He preferred the title Colonel to anything else. A prominent Republican, he had broken with the isolationists in his party in the spring of 1940, making a speech at Yale University that created banner headlines because he came out in support of President Roosevelt's programs for a draft to build up the American military and aid to Great Britain in her fight against Germany. As a result, Roosevelt had appointed him Secretary of War in June 1940, and although Stimson was then in his seventies, he served as, we would call it today, Secretary of both the Army and the Army Air Force (there being no separate Air Force at that time) throughout World War II with extraordinary wisdom, strength and integrity.

To me, Stimson was a man of truly heroic stature, one of the greatest men of the war, head and shoulders above Marshall. That's personal opinion, of course, or perhaps it's just one civilian sticking up for another, but I believe that Stimson saw changes in the wind, and the way the world would be in the future, before Marshall did. I also believe, and the evidence to date seems to prove the point, that Stimson stiffened Roosevelt's spine on a number of occasions, forcing Roosevelt to take immediate action rather than vacillate, as was his custom.

When the Pentagon was built, at first Stimson refused to move his office from the old War Department next to the White House, because he liked to have his windows open. The Pentagon was hermetically sealed because of its newfangled air-conditioning. Later, he relented and came to like it. As for me, I always propped my window in the Pentagon open with a coat hanger. No one could catch me doing this, since no one had the security clearance to enter the room and see what was going on.

The Secretary greeted Cramer, Bundy and me most cordially, as was his practice. He seated General Cramer next to him at his desk, placing Bundy and me across from him.

Stimson began outlining the problem that he saw in making the report of the Army Board public as it was written. The nation was clamoring for blood, and the Republican members of Congress were calling for the courts-martial of the guilty parties. Marshall could be charged. Hull's reputation could be destroyed. Preliminary leaks to the press about the contents of the Board's findings that alleged treason within the White House were igniting even greater public anger. But overall, there was the issue that the Board's criticisms appeared to be fatally flawed, because I suspected that the Board had heard perjured testimony, that crucial evidence had been withheld from it and that the general officers on it were unfairly prejudiced against Chief of Staff George C. Marshall.

Something had to be done, and done quickly, Stimson said. He then asked General Cramer, "What are your recommendations?"

Cramer hemmed and hawed. His comments were completely indecisive.

Stimson snorted and then fixed me with a steely eye. "Major Clausen, what do you think?"

My lunchtime preparation paid off.

"Mr. Secretary," I said, "it would be highly dangerous to release falsehoods to the public. We are fighting a world war, and winning that war is of paramount importance. General Marshall, whom the Army Board has harshly criticized in its newly finished report, and who will be the focus of great public anger, is working in the next room fighting the war. If he is to be court-martialed, like any defendant in a court-martial proceeding, he would rightly insist that his court-martial be held in a public forum. This would mean that we'd have to reveal to our enemies that we have broken their codes. That would be suicidal to our war effort."

"I agree," Stimson said. "Specifically, then, what do you recommend?"

"If you want to discipline Marshall," I said, "why not do what President Lincoln did when he gave an administrative reprimand to Secretary of War Cameron for gross dereliction of duty? Cameron's picture is hanging on that wall, there, Mr. Secretary.

"However, you can't do that," I continued. "In my considered judgement, you do not have all the facts of the case before you. It appears that a number of witnesses gave misleading testimony to the Army Board about our supersecret code-cracking intelligence. We don't know yet how misleading this testimony was, or why it was given the Board. Furthermore, only one week before the Board adjourned its hearings, because its authorized investigative time limit of ninety days was expiring, did the Board learn that the decrypts of the Japanese intentions were available to the Army *and* the Navy before the Japanese attack. The Board failed to investigate fully the issues raised by the availability of these decrypts."

Stimson sat bolt upright in his chair. I had his attention.

"Continue, Major."

"Well, sir," I said, "the Army Board, one week before its term was to expire, learned that while the Navy had been holding its own Court of Inquiry in the building next door, the Navy had introduced an exhibit from the earlier Navy Hart Inquiry in the form of testimony by a Naval Captain of Intelligence named Safford. In his testimony, Safford had revealed the names of Army personnel who were active in our Army G-2, War Department Intelligence. Safford said that these men knew about Japan's intentions before they attacked Pearl Harbor.

"That's a heavy charge, Mr. Secretary. We immediately requested Safford's testimony from the Navy Court for use by the Army Board. The Navy Court refused our request. We appealed the denial to the Under Secretary of the Navy Board. He upheld the denial. We then appealed to Secretary of the Navy Forrestal. He reversed the rulings of his Under Secretary and the Navy Court. And so we got Captain Safford's testimony, and our first knowledge of the code cracking.

"With Safford's testimony in hand," I continued, "the Army Board demanded of Army G-2, War Department, all the messages and details of these decrypted dispatches. General Russell of the Board was given copies of these documents. He was made custodian of this special file, to which only he had the combination. As the Assistant Recorder of the Court, I was not allowed to see the decrypts at that time. The next witnesses called before the Army Board were General Marshall and Colonel Rufus Bratton. They told us the gist of what the

Navy Court had refused to give us during our ninety days of hearings. What they had to say threw everything else we had taken testimony about into a cocked hat. The Army Board then went out of business because its statutory time limit expired. The Board's two reports were written and submitted without the Board's having properly completed its investigation. So the Board's findings are biased and incorrect, because the Board was suckered. Most importantly, the Board's findings, I believe, are way off the mark. To release them to the public as they stand would be a serious miscarriage of justice."

Stimson almost leapt from his chair. He walked swiftly to the window of his office overlooking the Potomac River and the Washington Monument, and then he wheeled on me.

"When I was the U.S. Attorney for New York," he said with real anger, "I always had all the facts. On cross-examination, I'd throw a lying witness out the window." He punched the air in the direction of the Potomac. "No witness ever lied to me and got away with it."

I rose and moved next to Stimson. He was upset, so I spoke softly. "If I can talk to you, Mr. Secretary, lawyer to lawyer, I, too, was an Assistant U.S. Attorney, although I served in San Francisco, and I know exactly what you mean about witnesses who lie."

Stimson took a deep breath, turned and pointed his index finger at my chest, saying, "Major, I want you to go back over the operations of the Army Board with a fine-toothed comb. Retake every bit of testimony that needs to be clarified as the result of our having broken the Japanese codes before Pearl Harbor. You are to follow any unexplored leads you consider necessary. Leave no stone unturned. You will report to me regularly via Mr. Bundy. I will give you all the support my office can provide. Just let me know what you need."

I was momentarily stunned by the enormousness of the assignment he was thrusting upon me. In effect, he was asking me to reinvestigate Pearl Harbor and giving me the discretionary authority to correct the faulty proceedings of the Army Board.

After a few seconds, I replied, "I welcome the opportunity, Mr. Secretary, and I hope to fulfill my duties to your satisfaction."

"Good luck, Major Clausen. And Godspeed." Stimson shook my hand with a powerful grip.

Our meeting was over. As we left the room, I pondered what might have occurred earlier. Obviously, Secretary Stimson had held meetings in high places about which I knew nothing. Nor did I ever learn what had transpired so that my name was put forward for the job. Everyone in the War Department knew I was a civilian at heart. I didn't give two hoots in hell for a military career. I had signed on for the duration of the war only. All I wanted after the fighting stopped was to return to my practice in San Francisco. The Army could have my body as long as the war lasted, but it could never have my heart. That belonged to the law.

Bundy, Cramer and I stood in the anteroom, chatting for a few moments, and then Bundy asked me to come into his office.

Folding himself into his chair, Bundy said, "I am delighted by the Secretary's solution to this problem of the Army Board's report."

"Thank you," I replied. "The Secretary certainly amazed me. I am deeply impressed and honored by the assignment. But it's a rather large order. It'll be difficult to do it properly."

I had good reason to feel both honored and apprehensive. I was being given a task usually assigned to a three-star general with a fully supportive court of inquiry and all the staff trimmings. I understood that the reputations of many men would depend on how effectively I performed my mission. I also realized that if I was careless in handling the decrypts now in my possession, I could cause terrible damage to our war effort.

The most important question would be how to conduct my investigation. I told Bundy that I preferred to act as an independent prosecutor, rather than convene a full court of inquiry. Since speed was of the essence in backtracking through the records and questioning witnesses who needed to be checked, the fastest and most secure way to do the job would be to act like an FBI agent. And rather than go through the time-consuming process of calling witnesses back to Washington from combat zones around the world, it would be better, I thought, if I went to them. I could take their statements and type them up in affidavit form, review the affidavits with the witnesses, then ask the witnesses to affirm and swear to their testimony to me as an officer of the court.

"I think that's a far better procedure than another high-falutin' Board with stars on their shoulders, all of them worrying about their chances of promotion," I said. "My mission appears to call for a careful, factual, judicial approach using extreme care to preserve the security of our code cracking."

"Excellent," said Bundy.

We agreed that there were other details I had to think my way through, so we decided to meet again in a couple of days.

That's how my investigation into Pearl Harbor began.

At the time, I was not aware of what was being hotly debated by Stimson, Secretary of the Navy James Forrestal and President Roosevelt about the release of the findings of the Navy Court of Inquiry and the Army Pearl Harbor Board. I was too busy working like a galley slave.

It quickly became obvious, however, that high-stakes politics were taking place. The result was that Forrestal reported to the nation that the Navy Court "had found there were errors of judgement of certain officers in the naval service, both at Pearl Harbor and at Washington." For his part, Secretary Stimson told the public, "So far as the Commanding General of the Hawaiian Department is concerned, I am of the opinion that his errors of judgement were of such a nature as to demand his relief from Command status. . . . In my judgement, on the evidence now recorded, it is sufficient action."

Stimson went on to say that he was still investigating other aspects of Pearl Harbor, but he didn't say why he was doing it, nor did he mention my name.

The statements by the Army and the Navy failed to satisfy a lot of people, most notably Sen. Homer Ferguson, a Republican from Michigan, about whom I will say a lot later. He was a staunch supporter of Admiral Kimmel, and a believer that the Roosevelt administration had forced the Japanese to attack Pearl Harbor to achieve Roosevelt's ambition to fight the Axis. (The Army Board report would have made him very happy.) Ferguson couldn't figure out how we had lost all those battleships and sailors at Pearl Harbor without somebody's having done something that was worthy of court-martial. Why hadn't heads rolled, either in the military or in the administration? He believed there must be a cover-up going on to protect people in high places: Roosevelt, Hull and Marshall, for starters.

Ferguson was partially right. There was a cover-up going on. But it was to protect our greatest secret: Magic. Ferguson was too partisan to be entrusted with the secret of Magic, as Marshall had done in the case of Dewey. He'd never keep the secret. And so the game of "blame, blame, who's to blame" had to be played out to the bitter end.

One of the greatest problems facing me was the question of how I was going to get people to tell me the truth. So, first I wrote a series of questions I would use as a cover, in that they dealt with every unanswered aspect of Pearl Harbor. Then I got the questions turned into an order for me to follow and had the order signed by Judge Advocate General Cramer. This covered one of my flanks.

The next thing was to get inside the Top Secret Purple group. This I proposed doing by carrying the decrypts of the most significant intercepted Japanese messages with me on my travels. Then, if a witness seemed to be evading my questions, I would simply haul out the necessary document and show it to him. He would comprehend that I was one of the Top Secret group, too, and that lying to me would be impossible. Bundy and Stimson thought this idea was "first rate." That covered a second flank.

Another tool would be my extraordinary power as the personal representative of the Secretary of War. I wrote a letter for Stimson's signature—which he signed with relish, I might add—that ordered *all* Army personnel to give me access to *all* records, documents and information within their knowledge, *whether requested or not*; to volunteer any information they might think I needed; and to answer fully whatever questions I might put to them.

I mean to say that this was some letter of authorization. It gave me tremendous leverage. It also made me feel quite humble, for such power must never, never be misused.

There was one possibility I had overlooked, however, and it was corrected one afternoon when I met with Bundy.

He called me into his office and without much preamble said, "Secretary Stimson is greatly concerned about the decrypts you're going to carry with you on your mission. He wants to make sure they are secure at all times. So we're going to use a method that involves strapping a special envelope to your chest. The envelope will hold the decrypts. Also a magnesium bomb. You'll have a cord that detonates the bomb when you pull it. If you are about to be captured, assuming you can't detonate the bomb at a distance, you will pull the cord and detonate the bomb closer. In any event, the bomb will burn the decrypts to a crisp."

Having just been told, admittedly in a very urbane way, how I was supposed to kill myself to avoid capture, I found myself speaking with some consternation. "Can I really detonate the bomb at a distance?" I asked. "If not," I suppose I will be crisped just like the decrypts as they waltz their way to heaven. I am not resisting your idea, I hope you understand. It's just that I fear some silly pilot might make me parachute into a jungle."

"I'm sorry, Henry," said Bundy. "There's no alternative. We have been ordered by Congress to conduct this investigation, and we will have guards for you at all the appropriate places. But if the enemy captured these decrypts, it would expose our greatest secret. So I must ask that you be prepared to take this extreme action.''

I paused for a moment to think it through.

"Okay, I understand all this, and I accept the order," I said. "I will become a walking bomb. When do I get this apparatus?"

"I have it here," Bundy said. My heart sank as he showed me the contrivance.

"Does it have a safety?"

"Yes. It's built so you can keep it on safety. But when you're in a war zone, the bomb must always be armed and the safety turned off."

In the months that followed, I was very unhappy to entrust my life to an unthinking device that, if it malfunctioned, would incinerate me in a flash. Strapped over my solar plexus, the damned envelope was stiff and uncomfortable to wear. And whenever I met a friend in a war zone and he slapped me on the back in greeting, I winced inwardly, waiting for the worst to happen.

2 ## "YOUR MISSION IS IMPOSSIBLE"

The morning after I picked up that infernal pouch from Bundy, and like a good lawyer who doesn't trust anything until he's tested the evidence, I went to the bomb range at Fort Myer. I carefully packed the envelope with fifty carbon copies of unimportant letters and detonated it from a distance. It flared up, like a million matches going off at once. Not a shred of paper could be found. I also deduced that not much of me would be found, either. But at least it would be effective and quick.

I then picked up another bomb pouch from supply and called on Maj. Gen. John Bissell, Acting Chief of Staff of G-2 (Intelligence). He was not pleased to see me. He became furious when I showed my letter of authority from Secretary Stimson and started to tell him what I needed.

He grabbed a piece of paper and in an act of intimidation wrote my name on it. "Your mission is impossible," he snarled, doubling his fists and banging them hard on his desk. Here I was, a lowly major, who behaved like a civilian, interfering with the Army's holiest secret of secrets.

He picked up the phone, saying, "I'm calling General Marshall to tell him what you're doing. That'll put a stop to this."

"Sir," I replied, "I wouldn't do that. The Secretary of War has ordered me to investigate the Army Command and Communications systems. You and General Marshall are potential witnesses. I don't think you'd want me to report to the Secretary of War, and through him to Congress, that you were stonewalling an investigation they ordered."

Bissell slammed the phone down. Then he shouted, "I'll be a son of a bitch!" He banged his fist on the desk again and again.

Finally, he ran out of steam. "Okay, you win," he said. "Tell me what you need."

Now that he had calmed down, I told him that I needed unlimited access to every decoded Japanese message the Army possessed. I also needed the intelligence evaluations for the twelve-month period before Pearl Harbor. I needed everything he could think of, internal memos, directives to Hawaii, responses from Hawaii, anything that related to Pearl Harbor.

Bissell turned puce while he listened, but at least he held his tongue.

"Come with me," he said, and took me next door, where I found myself back in the office of Gen. Carter Clarke.

"Give the Major whatever he wants," Bissell snapped. He turned on his heel and stalked out.

Clarke had a good sense of humor. He laughed heartily at the twists and turns I would have to follow, but he said he'd help in whatever way he could.

First, he showed me the special Top Secret oath that bound the people of G-2 who were working in code-breaking fields. I could understand immediately how they had been able to cross their fingers and lie to the various investigative boards before which they had testified. The oath demanded that they do so. (Nearly thirty years later, when the CIA's former director, Richard Helms, lied to Congress about the CIA's activities and was convicted for doing so, I had a real—and frightening—sensation of déjà vu.)

"Thank you," I said. "I understand. The Secretary of War has required these oaths for G-2 personnel, and in turn, he exempted me as his investigator, as his orders confirmed."

Well, I thought, if today's events are any indication of what it's going to be like to dig information out of these people, the Gilbert and Sullivan song was right: "A policeman's lot is not a happy one. . . ."

It took me days to review the many thousands of decrypts in Clarke's possession. Finally, I picked out forty or so messages I thought would be relevant to take with me on my travels. Clarke copied them and bound them in a special folder.

This time, I put them in my bomb pouch.

For the uninitiated, it is difficult to understand the significance of the decrypts that I picked out of General Clarke's files. The decrypts worked for me like the magic words "Open, Sesame!" But they would have meant little to the average person, because the military set up a variety of security systems to hide the meanings of the messages, so they were like a series of Chinese boxes, one hidden within the other.

Even today, historians are denied access to the full range of decoded Japanese intercepts from the months before Pearl Harbor. Many of the decrypts can be found in the thirty-nine volumes of the Pearl Harbor Hearings, assuming one can find copies. Even then, they are out of context, especially in terms of what I was doing. In my own report, which Congress published, one has to work hard to track the serial numbers of the decrypts identified in the affidavits I took, because the printer jumbled the order in which the decrypts were published. I had no control over this printing process, but it proves that the military's obsession with secrecy makes life hell for the historian.

Therefore, if my book now appears to contradict what historians have written previously, it does so only because, as a player in the game, I was working on the inside, while historians have used deductive reasoning to write their books.

Put it another way. The historians have seen only what has been released to the public to date. They have not seen what I have seen, nor perhaps talked with the people from whom I took sworn testimony. The decrypts the historians have seen are not always truly accurate in terms of when, precisely, the messages were received, or when they were decoded, or when they were distributed within the military chain of command in Washington (to say nothing of the distribution of this material to the State Department or the White House). Neither do the public records specify when the information in these decrypts was sent to the commanders in the field, nor how the information was then used by the various commanders. If the judgements I make in this book appear contrary to what has been written before, I ask the reader's indulgence, because I am basing my statements on my understanding of the system of codes and decoding according to the experts who made the system work.

Secret messages and eavesdropping on one's enemies and friends are facts of history. Polybius enumerated several codes used in ancient Greece. In about 1516, a writer named Trithemious wrote a famous treatise on the subject. Francis Bacon saw codes as a part of grammar. He devised an ingenious plan of deciphering, explaining that while ciphers usually consisted of letters, they could also be found in words. Thus, words collected from dictionaries might represent complete ideas. Also, numbers and other characters could be used as substitutes for letters.

For example, the dispatches of the Venetian ambassadors to England during Queen Mary's reign have only recently been deciphered. The diaries of Samuel Pepys contained codes to keep his servants from reading his innermost thoughts. In 1641, Wilkins, the Bishop of Chester, published a treatise called *Mercury, or the Secret of Swift Messenger*. And when the Earl of Argyle was trying to overthrow James II, the Earl wrote to his coconspirators in sentences of no apparent importance, the real meaning of which was found in words placed in sequence or at certain intervals.

An American named Herbert Osborne Yardley became a legendary contributor to this rich field of history. The son of a railway telegrapher, he was an outgoing, intelligent boy who could do almost anything. He was president of his high school class, editor of the school paper, a good public speaker and captain of the football team. He was a true, all-American boy. At the age of twenty-three, he left his home in Indiana to seek his fortune in Washington, D.C., starting as a code clerk in the State Department in 1912 and later transferring to the Army, where he organized the first code-breaking operation in the country.

Yardley eventually became the most famous cryptologist in the world, and it will always be a mystery how he accomplished some of his more legendary exploits. People have always wondered if he filched the texts of messages from the safes of foreign embassies or merely decoded the messages as they had been sent. It is known that he had coconspirators within the telegraph companies, and his abilities amazed President Wilson's administration when he successfully decoded messages sent to the President by his personal emissary, Colonel House.

At the end of World War I, Yardley was in Paris, working to develop cooperation with French code experts. He operated from two rooms in the Hotel Crillon, running a code bureau attached to the

American Commission to the Peace Conference, where his headquarters became known as the "black chamber." Yardley was called its father.

When Yardley returned to America after completing his assignment, the Army made an effort to retain him in its peacetime organization. Gen. Marlborough Churchill, the Director of Military Intelligence, asked him to report on code-breaking developments. Yardley's revelations excited the experts, and Gen. Payton C. March, then the Chief of Staff, brought the "black chamber" back to life. For reasons of security, Yardley set up his shop in New York, advertising the operation as a commercial translation office and code compilation company.

The Japanese then came out with a new code. In July 1919, General Churchill asked Yardley if he could break it. Yardley promised to do so within a year—or resign. The solution came to Yardley while he was asleep. As he explained it later, "My heart stood still, and I dared not move. Was I awake? Was I losing my mind? A solution? At last—and after all these heartless months."

It had taken Yardley only six months to find the solution. Meanwhile, America had called for a conference to limit naval armaments. "Tons and guns" was the way some Naval experts viewed the matter, and during the summer of 1922, the United States, Great Britain, France, Italy and Japan met to set the limit on the number of ships each nation could launch, as established by that nation's current naval strength. (It sounds somewhat like the long-range missile treaties of today.)

During these tense negotiations, Yardley deciphered the messages that Tokyo was sending to its negotiators about the minimum tonnage agreements Japan would agree to. (It is also claimed that Yardley was doing the same decoding of the instructions to the British, French and Italian delegations.) Because of the accuracy of Yardley's code breaking, the United States stood firm in the negotiations and succeeded in getting Japan to agree to the lowest possible tonnage Tokyo would accept. It was quite a victory for the code breakers in the "black chamber."

In 1929, Henry L. Stimson was named Secretary of State. Upon learning that the State Department was paying the bills for the "black chamber," Stimson made one of the greatest errors of his life. He called the operation "unethical" and ordered that the "black chamber" be shut down.

Needless to say, Secretary of State Stimson in 1929 was a totally different person from the man I knew in the 1940s. The Stimson I knew was always demanding that our code-breaking abilities be improved and expanded; he became a bear about making sure that our intelligence-gathering operations worked properly. As he explained it to me, "When I was Secretary of State, I had a different mission than I do now."

Because Stimson closed the "black chamber," he threw Yardley out of work. The result was exactly what the Army didn't want. The famous code breaker then toured America, lecturing to large audiences about what would happen to the nation if it continued to deprive itself of his special talents. He wrote books, too. One was called *The American Black Chamber*. Another was written with a young free-lance journalist, Marie Stuart Klooz. It was called *Japanese Diplomatic Secrets, 1921–22*, and it caused a major sensation in Japan by revealing how Tokyo had been snookered during the naval negotiations.

The first thing the Japanese did was to change their codes. Overnight, we lost a source of priceless information. Our military asked that special legislation be introduced to prevent leaks such as Yardley's from happening again. The issue was hotly debated, and a compromise bill was submitted to President Franklin D. Roosevelt. He signed it, and it became law on June 10, 1933.

Meanwhile, the Army had another code-breaking operation up its sleeve. Here, a remarkable man appeared on the scene, Wolf Frederick Friedman. He had graduated with honors from high school in his native Bucharest and, to escape anti-Semitism, had come to America to study agriculture at Michigan Agricultural College in East Lansing. His abilities in the field of genetics won him a scholarship to Cornell. He obtained his Bachelor of Science degree, then became a geneticist at the River Bank Laboratories in Geneva, Illinois.

The man who ran River Bank was "Colonel" George Fabyan, the heir to a large fortune, who dabbled in science: acoustics, chemistry, genetics and cryptology. It was his hope to prove that Francis Bacon was really the author of Shakespeare's works, and Friedman became interested in this venture. Soon he found himself heading up the Department of Ciphers, which began receiving assignments from an unexpected source: the American government.

World War I was looming on the horizon, and Friedman surprised everyone by decoding and returning in a matter of days the material Washington had sent him. Fabyan then offered the War Department the services of his Cipher Department. The offer was accepted five days before America declared war on Germany.

The Washington Department was formed, and a few months later, Friedman found himself teaching Army officers a cram course in cryptoanalysis. The first class only had four participants; later it grew to seven or eight. It was then that the War Department learned it had been sending material to River Bank in the belief that the lab was involved in cryptography, the making of codes, rather than cryptoanalysis, the breaking of codes. (It was not until 1921, however, that Friedman coined the term "cryptoanalysis," which covers all aspects of cryptology.)

Friedman was commissioned to the Army in 1918 and sent to France to seek a solution to the German codes. He was successful, and when he returned to America in 1921, he became head of the Signal Corps Codes and Cipher Section. He also revised the War Department Staff Code. At that time, he and one assistant made up the entire War Department Cryptographic operation. Our Signal Intelligence Service (SIS, and not to be confused with a British intelligence department boasting the same initials) was created by the Army in 1930. The chief signal officer was Friedman, whose duties and responsibilities were ordered by the Secretary of War. These included the preparation and revisions of Army codes and ciphers, and, in time of war, the interception of enemy radio and wire traffic.

In 1934, the world situation began to worsen, and Secretary of War Harry H. Woodring began building up the SIS. By the time the Germans invaded Poland in 1939, the SIS staff had grown to nineteen in number. When Japan attacked Pearl Harbor in 1941, the staff had grown to 331. The staff numbered about thirteen thousand by the time the war ended.

Meanwhile, our Navy had been involved in cryptology almost as far back as the first wireless transmission from a Navy ship in 1899. It, too, had a code and signals section in the Naval Communications Service (NCS). Then, in 1924, a thirty-one-year-old lieutenant, Laurence F. Safford, was ordered to head up a radio intelligence section, and he began building an intercept organization. By late 1930, the Navy's cryptological organization numbered seven hundred officers and enlisted personnel; it had listening stations in Washington State, Maine, Maryland, Hawaii and the Philippines, plus smaller stations in California and Florida, and on Guam and Long Island.

At that time, Japan was employing nine cipher systems. The most important of these was a machine-operated system called *Angooki Taipu A,* or Cipher Machine A. This code was for high-level diplomatic traffic.

In 1936, after a year of effort, Friedman and the Army SIS team broke the Japanese Type A code. Friedman gave the classification Red to the machine that broke the Type A code. A short time later, in late 1938, the Japanese changed their codes again. It was not until September 25, 1940, that Friedman's team created, seemingly by a miracle, its own machine that produced the first totally clear, ungarbled decryption of this new code, which Friedman classified as Purple. All of these code designations were lumped together by the American intelligence services into one catchall word: Magic. The very name, Magic, was fitting for the feat that Friedman and his team had achieved. The machine that they had built to break the Japanese Purple codes proved to be as efficient as the original that the Japanese had created, if not superior to it.

I believe that Friedman's accomplishments should have been honored by church bells ringing across America, because from the new Magic decrypts, it was obvious that the Japanese were preparing for war and we were being given the chance to prepare against whatever Japanese aggression might be coming. Instead, silence became the order of the day. The news about Magic was restricted to but a few key members of our government. Otherwise, it was feared that our breakthrough with Magic might be leaked back to the Japanese and we would lose the information that was so vital to our budding war effort.

Meanwhile, the British had been busy working on the codes used by the German military, and had succeeded in breaking the so-called Enigma codes (a name derived from a special code machine used by the German forces). Like the Americans, the British called their final product of breaking the Enigma codes by a special term: Ultra. (From now on, when I mention the messages derived from the American breaking of various codes, I will use the term "Magic"; when I discuss the messages derived from codes broken by the British, I will use "Ultra.")

It was obvious to the leaders of Britain and America that they would soon join in war against the Axis. In July 1940, Prime Minister Churchill wrote to President Roosevelt suggesting that secret information of a technical nature be exchanged between the two nations. The letter was delivered to the White House by Lord Lothian, the British Ambassador to Washington, in surroundings of the greatest secrecy.

Roosevelt approved of Churchill's idea, and the Prime Minister dispatched one of his top scientists, Sir Henry Tizard, to begin the discussions with the Americans. He met with Gen. George Strong, the Chief of our Army's Planning Staff, and Gen. Delos C. Emmons, of our Army Air Corps. It was Emmons who told the British War Office about our Magic breakthrough. I have never been clear as to whether he was authorized to do this by General Marshall or whether he did it unofficially. Needless to say, the British were extremely excited by this news. They had been unable to break the Japanese Purple code, and so London proposed that the exchange of information be widened to include a full exchange of cryptographic systems.

Upon returning to Washington, Strong and Emmons delivered a secret report to Marshall, recommending that Washington give London a Purple machine that would break the Japanese codes. (Later, our Assistant Chief of Naval Operations agreed that the exchange of equipment should also include the U.S. Navy's code secrets.) Marshall took the stance that since the Army had broken the Japanese Purple code, he needed no further authority about sharing the machines with our British allies. But when the news of this reached Admiral Anderson, the Director of Naval Intelligence, and Adm. Leigh Noyes, the Director of Naval Communications, they were furious that Marshall was not consulting them. They believed Marshall was giving the British far too much without getting anything in return, and they asked that, in exchange, the British give us their Enigma machine that broke the German codes.

A great amount of haggling took place. Marshall got his way, apparently believing that the British would reciprocate and give us their Enigma machine. But Marshall had been deceived. When the Americans went to Bletchley Park, the center for British code breaking, they handed over to the British two Purple machines, two Red machines, plus consular codes and other naval code-related materials. In return, the British gave Marshall nothing. They reneged on all their previous agreements, saying that it was against British policy to share code secrets with a neutral nation, which America was at the time, since the Japanese had not yet attacked.

What made the perfidity of the British even more galling to the Americans was that in giving our Purple decoding machines to England, we gave up a machine that had been destined for our Navy's use at Pearl Harbor.

The British have never officially acknowledged the story about how they fooled us into giving them our most secret weapon against Japan. But it certainly soured the feelings of many in the American Navy toward Great Britain. I fear it also is a major reason why there has been so much made about Churchill's supposedly having conspired to keep Roosevelt from knowing the Japanese were going to attack Pearl Harbor, which meant that America would automatically become a British ally in the war against Germany and Italy. During the course of my investigation, I visited Bletchley Park and reviewed the British decrypts of the Japanese Purple codes. Copies of these decrypts are included in the appendix as Exhibit No. 8 on pages 353–393. They prove two things. One is that the British intercepted approximately the same messages as did the Americans before Pearl Harbor. The second is that the British appear to have shared this information with the United States, which means that it is highly doubtful that the British conspired to allow the Japanese to attack Pearl Harbor.[1]

It is also important to remember that despite Friedman's having solved the secret of breaking the Japanese diplomatic Purple code, we never broke all the Purple messages we intercepted, and the more important Japanese naval codes were almost never broken. According to the Hewitt Investigation, which the Navy conducted simultaneously with my own, and about which I will write later, between January 1 and December 7, 1941, our radio intercept stations picked up 1,280 diplomatic messages between Tokyo and Washington. Of this number, we could decrypt only some six hundred, which gave us only a fragmentary picture of Japanese intentions. As for breaking the Japanese naval codes, I was told that we broke only about 10 percent, which didn't help our Navy very much at that time.

I also met, during the course of my investigation, Lt. Col. Frank B. Rowlett of the Signal Corps. While I was taking his affidavit, Rowlett told me in a disarming manner that "Friedman thinks he deserves all the credit, but I'm the guy who actually did the impossible trick with the 'Purple' machine."

"If that's the case," I replied, "you deserve ten stars on your shoulders." I meant it, too, because our system of rewards for people in the code-breaking and intelligence field was terrible. We never gave them enough money; we never gave them recognition; we never gave them the rank they deserved. We treated them shabbily. Later, I learned that what Rowlett had told me was, indeed, true. And he had also

---

[1] Letter from Clausen to Lee, Sept. 10, 1991.

spoken the truth when he said he preferred being a light colonel, because then he didn't have to worry about administrative responsibility. What he really wanted to do was to have time to think and let his genius run free.

Thus, it was Friedman and his SIS group who accomplished the miracle of re-creating the Purple decryption machine, although Safford's naval group, OP-20-G as it was called, was also involved in the project. The real problem was that the relations between the two groups were argumentative and controversial. Whenever one of the groups had decoded a special message, it couldn't wait to run to the White House or wherever, shouting, "Lookee, lookee at what we've got here!" Perhaps it's understandable when you consider that both groups were starved for funding and the only way they could get any attention was to show the President what they were accomplishing.

Nevertheless, as I found throughout my investigation, this caused a lot of duplication of effort. It was unseemly, too. Finally, the Army and Navy compromised. They exchanged everything that was intercepted by their ten or twelve interception stations. The Navy would then decrypt and translate the traffic on the odd-numbered days of the month, while the Army did the job on the even-numbered days. The absurd system went even further. In January 1941, the two services also agreed that they would service the White House with Magic on alternate months. The Army (G-2) would perform the service in January, March, May, July, September and November. The Navy (Office of Naval Intelligence, or ONI) would do the job in February, April, June, August, October and, presumably, December. (Navy documents conveniently seem to forget this month.)

All went well until May 1941, after the State Department had lost intelligence memo Number 9 in March. The Army (G-2) Chief, Brig. Gen. Sherman Miles, suspected that this loss had caused the Germans to tell the Japanese that their codes had been compromised. Fortunately, Tokyo ignored Berlin's warning, but G-2 clamped down even tighter on security.

This resulted in a check on the White House. Magic documents were found in the desk of Maj. Gen. Edwin M. "Pa" Watson, the military aide to President Roosevelt. Watson's desk and office were determined not to be secure. (This differs, of course, from earlier stories that crumpled-up Magic papers were found in Roosevelt's wastebasket.) As a result of this discovery, Army (G-2) decided unilaterally in May to stop providing the White House with Magic. Instead, G-2 provided Magic to the State Department, which G-2 believed to be the proper recipient for these intercepted diplomatic messages.

G-2's decision to stop servicing the Commander in Chief with such vital messages created friction between Roosevelt and the Army. Who was running the country? one might ask.

Meanwhile, a new Naval aide to the President was named, Rear Adm. John R. Beardall, and ONI kept servicing the Admiral with Magic. Apparently, the President had been asking Beardall what was going on, because Beardall kept telling Lt. Comdr. Alwin D. Kramer of the Navy's Translation Section to bring the original decrypts to the White House. Toward the end of September, with Army (G-2) still refusing to send Magic to the President, the President told Beardall that he wanted to see the original material Kramer was bringing him. Initially, Kramer told Beardall that he would have to check first with the Director of Naval Intelligence, Rear Adm. Theodore S. Wilkinson. Then, with Wilkinson's permission, Kramer contacted Col. Rufus S. Bratton, Army (G-2), and got his okay on the matter.

By November, Army (G-2) had determined that the leak in the White House had been plugged, and Brigadier General Miles was ready to service the White House again. It was too late to smooth things over with Roosevelt, however. The President said he didn't care if it was the Army's month to send material to him. He wanted the Navy to do the job from then on.

The distribution agreement between the Army and the Navy was modified again. From mid-November on, the Army gave its Magic information to the State Department, and the Navy solely serviced the President via Kramer to Beardall.[2] The entire system was a shambles, at least as far as my lawyer's logic was concerned. That the Army should have stopped giving the President the Magic information without explaining itself to the Commander in Chief is beyond belief.

From what I could see, by early December 1941, our communications intelligence community was like a series of small towns competing for dollars from the state government. The Army's SIS handled Japanese army military traffic, even though none might be decoded. In the meantime, the Naval OP-20-G group secretly handled Japanese naval ship traffic. Both groups still followed the odd-even-day formula for processing Purple. Meanwhile, the Coast Guard, the FBI and the

[2] Proceedings 5475,76; Bratton to Clausen; confidential briefings to Lee.

Federal Radio Intelligence Division were climbing into the act. (The last group claimed complete responsibility for radio interception and direction finding, if you can believe it.)

The finished, translated product of all the diplomatic Purple traffic was furnished to the War (Army and Army Air Force), Navy and State Departments. Parts of it went to the FBI. The Navy's ship intercepts were available in full only to the Navy Department, but summaries were furnished to the War Department for use only at the highest level.

As my investigation would prove, one of the worst aspects of the delivery system for Purple material was that no permanent record was kept of who had seen which decrypts or when. A courier would arrive without notice at an official's desk, and that official would have to interrupt his work, read the material immediately and give it back to the courier without time to reflect upon it. Any briefings on the information were oral. There was no comprehensive method for either disseminating or evaluating the material.

We might have possessed the genius to break the Purple code, but in 1941 we didn't have the brains to know what to do with it.

After Pearl Harbor, however, the military chiefs realized that the dissemination of Magic information was too important to allow the old, inefficient system to continue. From then on, the system was constantly improved, with better and better analysis added to the product. Thus, despite the early drawbacks and chaotic procedures that existed when we entered World War II, by the end of the war, we and the British were breaking virtually all the Japanese diplomatic codes, and the benefits were staggering. With precise information detailing the enemy's intentions, Allied forces accomplished military miracles.

In monetary terms, what we spent to break the Japanese Purple codes produced perhaps the best return on investment America ever made.

Churchill said the results were worth many, many more divisions. Adm. Chester Nimitz rated its value as the equivalent of another whole Pacific Fleet. Gen. Thomas Handy, Deputy Chief of Staff of the Army, claimed it shortened the war in Europe by at least a full year.

I have no reluctance to say that if our military had created a more efficient system for analyzing and disseminating our code-breaking intelligence in 1940 and 1941, the disaster at Pearl Harbor as we know it could have been avoided. At least, our defenders would have been ready to repel the attackers instead of being asleep at the crucial moment. My investigation for Secretary Stimson proved this conclusively, and Stimson totally agreed with my findings. Furthermore, if one studies our military actions subsequent to Pearl Harbor and the favorable results we achieved, one can see the truth of my statement. We learned a vital lesson at Pearl Harbor, and one cannot help being impressed by what we accomplished later on, when we were able to use Magic intelligence properly. For example:

- Only six months after Pearl Harbor, we were able to ambush the Japanese en route to attack Midway. Our Navy destroyed the most important aircraft carriers in the Japanese fleet. The Battle of Midway proved to be the turning point of the Pacific war.

- By breaking Japanese codes, our pilots were able to shoot down a plane carrying Adm. Isoruku Yamamoto, the Commander in Chief of the Japanese Navy. This angered General Marshall, who claimed that the secret of our having broken the enemy's codes was too important to be compromised by such an obvious indicator of intelligence sources and methods.

- Early on, America learned of the crucial decision by the high command in Tokyo that Japan would not join Germany in its war against Russia. This knowledge dictated our strategy throughout the war.

- The breaking of Japanese codes provided crucial information about the weak links in the chain of Japanese island fortresses in the Pacific, thereby aiding MacArthur's successful advance from Australia through the South Pacific and his retaking of the Philippines.

- Breaking the Japanese codes provided our Navy with incredibly accurate information about when Japanese merchant ships were to sail from port, including their routes and their destinations. It was the key to our successful submarine campaign. We also learned exactly how many ships Japan lost during the course of the war, where they were lost and when.

- Before Pearl Harbor, America knew that the Japanese Ambassador in Berlin had informed Tokyo that Hitler intended to attack Russia. The Russians were warned, but Stalin refused to believe the reports.

- The value of our breaking the Purple codes continued beyond Japan's surrender in 1945. General Bissell, who ended the war as the Chief of G-2 (Intelligence), War Department, sent a memo to Marshall saying that after the war, we persuaded the Japanese that we had never broken their Magic code. The Army also prevented the physical destruction of the Japanese diplomatic code systems, especially those that used the Purple machine. The Japanese then continued to use the Magic machines for their diplomatic traffic. Bissell said we were benefiting greatly from what we were learning and predicted we would learn even more in the future. We continued to read the so-called Japanese diplomatic mail until Congress decided, at the start of its hearings in 1945 into the cause of Pearl Harbor, to tell the public about our code-breaking abilities.

So when I took the package of decrypts from Carter Clarke in 1944, you can understand why the Army was unhappy with my mission, and why I was forced to carry the documents in a bomb bag that was strapped against my heart and stomach. The pouch itself looked like dirty canvas, with a strap that went around my chest and a small set of suspenders that fastened with buckles. The lanyard triggering the pouch was attached to the right-hand bottom corner, and if I was going into a hot spot of the world I always had the lanyard where I could pull it quickly, because the war effort was more important than my life.

The most important thing to me was that I had been entrusted with these papers that were so secret they could alter the course of the war. So I worked at keeping people from seeing any bulges under my shirt and that way they couldn't tell that the most important papers in the world were only an eighth of an inch from my skin.

When I was overseas, or traveling in America, I wore the pouch into the office of the person I was interviewing. If an individual appeared reluctant to talk, even after reading Stimson's letter of authorization, I would open up my shirt, unbuckle the pouch, and pull out the specific Magic document I wanted to ask questions about. That's what I did with Captain Layton, for example. The look of surprise on his face when I did my striptease act was worth the price of admission.

Other people I interviewed flinched visibly when I first showed them the papers I was carrying. Others began to drip with sweat. They understood that they were being questioned by someone who knew more than they did.

The result was that one by one they changed or amplified the stories they had told previously under oath. And the truth of why there had been a disaster at Pearl Harbor began to unfold before my eyes.

3 | "WITH YOUR BLESSING, I'LL ENLIST"

One morning, while I was getting ready to carry out my mission, Stimson called me into his office.

After greeting me and asking how things were going, Stimson said, "Clausen, the Navy has done it again."

"What's that, Mr. Secretary?"

"Whenever the Army and the Navy have a joint mission, the Navy usually tries to appoint a member who will outrank his counterpart in the Army," Stimson said. "This time they have outdone themselves. Secretary of the Navy Forrestal has informed me that the Navy will conduct a further investigation into Pearl Harbor such as you are doing. Furthermore, your opposite number in this operation will be a four-star admiral, the former Commander of the Mediterranean Fleet, Henry K. Hewitt."

"He certainly outranks me, Mr. Secretary," I said with a grin. "You can quickly correct it if you want to."

Stimson chuckled. "You should know, Henry, that at first it was recommended that we appoint a general officer to handle this mission. But your name kept coming up on top of the list. Your credentials are right for it. You're Republican, you're a good trial lawyer and you're an independent thinker. Your approach to this job is similar to being a special prosecutor. It's just the ticket.

"You may also be interested to know," Stimson continued, "that Mr. Forrestal told me on the phone that the Chief of Naval Operations, Admiral King, was furious at him for appointing Hewitt as your opposite number. King told him he was giving too much power and authority to one person."

I could only say, "Mr. Secretary, I appreciate your confidence in me."

And then Stimson let out a real whoop of laughter. "By God, Henry, I wish I could have been a fly on the wall in King's office when he heard that I had appointed a Major to do this job for me!"

I immediately set about meeting my opposite number by calling his assistant, Comdr. John F. Sonnett. He had been a brilliant and prominent New York lawyer and special assistant to Secretary Forrestal. He quickly arranged a meeting with the Admiral.

After shaking hands, I said, "Admiral Hewitt, I suppose this is the first time in your military life that your opposite number is a lowly Army Major."

"We are equal in that our first names are Henry," he replied.

"That is true," I said. "And even more so, because of the Secretary of War, whose first name is also Henry."

Hewitt's eyes widened slightly at this shot across his bows, and we never had any problems between our two operations. In fact, whenever I needed help from the Navy at one of its far-flung outposts, I would simply tell the head of the base to call Commander Sonnett at the Munitions Building, and from then on, I'd get the red-carpet treatment.

During the course of our investigations, Sonnett and I often traded information in the way that lawyers do. I have always believed that the Hewitt Investigation was the best one the Navy held. Hewitt bore down heavily on intelligence matters, as did I, and twenty-one of his witnesses never appeared before another inquiry into Pearl Harbor. His work should be reevaluated by historians in the light of his probing into previously unexplored areas. Like myself, Hewitt reached some conclusions that were not to the Navy's liking. He, too, concluded that Naval personnel had made mistakes that contributed to Pearl Harbor. He also found that Kimmel "did have sufficient information in his possession to indicate the situation was unusually serious. . . ."[1]

I believe the Hewitt Report forced the Navy, for the first time, to

---

[1] Hewitt Report, p. 176.

consider the issue it didn't want to think about: that Kimmel's actions before the Pearl Harbor attack were wrong.

As for me, the question has been asked, "Henry, how the hell did you ever find yourself in the Army in the first place?"

The answer is simple. I volunteered.

All Americans my age remember where they were when the bombs fell on Pearl Harbor that Sunday, December 7, 1941. I was in my law office in San Francisco, preparing for a jury trial the next day. I had recently won a major victory for Joseph Strauss, the engineer who had designed and built the Golden Gate Bridge, and the breach of contract suit I conducted for him produced a jury award of $250,000, plus a court award of $150,000 covering the costs of field investigation. This was real money in those days. But I was behind in preparing for my next case, hence a Sunday in the shop.

I was alone as I dug into the file, so when the phone rang, I was tempted not to answer. But it kept ringing and ringing, and I thought only someone who wanted to reach me desperately, like my wife, Virginia, would be so persistent.

It was Virginia. But the person I spoke to now was not the cheerful, composed mother of four whom I had kissed good-bye earlier. "Henry," she yelled. "A news flash on the radio says the Japs are bombing Pearl Harbor!"

"That can't be true," I said in typically husbandlike fashion. But Virginia put the phone next to her radio, and I could hear the news for myself. "I'll be right home."

I grabbed my jacket, stuffed the file for the next day's trial into my briefcase and drove home while further news reports on the radio made me almost explode in anger.

When I reached the house, the first thing Virginia said was, "What can we do to help our country?"

"I don't know beans about the military," I replied. "But with your blessing, I'll enlist."

"People will think you're crazy," Virginia said. "You're thirty-six. You have four small children. But I think it's the right thing for you to do, and of course you have my blessing."

Thank you, Lord, I thought. You have provided me with so wonderful a wife. . . .

I immediately wrote the Army, Navy and Marine Corps, offering my legal talents and giving my qualifications, including my several years of experience as an Assistant U.S. Attorney in the San Francisco area. A short time later, I received a letter from the Judge Advocate General's Corps in Washington offering me a captaincy. I took the forms in the letter to the San Francisco Presidio, passed my physical and was sworn in.

The most pressing problem was that I had to report in Washington within two weeks, and I still had to close down my law practice. I had fourteen years of hard work under my belt, and I was concerned for my clients. When I told my associate, Stanislaus Riley, that I had enlisted, he was thunderstruck.

"I'm too old to ever be drafted," Stanislaus said. "But I'll carry on for you, Henry, just the way I did for Bill Murphy in World War I."

I offered Stanislaus the compensation my cases would bring, but he wouldn't hear a word of it. "There'll be no deductions for fees or rent," he said. "I'll see you when the war's over."

We shook hands on the deal. That was all. There wasn't any contract. I knew Riley's word was as good as his bond, because he was ethics personified. He was an attorney for the Roman Catholic Archbishop, and many of us believed he would have been a marvelous priest.

I hopped a train for Washington, which took nearly a week in those days. Along the way I observed the many happy family groups on board, and as the miles rushed by, I wondered if I was doing the right thing. I became even more depressed on arriving in Washington and hearing a behind-the-scenes account of Pearl Harbor from Virginia's uncle, Capt. John Palmer, USN. We had visited him at Pearl Harbor when he commanded the target battleship *Utah* before the war. The *Utah* was sunk in the attack, but John had been reassigned before the attack as the Superintendent of the Navy Yard in Washington that built sixteen-inch guns and specialized in battle damage repairs. He was promoted later to Rear Admiral, but he preferred and always used the title Commodore. It was from John that I had learned earlier of the rivalry in the Navy between the big gun, battleship proponents and the new aircraft carrier types, plus the arrogance of the American military toward its Japanese counterparts, which was rudely shattered by Pearl Harbor and subsequent events in the Pacific.

At dinner that night, one of John's beautiful young daughters asked: "Why exactly did you volunteer? Cousin Virginia wrote that you were doing so well as an attorney."

I paused for a moment to reflect. "The motivation for both Virginia and myself was patriotism,'' I said. ''There's no other way to put it, although it probably sounds simplistic to some people.''

''The reaction of you civilians toward the war is proving a real surprise to those of us in the military,'' John said. ''I propose we drink a toast to them.''

For me, any doubts I might have had about doing the right thing were ended forever.

The next day I reported for duty.

The Judge Advocate General had his offices in a local armory, which was littered with boxes of dusty records of Army personnel that went back to our Revolutionary War.

My lack of military training became apparent at once. Instead of saluting Gen. Myron Cramer, the Judge Advocate General, I tried to shake hands. Thankfully, he was understanding and, after a series of personal questions, assigned me to the Military Justice System in his office.

My first duties involved reviewing sentences imposed at courts-martial. I was surprised by the drastic terms that were meted out for minor offenses. For example, one recruit was sentenced to a year at hard labor for calling his lieutenant a ''satchel-ass'' when the officer was riding in a vehicle and the recruit was humping a full field pack on a twenty-five-mile march. I recommended that the case be ''busted'' and returned to the original court for correction. The files were filled with similar cases. I busted them all.

A short time later, I was assigned to the Litigation Division of the Office of the Judge Advocate General, and was promoted to Major. Meanwhile, the staff in our office expanded with an influx of other volunteers and reserve officers from all over the country. Many had been prominent lawyers in their communities. Others were former judges, governors, legislators and the like. A number of them, including Leon Jaworski, who later was the independent prosecutor for the Watergate case against President Nixon, became close friends. Working with men such as these was for me like getting a graduate degree from Harvard.

After getting my bearings in the Washington area, I called Virginia. We decided to rent our home in San Francisco while she moved East with the children. We lived in a boardinghouse at first, then rented quarters. It was a grand adventure, especially for the kids. They quickly became acclimatized to the hot, steamy weather and their new schools, made lots of new friends and were impressed by the aura of the Capitol.

Then, tragedy struck. Virginia's father keeled over and died at home from a massive heart attack. Her mother was also in poor health, so we agreed that I should ask for emergency leave and we'd return home to sort out the family's affairs. Leave was granted, and friends offered to look after the children, who were in school.

Our arrival gave Virginia's mother a much-needed boost in spirits, especially since I fulfilled her request and as a Past Master performed the Masonic Funeral Service for a man whom I had loved dearly. Then, after winding up my father-in-law's business affairs, I was ordered to report to the Ninth Service Command in Salt Lake City.

While Virginia and the children loved the scenic beauty of the area, I quickly discovered that my new work was dull and dry. It wasn't litigation; it was paper pushing. I got my fill of it one day when I was ordered to process a claim filed by some loving mother against the Army for the sum of one dollar and fifty-eight cents. Apparently, she had mailed her son a home-baked cake and he never received it. She wanted to be reimbursed for the postage she had lost. Such a claim would take nearly two hours to process with all the forms needed for settlement. I offered to write a check to the lady from my own account. That was against regulations. Muttering, I filled out the forms.

Nobody else in the office seemed to mind this work. It was safe duty for them, but slow death for me; so without asking the permission of my commanding officer, I wrote Washington, requesting reassignment where my experience and qualifications would best serve the Army. Imagine my surprise when orders arrived assigning me to attend the newly organized Judge Advocate School at the University of Michigan. I fled Salt Lake City with the speed of an antelope, while Virginia followed in the car with the children.

Fortunately, the schoolwork was interesting, but not taxing, and it was easy to get good grades. Upon graduation, I was reassigned to the Litigation Division in Washington. Once again, I rushed off while Virginia and the children followed in the van.

I got a real break when I applied for membership in a motor pool so I could get around Washington and was assigned to the same vehicle as Lt. Col. William J. Hughes, who was the advisory head of the Military Justice Division, besides being the official troubleshooter for the Judge Advocate General. His father had been Solicitor General and author of the famous legal treatise *Hughes on Federal Practice*. Bill was a tall, friendly, learned and outstanding lawyer. He wore pince-nez glasses and was nicknamed ''Bill the Breeze'' for the way he moved in and out of meetings around town.

We liked each other immediately, and when Bill learned of my prosecuting experience as an Assistant U.S. Attorney, he asked, ''Henry, would you like to try cases acting as Trial Judge Advocate?''

''I'd be delighted for the opportunity,'' I said. ''It would make the most of my experience and qualifications.''

Bill immediately had me assigned to try a case brought against an Army major who had allegedly stolen Army property. I prosecuted. The Court found the major guilty.

My next case was, I believe, responsible for my being asked to investigate Pearl Harbor, because I made a number of friends in Congress as the result of my work, and they, too, were involved in the Congressional hearings into the disaster. The matter in question had been referred to the War Department by the Senatorial Committee headed by Harry S. Truman, who had investigated the faulty procurement of vital war materials. The Truman Committee had determined that Army personnel assigned to monitor the Wright Aeronautical Corporation's plant at Lockland, Ohio, had failed to properly inspect aircraft engines before they were shipped to various war zones. This meant that when the engines arrived in a combat zone, they had to be reinspected, often rebuilt and frequently scrapped as being totally unusable.

The Truman Committee had discovered that records either were not kept or were falsified at Lockland. Engine parts were not checked before assembly. Parts that were labeled defective were restamped as being usable. Worse, any zealous inspector who tried to do his duty was ignored and transferred immediately. It was a sorry record of war production failures. The Committee wanted the Air Force to court-martial the responsible officers. But fearing political fallout, the Air Force bucked the job to the War Department, and I was appointed Trial Judge Advocate for this hot potato.

So I called upon Harry Truman and met him for the first time. He was cooperative, but stiffer and more formal than I had expected. We reviewed the case. I said that to prosecute it properly, as he wished, I would need all the evidence his Committee had uncovered, plus both a Democrat and a Republican member of the Committee to testify and prove the prosecution was bipartisan. Truman nodded his approval to these ideas, but he didn't respond with any enthusiasm.

Then I told him: "When you were the Grand Master of the Masons in Missouri, I was Grand Orator of the Masonic Grand Lodge of California."

Hearing this, Truman literally jumped up from his chair, came around the desk and began shaking my hand vigorously. "You'll have my complete cooperation, Henry," he promised, and he immediately began to put his words into action.

He picked up the phone and called Hugh Fulton and Samuel B. Stewart, both of whom had been top-flight attorneys in New York before the war and had served as counsel to the Committee during the hearings. Truman introduced me to them and told them to give me whatever evidence they had assembled. He also instructed them to give me a list of all their witnesses, not just those who had testified, plus all the material gathered by the FBI and the names and phone numbers of the FBI investigators.

Truman then said: "I'll get Senators Albert Gore and Homer Ferguson to testify at the trial. They'll be perfect for you." (As I said earlier, Ferguson was the firebrand Republican who called for the Congressional investigation into Pearl Harbor; I will discuss my battles with him later on.) Truman also volunteered the services of another Army man whose name would become well known when Truman became President: Gen. Harry Vaughn, who would act as liaison between the Committee and my Court. "Keep me posted every day," Truman told Vaughn.

It took some time to study the documents the Committee had given us, and when my two assistants and I went out to Cincinnati to begin the trial, we carried huge briefcases bulging with documents. Because of our careful preparation, the trial became something of a cause célèbre that lasted three weeks. We examined ninety-four witnesses, introduced 190 exhibits, took more than three thousand pages of testimony and convicted all three defendants. It was the biggest trial to come out of America's four-year-long war production effort.[2]

My cross-examinations were severe at times, but that was because I had done my homework, and some witnesses were demolished. The reporters covering the trial nicknamed me "Bull Dog" or the "Methodical Major" in their stories, which made front-page headlines day after day. I sent the articles to General Vaughn for Senator Truman, because they told the story far better than I could.

---

[2] Memo for the Chief, Military Personnel, Oct. 3, 1945, from Col. William J. Hughes, p. 3.

As one result, Senator Truman wrote a glowing letter of com-
mendation in my behalf to the Judge Advocate General, who was
astounded to receive it. Usually, letters from Truman and his watchdog
committee singed the hides off whoever was named in them, and you
could honestly say that Truman's committee terrified the Pentagon.

As another result, I was named by the Judge Advocate General to
a Presidential Appellate Court, which President Roosevelt wanted set
up to review the trials of two groups of German spies who were
captured after being landed in America from U-boats. Thus, I had the
rare distinction of sitting on this Appellate Court and hearing Attorney
General Tom Clark, who would later become a Justice of the Supreme
Court, argue on behalf of the United States for affirmation of the spies'
convictions. The Court agreed that two of the eight spies who had
testified against their comrades should have their lives spared. The
other six were executed.

Meanwhile, by Joint Resolution on June 13, 1944, Congress directed that the Secretaries of War and the Navy were to investigate
Pearl Harbor and *court-martial any personnel found guilty of dereliction of duty, crime or offense against the United States.* The resolution
had been sparked by Senator Ferguson, who had testified in a perfect
manner for me as a prosecution witness in the Lockland case.

Having been involved in the Lockland case, I understood the
collective shudder that went through the War and Navy departments
when this Joint Resolution was passed. It didn't take long for the
people who supported General Short and Admiral Kimmel to start
beating the drums on their behalf. Issues of fact became subordinate to
political considerations. So did the issue of national security.

From a list of names sent forward by Chief of Staff Marshall,
Secretary Stimson appointed the famous, or infamous, Pearl Harbor
Board. It consisted of three general officers whom Marshall had re-
lieved of command at one time or another. I considered this to be a
fatal mistake by Marshall at the outset. The three were Lt. Gen. George
Grunert, Maj. Gen. Walter H. Frank and Maj. Gen. Henry D. Russell.
Col. Charles West was named Recorder for the Court; I was named
Assistant Recorder. General Frank requested that he be assisted by
Col. Harry Toumlin, who had been a patent lawyer in civilian practice
before the war. We were granted a staff, headed by an enlisted man
named Montgomery, and a number of secretaries.

Our quarters were in the old Munitions Building and rather spar-
tan. There was one large room for the generals, each of whom had a

desk. The hearings themselves were held in another room, around a large library table. There was an adjoining room for the secretaries and transcribers. Next to that was another room with desks for West and myself, plus desks for the aides-de-camp for two of the generals: Lt. Bob Hurt and Lt. Jim Murphy.

The hearings began on July 24, 1944, and Grunert, as Chairman, sat at the head of the library table. To his right were General Frank and Colonel Toumlin, plus the court reporters. To his left were General Russell, Colonel West and myself. Grunert and Frank had their aides-de-camp seated behind them. At the foot of the table was a solitary chair for the witness.

Throughout the hearings, Grunert sat like a majestic Buddha, with three stars on his shoulders and an imposing array of ribbons on his chest testifying to his long military career and well-known bravery in action. He was flanked by two other major generals and their aides, and their demeanor presented a formidable sight to anyone testifying before the Court. Appearances, however, can be deceiving.

The duties of the Recorder and Assistant Recorder for a Board of this nature would ordinarily include the preparation of questions for witnesses, plus assisting in questioning the witnesses and cross-examination. I was surprised to find that on this Board, the generals did most of the questioning themselves. Grunert and Frank were military men at heart. They usually wrote out their questions and read them off to the witnesses, which is not the right way to elicit truthful testimony. Russell, who had been a National Guard officer and an attorney in civilian life, worked from rough notes. Because of the way the generals ran the Court, West did not ask many questions; neither did I.

I, therefore, had a front-row seat for the parade of 151 witnesses who testified before the Board in Washington, San Francisco and Pearl Harbor. As I watched many of those testifying, I became aware that something didn't seem right. Questions about intelligence matters were not pressed home. Some witnesses, like General Miles, the head of G-2, appeared to be on the verge of saying one thing, but said another. It happened time and again. I couldn't figure out what was going on, because I didn't know about Magic.

When it came time for Chief of Staff Marshall to testify, for example, instead of Marshall's appearing before the Court, the Board went to his office. I was shocked at what happened next. Marshall asked the three generals into his office, refusing the allow West or me in on the meeting, and talked privately to them for the better part of three quarters of an hour. This wasn't just unusual. It was improper. Marshall should have known better. It was at this juncture that the Pearl Harbor Board really went off the rails.

Only later did I learn that Marshall had told the three generals in greatest confidence about our having broken the Japanese codes before Pearl Harbor. What was worse, he cautioned the Board that it would be wrong to reveal this information in Court or in their report, and urged the Board not to investigate this area of intelligence.

That was why the Board had refrained from pursuing intelligence matters. It was why the Board's final reports, the Top Secret of the two dealing with Marshall's revelations, were so badly skewed in their final analysis. The Board simply had not conducted a proper investigation.

In my opinion, Marshall really messed up the Army Board by choosing the wrong officers to sit on it, because they had grievances against him, and he also withheld the whole truth from them.

I don't believe historians have really understood what happened here. They have used the faulty reports of the Army Board as a basis for their interpretations of the Pearl Harbor disaster. In turn, this has caused great confusion about what really did happen and who was responsible. Yet, the historians are not to blame, because they have been writing from sworn testimony and supposedly authoritative reports. There was no way they could have known they weren't writing about what actually happened. Nor is there any way to explain the damage done by Marshall's miscalculation of how the truth should have been placed before the Army Board.

I believe that history will show that he hurt his reputation badly by all this. His motives were the best, but he did what he did knowing full well that it was improper. Worse, he did so without asking the advice of counsel. If he had asked Stimson, or me, what to do, I know we would have advised him to tell the Board the real facts of the case.

As I viewed the conclusions of the Army Board's findings, they represented a calamitous miscarriage of justice. Secretary Stimson was asking me to find out what had caused this. More important was the fact that by assigning me—a lowly major, who was a civilian lawyer at heart—to perform this task, Stimson was seeking his own independent investigation of why the Japanese had been successful in surprising our defenders at Pearl Harbor.

4 | WHO WAS TELLING THE TRUTH?

To explain how I approached my investigation, let me tell a story about the professor of law who began his class by writing the numbers 2 and 4 on the blackboard and asking: "What's the answer?"

Some students shouted "six." Others said "four." Some said "eight." Whereupon the professor shook his head with a look of sorrow. "None of you have given me the answer, which is: What is the problem?"

In other words, if I was going to proceed as an independent prosecutor and find out what had really gone wrong at Pearl Harbor, I'd damn well better focus on the hole in the doughnut. I suspected what the problem might be, but I still wasn't sure as to its scope, so I began rereading the hearings of the Army Board. Then I began mixing in the unknown quantity—the Magic intercepts, which had been denied the Board until the end of its investigation.

This resulted in a three-page memorandum with twenty-five questions that needed answering with a mixture of flexibility and discretion. But what the reader should know is that these were my "cover" questions that I spoke of earlier. Knowing how the Army, and the

Navy, really works, I submitted the memo to General Cramer; within twenty-four hours, I had on my desk, a "Memorandum for Major Henry C. Clausen, JAGD" that outlined the type of questions I would ask and pursue at my discretion, only now the questions were those of Cramer, the Judge Advocate General, himself. Needless to say, they gave me the opportunity to lift up the corner of any carpet I might find to see if there was dirt hidden underneath.

But now for the hole in the doughnut. The more I read the record of the Army Board hearings, the more convinced I became that there were four primary questions that needed answering. I went over them with Colonel Hughes in the privacy of our vaultlike office, simplifying them to essentials. The questions were these:

(1) What had Pearl Harbor *known* about Japanese intentions before the attack?

(2) What had Pearl Harbor *done* with this information before the attack?

(3) What had Washington *known* about Japanese intentions before the attack?

(4) What had Washington *done* with this information before the attack?

If I could find the answers to these seemingly simple queries, my investigation would be a success. And now that I had my agenda fixed in terms of knowing the road I would travel as an independent prosecutor, I was ready on January 24, 1945, to depose my first witness.

Before I begin my parade of evidence, it is only fair to warn the reader that, as in a real-life trial, evidence frequently comes before the court and jury in unusual, unexpected ways. From the very start, the reader will be presented with conflicting statements. I will try to point out the most glaring examples of such conflict during the course of my narrative. And at the end, in my role as independent prosecutor, I will summarize the case to avoid confusion.

Colonel Hughes came up with the suggestion that I begin with Brig. Gen. Kendall J. Fielder, who at the time of Pearl Harbor was a colonel serving as head of G-2 (Intelligence) in the Army's Hawaiian Command. At the moment, he was working in the Pentagon. (Hughes had one of the best ears for picking up rumors and knowing who was where, doing what and to whom that I could have asked for.) So I telephoned General Fielder, whom I recalled from watching him testify before the Army Board as being a rather slick, fast-talking public-relations type of fellow, and asked if he'd be willing to come to my office in room 4D852 for further discussion.

"I'd be delighted to," said Fielder. "Would half an hour be soon enough?"

"That would be perfect, General. Thank you." My goodness, I thought, imagine a general's being so polite. The grapevine must be working overtime.

Colonel Hughes and I rushed to secure all the Top Secret documents in our office, which was about twenty feet by fourteen, and Hughes then excused himself so that Fielder might feel more comfortable answering questions without a witness present. Why, one might ask, did we go to such lengths to make our office sterile? Well, I had a hunch that General Fielder, despite his having been the top Intelligence Officer for the Army at Pearl Harbor, had never been cleared for Top Secret Magic. What I needed to know was how he could have done his job properly, and kept his commanding general informed about what we knew about the Japanese intentions before the attack, without having had access to this type of information.

I couldn't let Fielder know that this was one of the major points of my interrogation. That isn't how a good lawyer works. First he needs to know everything he can before he starts asking questions. Then he has to employ the Socratic method, probing gently here and there, until he has laid the groundwork and can ask the all-important question. You win your cases by studying your books and working papers, and by thinking hard at your desk before you go into the courtroom. That's when you figure out what you know and what you don't know, what the answers of the witness might be, what you should ask the witness, and when you should stop asking questions. I was prepared for Fielder.

As it worked out, however, Fielder wasn't ready to be deposed.

He turned aside many of my questions, asserting that he would have to review his records, which were locked away in Hawaii—and since nearly four years had passed since the attack, he could no longer remember the specific details—and this would entail considerable research on his part. Meanwhile, he addressed certain other points, including these:

Commenting on a message he had sent to Washington on September 6, 1941, asking the G-2 office not to send him any more intelligence bulletins, because they duplicated what the Navy was already distributing, Fielder claimed that he was referring only to counterintelligence matters. He claimed his message had had "nothing to do with combat [intelligence]." Personally, I found his comment odd, because that was not what his original message said.

The message from Fielder contained three paragraphs. The first said that the Summaries of Information sent regularly by Army (G-2) Washington actually originated with Naval intelligence in Pearl Harbor and already had been given Fielder's office. The second paragraph said that the "cooperation and contact" between the Office of Naval Intelligence, the FBI and Fielder's own G-2 office at Pearl Harbor "is most complete." In conclusion, Fielder was telling Washington to stop sending Summaries of Information, "to avoid duplication of effort." In other words, Fielder was reassuring Army (G-2) Washington that everything was fine with his operation, that he was getting everything he needed to do his work properly from the FBI and Naval intelligence.

I suspected that this message was misleading, if not an outright lie. The Navy had withheld information from the Army Pearl Harbor Board until we went to the mat with them, as I earlier told Secretary Stimson. The question in my mind now was what the Navy had withheld from Fielder that he didn't know about. In turn, this led to the question as to whether or not Army intelligence at Pearl Harbor had done its job.

My suspicions were even further aroused when Fielder next said "he was not very well acquainted with" Comdr. Joseph J. Rochefort of Naval Intelligence at Pearl Harbor and that he had "maintained no liaison with him." Also that he was unaware of any liaison arrangements between Commander Rochefort and Col. Edward Raley of the U.S. Army Air Force. (At that time, the Air Force was under Army control.) He also stated that he had no knowledge of the Top Secret Magic material. When I asked Fielder if he had known about the Navy's intercepting such traffic, he said he understood this was being done, but that "it was talked about in whispers" and only on this basis did he know that we had broken the Japanese codes.

As I took all this down for the record, I could not help wondering at the significance of what Fielder was revealing, not about himself and how he ran his shop, but about the Army's system for handling these exceedingly important and sensitive matters.

How could he be G-2 for the commanding general at Pearl Harbor when he neither had training for the job nor was cleared for Top Secret Magic information? Some people in the Pentagon referred to this Top Secret Magic as "boogie-woogie." Now I could see why they called it that, because there was no apparent rhyme or reason in how it was disseminated. Even by January 1945, when I was interviewing Fielder and he had been promoted to brigadier general, he still hadn't been cleared for Magic. Because of this, I couldn't show him the decrypts I was using in my investigation. Instead, I had to paraphrase everything and ask him questions such as: "Were you ever aware of such and such a message of this date that said this . . . ?"

Again, Fielder parried my questions by saying he would have to check his records in Hawaii. (The reader may not understand my questions at this point, but they will become clear later on.) Fielder "understood" that his G-2 estimates of October 17 and 25, 1941, had been circulated to the Hawaiian Chief of Staff and to General Short. He also "thought" he had talked to General Short concerning an all-important warning from G-2 Washington of November 27. He claimed he did not see the Navy Intelligence Bulletin of December 1, 1941. He claimed he did not see a warning from the Military Attaché in Melbourne, Australia, of December 5–6, 1941. He stated that General Short had "assumed" that the Navy was conducting long-range reconnaissance by plane to warn Pearl Harbor of a surprise Japanese attack. He also said that he "didn't remember" a message, numbered 519, from G-2 Washington of December 5, 1941, that instructed the G-2 Hawaiian Department to contact Commander Rochefort immediately. As Fielder put it, the December 5 message "might have come in as routine," but that didn't mean he had to see it.

Once again, I suspected Fielder wasn't being completely honest. As a result, my research into who had seen this message number 519—or "old 519," as I called it—would take up a considerable portion of my investigation.

And there I left it. Since Fielder didn't have access to his files and notes, I wasn't going to get a signed affidavit from this interrogation, but my typewritten memorandum for the files would be incorporated in the final affidavit that I would take later, when I went to Pearl Harbor, making sure that Fielder was there, too. Nevertheless, Fielder had given me information of a very disturbing nature. My investigator's instincts were aroused, and I was worried.

The next morning, instead of going to the Pentagon, I drove out Connecticut Avenue to the Navy's code-breaking complex not far from Chevy Chase Circle. There, I took the affidavit of Navy Capt. Joseph J. Rochefort, who had been the Combat Intelligence Officer in charge of the Combat Intelligence Unit at Pearl Harbor. This was actually a field unit of the home office in Washington, and it was attached to the Commandant of the Fourteenth Naval District in Pearl Harbor, *not* the Pacific Fleet, which was commanded by Admiral Kimmel. (As it turned out, this designation of assignment would be important later on.)

Rochefort gave me no idea of the strain he had been working under. I did not know that he had been recalled to Washington because he had dared to disagree with his masters in Washington about their analysis of the Japanese battle plans before the battle of Midway. It was only when Rochefort and Capt. Edwin T. Layton, the Fleet Intelligence Officer, convinced Adm. Chester Nimitz, the new commander of the Pacific Fleet, as to the true meaning of the Japanese decrypts before Midway that our Navy fliers were able to score a stunning victory that miraculously changed the course of the entire Pacific war. Rochefort's independent thinking had proven the analysis of the strategic situation by the Office of Naval Intelligence in Washington to be totally wrong. This had infuriated the Washington command, who then punished Rochefort by bringing him back from his all-important combat command in Hawaii to give him an insultingly unimportant assignment. (It was only when Admiral Layton published his book, *And I Was There,* which made the front page of the Sunday *New York Times* on November 17, 1985, that Rochefort's accomplishments were recognized officially. The Navy posthumously awarded him the Distinguished Service Medal, which the President presented to his widow.)

Anyway, Rochefort appeared totally calm and collected to me, the epitome of how an intelligence officer should look and act. He spoke with a benign smile. His words were precise and exact. Thus, I was flabbergasted when Rochefort calmly began to contradict Fielder's statement to me of the day before.

"My opposite number in the Army at Pearl Harbor was Col. Kendall J. Fielder, G-2, Hawaiian Department," said Rochefort. "In the fall of 1941, arrangements were made between Col. Fielder and myself for liaison and exchange of intelligence information pertaining to our functions on matters of personal concern. . . . I had discussions with him and Edwin T. Layton, Fleet Intelligence Officer, at my headquarters. Thereafter, including the period of 7 December 1941, we maintained most cordial and close relations, meeting informally and frequently, and carried out these arrangements."

Great Scott—who was telling the truth? I reminded myself that both Rochefort and Fielder were intelligence officers, which meant they both knew how to lie convincingly. I wouldn't make any conclusion now about the conflicting statements, but I promised myself that I'd get to the bottom of it all sooner or later.

As an aside, when I say that I was flabbergasted by what a witness might be telling me under oath, that doesn't mean that I ever allowed the witness to see my surprise. Good lawyers have poker faces. We hear so many conflicting bits of testimony during the course of a trial that we have to keep a tight check on our emotions. When a wise lawyer appears angry in a courtroom, for example, he's pretending to be angry. If he isn't pretending, then he's lost control and, most likely, his case. So while Rochefort continued his statement, I kept my face blank.

According to Rochefort, his duties from the fall of 1941 up to December 7 did not include the gathering of information or intelligence from Japanese political or diplomatic sources. He knew this was being done in other places by joint units of the Army and Navy. (What Rochefort was really saying was that he was concentrating on another aspect of Magic: breaking the Japanese naval codes for flag officers.) I noticed a flicker of emotion behind Rochefort's eyes, however, when I showed him the Magic decrypts I had brought with me to the interview. He picked out five of them, saying that he knew their substance before Pearl Harbor, and he wrote his initials on the back of each one.

For reasons of security, when I produced my report back in 1945, I could not attach the Magic decrypts to an individual's affidavit so the reader could easily understand the secret part of the interrogation. This made it terribly difficult, if not impossible, for the historian. But for the reader of this book, I can say that the full text of the five messages that Rochefort acknowledged having known about before Pearl Harbor can be found in the appendix on pages 322 (SIS 25432), 322–323 (SIS 25392), 335 (SIS 25545), 335–336 (SIS 25787), and 339 (SIS 25640). As for the significance of these messages, let me explain briefly.

The first two messages constituted the basis for the so-called Winds Code, which has been a constant source of debate and irritation for half a century. On November 19, 1941, Tokyo used a low-grade code called J-19 to advise its diplomats in Washington to be on the alert for a special radio broadcast in the *"case of an emergency (danger of cutting off our diplomatic relations) and the cutting off of international communications."* (Emphasis added) Should this happen, a special warning would be added to the middle of the daily Japanese-language shortwave news broadcast.

Thus, if all normal forms of communication were cut off, the diplomats in Washington should listen to Tokyo shortwave radio. If they heard the words "east wind rain" in the middle of the news broadcast, they would know that relations with America were in danger. If they heard the words "north wind cloudy," they would know that relations with Russia were in danger. Similarly, if they heard "west wind clear," they would know that relations with Great Britain were in jeopardy. The two messages also said that when the diplomats heard these Winds Code words, they were to "destroy all [their] codes, papers, etc." In other words, if all normal communications were cut, and the Japanese diplomats around the world heard these messages broadcast by Tokyo, they were to destroy all their secret codes, their code machines and other means of secret communications in preparation for war.

The other three messages had nothing to do with the Winds Code. The third message was sent in the Purple code from Tokyo to Washington on December 1, but was not translated in Washington until December 5. This message told Washington to "discontinue the use of your code machine [Purple] and dispose of it immediately." Special emphasis was given to taking the machine apart and breaking up its important parts. Washington was also ordered to burn its machine (Purple) codes.

The fourth message advised the diplomats that if they had to destroy their codes, they should contact the Naval Attaché in that particular embassy and use the special chemicals the Attaché possessed to ensure that vital documents and equipment were properly destroyed. This message was sent by Tokyo on December 1 in the Purple code and was translated in Washington the same day.

The fifth message was also sent in the Purple code from Tokyo to Washington, on December 2. Translated on December 3, corrected on December 4, it gave specific instructions to the Japanese diplomats in Washington to burn all their Purple codes, plus all the other codes the embassy possessed. Only one copy each of two special codes were to be retained for future use. Washington was also told that it was to "stop using at once *one Purple code machine unit and destroy it completely.*" (Emphasis added) Meanwhile, a cipher specialist named Kosaka should have been returned to Tokyo on a Japanese ship that left the United States on November 28.

These last three messages were of extreme significance.

When a nation prepares to launch an attack and go to war, one of the most indispensable steps it takes is to make sure that its codes and code machines cannot be captured by the enemy should the enemy retaliate and raid an embassy for intelligence reasons. Washington knew from reading these messages that war would have to break out, with Japan attacking somewhere in the Pacific.

Therefore, the Navy in Washington alerted Kimmel on December 3 by sending two advisory messages that paraphrased the intercepts I have described above. The first message read as follows:

> **HIGHLY RELIABLE INFORMATION HAS BEEN RECEIVED THAT CATEGORIC AND URGENT INSTRUCTIONS WERE SENT YESTERDAY TO JAPANESE DIPLOMATIC AND CONSULAR POSTS AT HONGKONG, SINGAPORE, BATAVIA, MANILA, WASHINGTON AND LONDON TO DESTROY MOST OF THEIR CODES AND CIPHERS AT ONCE AND TO BURN ALL OTHER IMPORTANT CONFIDENTIAL AND SECRET DOCUMENTS.**

The second message to Kimmel read:

> **CIRCULAR TWENTY FOUR FORTY FOUR FROM TOKYO ONE DECEMBER ORDERED LONDON, HONGKONG, SINGAPORE AND MANILA TO DESTROY *MACHINE*. BATAVIA *MACHINE ALREADY SENT TOKYO*. DECEMBER SECOND WASHINGTON ALSO DIRECTED DESTROY, ALL BUT ONE COPY OF OTHER SYSTEMS, AND ALL SECRET DOCUMENTS. BRITISH ADMIRALTY LONDON TODAY REPORTS EMBASSY LONDON HAS COMPLIED.**[1] (Emphasis added)

Because the Navy paraphrased these warning messages to Kimmel, they differ somewhat from the messages that I carried in my bomb pouch, which I showed Rochefort.[2] Both the Navy warning messages to Kimmel are exceedingly important, but the second is the more important. The first implies that Tokyo has ordered its embassies and consulates around the world to burn their codes. But it is the second that says *without equivocation* that Tokyo has ordered its consulates to destroy their codes and *code machines*. Once code machines were

---

[1] Report of the Joint Committee, p. 100.
[2] See appendix, SIS 25787, p. 336; SIS 25545, p. 335 and SIS 25640, p. 339.

destroyed, there could be no turning back potential Japanese attacks. The consulates could no longer communicate effectively with Tokyo. War had to follow; it was inevitable.

This meant that Rochefort had seen vital intelligence warnings to Kimmel indicating that Japan was preparing to attack within a matter of days, or hours. It was imperative that I learn what had happened to this information within the Naval command at Pearl Harbor and how this information was passed to Short and his Army command.

As for the significance of the earlier Winds Code messages, from what I could determine, the three messages from Tokyo ordering the Japanese diplomats around the world to destroy their codes and code machines made a Winds Code broadcast unnecessary, since the required orders had already been given. I will speak about this later on. What I now needed to know was how Rochefort had communicated all the information about the Winds Code and the warning messages about codes and code machines from Washington to Colonel Fielder. (For the most authoritative analysis of the Winds Code, see the Appendix, The "Winds Code," on pages 447 through 470. No one can read this report and believe the claims advanced by Captain Safford.)

I recalled that Fielder had told me earlier that he was not well acquainted with Rochefort and that the two men had no real liaison about such information. So you can imagine my surprise when Rochefort continued his testimony to me by saying: "It was my practice to give Col. Fielder all the information of importance in which the Army and Navy were jointly interested and which came to my knowledge in the course of my duties. This was done so that Col. Fielder and I could keep abreast of intelligence developments in our common interests."

Rochefort cited examples to buttress his positions, not knowing that Fielder had never said anything about these things to me. First, Rochefort maintained that the Navy at Pearl Harbor had begun to monitor the Tokyo shortwave radio to see if it could intercept the so-called Winds Code. No such interception was ever accomplished, but he claimed he had discussed these abortive intercept attempts with Fielder. Next, Rochefort claimed that on December 4 or 5, he had given information to Fielder that the Japanese consul in Hawaii was destroying his secret papers (which differs from saying codes and code machines). Lastly, Rochefort said he had also shared this information with Robert L. Shivers, the FBI Agent in Charge in Honolulu, plus Rochefort's head office in Washington.

Upon leaving Rochefort's office, I pondered the unique command

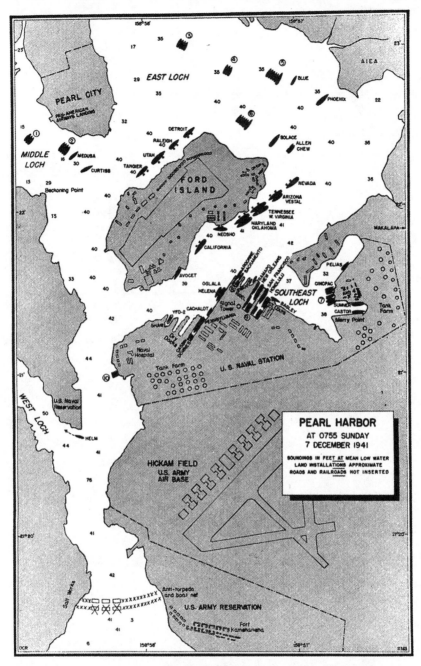

This map shows the disposition of the U.S. fleet at the start of the
Japanese attack. The battleships *Arizona, California, West Virginia*
were sunk. So was target battleship *Utah*. The *Oklahoma* capsized.
The *Nevada, Maryland, Pennsylvania* and *Tennessee* were damaged.
Hickam Field was devastated, its planes lined up wing tip to wing tip.
Fortunately, the Japanese did not attack the vital oil tanks.
(R. M. BERISH NAVAL HISTORICAL CENTER)

Captured Japanese photo shows torpedo tracks streaking toward moored battleships. The *West Virginia* and *Oklahoma* have been hit. Planes at Hickam Field burn in background. American naval experts had predicted that torpedoes could not be dropped from planes in shallow Pearl Harbor.

The view of ships exploding as seen from the Naval Air Station. Note the close proximity of planes to each other.

On April 9, 1942, President Roosevelt awarded CNO Admiral Stark a gold star. Roosevelt had favored the Navy over the Army in the dissemination of Magic decrypts. But the Navy failed at the crucial time to have a translator on duty to alert the commander in chief about Japanese intentions.

Secretary of the Navy
Knox (left) wrote
Secretary of War Stimson
in January 1941 about the
Navy's fear of "a surprise
attack upon the fleet . . . at
Pearl Harbor [by] . . . (1)
air bombing attack, (2) air
torpedo-plane attack. . . ."
Chief of Staff Marshall and
Secretary of War Stimson
(below) agreed and
alerted the Army's
Hawaiian Command to the
danger, saying: "The risk
involved by a surprise
raid by air . . . constitutes
the real perils of the
situation. . . . Keep clearly
in mind . . . that our
mission is to protect the
base and the Naval
concentration."

Secretary of State Hull (left) on November 27, 1941, told Stimson that further negotiations with Japan were impossible. Stimson helped draft this warning to General Short and the message was sent over Marshall's signature. Instead of preparing for an attack, Short put his troops on minimum alert.

Members and staff of the Army Pearl Harbor Board. Its three general officers hated Marshall. They heard perjured testimony and reached fallacious conclusions. Henry Clausen is at the far left.
(COURTESY OF THE AUTHOR)

WAR DEPARTMENT
WASHINGTON

6 February 1945.

MEMORANDUM FOR ARMY PERSONNEL CONCERNED:

      Pursuant to my directions and in accordance with my public statement of 1 December 1944, Major Henry C. Clausen, JAGD, is conducting for me the investigation supplementary to the proceedings of the Army Pearl Harbor Board.

      You are directed to give Major Clausen access to all records, documents and information in your possession or under your control, and to afford him the fullest possible cooperation and assistance. Inquiries made by Major Clausen should be answered fully and freely and the persons interrogated should volunteer any pertinent information of which they may have knowledge. Copies of any papers required by Major Clausen should be furnished him.

Henry L. Stimson

Secretary of War.

The extraordinary letter of authority that Clausen carried during his investigation for Stimson.

Brig. Gen. Kendall J. Fielder, G-2 to General Short. Fielder represented all that was wrong with the Army's intelligence system. He was not cleared for Top Secret. He had no intelligence training. Chosen for his job because of his social graces, he shunned responsibility.

Col. Moses W. Pettigrew initiated Cable 519 advising Fielder to contact Rochefort about the Winds Code. Fielder and Short claimed they never received the message, although another G-2 officer swore he saw it on Fielder's desk.

Capt. Joseph J. Rochefort, who played a major role in winning the battle of Midway, tried to mislead Clausen about how the Navy allegedly cooperated with the Army at Pearl Harbor. Rochefort also failed to exert maximum effort to break Japanese signal traffic that would have proven Pearl Harbor was a target. (NAVAL IMAGING COMMAND)

structure at Pearl Harbor as it existed in early 1941, when plans were drawn up for the defense of the Hawaiian Islands. The Army and Navy had agreed upon a method of coordination—called the Joint Coastal Frontier Defense Plan, Hawaiian Coastal Frontier—that was based on the concept of *mutual cooperation.* For those of us who were basically civilians in life and heart, when we joined the military in World War II, the concept of *mutual cooperation* between the various services was something that made us laugh or curse. If you train dogs or people to be fighters, when there is no enemy to fight, they compete against each other, and orders for *mutual cooperation* be damned.

Both the Army and the Navy had paid lip service to the concept prior to 1941. Plans were made during peacetime for every potential wartime contingency based on everyone's cooperating with everyone else. But things hadn't worked that way. If I was already finding conflicting stories about *mutual cooperation* among the worker bees, the men who were really doing the labors of the day in the field at Pearl Harbor, I guessed there might be even bigger conflicts ahead. And with these grim thoughts racing in the back of my mind, I returned to the Pentagon to prepare a paraphrase of Rochefort's affidavit. (The rules were such that Rochefort's comments had to be sanitized and safe-guarded under wartime security regulations.) Knowing it would take some time for Sonnett to review Rochefort's paraphrased affidavit, I continued my review of the historical records. Before my own investigation, there had been five major inquiries into Pearl Harbor:

(1) The Roberts Commission began on December 18, 1941, ended on January 23, 1942, and produced a 2,173-page report.

(2) The Hart Inquiry commenced on February 12, 1944, ended on June 15, 1944, and yielded a 565-page report.

(3) The Army Pearl Harbor Board, on which I had served, began on July 20, 1944, ended on October 20, 1944, and produced a 3,357-page report.

(4) The Navy Court of Inquiry started on July 24, 1944, concluded on October 19, 1944, and produced a 1,397-page report.

(5) Lastly, the Clarke Inquiry had two sets of hearings, September 14–16, 1944, and July 13 to August 4, 1945. This investigation yielded a 225-page report. (I read the latter portion as I concluded my own report.)

From these thousands of pages of testimony, I deduced that I would not need to take affidavits from Admiral Kimmel or General

Short. They had spoken fully and freely before these commissions and hearings. There was nothing further they could add to my investigation except more qualifying and self-serving statements that would muddy the waters. (As I said previously, a good lawyer knows when to quit asking questions.)

In terms of how poorly the concept of command of *mutual co-operation* had worked before the attack of Pearl Harbor, I was particularly struck by the testimony of Comdr. William E. G. Taylor, a Naval Reserve Officer, who, before Pearl Harbor, already had two years of war experience in England. As a fighter pilot, Taylor spent one year with the British Navy and a year with the Royal Air Force, during which he had access to and learned the air warning system that helped win the Battle of Britain, both ashore and afloat.[3]

According to Taylor, the Army had asked for the services of a specialist such as himself. He had been assigned to special duties to assist the Army "in an advisory capacity" to set up a radar early warning system for Pearl Harbor. His time was spent with various staffs in Hawaii trying to work out the liaison between the aircraft warning systems and the various commands. According to Taylor, although there was no permanent radar installation per se, the five mobile sets in use by the Army before the attack on Pearl Harbor were "adequate to do a fair job of early warning." The problem was that "the communications between the fighter-director officers', or controllers', positions, and the fighter aircraft were totally inadequate to control fighters more than five miles off shore."

The control and operation of the shore-based radar was the responsibility of the Army. But, General Short claimed, it did not have enough trained personnel to operate the equipment twenty-four hours a day. This was a complete contradiction of the Roberts Commission Report. Then, to save the equipment, General Short had ordered that it not be operated continuously. Said Taylor: "I feel, and felt then, that these stations should have been operating twenty-four hours a day, and the air warning system fully manned."

Among his attempts to get the air warning system operating properly, Taylor called a meeting on Monday, November 24, copies of the minutes of which were circulated the next day to the appropriate Army and Navy commands. Everyone present at the meeting agreed that the interservice operational structure was inadequate; measures needed to be taken immediately to correct the situation. But, as Taylor explained,

[3] Navy Court of Inquiry, pp. 461–475.

"very little was done as a result of this conference. We managed to complete our communication lines. We were not able to have either the Army or the Navy agree on an aircraft identification system. We were not able to get men to man the information center. We were able to get no more personnel and the information center remained as it was on 24 November. The fact that the radar stations were shut down, except for the period of 4:00 A.M. to 7:00 A.M., made it impossible to continue to train plotters and operators for more than three hours a day, which was not enough. That fact alone did more to slow down the development of the information center than anything else."

When asked if he had made a request to the proper Naval authorities for Navy liaison officers to work with the Army on an air warning system and an information center, Taylor said he had made a verbal request for this from "Commander-in-Chief, Pacific Fleet, staff, and Com 14's chief of staff [Capt. J. B. Earle], and also Admiral Bellinger." But, said Taylor, "The reply was in all three places there were no liaison officers available."

Had an information center been fully operational, the absence of these Naval officers would have prevented the communications center from operating properly. For without officers from both the Army and the Navy to identify which planes belonged to which service, the information center could not discriminate between friend and foe.

There were efforts on the part of the Army to make the system work, but only by two junior officers, both captains. "The two of them worked very hard and tirelessly," said Taylor, "but they did not have enough force [clout] to get what they needed from the various commands to get the station [information center] operating."

As it turned out, the radar station was operating on the morning of December 7, albeit only by radar operators who were being trained and who picked up the signals of the approaching Japanese planes some one hundred miles away from their designated target. At approximately the same time, however, a flight of Army B-17 bombers was supposed to be arriving from the West Coast. "But without some method of identifying the planes that came in, no one could have told whether the planes were friend or foe, and therefore no action would have been taken," explained Taylor. "Without the Army and Navy working together . . . it would have been assumed that [the planes coming in] were friendly. The information center is set up with its Army and Navy liaison officers for the single purpose of identifying the planes that are coming in."

As a result of the Pearl Harbor attack, said Taylor in his testimony, from the time after the bombs started falling, enough staff was supplied, and radars were on continuously, so any incoming plane was immediately identified; those that were not identified were declared hostile, and Hawaii's air-raid sirens were sounded.

Ah, me, I thought. This is a perfect example of the problems of command by *mutual cooperation*. I have always believed in the maxim proposed by Gen. Ulysses S. Grant, who declared: "Two commanders on the same field are always one too many." What had been needed at Pearl Harbor was a *unified* command under the control of one man who understood the problems and had the authority to correct them. The Navy turned off the radar on its ships when they entered the port of Pearl Harbor, because (1) the radar didn't work in port, since the anchorage was surrounded by high hills; and (2) the radar caused havoc with local civilian electronic communications on shore. In other words, the Navy turned off its early warning safety equipment, which was as effective as the Army's radar, not understanding that the Army's radar was often not operating. There must have been something wrong with a system that created such mistakes and inefficiency.

This was the point that Commander Taylor was trying to make in his testimony. The Navy's lawyers, however, were interested only in showing that it had been the Army's responsibility for making sure the land-based radar, on which the fleet depended, was working.

I wondered why the Navy hadn't demanded that the Army have its radar working. An admiral who made that demand, and forced the issue, thereby ensuring the safety of his fleet with an adequate early warning system, probably would have ended up a hero. For if the early warning system and identification center staffed by Army and Navy personnel jointly had been in place as Commander Taylor envisaged, someone most likely would have figured out that when the Army radar showed more than 130 planes approaching Pearl Harbor on that fateful morning, the images had to represent something other than a small flight of bombers expected in from the West Coast.

You can see the problem: Because mutual cooperation was the order of the day, the blame finders in the two services only wanted to discover if their opposite service had let them down. No one really wanted to focus on whether or not there might be something wrong with the overall system in which they were involved.

Another question that I would have to investigate was: What did Pearl Harbor know about the Japanese intentions before the attack on December 7? Pulling together all the various items of intelligence that had been sent Pearl Harbor from Washington, and what Pearl Harbor had acquired from its own activities, was an arduous task. More importantly, the material had to be arranged in chronological order lest the investigator lose track of what he was working with. Slowly but surely, the list began to take shape,[4] and I created a memo that bore the following heavy-handed title:

INFORMATION MADE AVAILABLE TO GENERAL SHORT
FROM WAR DEPARTMENT AND OTHER SOURCES
OF THREAT OF WAR WITH JAPAN
AND
OF THREAT OF SURPRISE ATTACK BY JAPANESE ON
PEARL HARBOR
ARRANGED IN CHRONOLOGICAL SEQUENCE

Some of the items were long, others short. Each item was given a separate page. All in all, there were fifty-six pages of information, beginning with the fateful letter from Secretary of the Navy Frank Knox to Secretary of War Stimson of January 24, 1941, which said: "If war eventuates with Japan, it is believed easily possible that hostilities would be initiated by a surprise attack upon the fleet or the naval base at Pearl Harbor. . . . The dangers envisaged, in their order of importance and probability, are considered to be: 1) air bombing attack; 2) air torpedo-plane attack; 3) sabotage; 4) submarine attack; 5) mining; 6) bombardment by gunfire. Defense against all but the first two of these dangers appears to have been provided for satisfactorily. . . ."

This correspondence was sent Hawaii, and by itself, the list was devastating in terms of attacking the claims of Admiral Kimmel and General Short that they did not have enough information to be prepared for a Japanese attack. In statistical terms, nearly 25 percent of all the warnings received by Pearl Harbor during 1941 arrived between December 1 and December 7. If anything, this sudden flood of messages should have alerted the Hawaiian commanders of the ever-increasing urgency of the dangers now facing them, as previously predicted.

Even more important, however, were the answers I was seeking: Who at Pearl Harbor had seen which Magic messages, and what had they done about them?

Another question I was going to have to solve was what happened

---

[4] See appendix, pages 422–447.

in Washington that Saturday evening and night of December 6, 1941, and during the Sunday morning hours just before the Japanese attack. There has been so much written about this subject, and so much of it is confusing, that the only way I can tell this story is by asking the reader to bear with me and follow the trail that I followed through my investigation.

The next affidavit I took was that of Col. Moses W. Pettigrew, Military Intelligence Service (MIS). From early August to December 7, 1941, he was the executive officer of the Intelligence Branch, G-2, at the War Department in Washington. More importantly, from November 1939 to August 1941, he had been the assistant to Col. Rufus Bratton in the Far Eastern Unit of G-2. (This was important, because Bratton was going to be a key figure in my investigation.) Pettigrew's duties consisted of reading various Magic intercepts of the diplomatic radio messages from Japan to its consulates and embassies around the world. They were in a variety of codes, such as Purple, High Level Diplomatic and J-19.

Pettigrew recalled seeing the so-called Winds Code messages that Tokyo sent out around the end of November. Then, on December 5, someone whom Pettigrew could not recall showed him an intercept of a message from Tokyo indicating that the relations between Japan and the United States were in danger even though regular communications had not been cut. He understood the intercept to mean that "anything could happen," so he prepared a secret cablegram for dispatch to Hawaii addressed to the Army G-2 there [i.e., Fielder], saying:

CONTACT COMMANDER ROCHEFORT IMMEDIATELY THRU COMMANDANT FOURTEEN NAVAL DISTRICT REGARDING BROADCASTS FROM TOKYO REFERENCE WEATHER

It was this message that became the infamous cable number 519. Because of statements made to him by various people in the Navy, whose names he could not recall, Pettigrew was sure that the Army in Pearl Harbor possessed the same information that he had received in Washington. Pettigrew also understood from these same Navy people, again nameless, that the Army in Hawaii had everything the Navy had in terms of decrypted intercepts. The Navy in Washington also falsely claimed to Pettigrew that Commander Rochefort was "monitoring and receiving these intercepts and breaking and translating the codes [in Hawaii] as well as Washington." As Pettigrew understood the situation, this was being done to save time, and by Hawaii's exchanging these decrypts with ONI in Washington, the translations could be checked: one message against another.

Pettigrew was a frustrating witness. He was one of those "I can't recall" people. I doubted that he was telling me everything he knew, because he kept saying that he couldn't recall things that he obviously should have remembered. He wasn't going to point a finger of responsibility at anyone, but I was sure that in his own way, the so-called Army way, he was going to tell me whom else I should talk to, and what compass direction I should follow on my journey. Pettigrew was so typically military, and so afraid to criticize his superiors in any way. And so wrong in his understanding of what was actually going on at Pearl Harbor. He knew far more than did the G-2 in Hawaii. But Pettigrew didn't realize that Colonel Fielder wasn't cleared for Top Secret, and didn't know anything officially about the interception of the Japanese codes.

Pettigrew said that on December 5, he took the draft of message number 519 around the office for approval. Colonel Bratton was one of the people who signed his initials on it, giving approval for it to be sent over the signature of General Miles. According to the outgoing message number—519—on the copy of the message that I showed Pettigrew, he stated that the message had been sent to Hawaii, but he had no knowledge of any action taken on it by the Hawaiian Department. He recommended that I interview personnel in the War Department Message Center, check the records in the Signal Corps files in Hawaii and see one Col. Carlisle Clyde Dusenbury, who also had been an assistant to Colonel Bratton. Without saying so, Pettigrew was sending me to a previously unknown source, a man who would prove to be one of the most important players in explaining what went wrong at Pearl Harbor.

After Colonel Pettigrew had signed his affidavit and left my office, I reviewed what he had told me. Instinct told me I had learned something important. Knowing how the Army grapevine worked, I wanted to strike while the iron was hot, so I immediately called Colonel Dusenbury to set up an appointment for the next day.

If things went as they usually did, I suspected that Dusenbury would run to his boss, General Carter Clarke, who would give him some briefing and instructions. I already had an earlier run-in with Clarke about how I would conduct my investigation. He always tried to keep his finger on everything, which is what made him such a good intelligence officer, and I had gone to him and said: "Listen, I want to be very sure you fellas don't tap my phone, and do not plant a bug in my office. Because if you do, the most astonishing things will happen. It's going to be very, very disastrous for you personally."

Clarke had promised faithfully that he wouldn't do anything of the sort. I don't think he ever did bug me, even though that's what intelligence officers are supposed to do. I believe I really scared him; he knew I didn't give a damn about having a career in the Army. And to protect the integrity of my investigation, I'd sound every alarm in the Pentagon if I found out that Clarke was messing around.

That doesn't mean that Clarke didn't know what Dusenbury was going to tell me, however, or that Clarke knew that Dusenbury had been kept under wraps since Pearl Harbor.

I cannot recall what Dusenbury looked like. But I remember that in giving his story, he stayed calm and collected the entire time, although he committed professional suicide before my eyes. He first explained how, during the course of the war, he had been Assistant Director of Intelligence, Southeast Asia Command, at Kandy in Ceylon, and was now on temporary duty in Washington. I decided to move slowly and began walking him through some of the material I had learned from Colonel Pettigrew the previous day.

For several months prior to, and after, December 7, 1941, Dusenbury had been serving as the Executive Officer of the Intelligence Group, Military Intelligence Division, in Washington; his duties were administrative, but also included the drafting and approval of outgoing messages. Dusenbury recalled cable number 519 of December 5, which Pettigrew said he had sent to Pearl Harbor. In fact, Dusenbury thought he had written the first draft of it. He recalled the reason for sending it as being twofold. First, there was danger indicated to the United States; second, "there was believed to be a lack of confidence by Edwin T. Layton, Fleet Intelligence Officer, as to Kendall J. Fielder, G-2, Hawaiian Department." (This was the first confirmation I had received that there had been some form of trouble between Layton and Fielder.)

Dusenbury understood that in early 1941, the Navy had about four or five hundred people working in Hawaii monitoring, breaking and translating "the Japanese diplomatic codes." He was wrong about the diplomatic codes, but correct in his belief that Commander Rochefort had been notified about our intercepting Tokyo's messages about the Winds Codes, plus other information, and Dusenbury believed that message number 519 would cause Fielder to go to Rochefort and get clued in.

Dusenbury had gained his background knowledge by working as assistant to Colonel Bratton since first reporting for duty in Washington in August 1940. For the first four or five months, Colonel Bratton received from the Signal Corps the translated Magic intercepts of Japanese diplomatic messages—about fifty to seventy-five of them a day—of which about twenty-five would be sorted out for distribution. Bratton would deliver these messages to Colonel Harrison, the aide to Secretary of War Stimson; John F. Stone, secretary to Secretary of State Cordell Hull; Col. Ralph G. Smith, Executive Officer of the Assistant Chief of Staff, G-2; plus Col. Walter Bedell Smith, the Secretary of the General Staff, and Col. Thomas T. Handy, or Col. Charles W. Bundy, in the War Plans Division. The decrypts that were not circulated were destroyed immediately. Those that were circulated were placed in binders and delivered to the recipients, who signed a receipt for the binder if it had to be held for a few hours. When the binders had been read and returned to Colonel Bratton, their contents and any receipts that had been signed for them were also burned. Only one copy of the decrypts that had been circulated was kept in a secure central file in G-2, but there was no record of who had seen the messages.

Bratton and Dusenbury began alternating the job of assembling and distributing the intercepts around February 1941. By December, Dusenbury was doing almost everything himself. (Bratton, apparently, was going to be sent to the General Staff College in preparation for a combat command and promotion to brigadier general.) But, said Dusenbury, no record of the deliveries that he made "is now available in G-2," and "none was kept because of Top Secrecy requirements."

Heavens, I thought, what a sloppy way to run a railroad. I couldn't run a business without keeping records. I'd go bust if I tried it, and all that talk about Top Secret requirements: that's just bunk, to cover your flanks. I'd better keep pushing. Something worse is hidden here.

The question in my mind was what had happened in Washington during the evening and night of December 6, and in the predawn hours before Pearl Harbor. As I explained earlier, the Army and the Navy had been dividing the work of decoding and translating the intercepted Japanese diplomatic messages. (It is important to keep in mind the responsibilities of the two services to decrypt and translate on the odd and even days in terms of the question: Did the system work?)

Early on December 6, said Dusenbury, it became apparent and ominous in Washington that something of great importance was happening. The Japanese were making their reply to the latest American proposal that had been set forth during diplomatic negotiations, which were aimed at peacefully halting Japanese aggression in the Pacific. By noon, the Army and Navy knew from a so-called separate pilot message that Tokyo was sending a fourteen-part message to its diplomats in Washington, asking them to keep the information secret for the time being. As to when it was to present the fourteen-part message to the U.S. government, Tokyo said that the timing would be wired in yet another message.

All the testimony I had read to date showed that both the Army and the Navy had collaborated on translating the decrypts of the first thirteen parts of the fourteen-part message, with the Navy doing the majority of the work. This didn't make sense to me at the time, because it wasn't the Navy's day for this task. Copies of the first thirteen parts were ready for distribution by nine o'clock that Saturday evening. (The fourteenth part of the message would be the conclusion of what Japan planned to do.)

Between nine-thirty and ten P.M. that December 6, the first thirteen parts of the message were given by a Navy courier to an assistant naval aide at the White House with the request that they be handed to the President at the earliest possible moment. They were presented immediately to President Roosevelt, who read them with his adviser, Harry Hopkins. The aide who delivered these first thirteen parts to the President had testified that, after both men had read the messages, "the President then turned toward Mr. Hopkins and said, in substance—I am not sure of the exact words, but in substance—'This means war.'

"Mr. Hopkins agreed, and they discussed then for perhaps five minutes the situation of the Japanese forces, that is, their deployment."

Once the President had finished reading the decrypts, the same Navy courier took them to the Wardman Park Hotel, where they were read by Secretary of the Navy Frank Knox. The courier then went to the home of Rear Adm. Theodore S. Wilkinson, the head of the Navy's Intelligence Division, who was hosting a dinner party that included Rear Adm. John R. Beardall, the naval aide to the President, and Gen. Sherman Miles, the Chief of the Army's Military Intelligence Division. All of these men read the thirteen-part message. The Navy courier then returned to the Navy Department at about one A.M. and, since the fourteenth part of the message, the conclusion, had not been received, went home to bed.

Meanwhile, another Navy messenger delivered copies of the thirteen-part message to the homes of Rear Adm. Royal E. Ingersoll, the Assistant Chief of Naval Operations, and Rear Adm. Richmond Kelly Turner, the head of the all-important Navy War Plans Division.

As for the distribution of the first thirteen parts of the message within the Army's chain of command, Col. Rufus S. Bratton had testified to the Army's Pearl Harbor Board[5] that he delivered the thirteen parts in the following order: First, he delivered them to Col. (later Lt. Gen.) Walter Bedell Smith, the Secretary of the General Staff, in a locked bag to which Marshall had the key. Bratton swore he told Smith that the bag contained very important papers, and that General Marshall should be informed of this at once so that he could unlock the bag and read its contents. Bratton continued, saying that he handed another copy of the thirteen parts to General Miles in Miles's office, and that he discussed the message personally with Miles. Bratton also claimed that Miles had done nothing about the message so far as he knew. Third, Bratton testified, he delivered a copy to Col. Charles K. Gailey, Jr., for Brig. Gen. Leonard T. Gerow, the head of the War Plans Division. Bratton further testified that he gave another copy to the watch officer of the State Department for delivery to the Secretary of State, completing the distribution to everyone who was supposed to see the material by ten-thirty that evening of December 6.

I had been wondering about the apparent discrepancy between Bratton's testimony, in which he claimed to have delivered the material to General Miles in his office, when I already knew that Miles had been having dinner that evening with Admiral Wilkinson. That was a delivery Bratton could not have made. Nor could he have discussed the Magic material with Miles, as he claimed. So I began prodding Dusenbury about his recollections.

Suddenly, my investigation flipped topsy-turvy.

Dusenbury remembered the night of December 6 all too clearly. As he told me his story, I could see his long and carefully nurtured Army career flying out the window.

The intercepts, "consisting of *fourteen* parts"—and it is crucial that Dusenbury told me *fourteen* and not *thirteen* parts—began coming in on the night of December 6 while he was on watch. Colonel Bratton

[5] Clausen Report, p. 250; PHA Hearings, pt. 39, p. 226.

was also on duty; he remained until about half of the message had been received, "whereupon he left and went home at about 9 P.M." Dusenbury stayed alone so that Bratton could get some sleep. The *fourteenth* part of the message, in which the Japanese declared a break in diplomatic negotiations with Washington, arrived "about 12 that night." Dusenbury solemnly swore he was so sure of this that on his affidavit, he scratched out his first words "11 or," leaving the hour of 12, midnight, shining forth like a beacon.

But once the fourteenth part had been received, Dusenbury went home—without distributing any of the fourteen-part message to anyone! All *fourteen* parts of the intercepts were in his possession, but he did not distribute them. He finally began distribution the next morning, Sunday, December 7, at about nine, and when he gave the copy for the Operations Department to Col. Thomas T. Handy, Handy read the message and said to Dusenbury, " 'This means war,' or words to that effect."

I asked Dusenbury why he hadn't delivered the material the night before, as Bratton had ordered. His reply has haunted me ever since: "I did not wish to disturb the usual recipients who were probably at home asleep, as I did not see the implications of immediate hostilities [in the messages]"!

Oh, Good Lord, I thought. All the earlier testimony about the thirteen-part message was nonsense. Dusenbury hadn't understood the significance of the fourteen parts. His failure to deliver them had put him in the Army's doghouse forever—he ended the war with the same rank he started it, a fate worse than death for a West Pointer—while Colonel Handy, who first read the messages, and immediately understood their import, ended the war as a full General and the Army's Deputy Chief of Staff. But the real significance of Dusenbury's failure to carry out orders was that he lost Washington a vital nine hours that could have been used to alert Hawaii and prevent Pearl Harbor.

5 | "HOSTILE ACTION POSSIBLE AT ANY MOMENT"

Dusenbury's affidavit was a bombshell. Was he telling me the truth?

When a man hurls himself down upon his sword and impales himself before your very eyes, it usually means he's telling the truth. I would have to make sure, however, and I would have to proceed with great caution, dotting all the *i*'s and crossing all the *t*'s. The reason was that because of Bratton's testimony to the Army Pearl Harbor Board, the Board had attacked General Marshall, saying that he had failed to tell General Short on the evening of December 6, or the early morning of December 7, about the critical information indicating that an immediate break with Japan was about to occur, "though there was ample time to accomplish this."[1]

In other words, the powerful, anger-making conclusions of the Army Pearl Harbor Board could well be wrong. But to prove them wrong, and wrong on the basis of tainted testimony, would require a lot of work.

[1] PHA Hearings, pt. 39, p. 264.

As to why Dusenbury hadn't understood the significance of the materials he was handling on the evening of December 6, my judgement is that some people just cannot reach the necessary conclusions from the facts they possess, even though they would be apparent to somebody else. It's a matter of intuition as well as brains. Dusenbury just didn't have it.

His testimony also gave me another problem. What was the true story of the time both the Army *and* the Navy received the fourteenth part of the all-important diplomatic message? All the previous testimony before the various investigatory bodies, until my interrogation of Dusenbury, had been that the vital fourteenth part hadn't been received and translated until around seven on the morning of December 7. But Dusenbury had told me that he had it in his hands around midnight on December 6. And if Dusenbury had it, and the Navy was also working on translating the message, that meant the Navy had to have it, too, no matter what its experts had testified to previously. The matter of the timing of the Navy's receipt of the fourteenth part would not be cleared up until after my own investigation had been completed, and even the final report by Congress on this is in error.

The truth of the matter, as I will show later, is that the Navy did possess the fourteenth part about the same time that Dusenbury had it (i.e., around midnight of December 6). Yet, the Navy did nothing about disseminating the fourteenth part, either—just like Dusenbury. But the Navy tried to hide the facts of this failure in the hopes that it wouldn't be found out.

What I was discovering was that our civilian government was being fed the most secret information by our military, but the military didn't do the job properly.

Then the people who received this Magic material never signed a receipt for it that was kept in a file. And I was learning more about the military's refusal to give Magic information to the President, because Army (G-2) believed that there was a mole who had access to the office of "Pa" Watson. I have mentioned this earlier. But can you imagine that at such a critical period in history, with war approaching, our Army for several months denied our Commander in Chief the most vital intelligence he needed?

I was not happy to be uncovering this.

There was another aspect to it all. The military wasn't presenting to its civilian masters the decrypts in the proper way. To explain: The decrypts often were not in clear English. The language was rather more like spasmodic verse. The intercepts missed words, or had garbled lines, and the translators frequently had to guess at what was being said. This made it impossible to summarize the decrypts properly. If you're the President of the United States, the material should not be given to you in its raw form. Experts such as General Miles or Admiral Wilkinson should be looking over the materials with the President and saying, "I believe this means . . . ," and the expert should then say what he thinks. He's not committing himself, except to say what he thinks, which is why he's wearing his stars and is what he's being paid to do. But in 1941, the military hadn't come to grips with this problem.

Meanwhile, I was checking around the Pentagon. With almost every person I spoke to, I'd ask, "Are there any other personnel with whom you think I might verify, or check, or who might explain the subject to me?" I was surprised at the number of leads that turned up, one of whom was Col. Clarence C. Jensen of the Air Corps. He opened up another line of investigation. I had asked Jensen some weeks earlier whether there was any foundation to certain of my suspicions that had been raised by the report of the Army Pearl Harbor Board. Reading it carefully, I had sensed a serious discrepancy in various bits of testimony. I suspected that Short's Hawaiian command had changed its standard operating procedure (SOP) before Pearl Harbor, and that the Hawaiian command had failed to alert Washington about these changes. If I was right, this failure would explain why Washington had been confused about the state of readiness of Short and his Hawaiian command in the hours before the Japanese attacked Pearl Harbor. It would also prove whether the Board's charges against Marshall were justified.

The facts of the situation were these: On November 27, 1941, both the Navy and the Army sent special warnings of war to their respective commanders at Pearl Harbor. The dispatch sent by the Chief of Naval Operations to Kimmel began with the fateful words "THIS DISPATCH IS TO BE CONSIDERED A WAR WARNING . . ." The message also instructed Kimmel to inform Short of the warning, and Short acknowledged, after the Japanese attack, that he had, in fact, seen that message.

On the same day, a dispatch over General Marshall's signature went to Short that read:

**NEGOTIATIONS WITH JAPAN APPEAR TO
BE TERMINATED TO ALL PRACTICAL PURPOSES
WITH ONLY THE BAREST POSSIBILITIES THAT**

THE JAPANESE GOVERNMENT MIGHT COME
BACK AND OFFER TO CONTINUE. JAPANESE
FUTURE ACTION UNPREDICTABLE <u>BUT
HOSTILE ACTION POSSIBLE AT ANY MOMENT.</u>
IF HOSTILITIES CANNOT, REPEAT CANNOT, BE
AVOIDED THE UNITED STATES DESIRES THAT
JAPAN COMMIT THE FIRST OVERT ACT. THIS
POLICY SHOULD NOT, REPEAT NOT, BE
CONSTRUED AS RESTRICTING YOU TO A
COURSE OF ACTION THAT MIGHT JEOPARDIZE
YOUR DEFENSE. <u>PRIOR TO HOSTILE JAPANESE
ACTION YOU ARE DIRECTED TO UNDERTAKE
SUCH RECONNAISSANCE AND OTHER MEASURES
AS YOU DEEM NECESSARY</u> BUT THESE
MEASURES SHOULD BE CARRIED OUT SO AS
NOT, REPEAT NOT, TO ALARM CIVILIAN
POPULATION OR DISCLOSE INTENT. REPORT
MEASURES TAKEN. SHOULD HOSTILITIES
OCCUR YOU WILL CARRY OUT THE TASKS
ASSIGNED IN RAINBOW FIVE SO FAR AS THEY
PERTAIN TO JAPAN. LIMIT DISSEMINATION OF
THIS HIGHLY SECRET INFORMATION TO
MINIMUM ESSENTIAL OFFICERS.
(EMPHASIS ADDED)

After conferring only with his Chief of Staff, Col. Walter C. Phillips, and within thirty minutes of having received this message, Short cabled Washington:

REURAD FOUR SEVEN TWO 27TH. REPORT
DEPARTMENT ALERTED TO PREVENT
SABOTAGE. LIAISON WITH NAVY. SHORT.

And now the confusion began. Short had ordered his Alert Number 1 as based on his revised SOP. But the SOP on file in the War Plans Division in Washington differed totally from what Short was actually doing. To explain: It appeared that on November 5, without telling Washington what he was doing, Short took it upon himself to rewrite the original SOP of July 14 (which was the SOP on file in Washington). In his new SOP, Short reversed the order of importance by which the alerts were numbered. What had formerly been the Number 1 Alert, and meant the highest form of readiness, was now the Number 3 Alert. Conversely, what had been the Number 3 Alert, which meant

the minimum alert possible, Short had now made the Alert Number 1.
The new alert system instituted by Short read:

> Alert No. 1: This alert is a defense against acts of
> sabotage and uprising within the islands, *with no threat
> from without.* (Emphasis added)
> Alert No. 2: This alert is applicable to a condition more
> serious than Alert No. 1. Security against attacks from hos-
> tile sub-surface, surface, and air-craft, in addition to de-
> fense against acts of sabotage and uprisings, is provided.
> Alert No. 3: This alert requires the occupation of all
> field positions by all units, preparing for maximum defense
> of OAHU and the Army installations on outlying islands.[2]

(This is a true copy of the controversial SOP; others as printed in the
reports of various investigations are frequently incorrect.)

Furthermore, by saying "Liaison with Navy" as a separate sentence, Short was telling Washington that he was in the process of
establishing with the Navy the liaison to effect the reconnaissance
necessary for a coordinated defense of Hawaii. Washington knew that
a successful joint defense would require "liaison" between the two
services, while a mere preparation for the prevention of sabotage would
not require any liaison between Short and the Navy.

I was never able to question Col. Charles Bundy, who was not
related to Secretary Stimson's special assistant Harvey Bundy, about
the matter. Colonel Bundy was the man responsible for coordinating
the replies to the warning message of November 27 for General Gerow
to pass up the line to General Marshall and Secretary Stimson. Bundy
was killed in a plane crash not long after Pearl Harbor, so his story
about these events was lost to investigators.

However, I believe my interpretation of why Washington was
confused by Short's fatally brief reply is correct (all the other commands in the Pacific area replied in detail about the status of their
defense alerts). And Short played down his changing of the SOP in his
testimony before the Army Pearl Harbor Board. I fairly concluded that
he misled the interrogator who asked him the question about these
alerts.

Otherwise, in his subsequent testimony, Short acknowledged that

---

[2] Clausen Report, p. 55.

he had ordered the air-raid warning system (i.e., radar) into operation, but only from four to seven A.M., and primarily on a training basis, in response to the order that he was to conduct reconnaissance. He also acknowledged that in ordering the minimum alert, in both instances, he had done so without consulting the Navy, even though he cabled Washington that he was in liaison with the fleet that it was his duty to protect.

As to why he had not prepared to defend Pearl Harbor from the probability of a Japanese air attack, which was the primary form of attack that Washington had foreseen and which Washington's directives had pointed out to Short time and again, Short could only admit before the Army Board: "I was wrong."

It was when Short sought to excuse his actions that things went badly. He claimed that he had sent his new SOP to Washington as required at the time he changed it. He also claimed that he assumed that the Navy knew the whereabouts of the Japanese fleet, and that the Navy would warn him in plenty of time if there was going to be an attack. He claimed that when he cabled the War Department that he was on the alert only against sabotage (which is not exactly what his cable said), Washington, by not saying that his alert was improper, had agreed to his operational plan. He also said that Washington had failed to give him additional warnings about Japan's intentions in the days after the cable from Marshall on November 27. Lastly, he claimed (falsely, as I would discover) that if he had ordered his forces to go on maximum alert to repel a Japanese attack, it would have interfered with the training program for his command, disclosed his intent, and alarmed the civilian population.[3]

Short's attempt to exonerate his failures was a counterattack that completely ignored the existence of Alert Number 2 (Security against air attacks from hostile subsurface, surface and aircraft, in addition to Alert Number 1), and the Army Board went to extraordinary lengths to bring in its witnesses. For example, the Board recalled from the field of battle Lt. Gen. Leonard T. Gerow, the commanding general of the Fifth Corps, which under his leadership had fought its way from the beachheads of Normandy to the Siegfried Line, to account for the confusion in Washington about the status of the alerts at Pearl Harbor.[4] In his testimony, Gerow acknowledged that, as head of the War Plans

---

[3] PHA Hearings, pt. 39, pp. 232–233.
[4] Ibid., p. 264.

Division at the time of Pearl Harbor, he had not personally checked the files to ensure that Short's message about his alert status was the proper SOP. Gerow accepted full responsibility for this failure, refusing to testify that his direct subordinate, Col. Charles W. Bundy, was the man charged with handling Pacific matters in the War Plans Division.[5] In its findings, the Army Board later criticized Gerow for his failure in this matter. But because he had demonstrated so clearly his superb qualities for battlefield command since Pearl Harbor, there was no cause to bring disciplinary action against him. Whereupon Gerow returned to Europe and led a newly formed Fifteenth Army until Germany surrendered.

As I have pointed out earlier, the Army Board was not so lenient with Marshall. It castigated the Chief of Staff on the grounds that he had failed in his relations with the Hawaiian Department to send additional instructions when he failed to comprehend that Short had misunderstood the warning message of November 27 and had not adequately prepared his command to repel an attack. In doing this, the Board did not take into consideration that it was not Marshall's job to do what his subordinates were supposed to have done. Nor did the Board take into consideration the basic fact that two wrongs don't make a right. Short had made the first error and had then claimed that it wasn't his fault. But if my suspicions were correct, *that Short had failed to notify Washington before the attack about his change of SOPs,* which had caused all the confusion in the first place, then Short's defense was without validity.

My question to Colonel Jensen was this: When had Short's Hawaiian command notified the War Plans Department in Washington about the revised SOP for alerts at Pearl Harbor?

As I sat at my typewriter and listed the sources Colonel Jensen had checked out for me, I could see that my suspicions had been justified. Jensen had done his research carefully, checking the records of the Operational Plans Division and its predecessor, the War Plans Division, the Adjutant General, the Army Air Forces, and the Registered Document Section of the Operational Plans Division, WDGS. In addition, Jensen had questioned Col. Robert Dunlop (now General), who in the months preceding Pearl Harbor had been the Adjutant General of the Hawaiian Command, plus a number of other individuals who were in the position of knowing when the revised SOP had been

[5] Ibid., p. 266.

sent to Washington. In summation, Jensen's research proved that Short's revised SOP was first received in Washington in March 1942, where it was receipted for and placed in a bound volume, Register Number 45, Operations Orders Hawaiian Department, 1941.

In other words, Short's revised SOP was not received by Washington until *four months* after the Japanese attack on Pearl Harbor.

Why the revised SOP was not sent earlier to Washington, as required by proper procedure, was not my concern. I now possessed a vital piece of evidence: The Army's Hawaiian command had made a major error, which it had tried to hide.

I would not understand until later why Short had unnecessarily revised the SOPs for the alerts. But his attempt to smear Marshall with the blame for his failures was unconscionable. (I was pleased with the eventual outcome of my report to Secretary Stimson in that it led to the Judge Advocate General's overruling the Army Board's improper criticism of Marshall.)

In reviewing my progress, after only a month of digging, I believed I had uncovered evidence leading to some root causes for the disaster at Pearl Harbor. More importantly, I knew the direction in which I was going was correct. I also believed that I could justify my recommendation to Secretary Stimson that he not make any public statement at the time about the guilt or innocence of General Marshall. Not only was the evidence beginning to build that Marshall was not guilty of the charges that the Army Board had leveled against him, but to bring such charges against Marshall in time of war would result in his asking for a court-martial. In that case, as I had pointed out to Secretary Stimson, Marshall would be entitled to defend himself and call for a public hearing, at which our penetration of the Japanese codes would have to be revealed. The situation would have been suicidal to our war effort.

I was also appalled at what I was learning: With a modicum of intelligence and enough business acumen to run a small cigar store, the disaster at Pearl Harbor could have been avoided. Most definitely, there was no reason why the Japanese attack should have been a surprise.

I reported to Harvey Bundy what I had found, and what I was thinking. He agreed with me. But one day, I found that he had a glazed look in his eyes before he started reading my interim report. Later, he said to me, ''You noticed that my eyes were so peculiar. I was going through the throes of death with General Groves about the atomic bomb.'' Groves was running the supersecret atomic bomb project, and sometimes he'd be in Bundy's office while I was there. Bundy always gave me all the time I wanted with him, but I respected the other problems that he worried about, so I tried to confine myself to only a few words that highlighted the testimony I had taken. Still, Bundy was a quick study. He'd zip through my reports and the supporting evidence. ''First class,'' he'd say. ''You're doing first class.''

It was from my investigation that the final examination of Short's performance was made. And it was Secretary Stimson who finally lowered the boom on Short and enumerated his shortcomings to Congress after the war.

In commenting on Short's claim that the warning message of November 27 was ambiguous, Stimson later told Congress:

> The fact is that it presented with the utmost precision the situation with which we were all confronted and in the light of which all our commanding officers, as well as we ourselves in Washington, had to govern our conduct. The situation was admittedly delicate and critical. On one hand, in view of the fact that we wanted more time, we did not want to precipitate war at this moment if it could be avoided. If there was to be war, moreover, we wanted the Japanese to commit the first overt act. On the other hand, the matter of defense against an attack by Japan was the first consideration. . . . [Furthermore], *all these considerations were placed before the commanding officers of their respective areas, and it was because they were thought competent to act in a situation of delicacy requiring judgment and skill that they had been placed in these high posts of command.*[6]
> (Emphasis added)

Stimson also pointed out to Congress that the warning message of November 27

> specifically mentions that reconnaissance is to be undertaken. This is to my mind a very important part of the message, not only because of its obvious desirability but also because we had provided the Hawaiian Department

[6] Stimson statement, Committee Record, pp. 14396–14397.

with what I regarded as the most effective means of reconnaissance against air attack and one to which I had personally devoted a great deal of attention during the preceding
months. I refer to the radar equipment with which the Hawaiian Department was then provided. This equipment permitted approaching planes to be seen at distances of
approximately 100 miles, and to do so in darkness and
storm as well as clear daylight. In the early part of 1941, I
had taken up earnestly the matter of securing such radar
equipment for aircraft protection. I knew, although it was
not generally known, that radar had proved of the utmost
importance to the British in the Battle of Britain, and I felt
in the beginning of 1941 that we were not getting this into
production and to the troops as quickly as we should, and
put on all the pressure I could to speed up its acquisition. By
the autumn of 1941, we had gotten some of this equipment
out to Hawaii, and only a few days before this I had received a report of the tests which had been made of this
equipment in Hawaii on November 19th, which indicated
very satisfactory results in detecting approaching airplanes.
I testified at considerable length with regard to this before
the Army Pearl Harbor Board.[7] When we specifically directed the commanding officer at Hawaii, who had been
warned that war was likely at any moment, to make reconnaissance, I assumed that *all means of reconnaissance available to both the Army and the Navy would be employed.* On
the same day a war warning was dispatched to the
Commander-in-Chief of the Pacific Fleet by the Chief of
Navy Operations. The standing instructions were that all
messages of this character were to be exchanged between
the Army and Navy commands.[8]

There you had it. By challenging Marshall, Short brought down
the wrath of his civilian bosses upon his own head. I will say more
about this later, but as Stimson pointed out, if he, as a civilian Secretary of War, could understand the importance of the newly invented
radar in terms of protecting Pearl Harbor, why couldn't a professional

[7] APHB, pp. 4064 ff.
[8] Committee Record, pp. 14398–14399.

military man such as Short understand it, too? And if a civilian Secretary of War could struggle to ensure that the most important military outpost in the American defense system was provided with such important equipment, why couldn't a general such as Short understand that he was to use the equipment to prepare for an attack that he had been warned might be coming at any moment?

Lastly, Stimson made the devastating point that "all messages of this character," meaning messages of extreme importance such as war warnings and critical intelligence matters, were automatically to be shared between the two commanders at Pearl Harbor. That didn't mean the messages were to be exchanged via couriers and then thrown away in the wastebasket. They were to be considered by the two commanders and discussed. This was how it was done in Washington between Stark and Marshall. It was the way it was supposed to be done in Hawaii. And Stimson was pointing out that Short had failed to do his job. (The reader will note that Stimson, ever the gentleman, did not stoop to a partisan level and criticize the naval command at Pearl Harbor about this even though such criticism would have been valid, as I will demonstrate later.)

A final determination about who created the errors that caused Pearl Harbor would be made, of course, by Congress. But even at this early stage of my investigation, I was becoming convinced that the failure of the Pearl Harbor command to have its radar fully operational (e.g., its primary reconnaissance) rested squarely on the shoulders of General Short. But this was not my only concern. There were other matters to be investigated.

One item that worried me was message number 519 that Colonel Pettigrew said had been sent to the G-2 of the Hawaiian Command on December 5, in which General Miles instructed Army (G-2) Hawaii to contact Commander Rochefort immediately.

During the hearings of the Army Board, the Hawaiian command claimed that it never received this message. (Short also swore he couldn't remember it.)

The issue had to be nailed down.

The next deposition I took was that of Margaret McKenney, the civilian clerk in charge of the Cable Section of the Assistant Chief of Staff. Her experience suggested that the December 5 message from General Miles had indeed been sent to Hawaii. The yellow copy of the message on file carried the number 519, which the Signal Corps code room had stamped on it when the message was first received from the

Washington G-2 office. Then there was the notation "SENT NO. 519 12/5" that was placed thereon. The numeral 4 in the lower left corner of the message indicated that it was the fourth message that went out from G-2 in Washington that day. This number was typed on the page along with the designation, the classification of the message, and the number 32, which was the number of the clerk, Mary L. Ross, who actually sent out the message. (I already had an affidavit from Mary Ross in which she said that she had sent it.) The receipt book in the files was also initialed "DG" with the number 519, showing that the message had been received by the addressee in Hawaii. Furthermore, the cross-checking system used by the Signal Corps showed that the Hawaiian Department on that day had sent its usual confirming message accounting for all the cable traffic it received each day by referring to the numbers assigned the messages. This showed that no repeat transmission was necessary for message number 519, meaning the message had been received by Hawaii.

So far as Washington G-2 was concerned, message number 519 of December 5 had been sent to Hawaii and received there. But, I wondered, what happened then?

On February 25, I took the affidavit of Col. George W. Bicknell, who, for the moment, was working in G-2, Washington. We met in my Pentagon office.

Bicknell was an interesting character. He was a Reserve Officer, without much polish. I wondered how he had been treated by the West Pointers in the days of the prewar Army. Not very well, I suspected, as I listened to him describe how he had been trained in G-2 work and, in the months preceding Pearl Harbor, found himself recalled to active duty in Hawaii prior to being made the assistant to Colonel Fielder.

According to Bicknell, in early 1941, he developed a close relationship with the head of the FBI in Hawaii, Robert L. Shivers, and also with then-Commander Rochefort, who was in charge of the Combat Intelligence Unit at Pearl Harbor. He also talked frequently with Capt. Irving H. Mayfield, the District Intelligence Officer for the Fourteenth Naval District, with then-Commander Layton, the Fleet Intelligence Officer of the Pacific Fleet, and local representatives of the British Secret Intelligence Service. Bicknell knew what Rochefort was up to, although he was *not* authorized to know what he knew, because he, too, was not cleared for Top Secret Magic at that time. Bicknell also made other sources of information available to himself, such as material from the local FCC intercept station, which was at that time against Federal law, plus interviews with visitors to Hawaii, the press and specific residents of Hawaii. In other words, Bicknell was what Fielder was not: a pro. I suspected this had worked against him, because the West Pointers might have considered him to be not an officer and a gentleman, but a cop. (To his credit, Bicknell never raised this issue with me, but I kept digging into the matter to see if I was correct.)

By late November 1941, and because he was trusted by the Navy as an intelligence expert, Bicknell knew that the Navy had intercepted and decoded Japanese diplomatic traffic. He also knew about the Winds Code message that was to be broadcast by Tokyo indicating the possibility of war between Japan and the United States, Russia, Great Britain or other nations. He said he learned about the Winds Code from Captain Mayfield. Later, to keep Mayfield out of trouble, he drew a line through this bit of testimony, but it is still readable in the original affidavit. Bicknell understood that a Winds Code broadcast would mean that the Japanese consulates and embassies were then immediately supposed to destroy their secret codes and papers.

I showed Bicknell the decrypts in my possession. He said that he had seen the ones about the Winds Code I was referring to, and he initialed them for use as evidence. He said that when he had first seen these messages, he took immediate action to have the FCC intercept station in Hawaii monitor the Tokyo broadcasts for any message that would make the Winds Code operational. And while later on he received a number of suspicious intercepts as a result of this surveillance, none of them was the one he wanted.

On December 5, Bicknell's attention was again drawn to the Winds Code, because he ''saw on Col. Fielder's desk'' a message that said in substance what General Miles had cabled Hawaiian G-2 in cable number 519. (It is interesting to note that Bicknell did *not* say that Fielder had shown him the message, but that he read the message off Fielder's desk, which I concluded to mean that he had read it upside down, as any good spook or reporter would do.) Bicknell immediately contacted Rochefort about the message, and learned that he, too, was monitoring the Tokyo radio broadcasts for the Winds Code execute signal. (Again, note that Bicknell did this on his own; he was *not* ordered to do it by Fielder.) Meanwhile, the information had been passed on to Shivers at the FBI.

Among Bicknell's duties was the preparation of weekly intelligence estimates based on the information that he had received from all his sources. These estimates were distributed to Short's Chief of Staff; G-2, Hawaiian Department; G-2, Hawaiian Air Force; G-2, Schofield Barracks; G-3, Hawaiian Department; the FBI in Honolulu; and the Office of Naval Intelligence, Hawaii. Bicknell's reports indicated the deteriorating situation in the Pacific, but he could not reveal the accuracy, or the secret source, of his information. This meant that his estimates were easy to challenge if anyone wanted to do so.

On December 3, Bicknell said Rochefort showed him the first message sent by the Navy Department in Washington to Kimmel at Pearl Harbor saying that Tokyo had ordered its diplomats in Washington, London, Hong Kong, Singapore, Manila and elsewhere to destroy their codes and secret papers. But Rochefort may have shown Bicknell the more important second message about the Japanese destroying their code machines. (Once again, to keep someone out of trouble, I did not identify Rochefort as being Bicknell's source.)

Later that day, FBI Agent Shivers told Bicknell "that the FBI had intercepted a telephone message from the Japanese Consulate" and the Japanese Consul General "was burning and destroying all his important papers." As Bicknell saw the situation at that moment: "Something warlike by Japan was about to happen somewhere."

That is exactly what Bicknell told the weekly staff conference three days later, on December 6, at the regular Saturday morning meeting conducted for General Short by the Chief of Staff. As Bicknell recalled it: "I told those assembled, which included the Chief of Staff, what I had learned concerning the destruction of their important papers by Japanese Consuls, and stated that because of this concurrent information which I had from proven reliable sources that the destruction of such papers had a very serious intent and that something warlike by Japan was about to happen somewhere."

But by waiting three days to make this rather wooden statement at a regular staff meeting, Bicknell may have defused the explosive nature of the information he had learned on the back channel from his Navy sources and only now was bringing to his superiors. No one present at the meeting asked him any questions. No one seemed to pick up on the fact that the Japanese Consuls around the world were burning their codes. (Bicknell did not use the words "code machines," and no one present comprehended that the generic use of the word "codes" includes the machines that create the codes.) The ho-hum attitude of the staff seemed to be in keeping with Bicknell's pedantic phrases and stolid delivery.

Late in the afternoon of Saturday, December 6, Shivers told Bicknell that the FBI had intercepted another Japanese phone call. This one was between a Dr. Mori, a suspected Japanese agent then living in Honolulu, and someone in Tokyo who appeared to be working for a newspaper. The phone call had been recorded. Shivers gave Bicknell a transcript. According to Bicknell, Shivers "was alarmed" by the potential military implications in the conversation: inquiries "by the party in Tokyo as to the fleet, sailors, searchlights, aircraft, weather conditions, plus reference to 'hibiscus' and 'poinsettias.'"

"My G-2 sense told me there was something very significant about this," said Bicknell.

It was about five-fifteen on Saturday evening, December 6, and Bicknell telephoned Fielder saying it was necessary that he see both Fielder and Short immediately. "I had something that I considered to be of utmost importance" was how Bicknell put it to Fielder. Bicknell was told that if he could make it to headquarters in ten minutes, Fielder and Short would wait for him.

Bicknell rushed over to headquarters and handed a copy of the transcript he had received from Shivers to Short, who read it with Fielder. But neither man was impressed. Both told Bicknell that he was too "intelligence conscious." To them the transcript appeared to be in order, and "there was nothing to be excited about." According to Bicknell, the conference was brief, about five minutes' duration.

Of course, that was the evening before Pearl Harbor. After the attack, Bicknell recalled, when he was waiting to testify to the Roberts Commission, Short approached him when the two men were alone and said, "Well, Bicknell, I want you to know, whatever happens, you were right and I was wrong."

This is pretty strong stuff, I thought. If it holds true, it's dynamite. The most important parts of Bicknell's testimony to me concerned what happened between December 3 and December 7. I made a mental note to concentrate later on what had really happened on those crucial days. Bicknell also gave me a number of leads that had to be checked out; one of them involved the operations of British intelligence in Hawaii.

I found myself rather liking Bicknell. He could not get out of his mind the idea that he had missed the secret meaning of the words "poinsettias" and "hibiscus." For all intents and purposes, his qualifications for intelligence appeared to be better than Fielder's. For example, while he wasn't cleared for Magic, the Navy and the FBI had been able to work with him on a matter of mutual trust, and this is invaluable, to have people trust you.

But I also worried that Bicknell might have been "shedded" by G-2 in Washington before he came to see me. By that I mean he had been coached, because in the old days, lawyers would bring their clients to court by horse and wagon, parking in sheds, and before they went to the courthouse, they'd discuss in the shed the points the clients as witnesses were going to talk about. You can always tell when a witness has been shedded about what to say on the stand. The Navy sometimes had the habit of sending witnesses over to the Army Board hearings. They would listen carefully to the questions and learn how, when the questioner finished, to perhaps take off their glasses and shine them up, then carefully put them back on and give a slow, deliberate answer. The best way to answer when you're being cross-examined is to think while the question is being asked and then give the answer immediately. Bicknell did this. But there had been times when he acted shedded, too. Was it merely because he was an intelligence agent? It gave me pause.

Not all my interrogations could be as exciting in terms of promising new discoveries as was Bicknell's. The following one proved the truth of the matter.

Major Edward B. Anderson of the Transportation Corps was the next person to come to my office. Anderson had been working in the Adjutant General's office in Hawaii before Pearl Harbor. His testimony was to the point. He did not remember seeing the December 5 message number 519 from Washington. But neither did he recall that it had been necessary that day to ask Washington to repeat a message because one was missing in the daily count.

I then took an affidavit from Brig. Gen. Robert H. Dunlop, who had been the Adjutant General in the Hawaiian Department from June 1941 until a considerable time after Pearl Harbor.

He clearly remembered an all-out alert that had been ordered by Maj. Gen. Charles D. Herron, who had preceded Short as Commander of the Hawaiian Department. The alert had lasted approximately six weeks. According to Dunlop, it hadn't alarmed the civilian population in the slightest. (This contradicted Short's testimony that if he had gone to a full-scale alert after having received Marshall's war warning directive of November 27, it would have scared the populace; I would have to follow up on this later with Herron himself.)

I then asked Dunlop about Short's revised SOP of November 5,

1941. Had Dunlop sent it to Washington before the attack on Pearl Harbor? He had no recollection of having done so. Perhaps I should have asked why he hadn't done so when the SOP was changed on November 5. But the fact that he hadn't sent either the SOP or the Operating Orders was all that was important at the time.

Dunlop vividly remembered the events of November 27. He was in General Short's office about two-thirty that afternoon when Col. Walter C. Phillips, the Chief of Staff, interrupted and, after excusing himself, said "that he had come in to show the Commanding General a very important message from Gen. Marshall, which he had just received."

Short read the cable and said in effect that "it certainly was a very important message." Directing his attention to Colonel Phillips, Short ordered him to put Alert Number 1 of the SOP into operation. The reader will recall that this alert was a "defense against sabotage and uprising within the islands, with no threat from without."

At four that afternoon, Phillips called a staff meeting at which Marshall's message was read aloud. Phillips then stated that the Commanding General had ordered into operation Alert Number 1 of the SOP, and asked if there were any questions. There was one, about an apparently minor matter, and there was no discussion about the possibility of going to a higher state of alert. The situation was cut-and-dried. An order had been given; an order would be obeyed. The meeting lasted about fifteen minutes.

I had had a couple of days to ponder my session with Bicknell. On the surface, it appeared that he had alerted Short about the importance of the Japanese Consul's burning his codes and important papers. But had he done all that he could have done? Even if he had not seen the second advisory to Kimmel? I was sure he had not. On December 3, for example, after learning about the first monumental advisory message from the Navy Department in Washington, why hadn't he gone running to Fielder and said: "Tokyo has ordered the Japanese in Washington and London and elsewhere to burn their codes, and this means war." Instead, he had sat on the crucial information for three days. Then he'd reported it without revealing the source at the regular Saturday morning meeting with the Chief of Staff, Phillips, saying merely that he had this information from reliable sources. That wasn't good enough. He should have gone directly to Short the moment he had the information from his Navy sources and told Short that he had seen the actual dispatch from Washington that Tokyo had ordered its posts to destroy their codes. To me that would have meant instant war and instant vulnerability of any military installation such as Pearl Harbor. It should have had the same meaning for Short, too. At least, he had testified that that kind of information was the most important he could have received.

It was obvious there was a conflict somewhere. On December 5, Fielder hadn't told Bicknell to get over to the Navy and check out the Winds Code with Rochefort. And had the Navy been completely clean about what it had told Short? That was another problem I would have to investigate. But for the moment, I had to worry about why Fielder was having a problem communicating with Bicknell. My belief was that Fielder just wasn't up to it. He'd simply think, "Well, our position is strictly defensive. All Bicknell worries about is 'combat intelligence,' and we're not in a combat situation."

As I explored the relationship between the two men, I could not help suspecting that if Fielder had showed cable number 519 to Bicknell and asked, "What do you think?" it would have opened up a line of communication between the two for Bicknell to say, "Well, this agrees with what Rochefort, Mayfield and the FBI guy are saying." Then the two could have had a dialogue.

The horror of it is when Bicknell does take the final risk and rushes out on December 6—possibly with a guilty conscience—to tell Fielder and Short about the Mori telephone intercept, he gets accused of being too gung-ho, too trigger-happy, too "intelligence conscious."

The same thing happened to Layton. When he'd go to the Navy Officers' Club, they'd kid him about when the Japanese attack would be coming. Under those conditions, a person is likely to clam up.

But Layton was an Annapolis graduate. He had access to Admiral Kimmel. Layton had clout.

Bicknell, however, was only a Reserve Officer, albeit an important one. And he found his way to Short blocked by his immediate superior, a West Pointer, who was denigrating him. Fielder was the one who wrote Bicknell's proficiency report. This could well have been why Bicknell didn't stick his neck out on December 3. Proficiency reports make a lot of Army officers timid. (They never meant a damn thing to me, because all I ever wanted to do was get out after the war was over and be a civilian lawyer again.) So when Bicknell had cataclysmic information in his possession on December 3, he didn't pass it on immediately. I believe he should have taken the bull by the horns, and risked everything to tell Short about this intelligence of overpowering, overshadowing importance. By failing to communicate properly, Bicknell failed to do his duty.

This is harsh judgement. And I confess that I never asked Bicknell why didn't he rush to General Short on December 3. My primary function was to determine facts: what had been done and by whom it had been done. But I couldn't help wondering . . . Was Bicknell afraid to reveal that he was privy to supercharged information that his superior, Colonel Fielder, wasn't even allowed to know about? Was he worried he might get his Navy friends in trouble? Or had Bicknell been assured by the Navy that it would pass the information on to General Short? There appeared to be errors of high command involved.

6 "PUT A PRIORITY TAG ON ..."

For some time, I had been worried about the decrypts I was showing to the people I interrogated. I found it difficult to figure out how they had been intercepted, or the dates the original message had been transmitted by the Japanese, and the time we intercepted them. Also to be considered was when they had been decrypted and translated, the problem being that some intercepts were decrypted more quickly than others. There were a variety of reasons for this, including the priority assigned them, the type of code they were in (there were a number of codes besides Purple), and whether there was sufficient staff available to do the work. I also wanted to know if Hawaii had copied any of the decrypts in my possession. Lastly, I needed a check on whether or not Tokyo had ever broadcast a Winds Code weather bulletin ordering the destruction of codes and code machines, and if so, whether it had been intercepted.

Thus, my next deposition was with Lt. Col. Frank B. Rowlett of the Signal Corps. The reader will recall that earlier in the narrative I identified Rowlett as being the man who did the impossible trick in terms of creating the brilliant machine that allowed us to break the

Purple code while serving as a civilian technical officer to the officer in charge of the Crypto-Analytical Unit of the War Department. At the time I took his affidavit, Rowlett was the Branch Chief of the Signal Security Agency.

Rowlett was extremely precise but diffident in his thinking and in the way he spoke. It was almost like listening to a computer whir, click and then talk. He could recall comments to the effect that a "Winds Code" broadcast had been intercepted, but his search of the files could not disclose any confirmation of this. (It was not until 1978, when the *Washington Post* revealed that a Japanese spy, Takeo Yoshikawa, who had been working undercover in Honolulu as a vice consul, claimed that he heard the broadcast while listening to a short wave radio broadcast from Tokyo as the bombs were falling on Pearl Harbor.[1]) But knowing Rowlett's penchant for accuracy, I found him a believable witness when he said that his search of the files had failed to confirm an interception of a "Winds Code" broadcast.

Rowlett had also prepared a special chart for me that answered my questions about when certain messages had been intercepted, when they had been decrypted and translated and whether or not the Army at Pearl Harbor had copied (or read) the messages. The chart is reproduced in full on page 104, and it is important to note that as far as Rowlett believed, the top leadership of the Army at Pearl Harbor had seen only *two* out of the 50 intercepts that concerned me. Of course, this chart represented only what Washington knew. As such, it seemed to support Short's claim that Washington had kept him in the dark about intelligence matters.

But I had already taken affidavits from Rochefort and Bicknell disputing this. Rochefort had acknowledged seeing at least five of the messages (Nos. 25432, 25392, 25545, 25787, 25640), and Bicknell had acknowledged that he knew about at least four of these messages, if not all five. As I explained earlier, these were the five most important messages of the fifty, because they included the warning messages about the "Winds Code" and the orders from Tokyo to its embassies and consulates around the world that they were to destroy their codes and code machines. (The generic use of the word "codes" includes the machine that creates the codes.)

By studying the chart, it became apparent to me that the Army in Washington had not understood what information was available to

[1] Ron Laytner, *Washington Post*, Dec. 10, 1978.

SIS No.	SOURCES*	DATE MSG	DATE INT	DATE TRANS-LATED	HONOLULU
23260	S	24 Sept.	24 Sept.	9 Oct.	No
23570	7	14 Oct.	15 Oct.	16 Oct.	No
23516	2,S,7,M,3	14 Oct.	14 Oct.	15 Oct.	No
23631	1	16 Oct.	16 Oct.	17 Oct.	No
23859	2,7,1	22 Oct.	22/23 Oct.	23 Oct.	No
24373	S(teletype)	5 Nov.	5 Nov.	5 Nov.	No.
25322	Navy Radio	14 Nov.	?	26 Nov.	No
25644	S	15 Nov.	?	3 Dec.	No
24878	S	16 Nov.	17 Nov.	17 Nov.	No
25773	S	18 Nov.	18 Nov.	5 Dec.	No
25817	1,2	18 Nov.	18/19 Nov.	6 Dec.	No
25392	S	19 Nov.	?	26 Nov.	No
25823	S,2	29 Nov.	?	5 Dec.	No
25040	S(teletype)	19 Nov.	?	20 Nov.	No
25432	S(teletype)	19 Nov.	?	28 Nov.	No
25138	S	22 Nov.	22 Nov.	22 Nov.	No
25435	1,6	26 Nov.	26 Nov.	28 Nov.	No
25344	S	26 Nov.	26 Nov.	26 Nov.	No.
25349	?	26 Nov.	26 Nov.	26 Nov.	No
25444	1,2	26 Nov.	27 Nov.	28 Nov.	No
25480	1,2	26 Nov.	26/27 Nov.	29 Nov.	No
25436	1	26 Nov.	26 Nov.	28 Nov.	No
25445	S,6	28 Nov.	28 Nov.	28 Nov.	No
25496	S(teletype)	29 Nov.	29 Nov.	30 Nov.	No
25554	Navy Radio	30 Nov.	30 Nov.	1 Dec.	No
25553	J, Navy Rad.	30 Nov.	1 Dec.	1 Dec.	No
25552	J, Navy Rad.	30 Nov.	1 Dec.	1 Dec.	No
25497	J ?	30 Nov.	30 Nov.	30 Nov.	No
25555	Navy Radio	30 Nov.	30 Nov.	1 Dec.	No
25787	British	1 Dec.	?	5 Dec.	No
25605	S(teletype)	1 Dec.	1 Dec.	1 Dec.	No
25545	S(teletype)	1 Dec.	1 Dec.	1 Dec.	No
25727	S,1	1 Dec.	?	4 Dec.	No
25783	S,Navy Radio	1 Dec.	?	4 Dec.	No
25659-B	1,2,7	2 Dec.	2 Dec.	3 Dec.	No
25660	7	2 Dec.	2 Dec.	3 Dec.	No.
25640	X,2	2 Dec.	2 Dec.	3 Dec.	No
25785	7	3 Dec.	?	5 Dec.	No
25807	W	4 Dec.	5 Dec.	6 Dec.	No
27065	S,5	2 Dec.	2 Dec ?	30 Dec.	Yes
25843	S(teletype)	4 Dec.	?	7 Dec.	No
25836	S(teletype)	5 Dec.	?	6 Dec.	No
25838	S	6 Dec.	6 Dec.	6 Dec.	No
25843	S	6 Dec.	6 Dec.	6 Dec.	No
26158	1,5	6 Dec.	?	12 Dec.	Yes
25846	2(teletype)	6 Dec.	6 Dec.	7 Dec.	No
25854	S	7 Dec.	7 Dec.	7 Dec.	No
25850	S	7 Dec.	7 Dec.	7 Dec.	No
25856	S(teletype)	7 Dec.	7 Dec.	7 Dec.	No
25866	2, Navy Rad.	7 Dec.	7 Dec.	7 Dec.	No

*Navy: J=Jupiter, Fla. S=Bainbridge Island, Wash. W=Winter Harbor, Me.
Navy Radio=Navy Overseas Interdept or British, X=photographs of
origina messages

Army: 1=Ft. Hancock, 2=San Francisco, 3=San Antonio, 4=Panama
5=Honolulu, 6= Manila, 7=Fort Hunt, Va.

SIS NO.	SOURCES*	DATE MSG	DATE INT	DATE TRANS- LATED	HONOLULU
23260	S	24 Sept.	24 Sept.	9 Oct.	No
23570	7	14 Oct.	15 Oct.	16 Oct.	No
23516	2,S,7,M,3	14 Oct.	14 Oct.	15 Oct.	No
23631	1	16 Oct.	16 Oct.	17 Oct.	No
23859	2,7,1	22 Oct.	22/23 Oct.	23 Oct.	No
24373	S (teletype)	5 Nov.	5 Nov.	5 Nov.	No
25322	Navy Radio	14 Nov.	?	26 Nov.	No
25644	S	15 Nov.	?	3 Dec.	No
24878	S	16 Nov.	17 Nov.	17 Nov.	No
25773	S	18 Nov.	18 Nov.	5 Dec.	No
25817	1,2	18 Nov.	18/19 Nov.	6 Dec.	No
25392	S	19 Nov.	?	26 Nov.	No
25823	S,2	29 Nov.	?	5 Dec.	No
25040	S (teletype)	19 Nov.	?	20 Nov.	No
25432	S (teletype)	19 Nov.	?	28 Nov.	No
25138	S	22 Nov.	22 Nov.	22 Nov.	No
25435	1,6	26 Nov.	26 Nov.	28 Nov.	No
25344	S	26 Nov.	26 Nov.	26 Nov.	No
25349	?	26 Nov.	26 Nov.	26 Nov.	No
25444	1,2	26 Nov.	27 Nov.	28 Nov.	No
25480	1,2	26 Nov.	26/27 Nov.	29 Nov.	No
25436	1,	26 Nov.	26 Nov.	28 Nov.	No
25445	S,6	28 Nov.	28 Nov.	28 Nov.	No
25496	S (teletype)	29 Nov.	29 Nov.	30 Nov.	No
25554	Navy Radio	30 Nov.	30 Nov.	1 Dec.	No
25553	J,Navy Rad.	30 Nov.	1 Dec.	1 Dec.	No
25552	J,Navy Rad.	30 Nov.	1 Dec.	1 Dec.	No
25497	?	30 Nov.	30 Nov.	30 Nov.	No
25555	Navy Radio	30 Nov.	30 Nov.	1 Dec.	No
25787	British	1 Dec.	?	5 Dec.	No
25605	S (teletype)	1 Dec.	1 Dec.	1 Dec.	No
25545	S (teletype)	1 Dec.	1 Dec.	1 Dec.	No
25727	S,1	1 Dec.	?	4 Dec.	No
25783	S,Navy Radio	1 Dec.	?	4 Dec.	No
25659-B	1,2,7	2 Dec.	2 Dec.	3 Dec.	No
25660	7	2 Dec.	2 Dec.	3 Dec.	No
25640	X,2	2 Dec.	2 Dec.	3 Dec.	No
25785	7	3 Dec.	?	5 Dec.	No
25807	W	4 Dec.	5 Dec.	6 Dec.	No
27065	S,5	2 Dec.	2 Dec. ?	30 Dec.	Yes
25843	S (teletype)	4 Dec.	?	7 Dec.	No
25836	S (teletype)	5 Dec.	?	6 Dec.	No
25838	S	6 Dec.	6 Dec.	6 Dec.	No
25843	S	6 Dec.	6 Dec.	6 Dec.	No
26158	1,5	6 Dec.	?	12 Dec.	Yes
25846	2 (teletype)	6 Dec.	6 Dec.	7 Dec.	No
25854	S	7 Dec.	7 Dec.	7 Dec.	No
25850	S	7 Dec.	7 Dec.	7 Dec.	No
25856	S (teletype)	7 Dec.	7 Dec.	7 Dec.	No
25866	2,Navy Rad.	7 Dec.	7 Dec.	7 Dec.	No

*Navy: J=Jupiter, Fla. S=Bainbridge Island, Wash. W=Winter Harbor, Me. Navy Radio=Navy Overseas Interept or British, X=photographs of original messages
Army: 1=Ft. Hancock, 2=San Francisco, 3=San Antonio, 4=Panama, 5=Honolulu, 6=Manila, 7=Fort Hunt, Va.

Short's command before Pearl Harbor. Yes, information was being shared on a low-level operational basis between the Army and the Navy in a back-channel fashion that violated the Top Secret regulations. But how was this information being relayed to the top, to Kimmel and Short? And were Kimmel and Short, or their top staffs, conferring on these crucial matters in accordance with Washington's expectations?

I found another problem in the chart. There were two intercepts with the same number, 25843. According to Rowlett, these particular numbers had been assigned by the Navy. But at the moment, he could not tell me which number was linked to which message, because number 25843 was the number of the fourteen-part diplomatic message that Dusenbury had failed to deliver to Marshall. The reader will see from the chart that one message number 25843 was not translated until December 7, while the second message numbered 25843 was sent, intercepted and translated on December 6. Dusenbury had sworn to me that he had all fourteen parts of the Japanese message in his possession at midnight on December 6. So I had a further question for Rowlett: Would he go back and recheck the numbers and see if Dusenbury had been correct?

Rowlett said he would do so.

Another question facing me was how would I deal with the discrepancies between the testimony of Colonel Dusenbury and Colonel Bratton? The latter was overseas as February 1945 drew to a close. There wasn't any point in tracking him down until I had taken the affidavits of those people to whom he had claimed, apparently falsely, that he had delivered the first thirteen parts of the fourteen-part diplomatic message on the night of December 6. If he was going to reverse his testimony, I would have to present him with such solid documentation that he'd know there wasn't any point in trying to wriggle out of the mess he had put himself in before the Army Pearl Harbor Board.

Maj. Gen. Ralph C. Smith was the first person I interrogated on the matter. Because there were two men with the name Smith involved in the chain of Magic distribution, I thought it wise to question both of them to avoid confusion. One was Walter Bedell Smith, the other was Ralph Smith, who had been a colonel before Pearl Harbor and had been Executive Officer in the offices of the Assistant Chief of Staff, which meant, in day-to-day terms, that he guarded the doorway to Brig. Gen. Sherman Miles, the head of Army Intelligence. It was to Ralph Smith that Dusenbury or Bratton regularly delivered the daily

binder of Magic in a locked pouch for Miles to which Smith had a key.
The usual practice was for Smith to unlock the pouch, scan the documents and give them to Miles. A few weeks before Pearl Harbor,
however, the routine was changed. Smith was preparing for a combat
assignment, and he turned his key over to Miles. So Smith no longer
saw the Magic decrypts, but merely took the pouch in to Miles, who
unlocked the material and read it.

I pondered the question of how Ralph Smith could be cleared for
Magic and also be sent off to a combat command when a man such as
Fielder was denied access to Magic. It seemed to me that the question
of who needed to know what, and who might be a security risk if
captured by the enemy, was not being properly applied.

Ralph Smith stopped working for Miles at noon on December 6,
and that evening at six, he boarded a train to Fort Benning, Georgia,
for a refresher course in infantry school. With him on the train was
Clarence R. Huebner, who ended the war as a lieutenant general commanding the famous Fifth Corps.

This took care of one Smith. I knew that Bratton could not have
delivered any of the fourteen-part diplomatic message to him on the
night of December 6.

The next affidavit I took went back to the issue of cable number 519
about the Winds Code, which allegedly had been sent from Washington to Hawaii on December 5 and ordered Fielder to contact Rochefort
immediately. Mary L. Ross, in 1945, was working in the Office of the
Assistant Chief of Staff, G-2, but in December 1941, she had been a
clerk in the Cable Branch in the Office of the Assistant Chief of Staff.
Like all such people, she was given a code name—in this case a code
number—so that her work could be identified. Her number was 32.

Ross remembered cable 519 of December 5. The yellow copy of
the message had been brought to her along with a buck slip with
handwriting on the bottom saying: "Important—please put priority tag
on . . ." Ross told me the writing belonged to Colonel Pettigrew. She
remembered that the person who brought the message to her had told
her that it was important and "its immediate dispatch was urgent."
Ross then made her customary entry in the office outgoing cables
receipt book, in which she typed "Ser. No. 4," plus her code number,
32. Ross then put a red priority tag on the yellow sheet, took it to the
Signal Corps code room and gave it to the clerk there, who signed his
initials on it, "DG." The yellow copy was returned to Ross the next

day with a new notation on it: "519" and "SENT NO. 519, 12/5." Ross then wrote the number 519 in the receipt book, which completed the process of sending and logging that particular message. (A copy of the outgoing cable log is found on page 110.)

Ross remembered it all clearly, because soon after Pearl Harbor she was questioned repeatedly about what she had done and she had helped assemble all the documentary evidence on the matter.

A week later, I took an affidavit from Col. Edward W. Raley, who, for about one year before Pearl Harbor, and on December 7, 1941, had been the G-2 for the Hawaiian Air Force (Army). Shortly after assuming his duties, Raley called on then-Commander Layton, saying he was representing the Air Force. He asked Layton for intelligence that might be helpful to the Air Force. During the months that followed, Raley said he had no more than six conversations with Layton concerning the subject of Raley's interest. Their last conversation about intelligence was around October 1941.

What had Raley learned from Layton? Not much. Layton was Raley's only Navy source, and Layton had told Raley that if there was any naval movement by Japan "which might imperil the Hawaiian Islands, he would inform me." The only specific information that Layton ever gave Raley in this regard were studies that Layton had made about a possible Japanese invasion of the Malay Peninsula, and of Japanese fleet installations in the mandated Marshall Islands. According to Raley, he received these studies about two months before the Japanese attack on Pearl Harbor, and he passed them on immediately to his Commanding General, Edward Martin.

In support of Raley's concern about the state of Japanese-American relations at the time, he showed me a letter he had written to his daughter back in the States, which she had returned to him. Raley told her he had invited Layton and Bicknell to his house for a few drinks before dining at the Officer' Club. Both Bicknell and Layton agreed with Raley that Japanese-American relations were deteriorating. As Raley put it in his letter, these relations "never were in a more critical state than they are at the moment. I don't say there necessarily will be a war between the two countries right now, but I do say that never in the past has there been a time when it would be easier to have one. . . ."

I was interested in what Raley was saying. It wasn't important that he and Layton and Bicknell had agreed the situation in the Far East was deteriorating. What was significant was that Raley had met only six times with Layton during the course of 1941, and that their last intelligence meeting had been two months before Pearl Harbor. I found myself wondering: What exactly was the value of the relationship between Layton and Raley as far as the Air Force was concerned? Apparently, in the crucial days before Pearl Harbor, Layton didn't tell the Air Force that the Navy had no idea where to find the Japanese carriers. Nor did Layton inform the Air Force about the crucial messages the Navy had received on December 3 about the destruction of the Japanese codes. So, despite the claims that everything had been smoothly coordinated between the various services, the evidence was starting to pile up showing that the sharing of intelligence between the Navy and the Army in Hawaii was far from what it should have been.

Before I could dig deeper into this, there were still some loose ends to dig up regarding the transmission of the Winds Code cable number 519 of December 5. I took an affidavit from Col. Edward F. French, who, at the time the cable was sent, was the Officer in Charge of the Traffic Division and Signal Center in Washington. His comments about the various notations on the file copy of the cable, and other documents, confirmed the previous testimonies of McKenney and Ross. But French was able to say exactly how Washington could have been sure that the message had been received in Pearl Harbor. The ultimate check occurred every midnight, when the sequence numbers sent that day were verified by the recipient to assure that all the messages sent had been received. French called this check the "good night service," saying that if the message had not been received, there would have been a break in the sequential numbers in the Pearl Harbor files, and the message would have been transmitted again. According to French, this system "was a long-time practice to assure and guard against lost messages." Accordingly, the loss of a coded message was possible but highly improbable. Furthermore, French said the staff in the code room could not remember ever having lost a coded message.

The net was closing around what appeared to be a false claim by the Hawaiian command that cable 519 of December 5 never reached them.

The testimony of the next person I deposed showed the difference between the way things worked in Manila and in Hawaii before Pearl Harbor. This affidavit came from Col. Joseph K. Evans. For two years

OUTGOING CABLES

*R/ Ser. No.	Message Center Number	Message Sent To	Clas.	Time Message Sent To Message Center	Clrk	Drafting Officer & Branch	SUBJECT
1	26	Mexico	r	9:30A	32	MA WMA/BAP	Col. Weeks will arrive about Jan 10.
				B.C			
2	Thru AGO	Comm. Inf.Schl Ft.Benning.Ga.		10:10A	32	TB XXX	FL AG 350-2(11-5-41)MT-B/ MID 350.2 Ref yr radio 12/3 To F/L Offcr AGO &AG letr 11/7 to C.G. Ft.Benning author attachmt Capt.Mahan & Sims Chilean & Unda,Mexican Army, for 2 months frm Dec 1, 1941.
3	707	Manila	s	10:45	40	RSM	I We desire amplifcctn of "Particulars of Airprts & Lndng Flds in the Phil.",as reqstd our 176 & 505. Radio explanation.
				B.C.			
4	519	Hawaii	s	11:35 A	32	RSB	I Comm.Rochefort who cn be locatd thru 14th Naval Dist hs sm info on Jap broadcsts in which wea rpts mentnd that you must obtn. Contact him at once.
				AS			
5	49	Bulgaria	r	12:10 P	40	RGW	210.492 F/A Bulgaria.authority visit only grantd.
6	627	London	s	1:25 P	32	A.F.527	Attn Col. Van Voorst. Advise whethr lavender prints of Brit training films "Cathode Ray Tube" ....
				DSK			
7	1	Kabul Afghanistan	s	2:30 P	32	RBR F	You may draw 12/6.Accrdng to yr l. $5000 trnsfrd to yr credit by Col. Dixon.
				DSK			
8	628	London	r	"	40	RBR	F FD 1402 incrsd $2000 reur 1271 FD1432 $10,0000.
				DSK			
9	43	Turkey	r	"	40	RBR	F Oct.acct not yet rcvd $6633 rprsnt ng Sept.rplcmnt & adtnl $4000 reqstd being trnsfrd to Fry's credit by Col.Dixon 12/5.Authority to.....
				DSK			
10	THRU AGO	USArmy Inspector, Gen.Motors Research Lab. Detroit Mich .		4:15P	86	FKL/FL	Permissn.grantd.for Gen.Nawton,Maj Durval Cpt.Ibsen........to make 1 day visit next wk.subj.restrictn

From #O-2   *R/S - Record Section   Date: DEC 5 1941

77/74

OUTGOING CABLES

*R SER. NO.	MESSAGE CENTER NUMBER	MESSAGE SENT TO	CLASS.	TIME MESSAGE SENT TO MESSAGE CENTER	CLERK	DRAFTING OFFICER & BRANCH	SUBJECT
1	26	Mexico	r	9:30A	32	MA WMA/BAP	Col. Weeks will arrive about Jan 10.
2	Thru AGO	Comm. Inf. Schl Ft. Benning, Ga.		10:10A	32	TB FL	AG 350-2(11-5-41)MT-B/ MID 350.2 Ref yr radio 12/3 To F/L Offcr AGO & AG letr 11/7 to C.G. Ft. Benning author attachmt Capt. Mahan & Simms Chilean & Unda, Mexican Army, for 2 months frm Dec 1, 1941.
3	707	Manila	s	10:45 B.C.	40	RSB I	We desire amplifctn of "Particulars of Airprts & Lndng Flds in the Phil.", as reqstd our 176 & 505. Radio explanation.
4	519	Hawaii	s	11:35A DJK	32	RSB I	Comm. Rochefort who cn be locatd thr u 14th Naval Dist hs am info on Jap broadcsts in which wea rpts mentnd that you must obtn. Contact him at once.
5	49	Bulgaria	r	12:10P DJK	40	RGM	210.492 M/A Bulgaria. Authority visit only granted.
6	627	London	s	1:25P DJK	32	A.F.527	Attn Col. Van Voorst. Advise whethr lavender prints of Brit training films "Cathode Ray Tube" . . . .
7	1	Kabul Afghanistan	s	2:30P DJK	32	BBR F	You may draw 12/6. Accrdng to yr 1, $5000 trnsfrd to yr credit by Col. Dixon.
8	628	London	r	" DJK	40	RBR F	FD 1402 incrsd $2000 rour 1271 FD1432 $10,000.
9	43	Turkey	r	" DJK	40	RBR F	Oct. acct not yet recd $6633 rprsnt ng Sept.rplcmnt & adtnl $4000 reqstd being trnsfrd to Fry's credit by Col. Dixon 12/5 Authority to . . . . .
10	THRU AGO	US Army Inspector, Gen.Motors Research Lab., Detroit, Mich.		4:15P	86	FNL/FL	Permissn. grantd. for Gen. Newton, Maj. Durval Cpt. Ibsen......to make 1 day visit next wk. subj. restrictn

Form #C-2   *R/S - Record Section   Date: DEC 5 1941 before November 27, 1941, Evans had been the Assistant G-2 in the Philippine Department, which was commanded by Gen. Douglas MacArthur. (Evans was currently working in Washington as the Pacific Ocean Area Specialist.)

According to Evans, there was good cooperation so far as he knew at his lower level between the Army and Navy at Manila. He obviously could not speak for the High Command. Manila had facilities for intercepting, decrypting and translating the Japanese Purple code. (Because the reception of Japanese radio traffic was so much better in the Philippines than in Pearl Harbor, and because Washington believed Manila to be in greater danger than Pearl Harbor, Manila was given these facilities.) Evans said the messages received and decrypted by Manila were approximately the same as those decrypts I had carried around for my investigation. The British Secret Intelligence Service was also represented in Manila. Evans said that I should see the British intelligence man, who had been there at the time, one Lt. Col. Gerald H. Wilkinson, who was currently working in room 303 of 630 Fifth Avenue, at Rockefeller Plaza, in New York City.

On November 27, Evans received orders to return to the United States, and he left the Philippines via the Army transport ship *H. L. Scott.* I could not help being amazed at how people's careers had been changed by virtue of their being transferred only a few days or hours before the outbreak of war. About two days before sailing, Evans learned from the British that their Secret Intelligence Service base in Singapore said that hostilities between Japan and America were "imminent, and that large Japanese naval forces were concentrating in the vicinity of the Marshall Islands."

For these reasons, the convoy in which Evans traveled did not take the usual direct route eastward from Manila to Pearl Harbor. Instead, it went by a circuitous route south through the Torres Strait, which separates Australia and New Guinea.

The convoy in which Evans traveled arrived at Pearl Harbor on December 15, eight days after the attack, and he spent a "number of hours" conferring with Colonel Bicknell and FBI Agent Shivers. Evans told the two men about the information that he had received from the British in Manila before sailing. Bicknell stated that he, too, had received this information "at the same time."

It was all becoming "curiouser and curiouser," I thought. The convoy leaving Manila on November 27 had exercised prudence. It altered its usual course on the basis of information from the British in

Singapore that the Japanese were massing in the Marshall Islands and might attack. Why had Manila been so cautious? And why hadn't Pearl Harbor shown the same alertness?

These questions carried me into yet another avenue of exploration. On the night of December 3, British intelligence in Manila (most likely Colonel Wilkinson) had sent an urgent cable to British intelligence in Hawaii, saying:

> We have received considerable intelligence confirming following developments in Indo-China.
>
> **A.** 1. Accelerated Japanese preparation of air fields and railways.
>   2. Arrival since Nov. 10 of addition 100,000 repeat 100,000 troops and considerable quantities fighters, medium bombers, tanks and guns (75mm).
> **B.** Estimate of specific quantities have already been telegraphed Washington Nov. 21 by American military intelligence here.
> **C.** *Our considered opinion concludes that Japan envisages early hostilities with Britain and U.S.* Japan does not repeat not intend to attack Russia at present but will act in South.
>
> You may inform Chiefs of American Military and Naval Intelligence Honolulu. (Emphasis added)

The distribution list showed that the British Secret Intelligence Service gave copies of this cable to Colonel Bicknell, FBI Agent Shivers and Captain Mayfield of the Navy.

I believe that many people are unaware of the significance of this message, but consideration should be given to its being either a part of the Winds Code or as part of the order from Tokyo of the similar date for its embassies to destroy their codes and code machines.

America and England had been following for many months the negotiations between the Japanese Ambassador to Vichy in German-occupied France regarding the former colony known as French Indo-China. Our Magic intercepts allowed us to comprehend the real meaning of Japan's proclamation of July 27, 1940, known as the Greater East Asia Co-Prosperity Sphere. Because Japan wanted to break her reliance on various Western powers for raw materials, especially oil, Japan was planning to take over the Dutch East Indies, Malaya, Burma, Thailand and the Philippines. To achieve this goal, Japan forced the Vichy government to accept that Japan would assume military control of French Indo-China, or what we later called Vietnam, both North and South. Thus, by late August 1941, Japanese forces controlled such important military staging areas as Hanoi, Cam Ranh Bay, Saigon and Phnom Penh.

With Japan having been fully prepared for war by the end of October 1941, the British and the Dutch had kept a watchful eye on the area, waiting for the attack they knew was coming. They only question was when it would be launched. Thus, the warning message from the British at Singapore, reporting the incredible buildup of Japanese forces in French Indo-China and that "early hostilities" were expected by Japan against Britain and America, with no concurrent attack on Russia, could only have been derived from British Ultra sources (the equivalent of our Magic sources). It should have received greater attention than it did from our combined commands in Hawaii, which had already downplayed the "war warning" of November 27 that had been received from Washington.

But if our commanders weren't going to pay much attention to Washington, I believe it fair to assume that they would pay even less attention to a warning from Britain.

It was the end of March 1945, just as the Allied forces were preparing for their final drive to the River Elbe, that I flew out to Pearl Harbor. Actually, it was my second trip, the first having been with the Army Pearl Harbor Board. On that occasion, we stopped overnight in California and I put a silver dollar into a slot machine and broke the bank. I had so many coins in my pockets, I would have drowned if our plane went down.

The C-54 landed safely, only there wasn't anyone to greet us. Pearl Harbor had all the advance information that these highfalutin generals were flying in, only they forgot about it. We joked among ourselves that if we had been the enemy, we could have bombed the hell out of them.

This second trip, because I was carrying all the supersecret decrypts, I got a special briefing on what to do if the plane went down. There was a special raft I could inflate, and a pouch with shark repellent. If I got hungry, I was supposed to drop a line with a lure overboard, plus crank a radio to call for help. It was all serious as hell. I asked if that might not be dangerous. After all, an enemy sub could be listening to me crank the radio and come up to capture me.

The major who was briefing me said, "You're not supposed to crank your radio with submarines around."

"Well," I asked, "how can I tell when submarines are around?"

"Oh, they come up at night for air."

I replied, "In that case, I want to make sure I get one of those special knives to clean fish. I might be out there a long time."

The major didn't think I was funny.

Anyway, I reached Pearl Harbor without having to inflate my raft, and the first person I called on was John E. Russell, the president of the trading firm Theo H. Davies and Co., Ltd. I wanted to ask him why, on December 4, 1941, his firm had contacted its shipping office on the West Coast and canceled orders that were in the process of being shipped to the Philippines.

The Davies firm was British-owned, so I couldn't depose Mr. Russell. He was a British citizen and also the Consul General. But the next day, he was kind enough to write me an official statement for the record. According to Russell, he telephoned C. V. Bennett, the manager of the Davies San Francisco office, on December 4, and told him "to cancel all outstanding orders for shipment to the Philippine Islands and to endeavor to stop shipments that were en route there."

Russell said that he had not received the message from Manila of December 3, but he saw a copy of a message that had been sent by one Colonel Wilkinson, "then working secretly for the British Government," to his agent in Hawaii. That agent, Harry L. Dawson, just happened to be sitting beside Russell as he dictated his statement to me.

As I read the document, I thought I had to get hold of Dawson. But Russell's next sentence shot me down in flames. Unfortunately, according to Russell, "Mr. Dawson finds that all his records of this incident were destroyed immediately after December 7, 1941." In polite terms, Russell was telling me that I wouldn't get any help from Dawson.

Apparently, the firm's agent in San Francisco, C. V. Bennett, also had his curiosity aroused as to how Russell had been so prescient in suddenly deciding to cancel shipments to the Philippines. But all Bennett got in the way of a reply was a letter from Russell saying that he could not "give any logical explanation as to why I had taken such steps. It just looks like one of those lucky hunches that one gets at times!"

What Russell was not saying, of course, was that the British had always pursued, were pursuing in 1941 and pursue today a linkage between their nation's commercial and intelligence interests. British intelligence and British business work hand-in-glove together. This has always angered many American military people. Later, I was to learn that Wilkinson's links to British business had inflamed MacArthur's command in Manila. The Americans believed that our way of colonizing was better, and provided greater freedom for the average local citizen, than did the British system, in which profits for British companies were linked to British intelligence at the expense of people under British rule.

Russell ended his statement to me by writing that he could not recall exactly what had been in the message of December 3, but he believed "it indicated some Japanese troops dispositions which were very illuminating in the light of diplomatic exchanges then taking place." Of one thing he was sure: "I do not believe that the message said that trouble would begin on December 7th; but as I told you today the general tone of the message was sufficiently alarming to cause a reaction in the mind of the businessman, strong enough to warrant the cancellation of a considerable volume of orders for delivery to the Philippines."

I could only agree with Russell, and wish that our commanders in Hawaii could have shared the same sense of danger as did a British businessman.

Having finished with the British intelligence people who had been on the spot when Pearl Harbor occurred, I made a note that I would have to check the central files of British radio intercepts in England. That would have to come later, however, and I set out to question Robert L. Shivers, who had been the FBI Agent in Charge at Honolulu since 1939. He was currently working as Collector of Customs for the Hawaiian Islands, having left the FBI during the course of the war.

Shivers looked Chinese. He was short, well built, dark complexioned, with very black hair. He was very frank with me. Actually, his affidavit had two amendments, because he kept adding material to what I had asked him.

He said that in 1940, he had established close liaison with Rochefort, Mayfield and Bicknell. He had weekly meetings with Bicknell and Mayfield, usually to discuss the problems inherent in the possibility of sabotage by the large contingent of Japanese who lived in the

Islands at the time. He said that Fielder attended some meetings, but not many.

Although he was not supposed to know what Rochefort was doing, Shivers knew he was in charge of the Navy's intercept radio station, a radio direction finder station and cryptoanalytical units. But Rochefort never gave Shivers any intelligence that was based on the Navy's information until *after* the Japanese attack.

About November 28, J. Edgar Hoover, the Director of the FBI in Washington, sent a radio message to Shivers saying that "peace negotiations were breaking down and to be on the alert at all times as anything could happen." Shivers passed this message on to Mayfield and Bicknell. Both said that they had received similar messages from their respective headquarters in Washington.

On two occasions, Captain Mayfield, the Intelligence Officer for the Fourteenth Naval District, passed on vital intelligence.

The first was when Mayfield told Shivers that the Navy was aware of the Winds Code the Japanese would use to announce its "war movements and break in diplomatic relations." Mayfield told Shivers: "If I suddenly call you and say I am moving to the East side of the island [Oahu] or North, South or West sides, it will mean that Japan is moving against the countries which lie in those directions from Japan."

Shivers passed this information on to Bicknell. But, he said, "at no time did Capt. Mayfield give me the code indicating such movement."

This was somewhat disquieting, I thought. It appeared that the Navy in Pearl Harbor had relied primarily on intercepting the Tokyo broadcast of the Winds Code message to learn about the imminence of a Japanese attack. What if the Navy missed the broadcast? What if there was no break in normal communications between Tokyo and its diplomats? There wouldn't be a need then for Tokyo to make a Winds Code broadcast. Should Mayfield have put so much reliance on a single intercept?

The other occasion that Mayfield called Shivers about was on December 3, when Mayfield coyly asked Shivers if the FBI could verify Naval information that the Japanese Consul General in Honolulu "was burning his codes and papers."

At the time Mayfield asked the question, Shivers thought he was referring to information that the Navy had obtained from tapping the phones of the Japanese Consul General's quarters in Honolulu. It wasn't until after Pearl Harbor that Shivers learned from Rochefort that Mayfield had been referring to the warning messages of that day that Washington had sent Admiral Kimmel saying that the Japanese were ordered to burn their codes in Singapore, Malaya, Washington and London, plus destroy their Purple code machines. About two hours after Mayfield's phone call, around noon, the FBI telephone tap intercepted a conversation between the Consul General's chef and an unknown Japanese person in Hawaii, during which the chef said that the Consul General was busy burning all his important papers.

Shivers immediately passed on this information to Mayfield and Bicknell.

Mayfield never told Shivers what he did with this information inside the Navy.

Bicknell told Shivers that he had passed the information on at the staff meeting of December 6.

Then, during the period between December 8 and December 12, Bicknell showed Shivers a paraphrased copy of a message the Army had intercepted on December 3 that had been sent by the Consul General in Honolulu to the Japanese Foreign Office in Tokyo. The message contained a system of light signals that had been devised by one Otto Kuhn for the Consul General, by which the movement of the American ships at Pearl Harbor could be flashed to Japanese submarines operating in the waters off Oahu and Maui Islands. But this message, which would have been a clear warning of the Japanese hopes to attack Pearl Harbor, had not been decrypted until after the attack. (The FBI found a copy of the message after it raided the Japanese Consul General's office on December 7; later, the FBI got an original copy from the Mackay Radio Co. in Honolulu, which it had transmitted to Tokyo.)

That was an important opportunity missed, I thought, but not the only one. What did Shivers recall about the full-scale alert that General Herron had ordered when he had been commander of the Hawaiian Department? "The civilian population of Oahu considered it routine Army maneuvers," replied Shivers, "and was not alarmed in any way."

This was another refutation of General Short's belief that his order for a minimal alert so as not to frighten the civilian population prior to Pearl Harbor was the proper action.

I also asked how the British operated their intelligence network in Hawaii before Pearl Harbor.

Shivers had it down pat. Around July 1941, Gerald Wilkinson had called on Shivers to say that he was a manager for Theo H. Davies and Co., but more importantly, he was the "representative in the Pacific area for the Special Intelligence Service of the British government, reporting direct to the British Foreign Office in London." Wilkinson wanted to identify for us another British citizen, Harry Dawson, who was the British Vice Consul for the Hawaiian Islands and would be the British intelligence person in Hawaii. Dawson was only working on "developing foreign intelligence information pertaining to the Japanese." He would do nothing to interfere with the internal workings of the Hawaiian Islands. To ensure we would leave Dawson alone, Wilkinson told Shivers that Dawson would pass on to Naval Intelligence, the Army G-2 and the FBI "information received from other [British] SIS operatives in the Pacific area."

The arrangement had apparently been approved by higher authorities in the Navy, and was in operation from that time on.

But what about the Navy's telephone taps on the Japanese Consul General's office? I asked Shivers. As I listened to his answer, my heart sank.

Around the end of November 1941, said Shivers, he discovered that the Navy, which for several years had been tapping the Consul General's phones in Honolulu, had missed a line that went into the cook's quarters. Shivers ordered a tap on that line, and it was from this tap that he learned on December 3 the Consul General was burning all his important papers. (But Shivers did not know that the Consul's actions were based on instructions that had come from Tokyo, or that other Japanese diplomatic posts around the world had been ordered to do the same thing.)

I then dropped the bombshell on Shivers. Had he known that the Navy had stopped tapping the telephones of the Japanese Consul General in Honolulu on December 2?

My question shocked him to the core. He had never heard this before. He seemed genuinely upset that his tap was the only one in operation in the days that immediately preceded Pearl Harbor. I thought he was a credible witness when he declared that Mayfield had never told him about the Navy's stopping its activities. "Had I known such ONI coverage had ceased," Shivers declared, "I would have caused FBI coverage in replacement."

I wondered what had gone wrong. After successfully tapping the Japanese Consul's phones for two years, why had Mayfield suddenly stopped the Navy's operation? And why, on December 3, hadn't May-field been more forthcoming with Shivers? If Mayfield had told Shivers that the Navy's information about the destruction of Japanese code machines, codes and papers had originated in Tokyo, and that the Japanese diplomats were following these orders in other countries, the two men might have been able to discern the value of the information they had in their possession.

My next stop was the Counter Intelligence Division (CID) in Honolulu. There, Lt. Col. Byron E. Muerlot described the conference that had been held in Colonel Raley's office at Hickam Field at two-thirty on the afternoon of November 29, 1941. Raley had called the meeting to discuss Marshall's warning message from Washington of November 27. According to Muerlot, the message had advised "that negotiations with Japan were at a stalemate, that hostilities might ensue, and that subversive activity might be expected." The upshot of the meeting was that "all practicable precautionary measures" would be taken to prevent sabotage. There was no discussion about what type of hostilities might occur. There were no questions.

The U.S. Army Air Force in Hawaii was doomed.

I then set out to track down what had happened to the Pettigrew/Miles message of December 5, old number 519, at Pearl Harbor. To say that flanks were being covered is to put it mildly. Col. O. N. Thompson, the Adjutant General, had put his staff to work trying to locate message number 519, which ordered Fielder to contact Roche-fort immediately about the Winds Code message. They were unsuc-cessful. The message was not in the G-2 files. (If that was true, how had Bicknell seen it on Fielder's desk?) Nor was the message in the master files of incoming radio traffic. (A master file record of incoming radio traffic was not started until January 25, 1942, I was told.) No record of message number 519 could be found in the Adjutant Gen-eral's decimal files. Lastly, no permanent record of incoming radio traffic was kept in the Signal Cryptographic Section.

I had run into the same dead end as had the Army Board. Pearl Harbor could not find the message. It was what I had expected; I would have to dig deeper.

Now the time had come for me to start digging into the Navy's activ-ities. I reported to the Naval Commandant at Pearl Harbor and showed my letter of authorization from Secretary Stimson. I also suggested that he might want to call Commander Sonnett at the Pentagon for further clarification. Sonnett always cleared the way for me in this regard, and within short order, I was given access to the Navy's code crackers at Pearl Harbor.

The first man I saw was Capt. Thomas A. Huckins, who on December 7 and for some time before that had been in charge of the radio traffic analysis. He was also responsible for the distribution of the Navy's radio intelligence summaries for the period of November 1 through December 7. According to Huckins, he had no liaison "with any Army officer," nor did he exchange any information with the Army about "his functions or duties." Lastly, before December 7, he had had no contact with Colonel Fielder.

As for Capt. Wilfred J. Holmes, his duties at the Combat Intelligence Unit prior to Pearl Harbor "included only the preparation of plots of positions of U.S. combat and merchant vessels, flights of U.S. trans-Pacific planes and positions of Japanese ships based on [radio] call analysis. . . ." According to Holmes, the information he produced went only to Admiral Kimmel. In other words, it was not shown to the Army.

I then spoke with Comdr. Jack S. Holtwick, Jr., who had been in charge of the IBM machine room and was assistant to the principal cryptoanalyst, as well as being the administrative assistant to Capt. Joseph J. Rochefort.

Holtwick verified for me, and showed me copies of, the messages that Rochefort had initialed for me earlier in Washington. These included the December 4 message from Washington to Pearl Harbor saying that Tokyo had ordered its embassies in Washington, London and other cities to destroy their Purple machines and important papers (codes) with the exception of one (code) system. Others included were the dispatches from Pearl Harbor to Washington that the Japanese would attack the Isthmus of Kra (on the Malay Peninsula) on December 1, plus the message of December 6 that said that the Japanese Consul in Hawaii had destroyed all his codes except for one system.

Holtwick showed me a cornucopia of other information that included the Navy's Intelligence Daily Summaries from November 1 through December 6. These summaries went *only* to Capt. Edwin P. Layton, the Fleet Intelligence Officer, for distribution to the appropriate Naval commands. The regulations for this distribution stated that "any request for additional copies . . . will be made to the Commander-in-Chief [Kimmel], and not to the Division of Naval Intelligence.'' Here was another vital intelligence channel that was not given to the Army.

Holtwick also confirmed that, in the months before Pearl Harbor, Rochefort's unit did not have the Purple machinery needed to decrypt the Japanese diplomatic radio messages. (His operation was trying to break the Japanese Fleet codes, a different proposition from the Purple code.) The Head of War Plans in Washington, Admiral Turner, had testified that he thought Pearl Harbor had a Purple machine. But the only code decryption machine Rochefort possessed was one that had been designed by Commander Holtwick for a Japanese code that had been abandoned in 1938; the machine was useless and had not been used since then.

In my view, this testimony was deadly. Admiral Turner had told the investigators in Washington that he believed Pearl Harbor possessed the machinery to decipher the Purple codes. As the head of the all-important War Plans Division, whose seniority Turner used to override the recommendations of the Office of Naval Intelligence, Turner had committed the classic blunder of failing to check to ensure that Hawaii had the equipment it needed to do its job. (I was told by Army experts that it would not have been difficult to build another Magic machine and have it flown out to Hawaii.)

On the other hand, perhaps Turner had forgotten that he had been involved in the debacle of trading Magic machines with the British in return for a copy of their machine that could break Germany's Enigma codes. The net result of all this was that Hawaii had been denied the ability that Manila possessed to decrypt the Japanese diplomatic messages. Meanwhile, Turner was testifying that he believed Hawaii had the machinery. It was a terrible state of affairs.

The historian and journalist, of course, wants to know why the Navy command in Hawaii didn't ask for the machinery. I can't answer that question. My best guess is that Pearl Harbor was terrified of Turner's temper. No one was willing to argue with this strong, determined man, who appeared to be trying to seize control of the Navy Department from the Chief of Naval Operations. It would have been professional suicide to say: ''Sir, you gave our Purple machine away to the British, and now we're up a creek without a paddle.'' That wasn't the way things were done in the peacetime Navy, or in the wartime Navy, for that matter. An Admiral such as Turner was God, even to Kimmel.

There were still some other matters I had to clear up. One of these required more checking into that infamous cable from Washington, old number 519.

To this end, I deposed Chief Warrant Officer Louis R. Lane, who had been assigned the task of searching the classified files for message number 519 of December 5, 1941. Lane had double-checked the records at Fort Shafter, including the Battles and Reports files of the Adjutant General, the Japan files, the Espionage files, the Military Information files and the Journals of the Adjutant General. According to Lane, "no record of the receipt by the Hawaiian Department of this message could be found." But Lane stated that the preceding messages, numbers 517 and 518, were located. The messages that followed 519, messages 520 and 521, were also located. Lane also suggested that I check the records of the local RCA office, because he believed, from reading the copy of the message that I carried in my bomb pouch, that message 519 had been sent via commercial cable.

To my prosecutor's mind, the missing message was very unusual and suspicious. Washington's "good night" service had verified the arrival of the messages numbered 517 through 521 on December 5. Bicknell had seen message 519 on Fielder's desk. Given Bicknell's actions, which had been corroborated by other witnesses, I could only conclude that message 519 had been received and buried, by either Fielder or Short.

The most important factor was that I believed any jury would convict on the evidence that I now possessed. But the question of the Winds Code, in my opinion, was not the primary object of my investigation. The Winds Code took on much greater proportions than I thought it should have. If someone wanted to create a role for the goddess of discord, and throw a golden apple over a fence to cause people to fight and waste time, the Winds Code was that golden apple. It was a red herring for men such as Safford, and Noyes, and Bratton and Sadtler to follow and let dominate their thinking.

It's the same as if a magician focuses your attention on what he wants you to see while he does something else you don't see. I can't say that the Winds Code was disinformation as the term is used today, but it comes close. It certainly caused havoc among our intelligence people.

I tend to agree with Admiral Ingersoll, who pointed out in his testimony that the Winds Code unnecessarily assumed gigantic proportions. The crux of the Winds Code, *if* it was broadcast (because ordinary communications were cut, or diplomatic relations were about to be ruptured), was that the Japanese embassies and consulates were then to destroy their code machines and their codes. The truth of the matter was that we had already intercepted and decrypted this very order on December 3, but in a different format. So, essentially, the Japanese never needed to broadcast an execute message for the Winds Code. Meanwhile, all our people were killing themselves to intercept the broadcast. If that isn't an apple of discord, or the reddest of red herrings, I don't know what one is.

The other item I needed to check up on was what had caused the Navy, on December 2, 1941, to discontinue its taps on the telephones of the Japanese Consul General in Honolulu.

Lt. Donald Woodrum, Jr., USNR, swore to me, on the basis of his knowledge of the events, there being no documentary evidence on the matter, that before November 1, 1941, the telephone surveillance of local espionage suspects and the Japanese Consulate was run by the local Office of Naval Intelligence under the command of Captain Mayfield. Transcripts of the conversations were given to the FBI almost on a daily basis.

So far, so good. But around November 1, the FBI learned that the telephone line to the cook's quarters at the Consulate had not been tapped. The FBI checked with Mayfield. He gave them permission to tap the cook's phone. According to Woodrum, it was the first such surveillance undertaken by the FBI in Hawaii.

Unfortunately, while making another routine installation, someone at the phone company discovered the FBI tap. The discovery was bucked up the line at the company and was ''casually'' passed to a member of the DIO (Naval District Intelligence Office). In the spirit of cooperation that existed between the DIO and the FBI, the DIO passed on news of the discovery to the FBI. At this point, everything unraveled.

Woodrum explained that Shivers, the FBI Agent in Charge, made a formal complaint at the phone company, claiming that the confidential nature of FBI operations had been compromised when the company told the DIO about the FBI's tap.

When Mayfield heard about the FBI complaint to the phone company, Woodrum said: "He was not only incensed at their [the FBI's] failure to consult with him before taking such action, but he considered that action to be a serious breach of security." Apparently, Mayfield was concerned that his instructions, which came from no less a personage than the Chief of Naval Operations, were to avoid "any possibility of international complications." Because of his awareness of the "explosive potentialities" of the surveillance he was conducting, Mayfield then ordered an immediate halt to all the Navy phone taps.

In stopping the taps, Mayfield did not tell Shivers what he was doing. This explains why Mayfield had to call Shivers on December 3 to ask if the sole remaining FBI tap had uncovered anything about the Consul's actions.

As I listened to this sad story of a childish dispute, a typical, everyday conflict between various law enforcement jurisdictions, I could not help asking myself what would have happened if Mayfield and Shivers had simply hung in there, discussed the matter calmly and kept the Navy's phone taps in place.

And I could barely repress a rueful smile when Woodrum assured me that Mayfield and the DIO had been so secretive about the operation that "very few people in the [DIO's] office even knew about the bugging anyway."

This depressing deposition ended one stage of my investigation in Honolulu. My next stop would be Guam, where I would take the affidavit of Captain Layton. I had prepared carefully for this, even going to the point of bringing Colonel Fielder with me from Washington, because if Layton was going to maintain that he passed on information regularly to the Colonel, I wanted to be able to confront him with Fielder, who had testified earlier that such was not the case.

Before I could fly from Hawaii westward to Guam, I had to send a cable listing all the people in my party. It would be just Fielder and myself, of course, but I knew that our names would be circulated to Layton via the jungle network, and he, being a smart intelligence officer, could figure out for himself what was up.

Layton was a guy who was fast on his feet. He had studied the Japanese language, served as a naval attaché in Japan and been on social terms with Admiral Yamamoto, with whom he played bridge. He could move around and pick up bits and pieces here and there, and make something of it all.

Fielder and I had a cozy plane ride out to Guam. I learned a lot more about him on the plane. He was an excellent magician. Not only did he do a lot of tricks for me and the crew, but he explained how he did them in lucid language. It didn't mean that I could copy him, however. I didn't have the manual dexterity. But I could see how his mind worked. Once, he let his guard down for a moment and told me that the key to his success was always to keep a clear desk—anything that landed on it was passed immediately to a subordinate for handling. It was for Fielder not to do the work, only to make sure that the papers cleared his desk—upward or downward—as fast as possible. Fielder was very proud of this system. But he failed to realize that in talking with me in this fashion, he had damned himself for proving that he didn't care a hoot about his job.

I made a mental note to check further into Fielder's background as we went along.

At Guam, I found my way to Captain Layton's office, which was a jumble of books and papers and maps. He was in full uniform, because he was on call to Admiral Nimitz at all times, and he talked very, very quickly. Before I knew it, he was telling me about the South Pacific and the Isthmus of Kra (on the Malay Peninsula). He was one of those "take charge" people. I began to suspect that he was not being straightforward when he started shoving an avalanche of material at me that he insisted I had to take. (I read it through, at a later time, of course, but it was about matters that were foreign to my inquiry.) And then I got the admission I had not expected to hear: Layton said that *the Navy could not give General Short any decrypts based on the Purple intercepts because of Navy regulations.*

His statement about Navy regulations simply was not true. But it proved that prior to Pearl Harbor, the Navy had placed itself in the predominant position of power in terms of holding on to intelligence and not sharing it with the Army, on whom it was codependent for survival. And it violated the agreement that said the two local commanders were supposed to share all important intelligence.

Layton phrased all this in typical Naval language. As he put it: "Liaison with other government agencies, including the Army, would normally be effected through established channels. . . ." He talked about the "interlocking yet independent" status of himself, Rochefort and Mayfield, who was Layton's "direct liaison" on Naval matters to other government agencies in Hawaii. (In other words, Mayfield was a "cutout," as they call it in intelligence.) Rochefort was head of the Combat Intelligence Unit under the direct orders of the Chief of Naval Operations in Washington, but was under the jurisdiction of the Commandant, Fourteenth Naval District (Hawaii), not the Pacific Fleet. He was Layton's direct liaison "in matters of Communications Intelligence." As for Layton: "My intelligence field was limited to the vessels and forces of the US Pacific Fleet and I was under the direct command of the Commander in Chief of that Fleet [Kimmel]."

And then Layton began to give testimony that was in total contradiction to what I had been given by Colonel Raley.

According to Layton, about three months prior to December 7, 1941, Colonel Raley "called at my office and informed me that he had been directed to establish with me an *Army* liaison and requested all information we possessed on airfields in Australia, Netherlands East Indies, Australian Mandated Territories, and any other Pacific Ocean airports and airways." (Emphasis added) Layton said that he gave Raley "all the information we possessed, confidential and secret." (But, I noted, nothing that was Top Secret.) From that point in time, Layton continued, either Raley or his assistant, a Lieutenant Brown, would request various items of intelligence. By mid-November, he claimed that the meetings between Raley, Brown, and Layton and his assistant, Commander Hudson, "increased in frequency."

At this point, a series of intelligence reports from various sources, including Washington and the Dutch, British and Chinese, indicated that Japan was on the move in a southerly direction along the China coast, "with concentrations being seen in French Indochina and South China." Layton said that the general tenor of these reports was "imparted to Col. Raley and we informally discussed and exchanged opinions on the general significance thereof."

Layton then went on to say: "In a period for about 2 to 3 weeks prior to 7 December, as my recollection serves me, I talked with Col. Raley on a general average every other day."

I kept my best poker face as I listened to Layton's recollections. I could recall Raley's sworn statement all too well: According to him, the last conversation between Raley and Layton had occurred around October. The two had met only six times in 1941. I began wondering whether I should have brought Raley with me to Guam as well as Fielder.

Layton continued his testimony. In the period of about ten days or two weeks prior to the Japanese attack, he claimed, he gave Raley specific Top Secret information from sources "that had previously been found to be completely reliable." But Layton did not tell Raley the "true source and concealed its true origin, in keeping with the Top Secret Oath by which I was bound." Furthermore, Layton told Raley that he would impart the information only if Raley promised that he would not make a copy of the information, nor write memos about it, and that he would tell it only to his commander, General Martin, who was the head of the Hawaiian Air Force.

Raley agreed to these strictures. So Layton gave Raley certain Top Secret items, including one about an intrigue in Thailand where Japanese leaders were circulating a false report about a Japanese invasion in the hopes of getting Britain to send some troops from Singapore to help the Thai government. Upon their arrival, Japan would claim that Britain had invaded Thailand, and the pro-Japanese faction in the Thai government would scream for Japanese assistance, which would make Japan's entry into Thailand easier and help in the Japanese invasion of Malaya.

Layton also recalled that he told Raley about the fact that the Navy was listening for the broadcast of "certain cryptic weather messages" (i.e., the Winds Code) that would "signal the breach of diplomatic relations, or the opening of hostilities between Japan and certain powers, namely, America, Britain or Russia."

What about telling Raley of the message that the Navy had received on December 3 relating that Japanese diplomats around the world *were* destroying their Purple codes and code machines? Layton could not recall whether or not he had passed on this information. It was, of course, another misleading statement on his part. I knew he had said nothing.

What did Layton know about what was going on in Honolulu in terms of what Captain Mayfield was doing?

Layton claimed he had not received any information from the dispatches sent by the Japanese Consul General in Honolulu—by commercial cable or otherwise.

Layton also claimed that he was never advised about the telephone conversation intercepted by the FBI between "Mori" and Tokyo.

Layton's story was that Captain Mayfield had called him on the evening of December 6, asking that he be able to see Layton the next morning at "my convenience." Layton continued: "I asked him if I should come down immediately as I was free, and he [Mayfield] replied, 'We cannot do anything about it now, as I do not have the material and will not have it until tomorrow morning.' "

Aha! I thought. Whaddya mean Mayfield didn't have the material? Bicknell had a transcript and a translation of the phone call in time to get to see Short and Fielder. Mayfield had it, too. I had caught Layton in so many inconsistencies that I thought I'd give him a breather.

We went back to the Japanese buildup in the Marshall Islands, the Carolines and the Marianas. They might appear as tiny specks on the average map of the world, but they were mighty naval bases in the Pacific. The Japanese were building airfields on all the islands and increasing their garrison forces. Layton had written several bulletins about all this for the Fleet High Commands and the Chief of Naval Operations.

Late in November 1941, the Army proposed making photographic reconnaissance of these islands. Layton said that he then held a series of conferences with Raley, giving Raley the latest information on developments in the area. (The missions were never flown, because the photo planes did not arrive in time.)

When I asked if Layton had ever discussed the so-called ABC Bloc (American-British-Chinese) with Raley, he replied that he could not specifically recall the term. However, he said, there might have been conversations about a geographic limit—a line drawn across the ocean—beyond which the British and the Dutch could not allow penetration by the Japanese without their going to war against Japan. Apparently, there was no assurance that the United States would help the Dutch, or the British, if the Japanese should cross this magical geographic line.

As for Layton's relationship with Colonel Bicknell, the only time Layton had ever had contact with him was when he met Bicknell at Raley's quarters at Hickam Field, when they discussed the deteriorating world situation and the Far East. Under normal conditions, claimed Layton, he wouldn't have any reason to contact Bicknell directly. That would be done by the Fourteenth Naval District, "through whom the Fleet dealt on all matters pertaining to shore-side business."

What about General Short? Did Layton have any contact with him?

Not really, was the gist of Layton's reply. From time to time, Layton was called into Kimmel's office to give a brief summary of the intelligence picture "at the time in question. I cannot state positively that Gen. Short was present at these times, but I believe he may have been." There were occasions when Short was present, however, and Layton did speak about "the general dispositions of the Japanese Fleet and Major Japanese Naval Air Units" based on all "available intelligence, including Top Secret."

Fine and dandy, I thought. Listen to what the man isn't saying. Sometimes that's more important than what he's talking about.

What Layton wasn't saying was that he never discussed in conference with Kimmel and Short the significance of the war warning messages of November 27 sent from Washington. Nor did he discuss in conference the significance of the information sent by Washington on December 3 that Japanese diplomats around the world, and in Honolulu, were destroying their code machines and codes. In other words, the vital intelligence briefings between the two commanders who were codependent on each other for survival *never took place*.

Well, then, what about Layton's links with his opposite number in the Army?

"I had no official liaison with Col. Fielder," declared Layton, "as I had presumed from Col. Raley's remarks when he first came to me and suggested setting up the liaison that he was then representing the Army, as the Hawaiian Air Force was a subordinate command of the Commanding General, Hawaiian Department."

Coming from Layton, who was a stickler for protocol and ran his office with an iron fist, this statement bordered on the absurd. He knew all too well that if the office, G-2 Army, wished to assign a surrogate representative, that man would have arrived with the proper credentials and introductions. But Layton knew how to play the game, and he played it to the hilt with me, explaining that Raley had told him that since the Navy and the heavy bombers of the Air Force represented the offensive weapons for carrying out the combined War Plans, he was directed to establish this liaison, because the Hawaiian Department saw itself as a defensive garrison.

This was a clever shot across Fielder's bow. Layton understood Fielder's character and his method of operating. And then Layton drove his attack home.

He gathered that "other liaison had been established [by the Army] with the Fourteenth Naval District." He also knew there was a specifically designated Naval Liaison Officer attached to Short's head-quarters, a young lieutenant named Burr. So, said Layton: "Inasmuch as I had no direct contact with Col. Fielder, I did not impart to him any of the information that I gave to Col. Raley. [In fact] Col. Fielder did not request any intelligence from me prior to 7 December 1941."

Only after the attack on Pearl Harbor, I said to myself. I remembered Fielder having told me that Layton wouldn't have given him any information even if he had asked for it. What did this conflicting testimony mean?

It seemed to me that Layton was trying to give himself maneuvering room by claiming that he was under the direct command of Admiral Kimmel and was concerned only with what happened in the vast expanses of the Pacific Ocean. He wanted to establish the concept that the responsibility for a link between the Army and the Navy in terms of sharing intelligence was solely a shoreside one, between Rochefort and Mayfield versus Fielder and Short, and that Kimmel and Layton were not involved. What Layton was saying was not true, in any manner, shape or form, because Short was entitled to all the information that Kimmel received from Layton, Rochefort and Mayfield. But Short did not get it.

That is why I use the term "codependent." No one else has used it. Each man, Short and Kimmel, was codependent on the other. Historians have used the term that they were to rely on "mutual cooperation," according to the terms of the Joint Action Agreements. But that's not the way to run a business, or an army and a navy. When people are codependent upon each other, it creates an error of command. There should have been one boss at Pearl Harbor, and only one boss. That way, there might have been a chance that the United States would have been ready to repel an attack.

As a final matter, Layton read over the decrypts that I carried with me. He claimed that he knew "the substance" of only two of them before Pearl Harbor. But they were crucial. One was SIS 25432 about the Winds Code. The other was SIS 25787 in which Tokyo told its embassy in London to "please discontinue the use of your code machine and dispose of it immediately . . ." At the bottom of this message Layton wrote: "Message not seen—but British reported that Japs had destroyed their purple machine in London. 26 April 1945. [signed] E. J. Layton."

Now it was confirmed that Kimmel's Fleet Intelligence Officer was fully aware of the facts regarding the Winds Code and Tokyo's ordering the destruction of the Purple code machine. This meant that Kimmel also knew.

But when it came to the war warning that Washington had sent Kimmel on November 27, and the subsequent warnings about the Japanese destroying their code machines that Washington sent Kimmel on December 3, Layton would not say a word.

Did he believe that his omissions would not be discovered? Or did he hope that by remaining silent on these matters he could protect Kimmel?

I held my judgement in abeyance and said farewell, taking with me the sixty-five pages of documents Layton gave me.[2] Later, as I

---

[2] Clausen Report, pp. 113–178.

read the papers in my quarters, I came to the conclusion that Raley had given me honest testimony, and Layton had not. Layton had said that he had violated Navy regulations in what he had told Raley, and I knew this to be untrue. The rules had been worked out in Washington that all important information was to be shared.

What I had discovered was the core of the Navy's practice of hoarding secret, vital information that it doled out to the Army only when, and if, it desired to do so. Apparently, this had been going on for a long time in Honolulu. And when you coupled this with an unworkable, double-headed command structure that required codependency and mutual cooperation, the defenses of Pearl Harbor had, from the start, been almost certain to fail.[3]

---

[3] Clausen letter to Lee, Mar. 13, 1991.

7 "I HAVE HAD TO BARTER LIKE A RUG MERCHANT"

I was deeply troubled during the flight back from Guam to Honolulu, but I could not let Fielder guess at what was bothering me. While he did his magic tricks, I thought about the problem.

If the Navy was guilty of hoarding secrets from the Army, who had the authority to explain the situation and make the charges stick? The Pacific Theater of Operations was, for all intents and purposes, a Navy command. Who had the strength to oppose the Navy in this brouhaha? There could be only one person, but would he help?

When our plane landed, I parted with Fielder, reminding him that he should be getting ready to give me his deposition, since he now had the time to review all the documents from his old command. Then I set about using secure phones to get the help I needed. There wasn't any guarantee that this help would be forthcoming, but my intermediaries in Washington promised they would do what they could.

Meanwhile, I went back to the essential details of the case.

Waiting for my return was a memo from Brig. Gen. C. A. Powell, who was in charge of the Signal Center at Fort Shafter. I had asked him, before leaving for Guam, if he would be so kind as to investigate three matters for me. The first concerned the infamous Winds Code message number 519 of December 5, 1941. Powell certified that, to the best of his knowledge, there were no copies of this message in the records at Fort Shafter. And he dropped notice on me that I'd never find the message, no matter how hard I tried.

"In fact," wrote Powell, "there are no copies of clear or coded traffic in the Signal Center prior to 1 July 1944. All coded traffic prior to 1 July 1944 and all clear traffic dated prior to 1 March 1945 have been destroyed by burning."

It wouldn't do me any good to appear angry about this, even though I was furious, because I'd never get anywhere trying to find out who had ordered the burning of this material, or why. It had been done. That was what mattered. All I could say was that I believed the Hawaiian command had covered up its mistakes as far as it could regarding this issue.

Powell was more helpful on other matters, however. This concerned another Japanese intercept, numbered Army 8007 and dated December 2, 1941. The message itself read:

> From: Tokyo (Togo)
> To: Honolulu
> December 2, 1941
> J-19 [the type of code in which the message was sent]
> #123 [Secret outside the department]
>   In view of the present situation, the presence in port of warships, airplane carriers, and cruisers is of utmost importance. Hereafter, to the utmost of your ability, let me know day by day. Wire me in each case whether or not there are any observation balloons above Pearl Harbor or if there are any indications that they will be sent up. Also advise me whether or not the warships are provided with anti-mine (anti-torpedo) nets.
>   NOTE: This message was received here (Washington) on December 23.
>   ARMY 8007 27605 (Japanese) Trans. 12/30/41 (5)

This was a vitally important intercept. Yet it had not been translated until three weeks after the attack on Pearl Harbor. Years later, in his book, *And I Was There*, Admiral Layton would charge that had he and the Navy at Pearl Harbor known about this intercept in time, they would have figured out that the Japanese had assigned Pearl Harbor the designation "attack target." Our Navy would then have taken a different attitude about defending the fleet.

Layton's analysis is only partially correct, however. This was one of the first indications I had seen that the Japanese believed they had the ability to attack Pearl Harbor, because Tokyo is asking the Hawaiian Consul General to report the status of our warships in Pearl Harbor on a daily basis. Furthermore, Tokyo needs to know if barrage balloons are being used (an indication that Japan might be considering an air attack), and if torpedo nets are in place around the American ships. (This was even more vital information, since the U.S. Navy believed that Pearl Harbor was too shallow for Japanese planes to drop torpedoes, which, in itself, was a fatal miscalculation of Japanese capabilities; the majority of the damage caused by the Japanese attack came from torpedoes especially modified for use in shallow water.)

Of Powell, I had asked: Why hadn't the intercept been translated sooner?

According to General Powell, the message had been intercepted on December 2 by the Army Signal Intelligence Service. It had been sent by Hawaii to Washington by air mail in a cumbersome process. Each day's SIS intercepts were gathered on a separate log sheet. The log sheets were then gathered, and when the SIS was notified that a Clipper (a Pan American flying boat) was about to depart Honolulu, an officer courier took the package of intercepts to the Clipper for transmittal to the West Coast. This particular message was sent by ship on December 11; the delay of nine days was because the Clipper was prevented from taking off first by rough weather and later by the outbreak of war. As to why the intercept hadn't been sent to Washington by radio, Powell could only say that the selection of messages for faster transmission had been the duty of the Signal Officer in charge at the time. But, said Powell, the J-19 code the Japanese had used was not considered a high-priority item according to the written instructions then in use for forwarding such intercepts to Washington.

The number 5 at the end of the message indicated that the intercept had been made by monitor station number 5 in Honolulu. At the time in question, the station was intercepting messages between Japan, Asia and Europe.

I could not help wondering how many more intercepts might have been missed because they hadn't been translated quickly enough. I would have to check this further.

The third question that Powell answered for me was one of extreme importance, and one that has puzzled historians for many years. My question to Powell had been about the monitoring of scrambled commercial telephone calls between Hawaii and California.

Powell stated that the Army had not monitored the scrambled phone lines between Hawaii and the mainland. Before 1937, he explained, the phone system used the same inverter for scrambling calls between Tokyo and San Francisco as did Hawaii and San Francisco. This meant, of course, that until 1937, Tokyo could monitor *all* the secret conversations between Hawaii and the West Coast. That is, until December 1937, when a new phone circuit was commissioned, giving what the Army called A-3 privacy. Not long after the A-3 system was installed, the Japanese technical operator in Tokyo asked the operator in Hawaii what type of new inverter was being used. He said openly that Tokyo was no longer able to understand the conversations between Honolulu and San Francisco. The operator in Tokyo was told that the only person who understood the new inverter was the Bell technician who had just installed it. Said Powell: "This was proof that Tokyo had in the past been monitoring the Honolulu–San Francisco radiophone circuit."

It meant more than that to me, however.

In 1940 and early 1941, Washington believed the Army's communications system was not as secure as the Navy's. This meant it was probable that the Japanese, between 1937 and 1941, had discovered the secrets of the A-3 inverter on the phone lines between San Francisco and Honolulu. In turn, this was the reason why General Marshall decided not to telephone Hawaii on the fateful morning of December 7 to warn Short that a Japanese attack might be coming. If the Japanese were monitoring the line, as they most surely were doing, they would have learned from a call by Marshall that we had broken their codes.

The story of how the final warning on the morning of December 7 failed to reach Short is a perfect example of the peacetime mentality of certain Army officers. What happened, as Congress determined later, was that after consulting with the Chief of Naval Operations, Admiral Stark, at around eleven-thirty A.M. Washington time, about the meaning of the fourteen-part Japanese message, General Marshall wrote out a radiogram that was to be sent to all the theaters of operations involved. These included Pearl Harbor, Manila and the Panama Canal Zone. The message read:

The Japanese are presenting at 1 p.m. Eastern Standard Time, today, what amounts to an ultimatum. Also they are under orders to destroy their code machine immediately. Just what significance the hour set may have we do not know, but be on alert accordingly.[1]

Marshall ordered Colonel Bratton to take his handwritten bulletin immediately to the message center for dispatch by radio. As Bratton was leaving the room, Admiral Stark telephoned Marshall, asking that the cable include *the usual request* to inform the Navy, so Marshall added: "Inform Naval authorities of this communication."[2]

As we were to learn, one P.M. Washington time was the approximate time of dawn at Pearl Harbor.

Bratton delivered the cable to Col. Edward F. French, who was in charge of the message center. On returning, Marshall asked Bratton how long it would take to encipher and dispatch the message. Not getting a clear answer, Marshall then sent Colonels Bratton and Bundy to the message center to get a better understanding of what was going on. They came back and told Marshall that the message should be in the hands of its recipients within half an hour. Even this answer did not satisfy Marshall. He sent the two Colonels back to the message center a second time. This time, they were able to confirm to Marshall that the messages would be received by everyone before the one P.M. deadline in Washington time.[3]

It was at this point that Murphy's law took over. (The law being: If anything can go wrong, it will.)

Colonel French personally saw to the dispatch of the message. First he learned that the War Department radio had been unable to reach Pearl Harbor since around 10:20 that morning. Without informing Marshall of this problem, French then decided to send the message via the fastest possible way, which was commercial cable. And so he sent the encrypted message by Western Union to San Francisco, from where it went by RCA commercial radio to Honolulu. The message was filed at the Army message center at 12:01 P.M. Washington time (6:31 A.M. Hawaiian time, and an hour before dawn at Pearl Harbor.) The Western Union teletype was completed at 12:17 P.M. Washington time (6:47 A.M. Hawaiian time). The message was received by RCA

[1] Committee Record, p. 224.
[2] Ibid.
[3] Ibid.

in Honolulu at 1:03 P.M. (7:33 A.M. local time, or at dawn, and the moment the Japanese were about to begin their attack). This was later than Colonel French had promised Bundy and Bratton. Worse, the teletype hookup between the RCA office and Fort Shafter was not operating at dawn that Sunday. The best the RCA office could do was to send a boy on a bicycle to Fort Shafter. But he sought shelter from the air raid and did not reach Fort Shafter until 11:45 A.M. Hawaiian time (or 5:15 P.M. Washington time).[4]

So much for the assurances to Marshall that all the recipients would have the message before one P.M. Washington time.

Testifying later before the Army Pearl Harbor Board, Colonel French said that the signal center had used similar commercial services before when there was important traffic and the radio link between Washington and Hawaii was not working. (The RCA broadcast station had forty watts of power from San Francisco, while the Army radio had only ten watts.) He also said that he acted properly within his authority, even though he did not tell Marshall how the message had been transmitted. (All the other messages reached their recipients in time.)[5]

When French was asked why he hadn't used the telephone, he said that he had never considered doing so. The telephone was *never* used by the message center. It was unsuitable for classified messages (the reason now being clear from General Powell's statements to me.) And then French said: "If they wanted to use the telephone, that was up to the individuals themselves, Chief of Staff, or whoever the individual concerned."[6]

Congress would later call Colonel French's actions on that December 7 "extremely regrettable."[7]

I personally believed it to be a good deal worse than that. Why didn't Colonel French tell Marshall that his radio could not contact Pearl Harbor that morning? French realized the importance of the message he was sending, and he knew of Marshall's concern that it reach all the recipients by a certain hour, so his actions will never be understood.

The fact of the matter is that Marshall tried to warn his sentries at the last minute, but his subordinates let him down.

---

[4] Ibid., p. 225.
[5] Ibid.
[6] Ibid.
[7] Ibid., p. 226.

Hard on the heels of the report from General Powell, I received an informational report from Commander Holtwick concerning his search for information about the possible interception of a plain-language broadcast of the Winds Code.

In 1945, only one officer was still in Honolulu who had been involved with the original project. Apparently, a watch had been established to monitor the Japan Broadcasting Company news broadcasts. Special attention was given to those that were broadcast on the hour, or half hour, since they contained the weather forecasts.

The monitoring watch *never* obtained any results. And as Holtwick laconically stated: "The monitoring watch was naturally secured immediately after it became obviously redundant." This was a nice way of saying that once the bombs started falling, we had more important things to do than listen for a Winds Code execute message.

The next affidavit I took was that of Theodore Emanuel, who was the Chief Ship's Clerk (USN). His was an innocuous-sounding title, but it covered a lot of deep goings-on. In reality, Emanuel was under the direct orders of the Chief of Naval Operations, and I got the distinct impression that Emanuel was reluctant to talk to me.

For two years before December 7, 1941, Emanuel had been assigned to the District Intelligence Office of the Fourteenth Naval District. His job included the tapping of the telephone conversations of the Japanese Consulate in Hawaii over five or six lines.

Emanuel also knew Colonel Bicknell. When Bicknell was called to active duty, the two men discussed what Emanuel was doing.

According to Emanuel, he would have the conversations recorded, translated and reported to the DIO, Captain Mayfield. The traffic averaged about fifty or sixty calls per day.

I was concerned that Emanuel said his operation had continued through December 7, when I had been told by other sources that Mayfield had cut off the phone taps on the December 2. After probing, I came to the conclusion that Emanuel was mistaken about the operation's continuing through the attack on Pearl Harbor, possibly because he did not want to be identified as the informant who broke the story that Captain Mayfield had prematurely ended the telephone surveillance of the Japanese Consulate.

I spent the remainder of April in Hawaii, writing up my preliminary findings, and celebrating the Allied victories that led to the fall of Berlin, Hitler's inglorious suicide and Germany's unconditional surrender. But the war was still raging in the Pacific. When I received orders to proceed to Gen. Douglas MacArthur's headquarters in Manila, I knew that our Sixth Army under General Krueger was still fighting a tenacious enemy only one hundred miles to the north of my destination. (Nearly one hundred thousand Filipinos were killed by the Japanese during the battle for Manila in a series of horrible atrocities; General Yamashita would later stand trial as a war criminal for the horrors committed by his troops.)

It was quite a shock to step from my comfortable seat in the C-54 on which I traveled to Manila. (Contrary to popular belief, not all our transports were equipped with bucket seats. Some even had sleeper berths.) The debris of war was everywhere. Fires still burned as the result of recent action by the Japanese diehards, and the sharp crack of ammunition "cooking off" in the flames added a sense of danger to my drive into the city.

After being introduced to MacArthur, and turning down his offer of a general's accommodations (I did not believe it would be conducive to good relations if I, a mere major, bounced some general from his room), I began my work.

Obviously, I was to have some vetting by the local command before I would be allowed to question MacArthur, so I first took the affidavit of Lt. Gen. Richard K. Sutherland. He was currently MacArthur's Chief of Staff, and had been a colonel doing the same job in the Philippine command prior to Pearl Harbor. As we talked, I could hear MacArthur striding back and forth in his office, a habit that got him in trouble with his pilots because his constant pacing threw the plane out of flying trim.

I showed Sutherland the complete files of intercepts that I had brought with me in my bomb pouch. It took some time for him to read through the material. When he was finished, I sensed that he was truly disturbed, although the official language of his affidavit did not show his dismay.

Adding the usual caveat, "to the best of his recollection," Sutherland told me that he had *not* seen any of these intercepts before Pearl Harbor. Neither had he known about the substance these intercepts contained, with the exception being some of the messages that related to the diplomatic negotiations in Washington before the Japanese attack. Nor had Sutherland seen the messages that described the Winds Code.

Sutherland also had never seen the British messages that Manila had sent Hawaii, especially the warning of December 1 that hostilities would soon break out. All Sutherland could say was that the source of the material appeared to be the mysterious Major (now Colonel) Gerald Wilkinson of the British Army, about whom I will say more later.

According to Sutherland, the Army SIS in the Philippines ran an intercept station at Fort McKinley before Pearl Harbor. The diplomatic messages the Army SIS intercepted in the Purple code were delivered in raw form to the Navy at Corregidor, where the Navy had facilities for decryption and translation. "Some or all of these messages"—a nice way of saying "not many"—were then returned to the SIS for delivery to the Army.

Among the messages that were intercepted, and that Sutherland recalled clearly, were reports by the Japanese Consul in Manila about the arrival and departure of ships in Manila Harbor. (This meant that Pearl Harbor was only one of the harbors where the Japanese were monitoring the movement of our shipping.)

As for disseminating this type of information, said Sutherland, his command didn't do it. Everything was done by the Army SIS.

Although Sutherland's testimony was bland on the surface, I knew that I was close to striking pay dirt.

I spent the next day with MacArthur, who was very frank. He said he had the same information Hawaii possessed, and that Hawaii had claimed this information was inadequate for the defense of Pearl Harbor, but he believed it was adequate for his needs.

I must acknowledge that I believed I was in the presence of a great man, a general who had fought back after a terrible defeat to thrash the enemy all the way from Australia to the Philippines. Yet, he was extremely courteous. He got up and paced back and forth across the floor, puffing his pipe, which was his way of conducting a conversation. I was so fascinated by all this that when I typed up the affidavit, I misspelled MacArthur's name, dropping the letter *a*. This caused a hullabaloo in Congress later, when I was called to testify about my investigation.

Sen. Homer Ferguson, who was a Republican from Michigan and tried hard to discredit me, asked me how to spell MacArthur's name, implying that because I had misspelled it, my work was unreliable. By then, I knew I had made the error, so I told Ferguson, "Well, Senator, I must refer you to Senator Jackson. He said it was a damn poor mind that could spell a word only one way." That stopped Ferguson dead in his tracks.

By now, MacArthur and I seemed to understand where we were both coming from. I asked him about the Navy's hoarding of intelligence. Was it true? Had it affected him, or how he performed his job?

Remember, we weren't doing the affidavit yet, just setting the background for it.

"I am going to ask [Major General] Willoughby to testify to those particulars," said MacArthur. "That's the best way to handle the matter. What I want you to do for me, Major, is to take a special plea back to the Secretary of War on my behalf. Tell Secretary Stimson that the intelligence-sharing problem is intolerable. I beg the Secretary to take drastic action to correct the situation. I have had to barter like a rug merchant throughout the war to get the intelligence I have needed from the Navy. All too often, they had no concept of what intelligence is necessary for me to save the lives of my men by avoiding concentrations of the enemy, or his air force. All the Navy can think about is protecting its ships. The system as it stands is wrong. Only Secretary Stimson, as Secretary of War, has the power to correct the situation. I urge you, as my emissary, to press this point of view home as hard as you can."

There was a method to MacArthur's madness in this. He knew I came direct from the Secretary of War. He knew that I would report forthrightly to Stimson about what he was saying. But MacArthur wasn't going to testify to that effect. He was going to let his intelligence chief sign an affidavit, and thereby keep the war for the control of intelligence in its proper channels. He was going to let the man who had really fought the intelligence battles carry the ball. And by standing behind him, like Banquo's ghost, MacArthur knew that this would carry more weight back in Washington than if he took to the parapets himself.

I felt a tingle of excitement as I listened to MacArthur. He was saying exactly what had been germinating in my mind. Rather than faulting individuals and seeking to court-martial them for what had gone awry at Pearl Harbor, it might be better if we started looking at the question of faulting the system, with one of the major problems being the Navy's arrogant hoarding of secret information and doling it out if and when it pleased. On the other side of the coin, if we were going to criticize the system, how would we change it? How could we make it better?

So here we were, sitting in MacArthur's office with the windows open and the sounds of ammunition exploding in the distance, some of it in the courtyard of the next building, talking about the Navy's hoarding intelligence. It seemed somewhat unreal. Finally, we got down to the General's affidavit.

For the record, MacArthur stated that he was the commanding general in the Philippines before and after Pearl Harbor.

He read my Top Secret Exhibit B of intercepted Japanese messages. "I have *no* recollection of seeing any of these before," said MacArthur. "I did *not* see the messages described as the 'Winds Code,' nor any activating or implementing message. . . . I have *not* previously seen the British [Secret Intelligence Service] messages. . . . I have *no* knowledge as to the basis or source of this intelligence, and I did *not* know that these or other similar messages were being transmitted to persons at Honolulu." (Emphasis added)

MacArthur did know that the Army's SIS operated an intercept station at Fort McKinley immediately before Pearl Harbor. But these messages were delivered in their raw, intercepted form to the Navy at Corregidor. "The Navy had facilities and personnel, not possessed by the Army, for such processing of this intelligence," declared MacArthur. And then he added the damning words, "Whether all messages were transmitted by the Navy to the Army I do not know. All transmission of this subject material was entirely in the hands of the Navy."

In ending his testimony, MacArthur stated for the record that he believed that his command had been given the correct warning by Washington to prepare for war. As he put it: "Dispatches from the War Department gave me ample and complete information and advice for the purpose of alerting the Army Command in the Philippines on a war basis, which was done prior to 7 December 1941."

This unequivocal statement was of extreme importance. First, it placed MacArthur at the side of General Marshall in terms of how MacArthur believed Marshall had carried out his duties as Chief of Staff before Pearl Harbor. (I was intrigued by this, since I knew all too well the bitter feud that had existed between the two men over the years.) Secondly, MacArthur repudiated the findings of the Army Pearl Harbor Board. Thirdly, his testimony challenged the arguments Admiral Kimmel and General Short had advanced that Washington had kept them in the dark about developments. Fourth, since the Navy controlled the flow of intelligence, MacArthur was saying that if any parties believed they had not received enough intelligence to have been prepared for war, their lacking this intelligence was the fault of the Navy.

No one else of MacArthur's stature had dared come to Marshall's defense so far. I suspected that MacArthur's statement would have wide-ranging implications, but I couldn't foresee at the time just how wide-ranging they would be.

We spoke again about the message MacArthur wanted me to carry to Stimson, and he said that he had tried time and again during the course of the war to have G-2 in Washington do something about the problem. Unfortunately, G-2 never seemed to understand what Mac-Arthur was getting at. I could believe this, because I had picked up rumbles in Washington that G-2 thought MacArthur was a chronic complainer, looking for another flag to wave from the grandstand. But MacArthur was right. Washington would have ignored the issue, not realizing the truth in what he said. Was MacArthur's support for Marshall a signal that MacArthur hoped would be understood by the Chief of Staff, and interpreted to mean that MacArthur's olive branch signified that the intelligence problem could be worked on harmoniously by the two former adversaries?

The issue was really joined the next day when I took the affidavit of Maj. Gen. C. A. Willoughby, which came in three parts: the primary affidavit; Appendix A, about British intelligence and Colonel Wilkinson; and Appendix B, about the Navy's hoarding of intelligence to the detriment of the Army. Apparently, Willoughby thought that it was best to split the subjects, then one appendix or another could be held back from prying eyes. It didn't matter to me how Willoughby wanted to testify. I was playing by the rules of a civilian investigator: Everything he said was going to be put on the record.

Prior to Pearl Harbor, Willoughby had been the Acting Chief of Staff, G-2 (Intelligence), for MacArthur's Philippine command. (He served as MacArthur's intelligence eyes and ears throughout the war, and I was told his work had been brilliant, allowing MacArthur to win campaigns with a minimum of casualties.) A tall, striking figure of an officer, wearing decorations that stemmed from an incident in which he was nearly captured, he carefully read through the intercepts I carried in my bomb pouch, and I could sense that this competent intelligence expert was upset by their contents.

Like so many others, he denied ever having seen any of the American intercepts. Nor did he have any knowledge of the Winds Code intercept. Willoughby did say that he had known about "isolated fragments" of the diplomatic message series, but that was all.

As for the British Secret Intelligence Service intercepts, Willoughby testified that he had not seen them before December 7. All he could say was that the material had been disseminated by Gerald Wilkinson. By the way Willoughby said the name, I knew he disliked Wilkinson intensely, and he said that he would say more about him in a separate appendix.

Willoughby also confirmed the testimony I had taken in the past two days: The Army had run a signals intercept unit at Fort McKinley, but all the intercepts had been handed over to the Navy for decryption and translation. As Willoughby phrased it delicately, "It was customary for the Navy, after these messages were decrypted and translated, to give the Army (Hq. USAFFE) such portion of the sum total of this intelligence, and the details and source thereof, as the Navy considered necessary to the functions of the Army." By this he meant that the Navy was arrogating to itself the role of running the Army, and this must have driven MacArthur up a tree; it also became grist for much of W. E. B. Griffin's best-selling novels (*Battleground* and *Line of Fire*) about the Marines nearly half a century later. The intercepts that Willoughby recalled seeing were the ones between Tokyo and Manila about the movements of military and commercial ships.

The Army in Manila kept no records of the dissemination of this information, nor did Willoughby think that any of this intelligence was sent to the Army in Pearl Harbor. That was "exclusively a Navy function."

In detailing his beliefs about the British intelligence operations, Willoughby wrote scathingly about Gerald Wilkinson in his Appendix A.

"The whole story is one of duplicity, evasion, bargaining, horse trading and a sort of E. Philips Oppenheim international intrigue," said Willoughby. He said Wilkinson was an untrained civilian and the British government gave him a military rank to protect him in case he was captured.

According to Willoughby, Wilkinson had married into the ultra-rich Davies family and represented his father-in-law as a sugar broker in Manila. But besides being a businessman, he aspired to become a British agent, reporting to the British Ministry of Information. Willoughby also said Wilkinson had violated American law in the Philippines by never registering as a foreign agent. Apparently, he had some relationship with the old Philippine G-2 staff, and after war broke out, he tried to build a relationship with Willoughby. The latter looked at the material Wilkinson was peddling and thought it outdated. But it appeared that Wilkinson had links with Hawaii and the local U.S. Navy, and he possessed his own cryptographic system and decoding clerks.

"I became convinced that his main purpose was to ingratiate himself into some official . . . recognition," said Willoughby. "But he was, and still is, an agent of the British authorities. . . . This [British] net of potential spies is world wide; it is still in operation; I employ [many] British, and find them loyal to no one but themselves and the Empire."

He then muttered: "Useful adjuncts of British commercial interests."

I asked Willoughby to evaluate the British intelligence messages Wilkinson had sent to Hawaii.

"My evaluation . . . is not high," he said. "A horse-trading operation, pure and simple. . . . The commercial deductions are obvious: Davies cancelled sugar contracts in the nick of time."

The use of Top Secret diplomatic/military intelligence for personal profit scandalized Willoughby. Later in the war, when Wilkinson had made his way from Hawaii to Washington and London, Wilkinson attempted to return to MacArthur's headquarters as "liaison," claiming even Prime Minister Churchill supported him for the post. Said Willoughby, "With his complete lack of military knowledge, such a position had its ludicrous side, *except for local espionage,* and we declined to have him." (Emphasis added)

According to Willoughby, the Briton was promptly demoted, stripped of his military status and returned to duty as a civilian with the office of British Information in Washington–New York.

Was Willoughby correct in his evaluation of Wilkinson? It was difficult to judge, but I interviewed Wilkinson later on in New York City. I found him to be something of a maverick, but one who produced better intelligence than someone like Fielder. I thought Wilkinson could be relied on. Meanwhile, the Pacific war, with all its ramifications for the former colonial powers operating in Asia, had its own political intrigues that were not included in the scope of my investigation. Willoughby derided the reputation of British colonial expertise. So I dropped the subject and moved on to the hole in the doughnut.

According to Willoughby in his Appendix B, the Navy had a highly efficient cryptological service in 1941 that specialized in Japanese material. Although the Army had participated in developing the service and its implementation of machines, the Navy somehow captured the lead in it. As a result, said Willoughby, "it can be said that the Navy enjoyed an almost monopolistic privilege." Worse, the Navy began "excluding other services," and kept all the operation a mystery, "rigidly centralizing the whole enterprise."

To explain how the system worked, and how it hurt MacArthur's operations, Willoughby carefully detailed how he got his intelligence information. Even as late as 1945, the cryptoanalysis for his Pacific area was being made in Melbourne, Australia, and forwarded to District Naval Intelligence of the Seventh Fleet. The operation in Melbourne was under the direct orders of the Navy in Washington. It "is not bound by any local responsibilities," said Willoughby, and "forwards [only] what they select, and when it suits them. The possibility of erroneous or incomplete selection is as evident now as it was in 1941."

What was the Navy's rationale for doing this? Power feeds on power.

"The only excuse the Navy has," said Willoughby, "is that its field is primarily naval intercepts, but there is a lot of Army traffic, or other incidental traffic." Willoughby's face became flushed as he continued and his anger boiled, because, in his opinion, it was this traffic that "is not always understood or correctly interpreted by the Navy."

Calling the problem "vexing and dangerous," Willoughby said the only solution was to create "a completely joint, interlocking intercept and cryptoanalytical service—on the highest level—with the freest interchange of messages and interpretation." (This point would be the heart of my testimony to Congress later on.)

Driving his argument home, Willoughby waved the decrypts I had brought with me, saying: "Had they been known to a competent intelligence officer with Battle Order and technical background, beginning with November 14th, [it] would have led instantly to the inescapable conclusion that Pearl Harbor naval installations were a target for attack!"

Willoughby went even further. He said that November 25 or 29 could have been chosen as the deadline for the Japanese attack, because it was obvious from the messages that there would be elapsed time involved in whatever was going to happen. To him, it meant "some sort of naval seaborne sortie."

That certainly plugged the hole in the doughnut. But, I reminded myself, it was plugging done from hindsight. All the documentation was spread out in logical order before the intelligence expert making the analysis. Back in 1941, it hadn't happened that way.

To give the Navy the benefit of the doubt, before World War II it was the Navy that was responsible for the defense of the oceans surrounding the United States and American interests outside the continent. At that time, an Army officer such as a division commander, or even a corps commander, was under the immediate instructions of the Secretary of War, what we now call the Secretary of the Army. If the Army was going to undertake long-range reconnaissance, the commander would get orders from the Chief of Staff to do it. The opposite was true in the Navy, in which the captain is in complete command of his ship. He doesn't listen to anyone in Washington telling him that he should have reconnaissance. He is responsible for the safety of his ship, and he makes up his mind about such matters for himself. And that was the vast difference between the Army and the Navy.

A ship's captain controls his ship, even though there might be an admiral quartered on board. Another thing: The admiral eats dinner alone. You wouldn't think of doing that in the Army, where the commanding general often surrounds himself with staff officers at meals, and if you can cheer him up, so much the better. I recall being with General Richardson for lunch (he succeeded General Short after Pearl Harbor), and he would say: "Tell us some stories, Clausen. We'd like to have a laugh or two." And I'd do my best to comply.

The Navy's point of view was that if its ships were sunk, America would be helpless, unable to defend itself. And through mischance, the Navy could be sunk within half an hour. The Navy believed that it was such a valuable asset to the country that it had a right to protect itself to the extreme, even to the point of being unnecessarily arbitrary and security-conscious. The problem with all that was, as Admiral Layton pointed out in *And I Was There*, the Navy itself was riven with internal feuding, frequently of a jealous nature, and this imperiled the nation in other ways. The Navy would have no concept that the way it disseminated intelligence was harmful and damaging to MacArthur's war effort. That notion simply wouldn't cross its mind.

Of course, the Navy's practice of hoarding information had to be changed, I thought. But how, and by whom? That, by golly, was going to be a tough question to answer. I began thinking of a plan.

After I had typed up these affidavits, I went back to get them signed. MacArthur signed his even though I had misspelled his name.

As I was putting the papers in my briefcase, MacArthur asked me some personal questions. I told him that when the war began, I had been the Grand Orator of the Masonic Grand Lodge of California, and I congratulated him, as I later did President Truman, on being made a thirty-third-degree Scottish Rite Mason.

He kept me in his office for nearly another hour, talking about how to expand in the Far East the moral principles of Freemasonry. Every dictator in history has tried to put the Masons out of business because they believe in freedom. MacArthur was positive that Hitler had poisoned the minds of the Japanese against the Masonic Order for this very reason, and that was why even the Constitution of Japan forbade anyone from joining the order. MacArthur promised me that if and when he got to Japan, he was going to make sure that provision was eliminated from any future Constitution. He did, too.

"Since we're talking in this fashion," I said, "may I tell you about the plight of some Masonic people in Manila? We have a lodge not far from here. I drove there the other day, and they don't have any pencils. They don't have paper. The Japanese confiscated everything. I went to the PX and got a load of groceries and gave it to one of the heads, and he gave me a ring to give to my wife. Would there be any objection, General, to my using the military mail to send over some implements that are used to start up the Masonic Lodge, items such as rods, Bibles and so forth?"

"Absolutely not," MacArthur said. "I'm a Mason. My G-2, Willoughby, is a Mason. We'll make the arrangements for you."

Well, Willoughby went overboard. He told me to send anything I wanted. So, when I got back to Washington, I thought that the first thing I should send was a master's hat, because the master of the Masonic Lodge wears a tall silk hat, plus the rods and other implements of the Order. The Masons in Washington thought I was nuts, but I managed to get everything that was needed to start the lodge going again, and shipped it to Manila. In later years, whenever Willoughby came through San Francisco from Japan, where he was stationed in MacArthur's occupation headquarters, he'd stop by and tell me about the Masons in Manila. MacArthur was also instrumental in getting the confiscated property in Manila and Japan returned to the Masons, and the Order has had the basis to flourish in both places and inculcate the spiritual values MacArthur recommended.

To get back to my investigation. When I had finished with Mac-Arthur and Willoughby, I had seen the hole in the doughnut. I returned to Pearl Harbor to take the testimony of Colonel Fielder, now a Brigadier General, and find out how he had viewed the situation in 1941, when he was G-2 in Hawaii.

Fielder testified that he took over the job as G-2, for which he had no training or knowledge, about four months before the attack on Pearl Harbor. His organization was small, but it's interesting to note how it was structured:

1) A small administrative section of one officer (Fielder) and two clerks
2) A public relations section with one officer and two clerks
3) A combat intelligence section of two officers and several clerks organized in such a way the operation could expand quickly in the event of war
4) A counterintelligence section of approximately twelve officers and thirty agents, which was called the Contact Office and was located in the city of Honolulu under the command of Lieutenant Colonel Bicknell

With the exception of Bicknell's group, the G-2 section was located at Fort Shafter, and most of the personnel performed dual functions, because the section was small and the duties varied from day to day.

The G-2 office had *no intercept facilities or other ways* to analyze Japanese communications. The section relied on information that was supplied by the War Department in Washington, on the local Naval command and on Bicknell's operations.

The principal mission Fielder undertook was to make sure there were no internal disorders or sabotage on the Hawaiian Islands. It was Bicknell's Contact Office that prepared the intelligence estimates for the Hawaiian command. To do this, Bicknell was supposed to use all the sources available to him.

In essence, what Fielder was telling me was that he took no responsibility for preparing the intelligence estimates that his commanding general relied on to defend Pearl Harbor. He had delegated that responsibility to the Contact Office while concerning himself with the 160,000 persons of Japanese ancestry who lived in the Islands, of whom 40,000 were aliens. During the last week of November and the first week of December 1941, Fielder spent his time inspecting the various military establishments to make sure that antisabotage procedures were adequate.

So, how did the real intelligence work get done? I asked the question in a gentler way, but that was what I wanted to know.

Fielder explained that the Contact Office under Bicknell's command was directly under G-2's authority, but Bicknell had direct access to General Short and the Chief of Staff. (This is a nifty way of saying that Bicknell was supposed to go directly to General Short or the Chief of Staff if he had any hot information, but if he did it without first telling Fielder, he'd get his legs cut off at the knees.) And then Fielder made the alarming statement that Bicknell's group was also in charge of what he called "combat intelligence." He said: "I refer to attempting to obtain and disseminate information of the potential enemy. In reality, from the Army viewpoint, there is no combat intelligence unless there is combat."

Now, this was one of the more unusual statements I had heard. I could barely believe what I was hearing. But Fielder then said: "You see, our mission out here was purely defensive."

I said that if you were going to be a good defender, you had to know your enemy and what he is going to do so that you could prepare your defense.

Fielder just chuckled at me. He had been more interested in his magic tricks, and his next golf game, than in trying to figure out the Japanese and what they might be doing. I guess it takes a magician to fool himself. He certainly managed to fool a lot of other people into thinking he was doing such a great job that he earned a star.

So, what else did Fielder do? Before the Japanese attack, there were weekly staff meetings. Bicknell was assigned to give a brief summary of the international situation. Fielder usually presented the latest information on the war in Europe. (I expect General Short would have learned more from reading the local newspapers than from listening to Fielder, but I kept quiet.) According to Fielder, the Contact Officer often reported items to Fielder, the Chief of Staff or General Short, while Fielder always passed on "everything that came to my attention regardless of its source." This was easy to do, because Fielder, the Chief of Staff and General Short had adjoining offices "and were in contact many times each day."

He was bucking for that star on his shoulder, I thought. It had to be one of the greatest boot-licking, butt-kissing games of its time. I would have to double-check, of course, but that's what it sounded like.

As to his relationships with the Navy, Fielder said they "were, in general, cordial, but none of their combat intelligence was passed on to me.'' (I thought this statement was unusual in view of Fielder's earlier comment about how the Army viewed ''combat intelligence'' when there wasn't any ''combat.'') He also said that the intelligence information he received from the Navy ''had to do primarily with counter-subversive measures. No information was given to me by anyone in the Navy which indicated in any way that aggression by the Japanese against Hawaii was imminent or contemplated. It was well known that relations with Japan were severely strained and that war seemed imminent, but all my information seemed to predict sabotage and internal troubles for Hawaii.''

What Fielder was telling me was a fib. He was covering his behind by saying that he was doing his job according to the book. He knew he was getting the other information about Japanese intentions from Bicknell, who said that war was about to break out, although he couldn't say where or when. All Fielder was saying was that he never got it from the Navy. He might be telling the truth, but he was not disclosing the whole truth. I certainly thought it was a very strange way for a G-2 to operate.

I showed Fielder my copy of message number 519 of December 5, 1941 (the cable that told G-2 Hawaii to contact Commander Rochefort about the Winds Code), and Fielder said: ''I have no recollection of having received the War Department radio, but had it come to me, I would in all probability have turned it over to Lt. Col. Bicknell for action since he knew Commander Rochefort and had very close liaison with Captain Mayfield, the 14th Naval District Intelligence Officer, particularly since the way it was worded it would not have seemed urgent or particularly important.'' (I loved the way Fielder said the wording of the message wasn't urgent; and I wondered what would happen to an enlisted man who didn't pop to attention the moment Fielder issued an order.)

Fielder went on to say that he never was told about the details of the Winds Code. He acknowledged that Bicknell might have talked to Rochefort about the matter. ''But,'' he said, ''I did not, and Col. Bicknell did not tell me if he did.''

There wasn't any point in showing Bicknell's statement about message number 519 to Fielder. He simply would deny ever having seen it, and then attack Bicknell for having seen it on his desk and not telling him about it.

So I went back and pressed Fielder again on his relations with the Navy. Again he said that he had no direct liaison with the Navy except for local or territorial concerns. "I believed the Pacific Fleet Intelligence Section to have excellent information of the Japanese fleet and assumed that [if] any information which I needed to know was possessed by Navy agencies, it would be disseminated to me," claimed Fielder. "I know now that had I asked for information obtained by the Navy from intercept sources that it would not have been given me."

Possibly for very good reason, I thought. Here was a case where MacArthur's plea to Stimson could be a sword that cut both ways. The Navy believed its officers to be superior to those in the Army. In this case, it could have been true. Would Fielder have understood what Layton might have told him? Would Fielder have been competent to handle the information properly and in a secure fashion?

The nub of the problem was that it was the duty of the intelligence officers of both the Army and the Navy in the Hawaiian command to cooperate, coordinate and evaluate information from all sources and of all pertinent types for their superiors. For one reason or another, they hadn't done it.[8]

Fielder tried to put a different interpretive spin on what he was telling me, however. He pointed out that even if Layton had given him information, the Navy Captain would not have revealed the source of it. (True, but bizarre, I thought, that Fielder had not been cleared for Top Secret at that time—what a comedy of errors.) But, claimed Fielder, Layton did give information to Bicknell without revealing its sources. (Perhaps Fielder was mixed up, because Layton testified that he met Bicknell only once.) "The Hawaiian Department was primarily a defensive command justified principally to defend Pearl Harbor Naval base," Fielder said. He pointed out that the Army's Seventh Air Force was the only Army unit capable of long-range defensive action, and that Colonel Raley was in liaison with Captain Layton about the matter, and that he had sworn Raley to secrecy about what the Navy told him. "Raley was honor-bound to divulge it only to his Commanding General," said Fielder. "It did not come to me, and I didn't know of the liaison until after the war had started."

Pontius Pilate lives, I thought.

I then discussed with Fielder the British intercepts that I was carrying. He could not "remember which, if any, were brought to [his] attention" before the Japanese attack. And he was definite that he did

---

[8] Pearl Harbor Report, p. 142.

not know the source of the information (Gerald Wilkinson) before the attack.

I showed Fielder the affidavit of Commander Rochefort, in which Rochefort claimed that he had discussions with both Layton and Fielder at the Colonel's headquarters. Fielder denied that he had received intelligence from Rochefort. (Given the testimony of Layton, I was inclined to let Fielder have the benefit of the doubt in this matter.) Fielder was sure that Rochefort was really referring to Bicknell, who did receive information from Rochefort. And then Fielder dropped another explosive disclaimer. "If any of it came to me indirectly [via Bicknell]," he said, "it was in vague form and *not recognizable as coming from reliable sources.* I certainly had no idea that Lt. Col. Bicknell was getting the contents of intercepted Japanese diplomatic messages. In any event, Rochefort did not give it to me direct." (Emphasis added)

The last bit of testimony I took from Fielder concerned the intercepts I carried in my bomb pouch.

Fielder said that he had never known of their existence before December 7, nor had he known the substance of the messages. The one exception was the message about the "destruction by [the] Jap Consul at Honolulu of codes and papers which was related by Col. Bicknell at the staff conference on December 6, 1941. I gave this information to Gen. Short the same day."

What would he have done differently if he had seen these intercepts before December 7? Fielder said that he would have gone to Alert Number 2 instead of simply Alert Number 1. (Alert Number 2 called for readiness against an enemy air attack, as well as an alert against sabotage.) "It is my opinion," said Fielder, "that if Gen. Short had seen these messages prior to December 7, 1941, he would have ordered Alert No. 2 without my recommendation. It is my recollection that the Commanding General ordered Alert No. 1 and then announced it to the staff."

Fielder had covered his flanks well. He could claim that Colonel Raley had failed to pass on vital information to him. But a competent G-2 would have found out from Raley what was going on. Fielder could also make the same claim against Bicknell, but again, Fielder didn't want to know what was going on. He was a one-man version of the three monkeys: see nothing, hear nothing, say nothing. I thought his performance as a G-2 was farcical. When I left his office, I knew his next phone calls would be to his military friends, asking them to help lobby for his promotion and a second star. But he was the Army's problem; I still had work to do.

The last stops I made before returning to Washington were the offices of the *Honolulu Advertiser* and the *Honolulu Star-Bulletin*. I had gone to them earlier to read through their clip files. When I said earlier that I thought General Short might have learned more from the local papers than he might have learned from Colonel Fielder, I wasn't being facetious. I had counted thirty-two major stories in both papers that had run between November 7 and December 6, 1941, and were remarkably accurate as to the state of Japanese-American diplomacy and Japanese aggression in the Far East. A majority of these stories appeared in the crucial days between November 27 and December 6, and they earned headlines such as these:

U.S.–JAPAN TALKS BROKEN OFF AS HULL REJECTS APPEASEMENT—FULL SURRENDER DEMANDED IN U.S. STATEMENT [Nov. 27]

EVACUATION SPEEDED AS PEACE FADES [NOV. 27]

U.S. REJECTS COMPROMISE IN FAR EAST— WASHINGTON INSISTS ON MAINTENANCE OF STATUS QUO, WITHDRAWAL FROM CHINA BY JAPAN ARMY [NOV. 29]

KURUSU BLUNTLY WARNED NATION READY FOR BATTLE—FOREIGN AFFAIRS EXPERTS ATTACK TOKYO MADNESS [NOV. 30]

LEADERS CALL BACK TROOPS IN SINGAPORE— HOPE WANES AS NATIONS FAIL AT PARLEYS . . . HAWAII TROOPS ALERTED [NOV. 30]

U.S. ARMY ALERTED IN MANILA—SINGAPORE MOBILIZING AS WAR TENSION GROWS [DEC. 1]

JAPAN GIVES TWO WEEKS MORE TO NEGOTIATIONS— PREPARES FOR ACTION IN EVENT OF FAILURE [DEC. 2]

U.S. DEMANDS EXPLANATION OF JAPAN MOVES— AMERICANS PREPARE FOR ANY EMERGENCY; NAVY DECLARED READY [DEC. 3]

JAPANESE PIN BLAME ON U.S.—[JAPANESE] ARMY PAPER CHARGES VIOLATIONS BY F.D.R. [DEC. 4]

PACIFIC ZERO HOUR NEAR: JAPAN ANSWERS U.S. TODAY [DEC. 5]

AMERICA EXPECTED TO REJECT JAPAN'S REPLY ON INDOCHINA—HULL MAY ASK PROOF, SUGGEST TROOPS RECALL [DEC. 6]

This was but a sampling of the news reports available in Pearl Harbor before the Japanese attack. I took them back to Washington, where I discussed them with Bundy and Secretary Stimson in conjunction with General Short's argument before the Army Board that he hadn't been kept fully informed by Washington of the breakdown of Japanese-American relations, and that the War Department's warning message of November 27 was too ambiguous to allow him to act properly.

Stimson was incensed. The Hawaiian papers had been remarkably accurate in their reporting. This led me to draft the following language for Stimson's final statement that was presented during the ultimate Congressional investigation on Pearl Harbor:

> Even without any such message [the War Department dispatch of November 27], the outpost commander should have been on the alert. If he did not know that the relations between Japan and the United States were strained and might be broken at any time, he must have been the only man in Hawaii who did not know it, for the radio and newspapers were blazoning these facts daily, and he had a Chief of Staff and an Intelligence Officer to tell him so. And if he did not know that the Japanese were likely to strike without warning, he could have read his history of Japan or known the lessons taught in the Army schools in respect to such matters.[9]

[9] Committee Record p. 145.

8 "IT WAS UNDERSTOOD . . ."

I cannot describe the joy I felt in returning to Virginia and the children, who were scampering about in the May 1945 sunshine on the old Hopkins homestead we had rented near Ashton, Maryland. War with Japan still raged, but Germany had surrendered, and the Allied forces were linking up with the Russian army all across Europe. We knew that peace would soon be coming.

Nevertheless, my work at the Pentagon continued at a breakneck pace. Secretary Stimson was deeply impressed by the affidavits I brought back from MacArthur, Sutherland and Willoughby. The Secretary told me that he already had started a complete reorganization of Army intelligence and these affidavits made him determined to do even more of a shakeup. I remember Stimson's reading the MacArthur material and slowly shaking his head in agreement, looking like a wise old owl. Of course, the concept of there being a single, centralized service for the handling of this "boogie-woogie" information was still nothing more than an idea. The OSS was going strong, but it wouldn't last for long. Nor did we have then, as we do now, the Central Intelligence Agency or the National Security Agency.

I didn't have much time to sit around at home.

With the war coming to an end, the Congress was going to hold its own investigation. Before this could happen, it was imperative that I finish my own work so that Secretary Stimson could make his report to the public and, we hoped, defuse the misleading findings of the Army Pearl Harbor Board. With the exception of some minor checking, I had covered what I needed to know about what had really happened at Pearl Harbor, and what the Army and Navy knew there before the Japanese attack.

Now I had to nail down what had really happened in Washington, D.C., on the fateful night of December 6, 1941. This meant tracking the movements of Colonel Bratton to discover whether or not he misled the Army Board about the way he claimed he had distributed the thirteen parts of the fourteen-part diplomatic intercept. So after a brief sojourn at home, I packed my bags again, said farewell to Virginia and the kids, strapped the bomb pouch to my chest and boarded another plane, this time to Europe.

Fifty years after the fact, in this era of jet airliners, I find it difficult to believe how long it took to fly across the Atlantic. I had plenty of time to reflect on my mission.

I had, of course, checked in with Commander Sonnett to find out what was going on in the Navy's Hewitt Investigation. We didn't swap secrets, as might be suspected. But we were frank with each other about the quality of the testimony that each of us had been exposed to, and I was gratified that Sonnett appeared to be thinking along the same lines as I was. He told me that Admiral Kimmel had testified that he had gotten a large part of his "diplomatic information from the newspapers." [1]

We commented on the fact that both Short and Kimmel were using this as a dodge. Their claim of being dependent on the papers ignored the all-important fact that information from Washington and British sources about the Japanese destroying their codes and code machines had been given them in early December, *after* they had received the vital war warning message of November 27. Kimmel finally had to admit that he did not act on newspaper information in preference to the cables he received from the Navy Department. From Sonnett's comments, I deduced that the Hewitt Investigation was finding discrepancies similar to those I was uncovering.

[1] Navy Court of Inquiry, pp. 306, 307.

I was concerned, however, that because America had won the war in Europe, and the war against Japan was also a foregone conclusion, the politics of a Congressional Pearl Harbor Investigation might be horrendous. America had undergone an incredible transformation in only four years' time. I feared Congress would forget the actual state of affairs that existed in 1941, when an isolationist Congress opposed our entry into the war until the enemy actually dropped bombs on American military bases. Just four years later, the American Army was now the largest in the world, with more than *five million* men under arms. But back in the late 1930s, Congress had so starved the Army for funds that, while our nation was one of the six most powerful in the world, our Army numbered fewer men than those of the Greek and Belgian armies combined.[2] When Marshall had taken over as Chief of Staff, there had been only 150,000 men in khaki uniform. Rifle bullets were rationed on maneuvers (the artillery was limited to four rounds per day), and there wasn't enough equipment to supply new recruits.

Marshall and Roosevelt had lobbied a rearmament program through Congress, but the isolationist, reactionary members of Congress had vowed revenge. (Even Roosevelt had backed away from Marshall's initial request for a 280,000-man Army, because, like everyone else, the President was looking at the forthcoming 1940 elections.) Only ten or eleven of forty-three Republicans who met with Marshall to discuss the issue of a draft were willing to risk the displeasure of their colleagues and vote in favor of the Democratic administration's selective service program.[3]

The isolationists had lost the vote on the draft in 1940, but they were bound and determined that they would defeat Roosevelt in the fall of 1941, when the Draft Act came up for a twelve-month extension. The antiwar lobby came up with the catchy OHIO slogan—Over the Hill in October—and the bitter battle about keeping drafted men in uniform beyond a year's term raged night and day on Capitol Hill, with the team of Roosevelt and Marshall winning by but a single vote.[4]

Although this had happened only a few years earlier, I was mindful there was a significant old-line isolationist group in Congress who, in 1945, were still seeking revenge. Roosevelt had died in April 1945,

[2] Leonard Mosley. *Marshall: Hero for Our Times*, New York: Hearst Books, 1982, pp. 107, 148.
[3] Ibid., p. 136.
[4] Ibid., p. 147.

just as the American Army's Second Armored Division reached the Elbe River with the orders to cross it and seize Berlin, but the memories in Congress were long and the knives even longer. Some influential senators and representatives still believed that Roosevelt had maneuvered America into the war. Others believed that Roosevelt had known the Japanese were going to attack Pearl Harbor and that he let them do so.

No matter that peace might be coming within the year, there were those in Congress who were going to start another fight for their own selfish purposes and discredit the memory of Roosevelt, plus the actions of men such as Marshall and Stimson, Hull and Knox. To do this, the Congress would rely on the false testimony given to the Army Pearl Harbor Board, and the improperly biased reports handed up by the Board that excoriated Marshall and, by implication, Stimson, Knox and the President.

As befitting a man of his gentlemanly nature, Stimson never once made the slightest mention to me, or to anyone in my presence, about these forthcoming Congressional pressures. Neither did Bundy. But I wasn't a dummy; anyone with half a brain could figure out what was going on behind the scenes. I knew I was working against the clock to get the evidence that would prove the two reports of the Army Board wrong, or should I say "misinformed." Perhaps even more important, I began to see the hope of creating something positive from my investigation, something that might prevent another Pearl Harbor from happening in the future.

For those readers who might complain that the next depositions I took are boring, I must say that I agree with their judgement. But if you are seeking to prove that someone may have misled a jury, you have to set the stage for the final confrontation, in which the lawyer faces down the witness and discredits that person's prior testimony. You must do this with care and precision. Colonel Bratton was now running Army intelligence operations out of Berlin, and he could dissemble like a master con artist. He would be a hard nut to crack.

So I sat down with my first witness in Frankfurt, Germany, Brig. Gen. Thomas J. Betts, who, in the months of November and December 1941, was the Executive Assistant to the Chief of Staff of Military Intelligence. Because of his position, Betts was aware of what was going on in terms of problems relating to Japanese intelligence before the war, and he knew of the operations of Bratton and his associate, Dusenbury.

Betts told me that, during the time in question, Bratton either showed or discussed with him "the gist of most of the Ultra material which he [Bratton] handled." Bratton also told Betts about the Winds Code and what it meant, but he never told Betts that a Winds Code broadcast had been intercepted. Neither did Betts hear from anyone else that such a message had been received.

Betts was a very straightforward type of fellow, as his deposition shows. No equivocation, just straight to the heart of the matter.

I then went to the office of Lt. Gen. Walter Bedell Smith, who was serving as Chief of Staff, Supreme Headquarters, Allied Expeditionary Forces (SHAEF). Back in 1941, he had been a colonel and served as Secretary of the War Department General Staff that served Marshall.

I first showed Smith my letter of authorization from Secretary Stimson. We chatted for a few moments, and I said that I would also like his authorization to question Colonel Bratton.

He said, "Just a moment," and immediately got on the phone to General Eisenhower, the Commander of SHAEF. I heard Smith tell Eisenhower, "I will order Bratton down here."

I could see all my plans going awry, and I interrupted: "Please, I don't think you should do that, General Smith. That would be pulling rank on him if you ordered him to come down here just to see a mere Lieutenant Colonel." (Someone had made a mistake back home and given me a promotion.) "It would be more polite if I went to see Bratton, assuming I can make the arrangements."

Smith repeated my comment to Eisenhower, and Eisenhower said, "I agree with Clausen not to order Bratton in."

Needless to say, Smith saw to it that arrangements were made for me to get to Berlin without exposing myself to capture and interrogation by the Russians. Smith reminded me of the German actor Eric von Stroheim. He looked like him, spoke like him and had the same quick arrogance. He was a perfect Chief of Staff: tough and determined.

Although Smith had been Secretary to the War Department General Staff back in 1941, at that time he was not allowed to handle Top Secret Magic material. The decrypts always came to his office in a locked pouch, to which only the Chief of Staff, Marshall, had a key. "I would always give the locked pouch to the Chief of Staff as quickly as possible," Smith said. And when Marshall was absent from his office, the pouch was always given to him first thing upon returning. Smith also recalled several occasions when the pouch was delivered to

Marshall ''at his home when the Acting Chief of Staff (G-2) considered the contents urgent.''

This was a most important point. It proved that there was precedent for delivering important Magic material to Marshall at his home after office hours. It was the failure to do this on the evening of December 6, 1941, that had helped create the disaster of Pearl Harbor.

Smith's testimony zeroed in on four areas.

First, he could not recall Colonel Sadtler's having come to him as Sadtler had claimed he had done in his testimony to the Army Board. (Sadtler claimed that he was not allowed to send a special warning message to Pearl Harbor about avoiding a sneak attack as had happened to Russia at Port Arthur.) Since Smith was not an Ultra officer at the time, it would have been impossible for Sadtler to reveal to Smith what upset him. (I still had to get Sadtler's affidavit.)

Second, Smith gave me a detailed description of how Magic pouches were sent to Marshall at home. Usually, the Duty Officer of the General Staff Secretariat would take the pouch to Marshall's quarters. ''On at least several occasions,'' said Smith, ''I recall definitely that I sent the G-2 officer to deliver the pouch to General Marshall at his quarters in the absence of a Duty Officer.''

Third, Smith declared: ''Both I, myself, and the Assistant Secretaries understood that these pouches contained information of such value and importance that they should be shown to the Chief of Staff without delay.'' In other words, if a pouch was delivered at any time, every effort had to be made to get it to Marshall immediately.

Lastly, Smith thought that he had left his office on the night of December 6, 1941, at his usual departure time of seven. He most certainly was not there after ten P.M., the time Bratton claimed he made his delivery to Marshall's office. Since the Duty Officer who took over after Smith left was fully aware of the importance of the information contained in the pouches Bratton delivered, if Bratton had brought the pouch around that evening as he had claimed he did, and if he had told the Duty Officer that the pouch contained material of ''urgent nature, it would have been delivered to the Chief of Staff [Marshall] in accordance with our usual prompt procedure, either by the Officer on Duty or by Colonel Bratton, himself.''

I believed Smith's statement would be most helpful when it came time for me to interrogate Bratton. For what Smith was saying was that Bratton had *not* delivered a pouch to the Duty Officer on the evening of December 6, although Bratton had testified unequivocally to the

Army Board that this is what he had done. As Smith put it, if Bratton had delivered the pouch, the thirteen parts of the fourteen-part diplomatic message would have been sent to Marshall at home without hesitation.

My next stop was at Cannes, France, to take the affidavit of Lt. Gen. Leonard T. Gerow, who had played such an important role in the Army Board hearings and was now in command of the newly formed Fifteenth Army. He had been brought back to Washington from his combat command, as I mentioned earlier, and I had thought it was wrong to bring a man back from the combat command of an Army Corps to make him give testimony.

I remember that after he had finished his testimony before the Board, he and I were the only people left in the room.

"May I get you a car from the pool?" I asked.

"I don't think I'm entitled to it," he replied.

"You mean a lieutenant general just back from combat on the Siegfried Line can't get a car from the motor pool?"

"I don't want to take the chance."

"In that case, General," I said, "may I drive you home in my own car?"

That's what I did.

So when it came time for me to take Gerow's affidavit in France, the General came to my scruffy quarters at ten in the evening just to make sure my bed was okay. If that was how he looked after his troops, no wonder he was a good combat commander.

Anyway, Gerow had taken the blame for the failure of his subordinate, Colonel Bundy, to check the adequacy of General Short's reply to Marshall's warning message of November 27. I wanted Gerow to amplify his testimony to the Army Board about this and other matters.

Gerow had been marked as one of Marshall's bright young men early on before the war. During November and December 1941, he had served as the Chief of the all-important War Plans Division. As such, he read all the Magic intercept material in its raw, unevaluated format. "I placed the highest degree of reliance on this form of intelligence," he said. But he never was allowed to keep a copy or notes of the material, having to return it to G-2 the moment he read it, which meant he had to keep it all in his memory.

When I showed Gerow my Top Secret file of decrypts, he acknowledged that he had probably seen them all. He remembered several specifically, especially one in which the Japanese Ambassador to Washington gave the details of a lengthy conversation that he had had with Rear Adm. Richmond K. Turner about the withdrawal of Japanese troops from China.[5] Gerow also recalled seeing the queries from Tokyo about the movement of ships at Pearl Harbor and the answers.[6] As he remembered, these reports were similar to what was being sent by the Japanese Consuls in Seattle, Washington and Manila. Gerow knew that these messages came to him from the Navy Department. He said: "I assumed that the Navy was fully cognizant, and would interpret this information in connection with Navy studies and estimates, and in connection with other information available to the Navy *and not given to me.*" (Emphasis added)

In other words, Gerow knew that the Navy was holding back certain items of information from the Army. This led him to conclude that if there had been a problem with the Navy's not warning the Naval commander at Hawaii that the Japanese were placing a bomb grid over the Pearl Harbor area, the fault lay with the way the Navy Department was interpreting the intercepts.

I then asked Gerow about Bratton's testimony to the Army Board in which he said that on December 4, he talked to Gerow about sending yet another warning to the overseas commanders. According to Bratton, Gerow had replied "sufficient had been sent." As a result of Gerow's refusal to act, Bratton had then conferred with the Navy and had sent the message number 519 of December 5 to Hawaii advising them to contact Commander Rochefort.

"I do not recall the incident," Gerow said. "[If Bratton had thought] my reaction inadequate, he could quite properly report the facts to his superior, Gen. Sherman Miles [the Assistant Chief of Staff], who had direct access to me and the Chief of Staff [Marshall] in a matter of such importance."

Next, I wanted to know more about the events of December 5: Colonel Sadtler had testified before the Army Board that he had told Gerow that the Japanese Winds Code had been broadcast and intercepted, signaling a breach of diplomatic relations, or war with Great Britain. Sadtler had also testified that he requested that General Short be notified, but Gerow had replied that he thought "plenty of notification had been sent."

---

[5] See appendix, Army numbers 5854, 23570 and 23516, pp. 315–316.
[6] See appendix, number 6991, p. 320; number 25773, p. 321; number 25817, pp. 321–322; number 7086, p. 329.

"I have no such recollection," said Gerow, "and I believe Colonel Sadtler is mistaken." He believed that it would have been most unusual for a Signal Corps officer such as Sadtler, who "was not concerned with the dissemination or interpretation of Magic," to be involved in such a discussion. Gerow was quite certain that he had never received any indication that a broadcast that would have been the "execute" message for the Winds Code had ever been intercepted. "If I had received such a message," he said, "I believe I would now recall the fact, in view of its importance." And in view of the major events that have occurred since that time during the course of the war, Gerow believed that written records on the matter should be the sole factor determining who was right or wrong on the issue.

Well, then, what about Colonel Bratton's testimony that, on the night of December 6, he or another person delivered to Gerow the thirteen parts of the fourteen-part Japanese diplomatic intercept?

"I did not receive, or see, any parts of the message mentioned until the morning of 7 December 1941, when a conference was held with the Chief of Staff [Marshall]," Gerow stated. "If I had received parts of the message on the night of 6 December, I would have immediately warned the overseas commanders and informed the Chief of Staff. Access to the Chief of Staff for such purposes *was always open to me.*" (Emphasis added)

As I continued taking his testimony, Gerow made a pertinent point about the complexities that the War Plans Division had faced in 1941. While the commander in Hawaii had the task of trying to move Army forces around the Pacific and get them properly trained, General Short's *primary* goal was to protect Pearl Harbor from surprise attack. The War Plans Department, however, was charged, as Gerow put it, "with global problems and considerations, involving possibilities of hostile land, sea, and air action against the United States by the Axis powers."

"In the months immediately before Pearl Harbor," said Gerow, "I did not receive any written or oral estimate from G-2, properly vouched for, which pointed to Pearl Harbor specifically as the attack target at the opening of hostilities with Japan or the other Axis powers." But he had received reports from numerous quarters that "one or more of the Axis powers would open with attacks on almost any of the many strategic points of United States or British territory in the Pacific areas."

And this is where I got the idea that, most likely, the duties of

General Short could be likened to the job of a sentry, ready to sound the alert at any moment, ready to defend his post against an attack from any direction, filled with the knowledge that he stood alone against the enemy, and ready to die to protect those he was guarding.

Gerow and the War Plans Division, however, were more like corporals of the guard. They tried to make sure that their sentries—stationed around the world—were awake, alert and ready to fight.

To use a sergeant's language, it may well have been true that Gerow should have kicked Short's butt to make sure his "sentry" in Hawaii was awake at his post. Gerow hadn't done that, and he accepted the blame for it. As for Short—the "sentry"—if he had been a private and behaved as he had, his sergeant either would have had him court-martialed or would have beaten the stuffing out of him, unofficially, behind the barracks. But Short was a three-star general, don't forget. The Army doesn't treat its generals the same way it does its privates.

But had Washington given General Short adequate warning of an impending attack? Gerow was both scathing and restrained in his response. "In my opinion," he said, "the War Department had sent ample warnings to the overseas commanders, including Gen. Short, to alert their respective commands for war."

Gerow went on to say:

> General Short did not send at any time any notice to the War Department which would indicate *that he was not fully prepared for an attack of the kind which occurred*. . . . The War Department had given him estimates and basic war plans which, in effect, *warned him to expect air and submarine attacks as preliminary threats* in a war with Japan.
>
> These *pre-battle plans and estimates,* with which I was very much concerned, were prepared, reduced to writing and given to General Short and other officers involved after a great deal of mature consideration by the best military brains available for that purpose. They represented the consensus of the belief and expert military opinions of the War *and* Navy Departments, *and* the Hawaiian Department. . . .
> I assumed that these fundamental concepts of primary threats from a surprise attack by Japan would govern General Short in his thinking and preparations in light of the

Col. C. C. Dusenbury testified to Clausen that he received all fourteen parts of the Japanese diplomatic message at approximately midnight December 6. He did not deliver these decrypts to Marshall as had been claimed, because he did not understand their importance and "did not wish to disturb the usual recipients." His actions lost nine vital hours to warn Pearl Harbor. Congress failed to ask Dusenbury to appear, thereby validating his affidavit to Clausen.

1st Lt. Frank B. Rowlett "did the trick" in creating the machine that broke the Purple code. He also confirmed that the fourteen-part Japanese message was in the Army's possession around midnight, December 6. Congress never asked Rowlett to testify either.

Col. E. F. French was ordered to send a last-second warning to Hawaii on December 7. But he failed to tell Marshall that the Army radio could not reach Hawaii, so he sent the message via commercial cable.

Robert Shivers, the FBI agent in charge at Hawaii, knew about the Winds Code. He also knew the Navy was tapping the Japanese consul's phone in Honolulu. But the Navy gave up their taps and never told Shivers, who would have continued them. (COURTESY OF FBI)

Capt. Edwin Layton was the Pacific Fleet Intelligence Officer. He falsely claimed that the warnings sent by Washington to Kimmel were too important to relay to Short. Not only did Layton "sucker the Army," he "tried to pull a snow job" on Clausen's investigation.
(U.S. NAVAL INSTITUTE)

Capt. J. S. Holtwick, USN, showed Clausen copies of the messages that Washington had sent Kimmel about Tokyo ordering its embassies to destroy their codes and code machines. Holtwick also confirmed that other vital Navy intelligence was not given to the Army in Hawaii.
(U.S. NAVAL INSTITUTE)

Maj. Gen. R. K. Sutherland told Clausen that before Pearl Harbor he had never seen any of the intercepts Clausen carried in his bomb pouch. As MacArthur's chief of staff in the Philippines, Sutherland had been denied this vital information by the Navy.

Capt. W. J. Holmes of the Navy's Combat Intelligence Unit was assigned to "plot the positions of Japanese ships based on (radio) call analysis." His information went direct to Kimmel, who never told Short that the Navy did not know the location of the Japanese carriers just before the attack.
(NAVAL IMAGING COMMAND)

Gen. Douglas MacArthur made a special plea to Clausen, asking him to tell Stimson that "I have had to barter like a rug merchant throughout the war to get the intelligence I have needed from the Navy." Said MacArthur: "The system as it stands is wrong."

Brig. Gen. C. A. Willoughby, MacArthur's intelligence chief, said the Navy gave the Army only what intelligence it selected, and only when it suited them. He said the only solution was to create "a completely joint, interlocking intercept and cryptological service—on the highest level" that would freely exchange vital intelligence. Clausen stressed this in his testimony to Congress.

The author, Henry Clausen, standing next to the wreckage of a Japanese plane in the Philippines. (COURTESY OF THE AUTHOR)

Lt. Gen. L. T. Gerow proved to be a brilliant combat commander. He knew the Navy was withholding intelligence. He believed that Short had been adequately warned to be on the alert for war.

Maj. Gen. W. B. Smith was Eisenhower's tough and determined chief of staff. He said that Colonel Bratton could not have delivered the vital intercepts to Marshall's office on December 6, because if he had, the material would have been given to Marshall immediately as standard operating procedure even if Marshall was at home.

Maj. Gen. J. R. Deane denied receiving from Bratton, or anyone else, on the evening of December 6 a pouch containing decrypts for Marshall. Deane also disputed the time Bratton claimed he arrived for duty on December 7.

Marshall (left) and Herron, who prepared the briefing book for Short about how to defend Hawaii. But Short read a novel, not the briefing book, and never asked Herron a single question about what his new job as Army commander in Hawaii entailed. In Herron's estimation, Short was not fit for the command.

warnings of imminent war. No notice ever reached me that
he would disregard these estimates or that he would omit
preparations against an outside threat. (Emphasis added)

Gerow still wasn't finished with his excoriation of Short. He
pointed out that Short's actions were outside the scope of regular
military operations. Gerow thumped his desk as he said: "General
Short at no time warned the War Department that he was not in full
agreement with War Department estimates and plans for the defense of
Oahu. If he was not in accord with these estimates and plans, then it
would have been quite reasonable to assume that he would have informed the War Department *in accordance with established military
practice*. I assumed also that General Short's liaison with the Navy was
such that he received *all* information of use to him and available to the
Navy at Pearl Harbor." (Emphasis added)

But why hadn't the War Department sent Short messages similar
to those the Navy sent Kimmel?

"It was inadvisable for the War and Navy Departments to send
identical or nearly identical messages to respective commanders at
Hawaii, for fear of compromising our codes," replied Gerow. "Hence,
it was understood that information sent by either Department [in Wash-
ington] which would be of use to the other service would be exchanged
between the two commanders at Hawaii."

"And this is what did not occur," I said. "A full exchange of
information never took place."

"Exactly," said Gerow.

I paused to reflect on the momentous impact of Gerow's words,
and then we explored the warning message sent to Hawaii over Marshall's signature on November 27. Gerow said that it should be considered along with all the Army and Navy messages that were sent to
Hawaii around that time, plus, and this is important, "whatever other
information was available to him [Short]."

Obviously, Gerow suspected that Short had received other information that Washington had not known about. He was right.

I asked him if he thought the Magic information had been handled
properly back in 1941. And should the Magic messages themselves
have been transmitted to Short?

Gerow said that, at the time, even he did not know how the
intercepts were procured. He believed it to be a vital necessity that
Magic not be compromised in any way. Because of this, he said, "it

was not the policy of the War Department to send these messages to overseas commanders. The wisdom of this policy has been proved by our recent victories.'' If the Magic intercepts had been sent to Short, they would have had to go to others, some of whom were in even greater peril of attack than Hawaii.

"This would have led to great danger of compromise,'' said Gerow. ''[It] might have lost for us [in] the present war the . . . best evidence of the enemy's intentions. This . . . would have been a great disaster, resulting in the prolongation of the war, increased bloodshed, uncertainty and expense, and possible defeats.''

As I said good-bye to Gerow, I could not help thinking that there was a great difference between a man who specialized in training soldiers, such as Short, and a man who led troops in combat, like Gerow. I wondered what Gerow would have thought if I had told him I had learned that Short changed his SOP alert list without telling the War Department. But I didn't want to upset Gerow any more than I had, so I left and hopped a plane to Rome.

I picked up a car and drove south to Naples and then east to Caserta. Perhaps that's why John Toland called me ''the peripatetic colonel''[7] in his book, but I didn't make that trip just to get a ride through Italy, I'll tell you that. I remember seeing a big sign on the road saying, ''Beware of Thieves.'' I thought it was somewhat out of place on the main highway. A number of former GIs stationed in Italy also remembered it many years later, which just goes to show what unusual things stick in your memory.

The man I had come to question, Col. Robert E. Schukraft, had been in charge of radio intercepts in Washington on December 7, 1941. When I showed him the decrypts I was carrying in my pouch, I could see a funny look go across his face. He knew I was a member of the Magic club, and he was obviously uncomfortable having me walk in on him.

Schukraft recalled seeing the intercept outlining the way the Winds Code was supposed to work. He had immediately ordered the San Francisco monitoring station to intercept all plain-text Japanese radio broadcasts and all news broadcasts from Tokyo. But he never received any weather forecast intercept with the wording necessary to execute the Winds Code. There were some intercepted telephone conversations that came from the Navy that Schukraft could not under-

---

[7] John Toland. *Infamy.* New York: Doubleday, 1982, p. 149.

stand, but he passed the information on immediately to G-2 and never heard anything more about it.

Essentially, Schukraft was a blind alley for my investigation. But I had to check his story, if only to show the tremendous amount of time that had been wasted trying to pick up a broadcast of the Winds Code.

I then flew to London to check the stories of two members of the State Department, George W. Renchard and John F. Stone. Both men had acted as personal assistants to Secretary of State Hull during November and December 1941; both recalled how the Magic intercepts were brought to the Secretary's attention. They verified that no receipts were ever given showing which messages the Secretary might have seen. No copies of the decrypts were ever made by the State Department. The moment after they were read, the decrypts were handed back to the messenger who brought them to the Secretary's office.

Because of the irregular delivery schedule for the Magic material, neither man could recall the exact, or even the approximate, time that the decrypts signaling the breach in diplomatic relations between Japan and the United States came to their attention. Nor could Stone recollect ever having been advised by a Naval officer that there was a possibility of a Japanese attack against Pearl Harbor.

What Stone was trying to say was that the situation was ludicrous when it came to Secretary Hull's reading the decrypts. The messenger carrying them would arrive unannounced, and the Secretary of State would have to interrupt whatever he was doing to immediately read twenty or thirty raw translations while the G-2 man breathed down the back of his neck. How could any Secretary of State do that and fully comprehend what he was reading? And relate it to decrypts that he might have read many days earlier? It's impossible. He wouldn't even know who was cleared for the information and who wasn't. With whom could he talk and rationally discuss the matter? It was a catch-22 situation.

After those two affidavits, I went to Bletchley Park, where the British had located their operation for breaking the German Enigma codes, and where their decrypt files were kept. I went through everything they showed me (see appendix, Exhibit No. 8, p. 353), and I didn't find any new decrypts that added anything to the nearly two hundred British intelligence items I had brought back to Washington from Hawaii. That closed the overall signals interception loop as far as I was concerned.

My next stop was Potsdam, where I took the affidavit of Maj.

Gen. John R. Deane. Back in November and December 1941, he had been an Assistant Secretary to the General Staff. On the evening of December 6, Deane said he left his office some time after five, and he said categorically that he did not receive from Bratton, or anyone else, that evening a pouch containing decrypts for General Marshall.

The next morning, December 7, Deane arrived for duty at the Munitions Building at the same time as Colonel Bratton. According to Deane, the time was between nine and nine-thirty.

It took only a short while to get this affidavit signed and sealed. Meanwhile, I took in what I could of the Potsdam Peace Conference. Deane was quartered in a house that had belonged to some former high-ranking Nazi, and it was flooded with our generals. All of them were supposed to be on R&R, but most of them had come to witness the proceedings (and politic for jobs after the war, I surmised.) I had never seen so many generals in my life—not even at the Pentagon. There were stars upstairs, downstairs, in the kitchen, in the pantry. You would have thought you were in heaven, there were so many stars.

Short though it was, Deane's affidavit was, as far as I could see, the last nail I needed to fasten down the lid on Bratton's coffin. But would Bratton cooperate now? Would he admit that he hadn't told the truth before the Pearl Harbor Board and thereby had contaminated its report?

I then flew to Paris, where I left the decrypts in a secure safe, and hopped a flight to Copenhagen. There, I borrowed a car and driver from the British for the trip to Berlin. (This was believed the safest way for me to move through Soviet-occupied territory.) As we reached the suburbs, I looked out my window and saw Colonel Bratton driving merrily along in the car next to us. I asked my driver to honk the horn, which he did, and I waved to Bratton to stop. He was extremely surprised to find me on his tail in such a manner, but with his usual professorial urbanity, he quickly invited me to billet with him at the quarters of the Berlin commandant.

I sent my British driver home and moved in with Bratton. He told me he'd be glad to cooperate, which was a relief. I told him that I had all these documents that I wanted to show him, but I hadn't dared bring them through the Soviet lines, in the event the Soviets might try to seize them. Would Bratton be willing to come with me to Paris, where we could do our talking in a more relaxed atmosphere?

The idea appealed to him immensely, and I waited around for a couple of days while he finished up some business he was running against Russian intelligence. I recall messing with Maj. Gen. James Gavin, who had been the commander of the Eighty-second Airborne. He looked like a young lieutenant, yet there he was with two stars on his shoulders.

I pondered how the fates had worked for one man and against another. Bratton had been supposed to report to Fort Benning a few days before Pearl Harbor, but General Miles, the head of G-2, had asked him as a favor if he could hang around a few days more rather than reporting immediately. Bratton was willing to do the favor. So, instead of reporting to Benning and getting his combat command, plus a general's stars on his shoulders, he got tossed into the meat grinder of Pearl Harbor and never recovered from it. I expected that every morning, Bratton woke up bemoaning the fact that he hadn't said no to Miles and gone to Benning along with Marshall's other bright boys when the chance was there to do so.

Bratton finally cleared his desk. When he told his staff he was leaving, he said, "I might not return," and secured his personal effects. We took a special military flight to Paris, where Bratton had rooms in a secure area. I was in the Georges Cinq—a delightful hotel, I might say—and that night we went out to a good restaurant and the Folies Bergère. Bratton seemed to enjoy himself. The next morning, I retrieved my bomb pouch from the safe at G-2, noting with pleasure that the triple-sealed wrappings I had used to secure it had not been tampered with. I took the package back to the hotel and sat down with Bratton. I gave him copies of all the pertinent affidavits to read. It took him some time to get through what his fellow officers had said about his testimony before the Army Board.

Bratton sort of exuded surprise and disappointment. He was a big man, solid and chunky, built like a wrestler, with very dark hair and bushy eyebrows, explaining his nickname: Togo. But as he kept on reading, he seemed to grow smaller, and he looked very sad and droopy, as if he had been caught out on something that he wished he could have avoided, like an impaled fish.

I had seen that look before: when I had a criminal dead to rights on the witness stand.

Bratton had the same look on his face as he read the record: Two-star General Deane, three-star General Gerow and three-star General Smith said Bratton had lied. He was trussed up like a Christmas goose. They and Bratton had been friends once. They used to pal around together. And now that Bratton could read what they said about him, he knew—now and for all time—that the jig was up as far as his career was concerned. He might as well kiss it good-bye. Never, never would he be given a general's star. I could see him posing the question to himself: "Do I now confess that I testified falsely to the Army Board?" He also knew that he was in a different category than those who had testified falsely because they were bound by the Top Secret oath. Bratton's testimony did not deal with the contents of the decrypts, but with his own modus operandi about delivering the decrypts on the night of December 6. He knew what this difference meant in legal terms. He had failed to do his duty, and lied about it. Finally, with a deep sigh, he said that we'd better get on with it.

"If you will dictate to me, I'll type it right here," I said, and I telephoned downstairs to ask the concierge to deliver the typewriter I had ordered earlier.

One of the first admissions or confessions I sought from Bratton was the fact that he had read and understood the ten affidavits I had taken previously from other Army officers in which they challenged the truthfulness of Bratton's testimony before the Army Board. Then, slowly and surely, I walked him through his activities before and during the hours leading up to Pearl Harbor.

Bratton confirmed that for several years before Pearl Harbor, he had received and reviewed the Japanese intercepts for distribution as military intelligence. From October to December 1941, the volume of these intercepts increased to such a great extent that Bratton asked permission from General Miles to use several of his assistants—Dusenbury, Moore, Schindel—to help in processing and distributing the information.

The material was distributed in raw, unevaluated form according to the instructions of General Marshall. The people to whom the material went included the Chief of Staff (Marshall), the Secretary of War (Stimson), the Secretary of State (Hull), the Chief of the War Plans Division (Gerow) and the Assistant Chief of Staff, G-2 (Miles). By agreement with the Navy, the President (Roosevelt) was furnished the decrypts solely by the Navy. The decrypts were delivered on a daily basis, and on the following day, the distributed decrypts and any receipts issued for same during the distribution process were burned.

According to Bratton, from October through November 1941, Army intelligence received from fifty to seventy-five decrypts per day. Only about ten to fifteen of the decrypts were judged to have intelligence value. These were the ones that were circulated. The trick in distributing the material, said Bratton, was arranging for various recipients to "receive their copies simultaneously."

What did Bratton remember about the Winds Code?

He remembered a meeting with General Miles at which Col. Otis K. Sadtler said that he had received verbal information from Admiral Noyes that there had been an intercept of a broadcast that might have executed the Winds Code. There had been several other false reports of December 1 and 3,[8] Bratton recalled. But the fact that messages had already been intercepted, decrypted and translated in which Tokyo ordered the Japanese embassy in Washington to destroy its codes meant that the " 'Winds Code' was superfluous and no longer of importance, *since the purpose would be to effect a destruction of the codes."* (Emphasis added) The truth of this statement became clearer later, when Bratton said he had verified that the Japanese embassy in Washington had begun burning important papers, apparently after receiving its orders from Tokyo to do so. Meanwhile, Sadtler was ordered to get from Noyes the verification of the broadcast implementing the Winds Code. But Sadtler never had returned with more information on the subject, Bratton said.

"At no time prior to 7 December 1941, although a thorough alert in this regard was in effect," Bratton declared, "did I ever see or hear of an authentic message implementing the 'Winds Code.' "

As for the testimony by the Navy's Captain Safford that such a broadcast had been intercepted, Bratton pointed out that Safford had said that the Navy sent two copies of the message to the Army. This was impossible, however, said Bratton, because "it was the customary practice for the Navy, when sending the Army material of this nature, to send six copies." And while, prior to December 7, Navy personnel had discussed with Bratton the "false alarms" regarding the Winds Code, no one ever discussed with Bratton the message that Safford said the Navy had received.

The most important factor in determining whether or not Tokyo alerted its embassies about forthcoming war via the Winds Code was the interception of the messages from Tokyo to its embassy in Washington telling the embassy to burn its codes and destroy the code machine. Bratton emphasized—and we know it to be true—that this particular information was distributed to *all* the people authorized to

[8] See appendix, SIS 25787, 25545, 25640, pp. 336, 335, 339.

read the Magic decrypts in the nation's capital, besides being paraphrased and sent to our military commanders overseas, especially to the Navy at Pearl Harbor.

By now, Bratton seemed to be fairly relaxed in dictating his answers to my questions. Confession is good for the soul, I thought, and I began to zero in on his previous testimony about the events in Washington of the fateful evening of December 6, 1941.

Bratton's memory had been refreshed by his reading of the affidavits I had shown him earlier. His story, as he retold it to me, changed dramatically from how he had testified before the Army Board. The thirteen-part message from Tokyo began coming in from the Navy during the evening of December 6. Bratton said he was on duty with Dusenbury, and the two men assembled and studied the thirteen parts, which Bratton believed had been received by ten P.M. Upon receiving the thirteenth part, Bratton said he telephoned the SIS duty officer, either a Colonel Schukraft or a Colonel Doud, to ask if there was any chance that the fourteenth part of the message would be coming in that night. Because there appeared to be a delay in the transmission by the Japanese, Bratton said he was told that it was unlikely.

Dusenbury and Bratton prepared the thirteen parts for distribution. Said Bratton: "I directed Col. Dusenbury to deliver the set for the Chief of Staff to his home at Fort Myer that night as Col. Dusenbury went to his home in Arlington. This was about ten o'clock." As for the other sets, Bratton said those for the Acting Chief of Staff, G-2, the Chief of the War Plans Division and the Secretary of War were *not* delivered that night, as he had sworn to the Army Board they were. Instead, they were delivered around seven the next morning, along with the fourteenth part.

Bratton's story was changing dramatically. Now he was saying he had *not* given the material to Col. Walter B. Smith, nor to General Gerow, Major Gailey, Col. Ralph Smith or Gen. Sherman Miles. (Nor could he have discussed the message with Miles, as he had sworn to the Army Board he did.)

"When I saw the Chief of Staff [Marshall] the morning of 7 December 1941," said Bratton, "he then had the fourteen-part message, which I had *not* given him." (Emphasis added)

So, what material had Bratton delivered that night?

"I took the thirteen parts destined for the Secretary of State," he swore to me, "and between ten and eleven P.M. delivered them to the night duty officer of the Secretary of State. I cannot recall who the night duty officer was. I told this officer that it was of the greatest importance that the papers be placed in the hands of the Secretary of State at once. He assured me that this would be done. This was the *only* delivery I made that night.''

After making this single delivery, Bratton told me, he went home and went to bed. He also said that he returned to the office about seven-thirty or eight the following morning, Sunday, December 7. (This statement conflicted with what Dusenbury and Deane told me, and I regret to say that I failed to question Bratton about the discrepancy.) The fourteenth part of the Japanese message reached his desk "about the time I reached my office." The message was processed "at once and it was sent to be delivered to the authorized recipients." Bratton said that he did not deliver any material that morning except for another intercept (SIS 25850), which was Tokyo's order to the Japanese ambassadors to deliver at one P.M., Washington time, the fourteen-part Japanese reply to America. Bratton claimed that he gave this message to Marshall between ten-thirty and eleven-thirty. This last message was also delivered to the Secretary of State by either Colonel Dusenbury or Lieutenant Schindel.

The time of this particular delivery, I thought, could never be verified, since the receipts for all deliveries had been burned.

I asked Bratton how he evaluated the importance of the fourteen-part message.

"Relatively unimportant," was Bratton's response, "in view of the other messages which preceded it, especially the one ordering the destruction of the Japanese codes and ciphers, and the one ordering delivery of the fourteen-part message at one P.M. [on Sunday, December 7]." According to Bratton, the fourteen-part message by itself merely signaled a break in diplomatic relations, which had appeared to be inevitable anyway.

What about Bratton's previous testimony that he had discussed the thirteen-part message with General Miles on December 6?

"I do not recall having discussed the . . . message with . . . Miles," said Bratton. Nor could he now remember how the decrypts he saw Marshall reading on the morning of December 7 had come into the Chief of Staff's possession.

Bratton had changed his testimony so dramatically that I added a special final paragraph to his affidavit to show that he was fully aware that his previous testimony to the Army Board had not been accurate. It would probably be wise to quote this in full here for the record, because of the importance of what he was now saying. This last paragraph read:

> Any prior statements or testimony of mine which may be contrary to my statements herein, including among other things as to the processing and delivery of material, and to whom and when, should be modified and considered changed in accordance with my statements herein. This affidavit now represents my best recollection of the matters and events set forth, and a better recollection than when I previously testified before the Army Pearl Harbor Board, and is made after having my memory refreshed in several ways and respects.

While Bratton signed the affidavit, I felt a brief sense of elation. His acknowledgment that he had lied to the Army Board was now legal fact. But my joy was short-lived. Bratton was obviously a beaten man, a true example of Shakespearean tragedy in which the inner flaws of the man eventually destroy him.

We carefully cleaned up my room. After hours of talking, we had made many notes. These we carefully tore up. We couldn't burn them in the wastepaper basket; if we had, we'd probably have burned down the hotel. So Bratton took them in small batches and flushed them down the toilet. The last handful went into the john with a grandiloquent gesture, and Bratton saying: "I consign thee to the sewers of Paris."

Fifty years after the fact, I am asked if I believe Bratton told me the truth. I believe he did. He impaled himself on the charge that he committed willful perjury. He also destroyed the edifice the Army Pearl Harbor Board created—its two reports, one Secret and one Top Secret—which so unfairly criticized Marshall, but which appeased those who hated the Chief of Staff and President Roosevelt.

Still, I couldn't dislike Bratton for what he had done. I separated the person from his misconduct. Nor could I leave him alone to brood about his day of testifying to me. We went up the street to a small café, something not very fancy, and had dinner.

When it came time to say good-bye, Bratton warmly shook my hand and said: "Colonel Clausen, there's one thing I want to tell you. You're the easiest lawyer to talk to that I've ever met."

I took the compliment as he meant it. I hadn't been out to scare him into changing his testimony. It had simply been a matter of logic and letting him look at the evidence for himself, which, in turn, made him decide to tell the truth.

After that, I followed his career, or what was left of it. I was told that he ended his days in Hawaii, living there in retirement, a heart-broken man, the picture of cruel remorse, another victim of Pearl Harbor.

9 "NO. . . . I READ A NOVEL"

I finished Bratton's affidavit on July 27, 1945, and returned immediately to Washington. I told Bundy that, in legal terms, I had uncovered enough evidence to refute the findings of the Army Board.

By August 1, I had a memo ready for Bundy and Secretary Stimson showing the importance of the changes in Bratton's contrasting testimony to me. They included the following points:

(1) Bratton had testified to the Army Board that the material I carried in my bomb pouch, which was labeled Exhibit B, had been delivered to the President, the Secretary of War, the Secretary of State, the Chief of Staff, the Assistant Chief of Staff in War Plans and the Assistant Chief of Staff in G-2.

But in his affidavit to me, Bratton swore he could not recall with any degree of accuracy who had delivered what to whom during the period in question. Nor were any records kept to prove what had been delivered or to whom it had been delivered.

(2) In his testimony to the Army Board, Bratton had also stated that he was the one who delivered the Top Secret radio intercepts to the officers concerned. In recanting his testimony to me, however,

Bratton changed his story to say that three other people—Dusenbury, Schindel and Moore—were also delivering this Top Secret material.

(3) In his testimony to the Army Board, Bratton testified that on the evening of December 6, he personally had delivered the thirteen parts of the fourteen-part Japanese message to the office of General Marshall and to the office of the Secretary of State. He also claimed that he had put the thirteen-part message on Marshall's desk. (In retrospect, this *never* could have been true, because Bratton would have had to hand over the material in a locked pouch to the Duty Officer. If the pouch was not transmitted immediately to Marshall, it would have been placed in the safe in Marshall's office. No Top Secret papers could be left on Marshall's desk, where unauthorized people might see them.) Bratton had named the following people as those to whom he had given the thirteen-part message: Col. Walter Bedell Smith for General Marshall; Major Gailey, for Lieutenant General Gerow; and Brigadier General Miles, the head of G-2. It was his recollection that these officers received all of this information that evening. He also testified that he had discussed the Japanese message with Miles.

In his contradictory testimony to me, however, Bratton confessed that the only package of the thirteen-part message he delivered on the evening of December 6 was to the Duty Officer of the Secretary of State. The other deliveries Bratton had said were made, in fact, were *not* made!

Nor could Bratton recall discussing the thirteen-part message with Miles, as he had claimed before the Army Board. He told me that he had ordered Colonel Dusenbury to deliver the thirteen-part message to Marshall at his quarters. But Bratton could not recall how the material Marshall was reading at his office desk the next morning came into the Chief of Staff's possession. (Dusenbury had admitted to me in his affidavit that he had not delivered the messages received on the evening of December 6 until after nine o'clock the morning of December 7.)

(4) Bratton had testified to the Army Board that on Sunday morning, December 7, he arrived at his office at about seven or eight. He further testified that he had tried to telephone the quarters of General Marshall at about nine A.M., but that the Chief of Staff did not arrive at his office until 11:25 that morning.

The affidavit of then-Colonel Deane, however, fixed the time that Bratton arrived at his office that morning as being between nine and nine-thirty. (This is confirmed by the affidavit of Colonel Dusenbury.) Thus, two witnesses dispute the time that Bratton claimed he came to the office, which destroys Bratton's claim that he tried to call General Marshall at nine that morning.

In his affidavit to me, Bratton changed his story again. He said that General Marshall was in his office between ten-thirty and eleven-thirty. This vital point, which placed Marshall in his office an hour earlier than Bratton had sworn to before the Army Board, and forty-five minutes earlier than the Final Congressional Report indicated (page 223), was supported by affidavits I had taken from Generals Gerow, Smith and Deane.

I believed it safe to conclude that all of Bratton's testimony prior to my interrogation of him was now highly suspect and could not stand up in a court of law. Some historians and writers of Congressional reports have ignored this fact, however. They have continued to misuse Bratton's earlier testimony to the Army Board, because it is more convenient in supporting their cockamamie theories about what happened at Pearl Harbor. This is a tragedy for the public. Perjured testimony must be identified as such, lest history become tainted.

The situation reminds me of the wonderful line in John Le Carré's book *The Honourable Schoolboy*, when the CIA man, Martello, asks George Smiley, "Which is it going to be, that's all. The conspiracy or the fuck-up?" [1] I can only say that what I was uncovering was not a conspiracy.

By now I also believed that I could put an end to the debate over the Winds Code. During my discussions in England with Capt. Edward Hastings of the Royal Navy, and after reviewing the signals files in Bletchley Park, I was unable to discover any evidence that the British had intercepted a broadcast from Tokyo that would have activated the Winds Code. The existence of an execute broadcast before the bombs fell depended primarily on the recollections of certain personnel in the U.S. Navy. Colonel Schukraft had claimed that he had seen an implementation that was in a form different from that reported by these Navy people, but when asked to produce the evidence, Schukraft could not do so. [2]

---

[1] John Le Carré. *The Honourable Schoolboy.* New York: Knopf, 1977, p. 518.
[2] See appendix, the Winds Code report, pp. 447–470.

As I said earlier, the action that the Winds Code was supposed to have triggered—i.e., the destruction of codes and code machines by Japanese diplomatic and consular representatives around the world in the event regular communications were broken down—had already been ordered via Magic by Tokyo in a message that was intercepted between December 1 and December 3. This meant that the execute message for the Winds Code *never* had to be broadcast by the Japanese. They already had achieved their required result.

Short's own staff gave him the information of the destruction of the codes by the Japanese diplomats before December 7. Yet Short testified before the Navy Court of Inquiry that he never knew about it. More importantly, Short swore that the news about the destruction of codes was the only important information in the message that Marshall sent him on the morning of December 7. But the affidavits I had taken from members of Short's staff proved that Short did in fact previously possess the ultimate, indispensable information he claimed he needed. If one takes Short's testimony before the Navy Court at face value, that the information of the destruction of the Japanese codes was the highest and most important information he could have had, the fact that he did possess it but failed to understand its importance explains why he ordered the wrong defense alert for Pearl Harbor.

As for Short's claim that the War Department's warnings to him had been inadequate, the affidavit of General Gerow crushed Short's argument to smithereens. Gerow told me that Short had been given adequate information of impending events. Furthermore, it should be considered that, for security reasons, the Navy Department restricted the information the Army could send in its messages. Also, the Navy had assured the Army that the Naval unit at Honolulu was intercepting and decoding the Japanese Purple messages from its own facilities.

I now knew the latter claim of the Navy was untrue.

There were also other questions. When did the fourteenth part of the Japanese message of December 6 actually arrive in Washington? What had happened to it?

Almost everyone who had read the first thirteen parts of the message, with the exception of Roosevelt, claimed that by itself the message was of little importance. The fourteenth part held the key. It read: "*. . . The Japanese Government regrets to have to notify hereby the American Government that in view of the attitude of the American Government it cannot but consider that it is impossible to reach an agreement through further negotiations.*" (Emphasis added)

So, after having accused the Americans of conspiring with the British and other countries ''to obstruct Japan's efforts towards the establishment of peace through the creation of a New Order in East Asia,'' the Japanese finally had broken diplomatic relations with America. Yet another short intercept of a separate, subsequent message ordered the news of this break to be announced by delivering the fourteen-part message to Secretary of State Hull at one P.M. (Washington time) on Sunday, December 7, 1941.

Reading the intercepts in sequence,[3] it becomes obvious that the fourteenth part, which said that diplomatic relations were to be broken off, clearly meant that war was going to begin. It was the final message, and again a separate message, saying when the fourteen-part message should be delivered, that gave a time when war might start. But it did not say where the fighting would first break out.

To my civilian, lawyerlike mind, the fourteenth part should have been enough to alert the Navy or the Army, or any intelligent civilian, that war was about to begin. Everyone to date had testified that the fourteenth part did not arrive much before seven A.M. in Washington on December 7. But in taking the testimony of Bratton and Dusenbury, I got the idea that the fourteenth part had been received in Washington much earlier than that. My suspicions having been aroused, I thought that if this proved to be true, the failure in Washington was far more devastating than anyone had considered, or dared suggest.

I might add that even the Congressional investigators failed to get the matter right in their final report of the Pearl Harbor Hearings, and many historians who have written about Pearl Harbor to date have failed to note this error. The significance of this will be developed later, when I comment on my recommendations to Congress about what should be done to correct the errors of Pearl Harbor that I had exposed.

Setting out on the final stages of my investigation, I felt more and more like Sherlock Holmes. I had dogs that barked, while others remained silent. Analyzing the clues would be tricky. The first person I took an affidavit from was Col. Otis K. Sadtler. He was the Signal Corps officer named as being involved in the attempt to send Honolulu the warning message of December 5 about the Winds Code.

One of the first things that Sadtler said to me ended a dispute that

---

[3] See appendix, pp. 342–352.

arose from his testimony to the Army Board. He had said that he learned from Admiral Noyes that the Navy had intercepted a broadcast that executed the Winds Code. Ordered to check back with Noyes, Sadtler now admitted to me that he had not made the check, nor to his knowledge had anyone else. He had assumed that Noyes would officially notify Army G-2 through channels that the implementation broadcast had been intercepted.

As Sadtler told me his story, I could understand his desire to quickly send a further warning to the Hawaiian Department. Sadtler gave me the text of the message he claimed he drafted for transmittal. However, Sadtler then admitted: "I have since checked with my office staff at the time and they have no recollection of the drafting of this proposed warning. I did not show it to anyone. I do not know where the message is now, and I made no copy at the time." I began to think that Sadtler was living in a dream world.

To make matters worse for himself, Sadtler then stated that the affidavits given to me by General Gerow and General Smith were, in fact, more accurate than his testimony to the Army Board. To cap matters off, Sadtler swore to me: "I did not see any execute message as contemplated by the so-called Japanese 'Winds Code,' and so far as I know there was no such execute message received in the War Department."

Sadtler went on to make other denials. I concluded that he was a sad, burned-out witness. He had reversed himself a number of times over the years, and from my point of view, it was time to close the charity office on him. He had consistently expressed himself in a dubious or ambiguous fashion. First, he reversed what he told the Army Board. Then, he told me that the affidavits of General Gerow and General Smith were correct, and he was wrong. Later, when he appeared before Congress, Senator Ferguson almost put the words in his mouth so that he could deny yet again what he intended to say. In later years, when people sought to ignore or criticize my affidavits, or vilify Marshall and Roosevelt, while extolling Sadtler's virtues, I thought it was the kiss of death to their claims as far as he was concerned.

Sadtler had also said that he wanted to send a message to the Pacific commands that they should take every precaution to avoid a repetition of Port Arthur (where the Japanese mounted a highly successful surprise attack against the Russians). He was going to say this message was based on *reliable information*. That was the talisman of those days: *reliable information*. The phrase possessed less value than the Good Housekeeping Seal of Approval.

My point is that *reliable information* didn't really mean anything. What was needed was someone to ask: Just how reliable is this information, and on what is it based?

If Short or Fielder had asked Bicknell this question, what would have come out was the complete background on the information that Washington had sent Kimmel. To make a point that people should comprehend, Sadtler or Bicknell should have said "most important information" or "most highly placed information." It's like an unattributed story in the newspapers. The source is often the real news.

When Bicknell went into the Hawaiian staff meeting on December 6 and began talking about the Japs' burning their codes "according to reliable information," he had said similar things so many times before. His cry of "Wolf!" was old and tired. The people at the meeting yawned and let it pass over their heads.

I have always wondered what would have happened if Bicknell had told the meeting on December 6: "I don't wish to jar you or upset you, gentlemen, but this is the most important, the *most* important information I have ever in my career received. . . ." What would have happened? Most likely, everyone would have woken up and said, "What the hell are you waiting for? Get in there and tell it to General Short the way you've told it to us!"

I don't think I'm being too harsh on Bicknell when I say that he failed in his chance to light a fire under Fielder and Short. On the other hand, after discovering the facts set forth in my next affidavit, I'm not sure any fire could have been lit under Short that might have prevented Pearl Harbor.

This conclusion is a harsh one. I reached it upon completing my interrogation of Maj. Gen. Charles D. Herron, who had been the commander of the Hawaiian department from October 1937 until he moved on to Washington and was replaced by Short on February 7, 1941. In Herron's affidavit to me, he said he knew it was crucial that Short be fully briefed about Herron's knowledge and experience of his Hawaiian appointment. It would be difficult to accomplish this, Herron knew, because Short was scheduled to arrive with his wife aboard the same vessel on which Herron was scheduled to leave for the West Coast. This meant that the two men would have less than two and one-half days to confer.

To make things easier for Short, Herron sent to San Francisco a complete briefing book, plus an agenda and exhibits for discussion. This material covered all the aspects of the Hawaiian command. Short was supposed to study it during his five-day voyage to Honolulu.

"Upon my meeting Short when he arrived," said Herron, "I asked him whether he had read the papers and material. He replied that . . . he had not given them much time while en route."

According to Herron, he did what he could in the limited time remaining to brief Short, including giving Short an evaluation of the officers and men in his command. According to Herron: "I told him of my estimate as to the efficiency of the staff officers and, with respect to G-2, that Col. George W. Bicknell, a Reserve Officer, was an experienced and qualified, efficient man for that position, and that it had been my intention to make him my G-2 [in charge of all intelligence]. I further told him [Short] of the G-2 work being done, of the liaison with the Navy, the FBI, and related sources of information, of the defense plans [for Pearl Harbor], of my experience with the *all-out* alert of 1940. . . ." (Emphasis added)

This trial alert had been ordered by the War Department on June 17, 1940, as an exercise based on war games that had shown that the best way for an unknown enemy to devastate the fleet in Pearl Harbor would be a surprise aerial attack. The actual order for the alert from Washington had read:

> Immediately alert complete defensive organization to deal with possible trans-Pacific raid, to the greatest extent possible without creating public hysteria or provoking undue curiosity of newspapers or alien agents. Suggest maneuver basis. Maintain alert until further orders. Instructions for secret communications direct with Chief of Staff will be furnished you shortly. Acknowledge.

The testimony of everyone to whom I spoke in Hawaii during my investigation was consistent: Herron had conducted these maneuvers successfully. The civilian population of Hawaii had been unconcerned.

I believe it fair to say, judging from past experience, that if Short had called for an all-out alert upon receiving the war warning of November 27, 1941, the alert would not have upset the civilians of Hawaii.

Herron reiterated to me his statement that he had briefed Short about "the relations and cooperation which had existed with the Navy, of the civilian population, of the Japanese situation, of the assumption that alien agents conducted espionage for the Japanese government.''

Herron also took Short around the island of Oahu. He showed his replacement the installations and ''gave him my ideas of possible attack and defense of that island.''

Then Herron dropped a bombshell. ''Following my talks with Gen. Short at the time,'' said Herron, ''he did not ever ask my opinion, or for information, or correspond with me on the subject of command or related problems.''

I gave a mental gasp at this statement, promising myself to dig into it later. I asked Herron if Short had been empowered to change the standard operating procedures relating to the various stages of alert for an enemy attack without consulting with, or reporting it to, the War Department.

Herron looked me straight in the eye and without a flicker of emotion drove a nail into Short's coffin. ''The Commander,'' he said, ''may and should take whatever action he believes dictated by necessity, but must so report to the War Department at the earliest possible moment.''

As we know, Short had reversed the SOP for staging the alert, but he failed to inform Washington of the changes.

Thus, it is easy to understand how Washington was confused by Short's reply to the warning of November 27: His message saying he was in liaison with the Navy indicated that he had ordered an alert to repel a surprise attack when, in fact, he had only gone to his revised minimum stage (i.e., protect against sabotage). This meant that Pearl Harbor was ripe for a surprise attack, but Washington did not know it.

After testifying and signing his affidavit, Herron and I discussed in general terms the material he had prepared for Short to read on his voyage to Hawaii. Herron was positive the briefing book was in really shipshape order. *Everything* was spelled out for Short, but Short ignored it all. Herron was a no-nonsense type of fellow, who believed in letting the chips fall where they may.

Herron said he asked Short if he had read the briefing book. Short replied: ''No, I did not. I read a novel, *Oliver Wiswell.*''

Herron said that Short's statement absolutely flabbergasted him. His immediate reaction was that Short wasn't up to the job. According to Herron, Short was in the last post of his career. He was a specialist in training troops, but he did not want the Hawaiian command. He thought it beneath him. Apparently, Short was supported in this by his wife. She believed that she had served her time as an Army wife and deserved better than to be taken away from her friends and relatives and isolated in a distant base at Honolulu. Both she and her husband had been hoping for a post at Fort Myer, outside Washington, or at the Presidio in San Francisco.

After Herron returned to Washington, he said he received back-channel reports about the nonchalance with which Short attended to his duties in Hawaii. This was exacerbated by the fact that Short's wife would frequently call her husband on a busy day at the office and complain vehemently about life in general. Short would then put on his jacket, abandon the office and go home to placate his wife.

I was astounded by what Herron was telling me. I immediately made separate notes for the file about what he said. I have them in my records today. But all that appears in Herron's affidavit is his laconic comment about the briefing book and exhibits: Short "had not given them much time while en route."

This answered the question about why Short had promoted an inexperienced officer like Fielder to be his G-2 over the head of the more experienced Bicknell. There were two reasons. One, Bicknell was a Reserve Officer, recently called to active duty, a rough-tough man who was more like a cop. Fielder was a graduate of West Point, smooth, polished, urbane, a ten-handicap golfer and a good dancer. When Short was involved with official business in the evening that precluded entertaining his wife, someone else had to take care of Mrs. Short during dinnertime. That person was, of course, Fielder. The more professional, job-oriented Bicknell was considered a bit uncouth to be Mrs. Short's companion.

Such were the problems of the peacetime Army of 1941.

I have often wondered why no historian ever probed more deeply into the subject. Only Gordon Prange, who wrote the best-selling *At Dawn We Slept,* ever interviewed me, and he never asked a single question about my views of the readiness of the Hawaiian command to resist a surprise Japanese attack. But when you tie in the comments by Herron with the report by the Inspector General as to the effectiveness of the Hawaiian command under Short's tenure, you will understand the scope of the problem I had discovered.

One item I had brought home with me from Pearl Harbor in May was a copy of a special investigation by Col. H. S. Burwell, AC, dated July 1941. It reported to Short the many deficiencies existing in his command. Perhaps the most important problem it noted was that the mind-set of both the Hawaiian Department and the Hawaiian Air Force, plus the air base at Hickham Field, was seriously deficient. Not only were the various Air Force staffs unable to understand the immediate need for steps to prevent sabotage, but "a considerable portion of the Command" failed to comprehend the realities of modern warfare. As Burwell had put it: "[They] do not see the mental picture of the interplay of relations now existing between intercontinental theatres of war and our local sphere of action."

Burwell went on to point out that the Hawaiian command was not alert to the possibility that the American Forces in Hawaii might have to react quickly in the event of a surprise enemy attack. This was especially true in the event of "an abrupt conflict with Japan."

The causes for these failures, declared Burwell, were those of the ingrained habits of peacetime. There was a carefree sense of "no worry" that was created by the isolation of a tropical island with a large force of troops stationed on it.

This meant that operations and supply functions received priority attention from Short's staff, and there was "relative inattention accorded in peacetime to intelligence functions."

In turn, the troops had lost their "aggressive initiative." The posture of the command was one of a purely defensive attitude. Nor was there any evidence by which Burwell could ascertain that the command itself had any "critical concern for the future."

In other words, Burwell's inspection report said that Short's command was lazy and ill prepared for the outbreak of a war that everyone believed was coming. Worse, nothing was being done to change the situation. The Army's Hawaiian command was a perpetual happy hour.

If Short did anything to make his command better prepared for war, and more alert to repulse a surprise aerial attack by an unknown enemy, the evidence that he chose his new staff wisely is missing. We have seen how Short chose Colonel Fielder to be his G-2 instead of Colonel Bicknell, the man recommended for the job because of his experience in intelligence matters that dated back to World War I. And we know that on November 5, 1941, Short designated Col. Walter C. Phillips to be his new Chief of Staff.

The testimony before the Army Board is replete with numerous views of Phillips by witnesses. Their replies ranged from a total reluctance to answer to flat statements that Phillips was unqualified for the job. It was said that Short did not treat Phillips as he would have treated a more experienced Chief of Staff. For example, Phillips was excluded from important conferences with the Navy. The Army Board never probed the matter more deeply, so the ultimate conclusion I could reach was simply that Phillips was not fully qualified for the job.

I cannot help believing that if Phillips had been better qualified, of stronger character and more conversant with the primary mission assigned to Short (to defend Pearl Harbor from surprise attack), then Phillips might have advised Short to go on alert to prevent an enemy aerial attack instead of simply making an arbitrary decision to be on alert only for sabotage.

If I were to fault General Marshall in this, it would be for his decision to send Short to Hawaii when it was apparent that Short didn't want the job. Of course, Short hadn't specifically told Marshall about his objections to the posting, although he hinted them to Marshall fairly clearly. But the Chief of Staff needed someone there to get the troops trained to fight. Short had a great reputation in the Army for this. Also, he was a moral man, not a hard drinker, and these are the many things that Marshall must have considered when he was appointing a commander for the Hawaiian Islands. I also doubt that Marshall ever knew the full extent of Short's problems at home.

The choice facing Marshall was typical of the pre–World War II Army. Everything is different today. There are all kinds of support programs to ensure that husbands and wives are fit for their assignments abroad. But back in 1941, if General Herron believed that General Short was not prepared to take over as commander of the Hawaiian District, he just couldn't go to Marshall and say, "You've made a mistake." This problem with personnel was a real nightmare. Marshall kept a little notebook in which he wrote the names of officers he discovered in peacetime who should be promoted over the heads of the older, but inefficient, peacetime commanders when war broke out.

More was needed than that. When I finished my investigation in 1945, I was asked to head up a new department in the Army, in which anybody could make a complaint against a superior officer directly to the commanding general. This office would have been more than that of an ombudsman, because it would have to not only judge the validity of the complaint, and recommend what needed to be done about it, but also protect the person who had made it. (So, you can see that the Army learned from its mistakes at Pearl Harbor.) But I replied, just as I told everyone, that all I wanted after the war was to be a civilian and resume my law practice.

10 "IT WAS CUSTOMARY AND EXPECTED"

The war in the Pacific was ending more quickly than anyone had anticipated.

The first atomic bomb exploded over Hiroshima on August 6, 1945. Three days later, a second atomic weapon destroyed Nagasaki. That same day, August 9, the Russians invaded Manchuria, and the Japanese Supreme Council for the Conduct of the War convened to discuss the severity of the situation facing Japan. The Russian invasion of Manchuria was of greater concern to the Council, because the enormity of the disaster caused by the atomic bomb at Hiroshima had not yet been grasped by the Japanese government. The military members of the Supreme Council still argued that Japan should resist the Allies until the bitter end. They wanted a fight to the death. This threw the Council into a stalemate. The civilian members who wanted to sue for peace were not strong enough to override the military presence.

The issue—whether to continue fighting or surrender—went to Emperor Hirohito, the only person capable of facing down the military and making such a decision stick. On August 10, the Emperor decreed that Japan would surrender according to the Potsdam declaration.

It took another four days for the surrender terms to be negotiated and transmitted. Meanwhile, the Emperor survived a coup against his decision to surrender by hard-line Army officers who tried to seize control of the Imperial Palace. They failed, and many of the rebels committed ritual suicide. On August 15, the Emperor broadcast the notice of surrender to the Japanese people.

I cannot describe the sense of euphoria that swept through the Pentagon. It was such an awesome feeling of relief, of sheer, unadulterated joy that the moral questions about dropping the atomic bombs were swept aside.

The war was over!

That was all that mattered.

My wife, Virginia, had come to the Pentagon for a party on the evening the surrender was announced. I cannot for the life of me recall now why, or for whom, the original party was being held. We were all overwhelmed by the emotions of the moment. One thing I knew, however, was that as soon as I could complete my investigation for the Secretary, I would ask for the relief he had promised me and we'd go back to California as quickly as possible.

It's odd, in a way, how the human mind turns from a complex task such as a war and immediately begins thinking about something else. I guess it's because future pastures are always more inviting. But I was still in uniform, and there was work to be done.

As a result, I found myself in Boston on August 16, taking the affidavit of Maj. Gen. Sherman Miles, who, in the run-up to Pearl Harbor, had been the head of Army intelligence (G-2) in Washington. At the moment, Miles was the Commanding General of the First Service Command, and there was almost a sense of déjà vu in taking down his words literally only hours after the surrender of Japan.

That didn't mean I wasn't going to be jolted by what Miles would tell me, because while I expected something of the nature of what he was going to say, I had no idea just how forthright he would be about it.

First of all, Miles said he wanted to correct his testimony before the Army Pearl Harbor Board. He acknowledged that he had avoided making any statements during that testimony ''concerning details of information and intelligence which I had derived from Top Secret sources then called 'Magic,' or any intimation that such sources existed.''

In other words, the head of Army intelligence was telling me that notwithstanding the implications of perjury, he had deliberately misled the Army Board. If that didn't help throw the Board's findings into Boston Harbor, nothing would. But why had he done it?

As Miles explained to me, Brig. Gen. Russell A. Osmun and Col. Carter W. Clarke (my old nemesis) told him not to reveal anything about Magic to the Army Board. According to Miles, Osmun and Clarke said that these instructions came from no less a personage than the Chief of Staff, General Marshall, the very person who was ultimately judged—and found wanting—by the Board. Said Miles in his laconic fashion about the orders he had received: "Accordingly, I obeyed that instruction."

I was flabbergasted when Miles told me this. He had been a brigadier at the time. He was G-2, the head of intelligence. He was in a position to go into anybody's office and say: "Listen to me! I disagree. What you're doing is wrong." But he didn't do it.

Although I hate to admit it, I probably would have agreed with him. But I don't think he should have done it the way he did. I recalled that when Miles testified to the Army Board, he'd give that little secretive smile, along with his bland, false denials, and I'd think that something wasn't right here. I had no idea then what was right or wrong, because even though I was a member of the Army Board, I hadn't been told and did not know about the existence of Magic.

Now, if there was any reason for Congress to be angry at Marshall, Miles had just given it to me. Marshall had blocked information from a congressionally appointed committee, a board that should have been vested with the power to hear Top Secret information that was known to other members of the Army. Marshall shortchanged me. He shortchanged the Army Board. He shortchanged Congress. He also severely damaged his reputation.

I was not happy to have this problem dumped in my lap.

After the war, when Congress began to dig into Pearl Harbor for itself, Congress made the mistake of not assiduously studying my affidavits. The big furor in Congress was over where General Marshall had been on the evening of December 6, 1941. Because he could not recall his exact whereabouts, the congressmen were out to blame him for Pearl Harbor for the wrong reasons. They took the position ipso facto that he was not on duty, ready to read and take action on the thirteen-part Japanese message that had been intercepted that evening.

Of course, Marshall could have answered his critics so easily by saying: "Well, we all make mistakes about time and place, but my best recollection, after checking with my wife, my aides and everybody else, is that I was home that evening." But he never did that. Who misadvised him? I regret now that I never asked, but that was not the point of my investigation.

I'll discuss the legal ramifications of the question later on. What I want to point out here is that by focusing on Marshall's whereabouts on the evening of December 6, Congress missed the real issue: Marshall had ordered his subordinates to lie to the Army Board, and they had complied.

Now, Marshall's reasons for this shocking deception were based on a claim of national security. He believed, and so did many others in the military and civilian command structure of the time, that the secret of Magic should be protected at all costs. The decision to tell the public that we had broken the Magic codes was made by the United States Congress during its investigation of Pearl Harbor after the war. It was Congress that blew the whistle on our code-breaking capabilities. The Army and Navy were in agreement on this and were totally opposed to letting this secret ever become public. So were the British. They didn't allow word of how they had cracked the German Enigma codes to become public knowledge until twenty-five or so years later.

If Congress had calmly, coolly debated the matter and concluded that the news of our breaking the Japanese codes was of vital national interest, its action would be understandable. But I concluded that Congress wanted to make the secret about Magic public knowledge mainly for purely partisan gain. Certain Republican members of Congress hoped that by uprooting the tree that bore the Magic fruit, they could place the blame for Pearl Harbor on Washington, discredit the Roosevelt era, vilify and destroy the continuing career of Marshall, and throw our new Democratic President, Truman, out of office.

But I am getting ahead of myself. I will discuss the ramifications of these issues later, when I find myself testifying before Congress. Let me return to the affidavit of General Miles, who had just admitted to me that he had been ordered to mislead the Army Pearl Harbor Board and had done so.

Continuing his testimony, Miles stated that his comments before the Army Board should be reconsidered on the basis of his newly acknowledged falsehoods. Now he wished to change his story. He affirmed that in the months preceding Pearl Harbor, the intercepts of the Japanese diplomatic codes had been available to both the Navy and the Army. He also affirmed the actions of Bratton and his subordinates according to the testimony they had given me. (In other words, he also confirmed that Bratton had misinformed the Board.) He affirmed that the intercepts had been given to the proper recipients in locked briefcases, and that after the intercepts were returned to G-2, they and all receipts for them were burned. No records were kept of what material was delivered or to whom. In fact, said Miles: "I do not think that any such records were made at the time."

I reviewed with Miles the file of intercepts that I carried in my bomb pouch. He thought that before December 7, he had seen all the messages in my exhibit, with one exception. So, without equivocation, Miles acknowledged to me that as the head of Army intelligence, he had seen the Magic decrypts in their entirety.

My question, then, became: How had he interpreted the intercepts that related to the reports made by the Japanese Consul in Hawaii and the inquiries from Tokyo about ship movements at Pearl Harbor? Also, there was the dividing of Pearl Harbor into a series of grids or districts to aid such reporting that I had discussed earlier with General Gerow.

Miles replied that this was "primarily of Naval interest and what might have been expected." He pointed out, correctly, that the Japanese were following the movements of our major ships in various ports as best they could, just "as we were doing as regard to their ships." Miles continued: "Since I knew the Navy was getting the messages mentioned also, they [the Pearl Harbor ship movement messages] did not leave any impression on my mind which has endured for four years [of war]."

Miles clarified what I had long been thinking. He had been reading Magic on the basis of what it meant to the Army. He knew the Navy was reading the intercepts on the basis of what was best for the Navy. Given that the defense of Pearl Harbor was based on the concept of mutual cooperation—or codependency, as I called it—no one appeared to have been taking an overview of the Magic decrypts and asking the fateful questions: What does this mean in *overall* terms? How do you in the Navy read this? How do you in the Army read this? What do all these decrypts mean when taken as a whole?

I felt a surge of excitement, but I held it in check. Miles had just confirmed what MacArthur had told me earlier. There was a crying need for a centralized intelligence service.

We continued. Miles said that he knew of the Joint Action Agreement of the so-called ABCD (American-British-Chinese-Dutch) Bloc, about which so much has been written, often with inflammatory comments. But Miles did not believe that this agreement had any real binding effect on American military policy. Why? For the simple reason that Congress never ratified it. Our allies might have "hoped" that the American Navy would come to their defense if the Japanese had crossed a certain line in the Pacific without first declaring war on America. But since Congress had never so said—that we should uphold the ABCD Joint Action Agreement—the issue was moot from the military's view.

We then tackled the question of the thirteen-part Japanese intercept of the evening of December 6. Miles acknowledged that he was aware of this intercept, "because I was dining at the home of my opposite number in the Navy, Admiral Wilkinson." The thirteen-part decrypt was carried to Wilkinson's home by Admiral Beardall, the President's aide. Wilkinson had read the thirteen-part message, then handed it to Miles.

Now I had confirmation that the heads of intelligence for both the Army and the Navy had read the all-important thirteen-part decrypt on the evening of December 6. Yet, neither of them had seen anything as sinister in the message as had the President, who said it meant war.

Miles told me he did not believe the thirteen-part message to be important enough to warrant his telephoning Marshall at his quarters to check whether or not the Chief of Staff had seen the material. He hadn't, as I knew.

This means that despite the failures of Bratton and Dusenbury to deliver the thirteen-part message (or fourteen-part message, as Dusenbury claimed it to be) to its proper recipients that evening, the chief of the Army's intelligence had, by chance, seen the material, and it had failed to move him to take action.

Why had Miles been so complacent about the matter? As he explained it to me (and his thinking is important), "It was my belief in the period preceding 7 December 1941 that the Navy was intercepting, decrypting, decoding and translating this material, consisting of Japanese diplomatic and consular messages *at Hawaii for use in connection with the fleet. . . .*" (Emphasis added)

Why was Miles so sure of this?

"I was given so to understand by Naval sources, but I do not recall who told me," he said.

I could accept this.

Given that Admiral Turner, the head of the all-powerful War Plans Division, also mistakenly believed that the Navy at Pearl Harbor was breaking and reading the Purple codes, why shouldn't Miles make the same error?

I made a mental tick that here was yet another reason to establish a centralized intelligence agency.

Switching gears on Miles, I asked him if he remembered the conversations he was alleged to have held with Bratton and Sadtler about the possible interception of a broadcast from Tokyo that would have executed the Winds Code.

Miles couldn't recall the meeting clearly. But he acknowledged that it might have been the catalyst for message number 519 of December 5 to Hawaii, instructing the G-2 there to contact Commander Rochefort about the Winds Code. Miles was more positive when it came to the so-called broadcast that would have executed the Winds Code. He said: "In the event of the receipt of such a message, I was prepared to transmit it immediately to the Chief of Staff [Marshall] and to WPD [War Plans Division]." Miles also set up a special alert for the broadcast via the Far Eastern Section of G-2. He remembered that several broadcasts were intercepted that appeared at first to be the vital one. On further analysis, however, they were found "not to be authentic."

I no longer had any doubt as to whether or not the Army had exhausted all its resources in trying to intercept the execute message for the Winds Code. I concluded that everything that could have been done had been done. The fact that several intercepts at first appeared to be what everyone was searching for, but later proved to be false leads, explained satisfactorily why, even today, there are those who believe that a Winds Code broadcast was intercepted before the attack. The facts show otherwise.

Another vital point on which I needed Miles's memory was that of his first meeting with Marshall on the morning of Sunday, December 7.

Miles pinned the hour at "about 11 A.M."

I then asked him how aware he had been about the possibility of a surprise attack on Pearl Harbor.

Miles drew his shoulders erect and replied in a cold, general's voice that he would like to refer me to his service in the Hawaiian Department as G-3 (Operations Officer) from 1929 to 1932. During those years, Miles prepared and distributed a General Staff Study that "emphasized the advantage which an attack on Oahu, particularly by surprise, might give Japan." The simulated attack, as programmed by

Miles, called for an unknown enemy to attack with little or no warning. It was supposed to be "out of the blue," said Miles. "I remember one situation we war-gamed, that of an attack 'out of the blue' on Sunday morning."

So if General Short had forgotten that his command would have been most vulnerable to surprise attack "out of the blue" on a Sunday morning, General Miles wanted to make sure the record showed that he, at least, had never forgotten.

To make sure that Miles really believed this, I asked him whether or not it was correct military practice for Short to have changed his SOP and acted contrary to the estimates of the War Department, such as those sent to Short before the attack, without consulting or reporting to the War Department.

Again Miles drew himself up, but even higher this time.

"The Commanding General was responsible for the successful execution of his mission," Miles said. "He could not act contrary to War Department estimates of the situation, but at his own risk. . . . Custom and doctrine of command would require him to report his action and the reasons therefore promptly to his superiors."

Continued Miles: "In my opinion, the messages sent by the War Department to Gen. Short prior to 7 December 1941, especially the one dated 27 November 1941, were definitive directives that a war alert was required by the situation, and there was an immediate threat from without as well as danger from sabotage."

And so, without the slightest equivocation, the former intelligence chief of the U.S. Army said that Short had to bear the blame for Pearl Harbor.

One final matter: I had learned from Commander Sonnett that a member of the Army's code-breaking team had testified to Admiral Hewitt's board that General Marshall had ordered certain records of Army G-2 destroyed. This was in reference to the so-called Winds Code broadcast that had not been intercepted. There were those who still believed that at least one of the preliminary intercepts that Miles had mentioned was, in truth, the real broadcast, or the execute message. It just goes to show how the mistaken story persisted.

I asked Miles if any records pertaining to this issue were destroyed. "To my knowledge," replied Miles, "no records of G-2, War Department, pertinent to Pearl Harbor were ever ordered destroyed by General Marshall or any other person." Miles was also positive that the Army had never destroyed any records related to Pearl Harbor that were derogatory to the Army. As he put it, if the records had been ordered burned, he would have known about it.

I doubt the debate will ever end about whether or not the Winds Code broadcast was intercepted. The issue is too attractive to those who believe in conspiracy theories, or insist that the Roosevelt administration maneuvered us into a war with Japan. They will never drop the bit from their teeth. Their theories are simply that: theories, on which they make money. When faced with sworn testimony, their theories collapse. In other words, I believed Miles. In the end, he had confessed his sins and told me the truth.

It was more than fifty years ago that I took that affidavit from Miles. When I pick it up today and read it over, I get even angrier than I was when I took it. When Miles testified before the Army Pearl Harbor Board, I had a hunch he was lying, because he looked like the cat that had swallowed the canary. He was asked several times by the generals on the Board, who knew better from having been alerted about Magic by Marshall: "Now, you're sure you didn't have any other means of intelligence available to you?"

Miles would pause in his testimony, and you could almost read his mind that, yes, there was a source, but he wasn't going to reveal it. So, what was the charade about?

You see, Miles's affidavit to me was a terrible indictment of Marshall.

Let's put it this way. Secretary Stimson assures Congress that he is going to convene the Army Board according to the instructions of the joint resolution of Congress. He convenes the Board and is faced with the fact that the officers in his Army have agreed not to testify truthfully. It's a conspiracy to commit perjury on the parts of Marshall and Miles, even if in the name of national security. I don't condone what Marshall did, but I can understand why he did it. His explanation is simple, direct. But, according to the law of the land, he was wrong, and I told him so later on.

Anyway, the time had come for me to take the testimony of the Chief of Staff, George C. Marshall.

We met alone in Marshall's office. It was a large one, comparable in size to that of Secretary Stimson. Marshall was tall and slim, a fast talker who liked helpers fast on their feet and who used words precisely. (He had told me earlier that he hated conversing with Secretary of State Hull; Hull spoke so slowly and ponderously he drove Marshall frantic.) One of the things that worried Marshall about my investigation, or any investigation into Pearl Harbor for that matter, was that so many people made statements based on what Marshall called their "backsight." This was his way of saying that people tended to show how smart they were by virtue of their hindsight. I believe he made a real effort when he spoke to me to say precisely what he had thought at the time Pearl Harbor occurred without resorting to "backsight." He just seemed to possess that rare type of integrity.

The first issue we covered in his affidavit was what Marshall had said to the General Officers of the Army Board when he asked them to meet him in secret before his first round of testimony. This secret meeting had lasted fifty-seven minutes on August 7, 1944. Marshall acknowledged to me that he had told the General Officers, while hiding it from the Board and the people, the Recorders and the Congress, "about the character of information that had been derived before 7 December from Top Secret sources called 'Magic.' " He told them of the interception, decoding and transcription of the Japanese diplomatic messages.

"I further stated," said Marshall, "that neither this information, nor the source thereof, should be made public because it would result in at least temporarily, if not permanently, extinguishing this source. This would have meant that our enemies concerned would certainly have changed their systems of communication and would thus have terminated this most vital source of information which has continued to be available up to the present hour. Many of our successes, and the saving of American lives, would have been seriously limited if the source of intelligence mentioned had been so compromised."

I said that I should warn Marshall that I believed, in legal terms, he had done himself a disservice in giving this information to the General Officers while eliminating the Recorder of the Court and the System Recorder from the meeting.

"Well," he said, "I had in mind the war effort, on trying to win the war. I have done things that might be highly questionable, such as permitting a whole troop convoy to sail into a nest of enemy submarines rather than ordering them to skirt around it. But if I had given the order it would have compromised the source of my intelligence."

As a lawyer, I had to admit that he gave a hell of a good answer. "Another place where I believe you did yourself a disservice," I said, "was appointing a board consisting of General Grunert, whom you relieved as Commanding General in the Philippines in favor of Mac-Arthur, and General Russell, whom you relieved on the training field and sent to Columbus, Ohio, and General Frank, whom you relieved as commander in Dayton, Ohio, and thereby prevented him from getting his third star. Each man had an axe to grind with you. I'm not saying they were dishonest, but if I were trying a lawsuit, I would eliminate them by challenge from serving on any jury with which you or your interests were involved.''

"Colonel Clausen, the sole reason I picked those men to serve on the Army Board was their availability for the job at hand,'' Marshall said.

I thought that was very patriotic, though somewhat naive. Yet, it was typical of the type of man Marshall was. He picked those fellows because they could be spared for the job, not for his own purposes. But it explains the derogatory reports of the Army Board and the confusion they have given historians over the years.

Marshall did not deny that Miles, Bratton, Sadtler or others had been ordered to mislead the Board. But he said that he personally did not see these men "prior to or after their testimony." In other words, Marshall himself did not order these men to dissemble to preserve the secrets of Magic.

"It was not until it developed that the 'Magic' papers were being disclosed before the Navy Court of Inquiry," said Marshall, "that the Army officers concerned were authorized to go into all the details regarding 'Magic' before the Army Pearl Harbor Board."

Now, this meant, as I had explained at the outset of my investigation to Secretary Stimson, that the Board heard tainted testimony about some Magic, and the truth about other Magic. The situation was further confused by Marshall's now telling me that on his second appearance before the Board, he "discussed with the Board at length the general problem concerning the method of including 'Magic' in the report of the Board, and also the availability to the Board of any officers concerned for the purpose of giving testimony on the Top Secret 'Magic' phases on the investigation." (It was around this point in time that I had first learned about Magic.) Marshall even suggested to the Board that Colonel Bratton was available to testify before them. But how was Marshall to know that Bratton would lie?

This was how Marshall boxed himself into a no-win situation by trying to handle problems in the "Army way" instead of coming clean with the Board's lawyers. The Board itself is guilty for falling into the same trap, like Groucho Marx, who said: "I never make a decision without ignoring my lawyer." Thus, the Board issued reports that were improperly biased on tainted evidence, faulty by virtue of the fact that the Board itself was prejudiced against Marshall, and improperly critical of Marshall because he had, without malice, caused perjured testimony to be presented to the Board.

Marshall understood this now. But how could it be explained to the public?

The problem was that Marshall was a soldier first, last and always, and an innocent when it came to the law. That was not a good situation when so many lawyer-type congressmen were going to try to pillory him in their forthcoming investigation.

First things first, however. I reviewed with Marshall the intercepts I carried with me. He said he believed before Pearl Harbor that Short was aware of some of this information, and that Short was also receiving some other information from facilities available only in Hawaii. (By this, Marshall meant the messages from British intelligence that I had picked up in Hawaii.) As for Short's earlier testimony that the most important information he could have received would have been the news that the Japanese were destroying their codes, Marshall referred me to Bicknell's testimony. You will recall that Bicknell had told me that the Navy had shown him on December 3 a cable from the Navy Department in Washington which read:

Highly reliable information has been received that categoric and urgent instructions were sent yesterday to the Japanese diplomatic and consular posts at Hong Kong, Singapore, Batavia, Manila, Washington and London to destroy most of their codes and ciphers at once and to burn all other important confidential and secret documents.

Marshall reflected on this message and said: "It was customary and expected that information of this character would be exchanged between the respective services at Hawaii."

This puts the icing on the cake, I thought. I have taken the testimony of Captain Layton, the Pacific Fleet Intelligence Officer, who swore that it was against regulations to exchange this type of intelligence with the Army. Yet, here I have just heard the five-star general who has served for six years as Chief of Staff of the U.S. Army say that it "was customary and expected that information of this character would be exchanged between the respective services at Hawaii."

It attributes the lie or violation or disobedience to Layton—and to Kimmel—in the most sweeping terms imaginable.

I must digress here for the moment. I don't believe any historian or any politician ever picked up on this point of who was telling the truth about these vital matters: Layton and Kimmel or Marshall. The reason for not doing so is obvious. In a single sentence, Marshall destroyed Layton's and Kimmel's arguments by showing how Layton and Kimmel had failed to do their duty. If you had Layton and Marshall testifying on this matter in a trial, the jury would side with Marshall, as it should. But the historians and politicians continue to ignore this, because it does not fit into their preconceived notions of conspiracy theories, or their ill-conceived plans for political revenge.

But to get back to Marshall's testimony: The Chief of Staff would not elaborate on his statement to me. Nor would he make further comment on the fact that the Navy at Pearl Harbor had kept the second message of December 3, as well as the first one, from going directly to Short. Marshall was not going to engage in hindsight or speculation. He would deal only with fact. Marshall had already pointed out that Kimmel and Layton had failed to do their duty, and he rightly pointed out that Bicknell had also failed, even though he had had to rely on back-channel information that violated Top Secret regulations. Bicknell waited three days to present his news at a regular staff conference and then had watered down his report, as I have pointed out earlier.

The real problem, which Marshall advanced with deadly clarity, was this: There were no relevant intelligence communications between Layton and Fielder, or between Kimmel and Short. The Pacific Fleet at Pearl Harbor had wanted to have everything its own way. It wanted to control intelligence information, and it did not share the information with Short's command, yet it wanted the Army to protect the fleet at Pearl Harbor. From my point of view, any further defense Layton or Kimmel might propose of their actions would be ludicrous.

As for the types of warnings Marshall had personally given Short about the defense of his command, Marshall referred me to two letters he had sent Short. The first was dated February 7, 1941, and it said:

> My impression of the Hawaiian problem has been that
> if no serious harm is done us during the first six hours of
> known hostilities, thereafter the existing defenses would
> discourage an enemy against the hazard of an attack. The
> risk of sabotage, and the risk involved in a surprise raid by

air and by submarine, constitute the real perils of the situation. Frankly, I do not see any landing threat in the Hawaiian Islands so long as we have air superiority.

A second letter from Marshall to Short, dated March 5, 1941, said:

I would appreciate your early review of the situation in the Hawaiian Department with regard to defense from air attack. The establishment of a satisfactory system of coordinating all means available to this end is a matter of first priority.

Marshall went on to point out that "estimates to the same general effect were sent to General Short by the War Department." The replies and other communications that the War Department received from Short indicated "that he was then alive to the danger of the possible surprise air attack against Pearl Harbor."

Marshall said all this with calm precision. His voice did not rise. Nor did anger show on his face. He delivered the coup de grace to Short by saying: "He participated in plans and exercises against such a possibility [of surprise air attack]. At no time did General Short inform me, or, to my knowledge, anyone else in the War Department that he was not in full agreement with these War Department estimates and plans for the defense of Oahu, which, in effect, warned him to expect air and submarine attacks as primary threats in the event of war with Japan."

What about Short's changing of the SOPs without having notified Washington? I asked.

Said Marshall: "The doctrine of military command required that the Commanding General of an overseas command, such as the Hawaiian Department, must not act contrary to War Department estimates of the character mentioned, unless he believed such action to be dictated by necessity, and unless he immediately reported and gave full details and reasons to the War Department."

Since Short had changed the SOPs and reversed their order of importance without informing Washington, any confusion created by this, Marshall was saying, was Short's personal responsibility. Short's command's trying to hide the fact that these changes had been made without notifying Washington only made the situation worse.

I also believe that the two personal letters of instruction that Marshall had sent Short were ample directives to any general fearful of what to do, or unsure of what he was supposed to do. They were definitive in the respect that they predicted the exact thing that occurred, namely, a surprise air attack. Short should have been prepared to defend against an air attack by using long-range reconnaissance, whether by plane or by radar.

As it turned out, the Army's radar was not fully operational on December 7 when the attack occurred. Nor had an integrated air defense command system been established. Neither did Short make any effort to learn from Kimmel about the Navy's plans, or lack of plans, for long-range reconnaissance.

The debacle at Pearl Harbor was the result of Short's and Kimmel's being asleep at the switch.

Think of what would have happened if Short and Kimmel had been ready to fight.

When the Japanese attacked, they would have been met by our fighters in the air and antiaircraft guns blazing away from below. The Japanese might have sunk some of our ships, but our defenders would have been like the men at the Alamo, ready for an attack. If they were overwhelmed and killed, they would have been heroes. If they had kept the casualties down and saved some of the battleships from sinking, they would have been even greater heroes.

The fact of the matter was that our commanders and their forces were caught with their pants down. In war, you can't have it both ways. You can be a hero if you're ready to repel a surprise attack. You can't be a hero if you fail in your primary mission and suffer the casualties in personnel and the loss of matériel that we did.

From what I had learned during my investigation, Short and Kimmel deserved to be relieved of their commands. Did they deserve harsher punishment? I believed so. According to law, they appeared to be guilty of criminal negligence and dereliction of duty.

Since this has been such a controversial matter for the past fifty years, let me pause a moment to explain. Let us use an auto accident as an example. Say you have a car that is defective. You put a bad driver in that car, and there is an accident. Had the driver been attentive, he might have avoided the accident. But, according to law, the driver should have known he had to be careful and look out for potentially dangerous situations; therefore, the accident occurred because the driver was violating his duty, and he is liable under the law. Now, the system that Kimmel and Short were operating under may have been faulty—indeed, I believe the system of handling Magic was improper —but both men were *ex industria* warned to be careful and avoid an accident, such as a surprise aerial attack. Neither man avoided the calamity. And, as I shall show later, neither man tried to communicate with the other about the potential dangers they jointly faced.

Let's put it another way: Kimmel and Short were like two sentries on duty who either did not look, and hence did not see, the tank that overran them, or who looked and still failed to see it. In either event, they were guilty of having failed to warn their comrades, and hence of dereliction of duty, just as a sentry on duty in time of war would be guilty and subjected to court-martial with the possibility of capital punishment.[1]

Whether the military could accept this judgement remained to be seen. I was certain, however, that other civilian lawyers, such as Secretary Stimson and Harvey Bundy, would agree with me. Indeed, they did.

If there was one mitigating factor in favor of Kimmel and Short, it was that, while they might have been sentries, it wasn't during a time of war that they failed in their duties, but in a time of peace. One might call it the result of the Pearl Harbor syndrome. Stephen Coonts is one of the first ex–military writers to touch on this, which he does in his recent best-selling novel *Under Siege*. Coonts's hero, Jake Grafton, explains why governments are caught with their pants down. "They weren't unprepared," Grafton says. "They just weren't ready, if you understand the difference. It's almost impossible for people who have known only peace to lift themselves to that level of mental readiness necessary to immediately and effectively counter a determined attack. . . . We refuse to believe."[2]

Although the affidavit from General Marshall was the last major piece of testimony for my investigation, there were still some minor players I had to call upon.

One of these was Col. Rex W. Minckler, who in the months before Pearl Harbor was the Officer in Charge of the Signal Intelligence Service. This meant he had direct supervision over the receipt and dissemination of intercepted radio messages.

---

[1] Clausen to Lee interview, Jan. 29, 1991; Clausen letter to Lee, Apr. 2, 1991.
[2] Stephen Coonts, *Under Siege*, New York: Pocket Books, 1990, p. 35.

Minckler recalled the action taken to monitor Japanese radio broadcasts for the execute message of the Winds Code. Again, I asked: Had a Winds broadcast been intercepted?

"I never saw, or heard of, an authentic execute message of this character before, or since, 7 December 1941," said Minckler. "It is my belief that no such message was sent."

Minckler confirmed that there had been one or two "false alarms," which he discussed with the Navy and G-2. There was one message that indicated a possible breach in relations between Japan and Great Britain, but even that was not verified.

Minckler also said, confirming earlier testimony by others, that it was normal procedure in sending messages between the Army and the Navy to send six copies.

I showed Minckler two decrypts I had carried with me during my investigation, which have caused considerable consternation to historians because they were intercepted just before Pearl Harbor, but were not translated until the day after the attack. The first message read as follows:

> From: Hon [Honolulu]
> To: Tokyo
> Dec. 6, 41
> PA-KY
> #253 release p5————123a
> 1. On American continent in Oct. Army began
> training barrage balloon troops at Camp Davis, N.C.
> 400,500 balloons considering use in defense of Hawaii &
> Panama. So far as Hawaii concerned through
> investigations made, they have not set up mooring
> equipment, nor have they selected troops to man them.
> No training for maintenance balloons. No signs barrage
> balloons equipment. In addition, it is difficult to imagine
> that they have actually any limits to barrage balloon
> defense. I imagine that in all probability there is
> considerable opportunity left to take advantage of a
> surprise attack against these places.
>
> In my opinion battleships do not have torpedo nets.
> Details not known; will report results of investigation.
> Army 718 258777 2a Trans 12/8/41 (2-TT).

The second message read:

From: Hon [Honolulu]
To: Tokyo
Dec. 6, 41
PA-K2
#254

1. On evening 5th, among battleships which entered port—one sub tender. The following ships observed at anchor on 6th.

9 battleships, 3 light cruisers, 3 sub tenders, 17 destroyers, in addition 4 light cruisers, 2 destroyers lying at docks (heavy cruisers & air plane carriers all left).

2. "It appears that no air reconnaissance is being conducted by the fleet air arm."
Army 7179 25874 Trans 12/8/41 (2-22) 3 a.

Minckler confirmed that both messages had been intercepted on December 6 but had not been translated until December 8, the day after the Japanese attack. He also confirmed that this was the proper amount of time for normal decryption and decoding the code in question, PA-K2.

Minckler also said that when such messages came in, they were automatically sent in raw form to the Navy.

I knew that the Navy had intercepted at least three more, similar messages from the Japanese Consul General in Honolulu. These were intercepted in enough time for decryption and translation to give ample warning of an attack. It wasn't until much later, however, that I learned why they had not been processed in time.

One of the things I had done when I was in Hawaii was to go to Mayfield's District Intelligence Office and get the Consul's answers to Tokyo's requests for the movements of ships at Pearl Harbor. They were in the form of intercepted cables that had been sent via commercial RCA traffic. When David Sarnoff, the president of RCA, had visited Hawaii in November 1941, Mayfield persuaded him to let the Navy have copies of the cables the Japanese Consul was sending. This was in violation of the law at that time. After the Consul had destroyed his code machines and codes, with the exception of one system, on the December 3 order from Tokyo, the RCA code link was the only one left to the Consul for sending messages. This meant commercial cable traffic, but neither the Army nor the Navy thought to upgrade the priority to hasten decryption and translation of this code traffic because of its new importance. This is where an array of hideous errors occurred.

One of the other messages sent and intercepted on December 3 read:

R.C.A.

No. 362   3 DEC 1941
From: Kita
To: Foreign Minister Tokyo
      Consul San Francisco
URGENT REPORT
1. Military transport (name unknown) departed for mainland on 2nd.
2. Lurline arrived from San Francisco on 3rd.

Another message on December 3 read:

R.C.A.

No.   3 Dec. 1941
From: Kita
To: FM Tokyo #363
Wyoming and two seaplane tenders departed third.

Another message went out on December 4, reading:

R.C.A.

No. 364   4 Dec. 1941
From: Kita
To: FM Tokyo
PM/3rd one British warship arrived Honolulu and departed early morning fourth X approximately 100 tons one stack one four inch gun fwd and aft X Fueled?
Immediately after arrival enlisted rating(s) received mail from British consulate.

This precise surveillance ended any doubt I might have had that the Japanese had established competent naval observers in Honolulu.

But even as late as 1946, when Capt. Arthur H. McCollum, the head of the Far Eastern Section of Naval Intelligence (Washington), testified before the Congressional Committee investigating Pearl Harbor, he contended this was not true, saying: "It was my feeling then, and is my feeling now, that the Japanese had been unable to put Naval observers into the Consulate General in Hawaii.'' McCollum admitted that the Navy knew the Japanese had such observers in Seattle, San Francisco, the Los Angeles–San Diego area and Panama. But how the former Chief of the Far Eastern Section of Naval intelligence could swear to Congress that the Japanese didn't have such an observer in Hawaii is beyond my comprehension, especially when he said he knew that the Japanese Consul in Honolulu had received specific instructions from Tokyo to report on the movement of our ships.[3]

Thus, Kimmel had in his possession—via his subordinates Admiral Bloch, Commandant of the Fourteenth Naval District, Captain Mayfield and Commander Rochefort by their receipt of these five Japanese messages from RCA—derivative knowledge that the Japanese were keeping close watch on Pearl Harbor. And Captain Layton, the Fleet Intelligence Officer, had acknowledged to me that he knew of the arrangement whereby RCA was turning these cables over to Captain Mayfield.

Why weren't the cables translated quickly, because of their new-found importance (the PA-K2 code being the only one left for the Japanese Consul to use)? According to Captain Safford's testimony to the Hewitt Inquiry (page 109), the system had been used for several years and was easily read by our code breakers. I concluded every effort should have been given to breaking these messages.

The reason this effort was not made was that Rochefort was overwhelmed by his concentration on cracking the unbreakable Japanese Naval Code for flag officers, which was introduced on December 1, 1940, and the pressure to locate the Japanese fleet. He wanted more personnel to help handle the workload, but to avoid acrimony, he refrained from asking Washington for this help. Next, Rochefort found that among the important PA-K2 code messages there were a lot of "garbage cables." This made him reluctant to assign staff to wade through so much rubbish. Finally, he told a warrant officer named Woodward to do the job. Woodward was able to read the PA-K2 code, but he erroneously stacked the pile of cables in inverse order of date, making the code sequences impossible to crack. It took four days for him to discover his error, by which time the attack had already occurred.[4]

---

[3] PHA Hearings, pt. 8, p. 3391.
[4] PHH 26/363; Edwin P. Layton, *And I Was There*, New York: Morrow, 1985, pp. 162–163, 244, 278 ff.

The most telling point in all this was the fact that Kimmel possessed within his own command information identical or similar to the information he so vociferously claimed Washington had denied him.

I will never forget sitting in the Hawaiian office of the Navy's Fourteenth District Intelligence Officer assembling all this documentary proof. I wondered why the Army Board and others had failed earlier to do the work I was now doing. And I remembered how Warrant Officer Emanuel told me that when he executed Mayfield's order to stop tapping the telephones of the Japanese Consulate, he closed out his log by writing *"Sic transit gloria mundi."*

11 ‖ NOT ON DUTY

The war might have ended and my search for witnesses might have been nearing its end, but in 1945 the controversy about the Winds Code was still going strong.

Captian Safford had testified to the Navy that a broadcast that implemented the Winds Code had been intercepted but ignored. He also claimed the records of this interception had been destroyed. So, despite all the evidence to the contrary I had dug up to date from my Army witnesses, there were still some loose ends to be tied up.

One of these was Col. Harold Doud. Before Pearl Harbor, he had been in charge of B Section of the SIS, which was the Code and Cipher Section. His duties were to supervise the "solution" (the breaking and translating) of Japanese radio intercepts for both the diplomatic and the military sides.

We discussed the original Winds Code message of November 19, 1941.[1] Doud said that when the intercept was translated, the Army immediately made arrangements to monitor Tokyo radio for a broad-

[1] See appendix, SIS 25432, p. 322.

cast that would be the so-called execute message. But, said Doud, "I did not see any execute message as thus contemplated and, so far as I know, there was no such execute message received in the War Department."

I asked Doud to review Safford's testimony to the Navy that the execute message had been intercepted. Safford had even gone so far as to say that Doud might have had knowledge of the execute intercept. Doud refuted Safford.

"I do not know the basis for this testimony by Captain Safford," Doud said, "as I do not have any information of an execute message."

Doud also confirmed for me that it took an average of two days for the Army to process the PA-K2 codes, which led me to conclude that the only way the Army could have processed the two intercepted messages of December 6 any faster would have been to have machines doing the work. This was something I would have to check out.

Another item Doud mentioned confirmed my belief in Dusenbury's story about having received the fourteenth part of the Japanese diplomatic message on the night of December 6. This meant, of course, that there had been a truly great failure in Washington to distribute that vital fourteenth paragraph. If Washington had received the message at around midnight on December 6, we would have had an additional nine hours of warning. But for reasons yet unknown to me, we had failed to use the time.

The problem was that I couldn't track this down all by myself. It was more than an Army matter.

The Army's responsibility for distributing intercepted Japanese messages ended at midnight on December 6. Because of the crazy way the "boogie-woogie" distribution system was set up, the responsibility for translating the Magic decrypts became the Navy's starting at 12:01 A.M. (or 00:01 hours military time) on December 7, 1941. Digging into what the Navy would consider its own secret internal affairs was not within my authority. But there's more than one way to skin a cat, I told myself. The trick was finding the right way to do it. It would require time and patience.

I then took a second affidavit from Lt. Col. Frank B. Rowlett, whom I had asked to do some additional checking for me. I had asked him to study the time it took to process the messages in the PA-K2 codes, which was how the Army had designated the codes in which the two messages of December 6 from Honolulu to Tokyo were sent.

The average processing time for nineteen intercepted messages within the period of November 1 to December 6, 1941, was three and a half days. This figure was based on the number of messages that were actually "published," or distributed throughout Army channels. In other words, there had been little or no chance that the Army—or even the Navy—might have processed a message intercepted late in the day on December 6 so that adequate warning could be gained from it.

Rowlett also confirmed for me that we were unable to read totally any Japanese army or Japanese Military Attaché codes before the outbreak of war. (Our Navy had been equally unsuccessful in breaking the Japanese J-19 naval code up to that time.)

I was interested to know how the Army had processed the all-important messages of December 6, including the fourteen-part diplomatic message. Rowlett recalled the day, saying it was the first time the Army had used a teletype to transmit intercepted material between San Francisco and Washington.

I thought this was rather unusual, what with the speed of processing seemingly so important, but Rowlett was definite that "this was the *first* time the Army had used teletype facilities to forward traffic to Signals Intelligence." He had actually helped to operate the equipment in the old Munitions Building that day, and he remembered that the first call to initiate the circuit was placed sometime after six P.M. on December 6. (The situation was even more bizarre because it was a Saturday. His operation usually only worked until midday on Saturday, which meant that people had to be called in from home.)

Washington's request for teletype service of that day's intercepts caught San Francisco unaware. They already had forwarded all the current intercepts via air mail, and they complained that they would have to use the station's file copy to prepare the intercepts for teletype. This required punching tape, and it took some time to get the tapes ready. To the best of Rowlett's recollection, this intercept traffic was received from San Francisco just after midnight Washington time.

As I have said earlier in my narrative, Rowlett struck me as being one of those totally honest, precise, creative code-breaking experts. He had double-checked the chart as I had requested (see page 104). He tacitly agreed that the second message numbered 25843 was the entire fourteen-part diplomatic message and that it had been received in its entirety around midnight on December 6, give or take fifteen minutes on either side. Now I had documentary evidence that supported Dusenbury's shocking statement to me that he had *all* fourteen parts of the message in hand that night, but had failed to deliver them as ordered to General Marshall.

Rowlett gave me some additional leads. I next interviewed Capt. Howard Martin, who had been the Non-Commissioned Officer (NCO) in charge of San Francisco's station number 2 on the evening of December 6, 1941. He remembered being in his quarters at Fort Scott about eight P.M. San Francisco time when the phone rang. The man on duty at the station said that Washington had called via teletype, asking for a transmission of all that day's intercepted traffic. It was Saturday night, Martin recalled, and he had only one man on duty. The other personnel were not easy to reach. In other words, they were off base with weekend passes, so Martin went to the station immediately and began punching tape to transmit all of Saturday's raw intercepted traffic. (The original traffic had been air-mailed as usual to Washington at four that afternoon.) Martin was also positive that the teletype, or TWX (pronounced "twix") machine had never been used before to send intercepts. As he blandly put it: "Because the following day the Japanese bombed Pearl Harbor, I have always associated [those] things in my memory."

Well, well, I thought. Here we have a man who did things right on December 6. He was once a sergeant, now he's a captain. I recalled an old saying: It's the good sergeants who really run the Army.

In a roundabout way, I was zeroing in on what I wanted to know: the significance of the Army's use of the TWX machine.

I then deposed Mary J. Dunning, who was currently working for the Signal Security Agency. She, too, remembered the evening of December 6 with great clarity.

Her shop in Washington usually closed down at one P.M. on Saturdays, and that day she left at the usual time to go home. Around two-thirty that afternoon, Colonel Minckler's office phoned, asking that she return as soon as possible. By three P.M., she was back in Minckler's office, "ready to work." She remembered the time precisely, because later on she was asked to come back on Sunday, December 7, at the same time. She asked if she could come in at five P.M. instead, since she was planning to drive out of town.

"I can't recall being told why we were called back to work [on December 6]," she told me, "but the general assumption was that we wanted to process traffic without delay since the Japanese Ambassador was in conference with the President." This wasn't exactly the case, of course, but it was close enough, I thought. It just went to show that if the Army wanted to spend the time and money to do something properly, it could darn well do it. But why hadn't it put this type of priority on handling the intercepts before this?

Ms. Dunning recalled: "I was asked to work in the 'cage' [a room where machine traffic was processed—so called because it had grill-work at its entrance to restrict admittance], where I had not worked for some time. I think that as I entered the room, I was surprised to see a teletype machine. How long it had been installed, I don't know, but it could not have been for more than a few hours, since I often had occasion to go to the door of the cage and it was clearly visible from the door."

Around four P.M., the teletype company sent some representatives around to instruct Dunning and the others on how to use the machine. After that, everyone practiced using the TWX.

Dunning said that waiting for something to happen always seems to take longer than it actually does, and she was expecting traffic from San Francisco at any moment. She was getting hungry, but could not leave the cage because no one knew when San Francisco would begin transmitting. She couldn't even take time to go out and buy a sandwich. She recalled asking Minckler about it, because she was joking with him "about my teaching *him* to operate the teletype."

A full-bird colonel learning how to use a TWX machine, I thought. Now, that's a refreshing change. Another good man.

When did the transmission from San Francisco end?

That is the key question, as we will see later.

"I believe I went home around midnight or 1 A.M.," said Dunning. There was nothing more to do.

Dunning also recalled processing traffic from San Francisco, the Philippines and Honolulu that evening. "I cannot say, however, whether it came to us by teletype or not, since the Message Center had been asked to deliver traffic to us as soon as it arrived," Dunning explained.

I was positive that the fourteenth part was received around midnight on December 6, just before Dunning went home. Once again, it was just as Dusenbury had sworn in his testimony, which has never been contradicted in the past fifty years.

Before I delve further into the matter of what happened to the fourteenth part of the all-important diplomatic message, let me conclude my investigation with my final witness, Louise Prather of the Signal Security Agency.

She, too, clearly remembered the night of December 6, 1941. As she recalled: "I was called at home and told our unit was being placed on a 24-hour basis immediately and that I should report for work at 7 A.M. the following morning, 7 December. When I arrived at the office at this unusual hour, I learned that the teletype was being operated and the reason for the urgent call had been to process this and other traffic as rapidly as possible."

The material Prather spoke of was yet another intercept from Tokyo instructing the Japanese diplomats in Washington to deliver the fourteen-part message about the break in relations between the two countries to our State Department at one o'clock that afternoon (Washington time), which would be approximately dawn at Pearl Harbor.[2] This meant the vital delivery time was in hand at least six hours before the bombs started falling.

I was concerned that the Army had not used the teletype before this to transmit important intercepts to the War Department. The Navy had been using teletypes. Why hadn't the Army? Why hadn't it been more on top of the situation? I regret to say that I didn't learn the answer right away, possibly because the discovery of what had happened to the fourteenth part of the diplomatic message was more important than deciding what was wrong with the system of intelligence processing used by both services.

During the course of my investigation, I had passed on to Sonnett, the Chief Counsel for the Hewitt Investigation, what I had learned from Dusenbury about the fourteenth part of the diplomatic message. In turn, Sonnett had pressed that inquiry into areas that made some people in the Navy highly uncomfortable.

According to these Navy witnesses, the fourteenth part of the diplomatic message, the notice that the Japanese were breaking off relations, was in English, and the Navy officer on watch thought he had delivered it to the Army sometime after midnight, which also supports Dusenbury's story.[3]

The message telling the Japanese diplomats in Washington to hand over the fourteen-part reply at one P.M. Sunday came in sometime between 3:05 A.M. and seven A.M. on December 7. It was processed by the Navy and sent to the Army for translation from Japanese into

---

[2] See appendix, SIS 25850, p. 351.
[3] PHA Hearings, pt. 36, p. 532.

English at seven A.M. on December 7. The Army translated the message and returned it to the Navy at about ten that morning.[4]

The question that kept niggling at me was this: It appeared that the Navy had broken the agreed-upon rules for translating the Magic material. The Navy was supposed to handle these translations on the odd-numbered days of the month, and December 7 was an odd-numbered day. Why didn't the Navy have a translator on duty from midnight to seven A.M. at the Navy Department?

The man who handled these translation duties, Capt. Alwin D. Kramer, testified to Sonnett that it would have taken him only "about two minutes" at 3:05 A.M. to translate the final and separate message instructing the diplomats to deliver the fourteen-part message to Secretary Hull at one P.M. Sunday.[5] But Kramer had gone home to sleep that night after having delivered the first thirteen parts of the fourteen-part message to the White House, Secretary of the Navy Knox and various admirals. (His wife drove him around town in making these deliveries.) Before going home, Kramer testified, he checked back with the office, found no new intelligence had come in, and ordered the watch officer to telephone him immediately upon the receipt of *any* further Japanese message. This had been done several times in the past. He lived only ten to fifteen minutes away from the Navy Department. A trip back to the Department was easy.[6]

No one called him.

So, once again, while Washington slept, from three to nine precious hours were lost, this time by the Navy, in terms of our having one last chance to alert our forces in the Pacific.

Kramer insisted that he understood the significance of the final part of the fourteen-part message, and also the meaning of the one P.M. delivery time. It meant war.

Instead of delivering these available messages in the predawn hours of Washington time, it was not until around nine A.M. on December 7 that Kramer returned to the office to deliver both messages simultaneously to Captain McCollum in Admiral Stark's office. The two men conferred. There was a map on the wall of Kramer's office showing the different time zones around the world, and he pointed out to McCollum that one P.M. Washington time would mean seven-thirty in the morning Honolulu time, or approximately sunrise. It would also

---

[4] Ibid.
[5] Ibid., p. 349.
[6] Ibid., p. 348.

be two A.M. in the Philippines. The exact significance of these Pacific times was not understood, but if an attack were coming, it looked as if it were timed for operations in the Far East, or possibly on Hawaii.[7]

McCollum took the messages from Kramer and gave them to Stark, telling Stark about Kramer's comments on the time zones and the potential threat of attack. McCollum testified: "We had no way of knowing, but because of the fact that the exact time for delivery of this note had been stressed to the ambassadors, we felt there were important things which would move at that time, and that was pointed out . . . to Admiral Stark. . . ."[8]

In making his other deliveries that Sunday morning, Kramer pointed out the importance of the time zones to Secretary of State Hull's private secretary and to Colonel Bratton (who also happened to be in Hull's outer office at the moment). All in all, Kramer said he told about eight to ten people of the significance of the timing for the Japanese reply.[9]

What all this meant was that when Kramer began his deliveries after nine A.M., there were only three hours left to warn Pearl Harbor. It might have been enough time if all had gone well in Marshall's office and with his attempt to send a last-second warning to Short. But two other truly fateful errors had been committed earlier: one was Dusenbury's failure to deliver the decrypts to Marshall, or the other Army recipients, and the other was the Navy's failure to have a translator on hand at the crucial moment after midnight on Sunday morning.

The question of why the Navy was processing the diplomatic messages on December 6 still hadn't been answered to my satisfaction, however. The Army was supposed to process the intercepted material on the even-numbered days. And Kramer went so far as to mislead Sonnett by swearing that "the Navy was responsible [for the sixth of December], [the messages] being in the key that the Navy was handling that day." This was false testimony.

It wasn't until much later, after I had read all the testimony before the Hewitt Board and the Congressional Committee, that I understood. The key that Kramer spoke of had nothing to do with the matter at hand.

It all came back to the fact that before December 6, the Navy was

---

[7] Ibid., p. 531.
[8] Ibid.
[9] Ibid., p. 532.

receiving intercepts from its listening posts by teletype, while the Army was still using air mail.

To explain: The Navy received the first intercepts of the fourteen-part diplomatic message via teletype on December 6, and began processing them instead of sending them immediately to the Army.[10] Apparently, this was done on the orders of Rear Adm. Leigh Noyes, the chief of the Navy's Communications Division.

According to Safford's testimony before Congress in 1946,[11] the first "five or six parts of the long 14-part message were received in the Navy Department, I believe, about ten minutes to twelve, just before noon [on Saturday, December 6]." The Naval Duty Officer telephoned his Army counterpart and learned that the Army was securing (closing down) its office at one P.M. "because they were observing the normal working hours prescribed by the Civil Service Commission."

According to the working agreement between the Army and the Navy dated November 12, 1941, the Army was supposed to process the messages on the even days of the month and the Navy on the odd-numbered days. This meant that only one service at a time was supposed to do the decoding, the "exclusion" of the code, the translation and the final preparation for delivery. (The Navy made all deliveries to the White House, and the Army to the Secretary of State.)

This explains the callback of the Army communications people to their offices on Saturday, December 6. The Navy was running on all eight cylinders; the Army was playing post office. It also explains the Army's belated installation of a TWX machine at headquarters to communicate with its intercept stations. But while the Navy had properly evaluated the situation on December 6, it could not handle by itself the mass of material that flooded in. It had to call on the Army for help that afternoon in processing portions of the first thirteen parts of the fourteen-part message.

The culmination of all this was that while Noyes was right to order the Navy to work on the intercepts on December 6, even though it wasn't the Navy's day to do so, the Navy did not have the requisite number of translators to handle the load on December 7. Kramer was a one-man band. He had to go home and sleep, relying on the watch officer to wake him. But this the watch officer failed to do.

[10] PHA Hearings, pt. 8, p. 3744.
[11] Ibid., p. 3558.

So, when Congress pinned down this failure, the testimony went like this:

> Mr. Murphy [Counsel to the Committee]: Is it not a fact that shortly after 5 o'clock (A.M.) [on December 7], or 7 hours before Pearl Harbor, in your department, while you were not in your department, they knew that the warning was given that 1 o'clock (P.M.) was the deadline? Isn't that right?
>
> Captain Safford: Brotherhood [the watch officer] did, that is correct. . . .
>
> Mr. Murphy: Where were you at 5 o'clock in the morning [of December 7]?
>
> Captain Safford: I was at home.
>
> Mr. Murphy: At home. The fact is further that the 7th was the Navy day for translating, was it not?
>
> Captain Safford: Yes.
>
> Mr. Murphy: There was no interpreter who knew Japanese in your department, was there?
>
> Captain Safford: There was not.
>
> Mr. Murphy: And you are over at home at a time when you think war is coming, because you have told this committee that war was coming on Saturday or Sunday, you knew that there is going to be a time fixed which will fix the deadline and you leave on Saturday afternoon at 4:30, and you do not inquire as to anyone under you until after the war has started; that is right?
>
> Captain Safford: That is right. . . .
>
> Mr. Murphy: The fact is that you had no interpreter there on the day you expected war to start, did you? Kramer was a subordinate of yours. You had no interpreter there, did you?
>
> Captain Safford: We had no interpreter there at the time.
>
> Mr. Murphy: The 7th was the Navy's day?
>
> Captain Safford: Yes, sir.
>
> Mr. Murphy: And it was the day that you expected war to start, wasn't it?
>
> Captain Safford: Yes, sir.
>
> Mr. Murphy: And you are still in your pajamas having breakfast at 2 o'clock [Sunday afternoon]?

Captain Safford: Yes, sir.

Mr. Murphy: Do you have any sense of responsibility for the failure of this 1 o'clock message to get to the proper people in time? Do you feel responsible?

Captain Safford: Not in the least. . . .[12]

Now, that is a pretty rough bit of cross-examination. And, in fairness to Safford, he claimed he went home on Saturday because he was totally worn out. Physically, he didn't believe he could have done any more. The greatest problem in his professional assignment was that of mental breakdowns. There had been several in his department. Safford was afraid he might be next. His not feeling any responsibility for the failure to handle the intercepts more expeditiously, however, was to my mind another symptom of the Navy's arrogance in its handling of intelligence.

On the other side of the coin, one must say that if Washington had relied solely upon Army intelligence, and its penny-pinching air-mail delivery of crucial intercepts, the fourteen-part diplomatic message and the all-important final message saying when the news should be given to our State Department would not have been decoded, translated and delivered until *after* Pearl Harbor.

The point I wish to make is that the intelligence-gathering process of the time was not up to the job. The system for handling communications intelligence was neither operationally efficient nor accurate in its analytical predictions. And while the two services might have paid lip service to the concept of mutual cooperation, when it came to the crunch, their good intentions were nothing more than that. Their rivalry had to be stopped. A single, centralized intelligence service had to be created. God forbid that because of a similar intelligence failure, we might endure a second Pearl Harbor. One with nuclear weapons.

[12] Ibid., pp. 3716–3717.

12 | SENTRIES WHO FAILED

At last! I was finished taking affidavits, the war had ended, and I was champing at the bit to return to San Francisco and resume my law practice. But I still had work to do for Secretary Stimson.

First, I had to prepare all the documents and exhibits that were to be included in my report. When I completed this task, I submitted the three Top Secret volumes it comprised. Within forty-eight hours, I received a call from General Marshall's office commending me, and asking that I serve as Marshall's lawyer before the forthcoming Congressional hearings.

"I'm sorry," I said, "but much as I am honored and might like the assignment, I should not accept the request. I am sure General Marshall will understand. I was appointed an investigator with judicial powers. Having exercised these judicial powers, it would be improper for me to represent the General before Congress. Please thank the General and explain why I must decline."

I also smelled a trap. As an attorney for Marshall, I might not be able to testify fully before the Congressional or any other hearings, my lips being sealed because of the attorney-client relationship.

The next day, I received another call from Marshall's office. The General understands your position, the caller told me. He agrees with it completely. Meanwhile, he wants you to know that he believes your report is superb.

I was pleased by the accolade.

Next, Colonel Hughes and I had to draft for the signature of the Judge Advocate General rebuttals to the two Army Pearl Harbor Board reports (one having been given Secret categorization and the other Top Secret). Our drafts would be reviewed by all the powers that be in the Army, but would bear the final signature of Judge Advocate General Myron Cramer. Lastly, we would have to draft a concluding statement that Secretary of War Stimson would release to the public concerning his inquiry into Pearl Harbor.

I have been asked why I did not write a conclusion to my own report. There are a number of explanations. First, I was working for the Army, which means that one often does things in ways that are not compatible with writing history. For example, I could not openly criticize the Navy. On the other hand, no one has known until now that I actually wrote the statements signed by the Judge Advocate General and the Secretary of War, either. I can only say that these statements are excellent summaries of my conclusions, with the exception that the penalty imposed on General Short (and also on Admiral Kimmel) was less than what I, and Secretary Stimson, believed was called for.

Secondly, Colonel Hughes and I hoped that historians would read the report and make up their own minds about it. I can see now, though, that without help in wading through its complexities, this could be a daunting task, and might discourage anyone who failed to ask for guidance. And, as I said earlier, no one ever asked.

Lastly, when I finished my report in 1945, any conclusion I might have written would have imperiled our continuing intelligence operations, especially since under General Bissell, the Army had continued breaking the Japanese diplomatic codes after the war's end. This proved to be most useful in the way General MacArthur governed newly defeated Japan. (The Army had successfully kept from the Japanese the news that we had broken their diplomatic codes, and we encouraged the Japanese to keep using their so-called unbreakable Purple machines. This the Japanese did until Congress took it upon itself to reveal that we had broken the Purple codes.)

Anyway, there I was, back in room 4D852 of the Pentagon in September 1945, talking with Colonel Hughes about the possible punishments to be inflicted on the individuals responsible for Pearl Harbor. After all, Congress had ordered the Secretary of War to seek courts-martial against the guilty parties. Among the subjects we talked about were that such guilt could have involved perfidy, dereliction of duty or errors of judgement.

It was then that I told Colonel Hughes about my theory that Short and Kimmel were like sentries who had failed in their duty. "A sentry is supposed to be posted as a guard of a group to warn them of danger," I said. "Being alert, the sentry would give such warning. If we strip from the case all the military jargon that's been loaded into it, we find that Kimmel and Short were supposed to be sentries. It all boils down to that single, simple issue. The fact is that they failed to do their job."

Hughes, who knew far more about Army procedures than did I, said he could accept my analogy. He was sure that the Judge Advocate General would, too. It would also be proper to include this concept in any recommendation that might be made to the Secretary of War. We were both aware that the Army's practice of removing a man from command was considered by the military a harsh enough penalty to prevent any further indictment. We also knew that we were dealing with the worst defeat in American military history, and who could tell which way the sword of justice would fall in a public trial?

A few days later, on another bright, clear, Washington morning, Harvey Bundy called me into his office to meet with Secretary Stimson and review what we had proposed for his statement to the public.

When the Secretary came to the portion of the statement that discussed the concept of Short and Kimmel as sentries, even though we were supposed to deal only with Army issues, Stimson asked me to expand on my concept. I explained it to him, including the comment by a veteran of World War I who told me that his outfit had always picked cowards to serve as sentries because they were too afraid to fall asleep at their post. I then gave it a little more erudition. Kimmel and Short, I said, were like the shut-eye sentries in Kipling's famous poem "The Shut-Eye Sentry":

> ". . . So it was 'Rounds!' What 'Rounds?'
> At two of a frosty night.
> 'E's 'olden on by the Sergeant's sash, but, Sentry,
> shut your eye."

Bundy laughed: "First rate, Henry!"

Stimson also laughed, saying: "Yes! I'll adopt that. Those men *were* sentries, if you consider all the ramifications, the tremendous responsibilities that both men shared, with vast, interlocking critical operations, and the fact that both men were surprised. 'Surprise loomed like a giant ogre,' " he quoted. "I have searched my mind for the twist of brief illustration in this matter, and I think what you have proposed is perfect. In reality, the American nation first and foremost depended upon those men to prepare for war. Instead, they both confessed surprise."

"They were like the drivers of automobiles who, after an accident, would try to excuse themselves and say, 'I did not see the other car,' " I said. "In law, they must still be held responsible. It is no excuse if they looked, but failed to see. The law says that to look is to see. Our field commanders said they looked, but did not see, so they were the equivalent of shut-eye sentries."

Stimson nodded in agreement.

"Our real problem," I continued, "is what charges we should bring against General Short. I believe we should consider whether he is guilty of perfidy, or dereliction or neglect of duty, along with Kimmel and some others. On the other hand, I am sure the Judge Advocate General, after considering the far-reaching instance of secondary fault (such as the failures I discovered of the Navy to share intelligence with the Army), will decide differently. He will recommend that for a distinguished soldier such as Short, after a long and successful career, relief from command is an electrifying and satisfactory punishment. We also have other factors to consider. We cannot impose punishment on a military man in the same way we would a civilian. Lastly, we have the problem of national security. If we convene a court-martial, Short will have every right to disclose our interception and decoding of Purple as part of his defense. We cannot allow that to happen, especially when General Bissell has convinced the Japanese to continue using Purple for their diplomatic codes. At this time, we are monitoring their traffic for the benefit of General MacArthur's headquarters.

"My recommendation, therefore," I continued, "is to let Short off with what many might consider a mere slap on the wrist: relief from command because he was guilty of serious errors of judgement. But the strength of the language in your final statement for the public will provide a final, damning, unanswerable fitness report that neither General Short nor Admiral Kimmel can evade in the years to come."

Stimson gave me a long, hard, judicial look.

"I believe you may be correct, Henry. I'll consider the question of culpability further, for I, too, believe that the punishment shall fit the crime." He paused, then continued: "I also believe you have a valid point about not judging military men according to civilian standards. They are separate worlds. Your comments about national security are irrefutable. But I need time to think about this."

I could see that the matter was causing Stimson deep concern. I withdrew and returned to my office.

A few days later, Stimson called us back into his office to announce that after much deliberation, he had decided to find Short guilty only of errors of judgement. Portions of his statement to the public would contain the following phrases: "The end of hostilities now makes it possible for me to make public much more fully my conclusions without such serious danger to the public security as to outweigh the desirability of such publication. [However], it is still not in the public interest to disclose sources of information. . . ." Thus, my report would be classified Top Secret and unavailable to the public.

Stimson had accepted all my recommendations about the failures of the Hawaiian commands of the Army and the Navy to adequately perform their duties. He also agreed with my findings that the two reports of the Army Pearl Harbor Board were inaccurate and should be rebutted by the Judge Advocate General, giving chapter and verse for why this should be done without breaking security.

Among the findings of my report that Stimson agreed to make public were the following:

- General Short had the primary and immediate responsibility for the protection of Pearl Harbor.
- General Short was repeatedly and sufficiently advised of the critical developments with Japan, and that a break in diplomatic relations between America and Japan might occur at any time.
- General Short had been adequately informed that the defense of his command was paramount to all other considerations.
- General Short was ordered to take such measures of reconnaissance as he deemed necessary, but failed to do so.
- General Short acknowledged in his testimony that it was traditional policy for the commanding officer to anticipate and be prepared for the worst form of possible attack. He acknowledged that he had been told by the Army's Chief of Staff, Marshall, that a surprise air raid and submarine attack constituted the principal perils to Hawaii. Yet, he failed to prepare against such attacks.

- General Short failed to use fully or properly the radar air warning service.
- General Short failed to discover what reconnaissance the Navy was carrying out, or to collaborate as ordered with the Navy in this regard.
- General Short failed to have his antiaircraft defenses manned or provided with ready ammunition.
- These failures resulted from vital errors of judgement.

In fairness to Short, it must be remembered that the belief that Japan would not attack Pearl Harbor was widely shared, including among some of his superior officers in the War Department in Washington. Short also knew that the Naval command at Pearl Harbor, which he thought to be better informed than he was because of the Navy's wide-ranging facilities, also believed that an attack on Pearl Harbor was unlikely. Yet, Short knew that an air attack on Pearl Harbor, even if improbable, was possible. He was the more responsible defender of Hawaii. He had no right to subordinate himself to the guesstimates of another service about his duty to be prepared against what he knew to be the most dangerous form of attack on his outpost.

Stimson would continue his report, saying:

- Certain information existed in the War Department that was not sent to General Short. If it had been sent, it might have sharpened Short's perception of the imminence of war. But portions of this information had been sent to Admiral Kimmel by the Navy. I had written the following for Stimson, and he included it verbatim: **"It was the rule that all such information should be exchanged between the Army and the Navy at Pearl Harbor, and the War Department had a right to believe that this information communicated to Adm. Kimmel was also available to Gen. Short. While Adm. Kimmel and Gen. Short were on very friendly terms and in frequent communication, the exchange of information as well as consultation in other respects at Hawaii between the Army and the Navy were *inadequate*."**
- Colonel Clausen's report proved that the information the Army Pearl Harbor Board claimed Short did not possess had, in fact, been given to General Short by his staff before December 7, 1941.
- Colonel Clausen's report proved that the Army Board's criticism of Chief of Staff Marshall was wrong.
- Lastly, the "theatre commander such as General Short, who was

like a sentinel on post and whose attention and vigilance must be entirely concentrated on the single position which he has been chosen to defend and whose alertness must not be allowed to be distracted by consideration of other contingencies . . . failed in his mission.''

Stimson's report carried the case against Short and Kimmel as far as national security would allow. Stimson did not reveal that we had broken the Japanese codes before the war. He did not breach faith with the fact that, under General Bissell's orders, we had kept the Japanese supplied with Purple code machines after the war and were monitoring the secret diplomacy of the new Japanese government operating under the rule of General MacArthur. Stimson did not seek any form of court-martial or other disciplinary hearing, even though Congress had ordered that this be done.

As my good friend Leon Jaworski, the Watergate prosecutor, used to say: Don't indict and go to trial unless you have a better than even chance of winning before a jury. Given the inhibition or impossibility of compromising vital secrets that would be necessary for a full presentation of evidence at the time, September 1945, Stimson's course of action was the wisest one to take.

Nevertheless, I believed then, as I still believe now, that Short and Kimmel were guilty of more than errors of judgement.

Although vested with high commands and responsibilities, they were surprised by the attack. They were unprepared for war. Thus, they were really guilty of criminal neglect of duty.

13 ‖ ERRORS OF JOINT COMMAND

Now, if we were to have waived our inhibitions about national security, and if a case were to have been made against Kimmel and Short, this is how I would have presented it.

The primary duty of Short and Kimmel was to protect the fleet.

This was made clear by the Secretary of the Navy, Frank Knox, who wrote a letter to his counterpart, the Secretary of War, Henry Stimson, on January 24, 1941, which said:

> If war eventuates with Japan, it is believed easily possible that hostilities would be initiated by a surprise attack upon the fleet or the naval base at Pearl Harbor. The dangers envisaged, in order of their importance and probability, are considered to be (1) air bombing attack, (2) air torpedo plane attack, (3) sabotage, (4) submarine attack. . . .[1]

The fears of the Navy in Washington could not have been expressed more clearly.

[1] APHB, p. 369.

Stimson agreed with this assessment. He replied by letter to Knox on February 7, 1941, saying: "I am forwarding a copy of your letter and this reply to the Commanding General of the Hawaiian Department [Short], and am directing him to cooperate with the local naval authorities in making these measures effective."[2]

If Short had difficulty understanding what the civilian heads of the Navy and War Departments wanted him to do, he was given additional instructions by Chief of Staff Marshall.

On the same day that Stimson replied to Knox, Marshall wrote to Short, saying: "My impression of the Hawaiian problem has been that if no serious harm is done us the first six hours of known hostilities, thereafter the existing defenses would discourage an enemy against the hazard of an attack. The risk of sabotage and the risk involved in a surprise raid by air and by submarine constitute the real perils of the situation. . . . Please keep clearly in mind in all your negotiations that our mission is to protect the base and the Naval concentration. . . ."[3]

A month later, on March 5, 1941, Marshall again wrote Short, to say: "I would appreciate your early review of the situation in the Hawaiian Department with regard to defense from air attack. The establishment of a satisfactory system of coordinating all means available to this end is *a matter of first priority*. . . ."[4]

There can be no claim by Short that he didn't know what his primary mission might be. He acknowledged this in his testimony before the Army Board.

First, the Board was shown the Joint Air Operations Agreement that was a part of the Joint Coastal Frontier Defense Plan, which had been signed by Short. Addendum 1 of the Agreement read as follows:
(a) A declaration of war might be preceded by:
 1. A surprise submarine attack on ships in the operating area.
 2. A surprise attack on Oahu including ships and installations in Pearl Harbor.
 3. A combination of these two.[5]

In view of the Defense Plan, which had been agreed to by Washington, Short was asked a specific question.

[2] Ibid., p. 368.
[3] Ibid., pp. 13–17.
[4] Ibid., p. 101.
[5] Ibid., p. 388.

General Grunert: You were fully aware, then, of the possible surprise air attack?

General Short: Oh, yes.[6]

So, if Short was aware of his primary duty, where did he start to go wrong? Let us examine the testimony of General Martin about the Joint Air Operations Agreement.

General Grunert: Now, in there was an estimated possible enemy action, and you stated the high probability of a surprise dawn attack. Now, that was in the mind of you airmen at the time you drew up the agreement?

General Martin: Yes, sir.

General Grunert: Now, what was done to avoid such a surprise attack that you people thought was highly probable?

General Martin: Well, nothing more than what I stated. The search of the area was in the hands of the Navy.[7]

It was here, my investigation proved, that the lack of cooperation between the two services began its downward spiral—no joint action to provide radar reconnaissance, no joint action on air reconnaissance, no joint action to create an aircraft identification center, no antiaircraft ammunition deployed to the Army gunners. Above all, there was no effective, systematic liaison initiated by either Short or Kimmel between the Army and the Navy.

This was the complete opposite of what Washington had expected the two commanders to achieve.

What, then, about the fact that Kimmel and Short were supposed to cooperate with each other on a one-on-one basis?

My investigation proved that on at least eleven occasions, Kimmel withheld from Short vital intelligence information that, if it had been passed on properly, might have caused Short to go onto a full war alert. Let me list these examples:

1. Japanese carriers in Marshall Islands. On November 26, 1941, the Commandant of the Fourteenth Naval District (Hawaii), Adm.

[6] Ibid.
[7] Ibid., p. 1823.

Claude C. Bloch, sent a memo to the Chief of Naval Operations, Adm. Harold R. Stark, in Washington, giving his evaluation of the current situation. On the basis of radio intercepts, Bloch believed that a strong concentration of Japanese air groups and submarines (at least one carrier division and one-third of the overall submarine fleet) were located in the vicinity of the Marshall Islands. This meant that there was a definite threat to Hawaii.

Kimmel did not discuss this potential threat with Short.[8]

2. Long-range reconnaissance. As we know, the local agreement for joint action in the defense of the Hawaiian Islands stated that the Navy assumed responsibility for long-range aircraft reconnaissance.

It was also mutually agreed that the trigger to begin these flights would be the moment Kimmel and Short agreed that an enemy threat was imminent.

On November 27, Washington sent a special warning message to each commander. These messages should have triggered the agreement that an enemy threat was imminent and the requisite reconnaissance flights.

As my investigation proved, Short was ordered on November 27 to start reconnaissance and liaise with the Navy.

For his part, Kimmel was sent a specific "war warning" message that ordered him to effect an appropriate defensive deployment (meaning reconnaissance).[9]

Kimmel ordered his Fleet Intelligence Officer, Captain Layton, to "get this [message] to General Short right away." Instead of following orders and delivering personally the dispatch from Washington, which would have made a great impression on Short and perhaps given Layton and Short time to talk about its significance, Layton gave the message to an Army captain named Earl, to be given to Short when Earl returned to Fort Shafter. As Layton wrote in *And I Was There:* "It had displeased Kimmel when he later found out that I had not carried out his orders precisely."[10] But Layton salved his conscience by saying that he was sure that Short had received the message.

The importance that Kimmel had placed on an impressive delivery of the "war warning" was lost by Layton's obvious desire to step

---

[8] PHA Report, p. 133.
[9] Ibid., p. 116.
[10] *And I Was There*, p. 216.

aside and not be involved in the matter. (I will speak more about Layton's role in all this later.)

As we know from my investigation, Secretary Stimson had gone to extraordinary lengths to provide Short with radar that could spot planes at a distance of 130 miles from Hawaii. The use of radar reconnaissance for the protection of Pearl Harbor was Short's responsibility. He failed to exercise it.

Kimmel never asked Short if he had turned his radar on.

Nor did Kimmel tell Short that he had decided, on his own, not to conduct long-range reconnaissance flights.[11]

I had concluded during my investigation that Kimmel should be named as the party responsible for this overall failure. But I could not say so in my report, even though Stimson said some of it for me. Thus, I was gratified later when the Congressional report agreed with my analysis. The Congress found:

> The very fact of [Kimmel's] having made such a decision [not to conduct reconnaissance flights] placed upon him the responsibility that every other available means for reconnaissance was being employed to protect the fleet. His determination not to conduct long-range reconnaissance is of itself a recognition by him that it was his obligation to provide such reconnaissance. He knew that the Army was depending on him for certain defensive measures. Further, the fact that there was an agreement with the Army at Hawaii whereby the Navy was to perform distant reconnaissance placed upon Admiral Kimmel the obligation of advising General Short that he had decided not to conduct such reconnaissance. . . . Admiral Kimmel's clear duty, therefore, in the absence of Navy reconnaissance, was to confer with General Short to insure that Army radar, antiaircraft and planes were fully utilized and alerted. None of these things were done. . . .[12]

3. Kimmel and the Winds Code. On November 28, the Commander in Chief of the Asiatic Fleet, Adm. Ernest J. King, sent a dispatch to Admiral Stark in Washington—with a copy to Kimmel for his infor-

---

[11] PHH 7/3043: 32/254.
[12] PHA Report, p. 117.

mation—concerning the creation of the Winds Code by Tokyo. The Navy in Hawaii was ordered immediately to monitor future Japanese broadcasts for the broadcast that would have executed the plan.

Kimmel did not discuss the matter with Short.

4. More Winds Code. On December 1, Stark sent a dispatch to the Commander in Chief of the Asiatic Fleet (King)—with a copy for Kimmel—that gave the frequencies on which Tokyo would broadcast the execute message for the Winds Code.

Again, Kimmel didn't discuss the Winds Code with Short.

5. If war breaks out . . . On November 30, Kimmel instituted a daily memo called "Steps to Be Taken in Case of Japanese-American War Within the Next 24 Hours."

Kimmel did not send a copy to Short.

The memo was continued daily up to the time of the Japanese attack. But even by December 7, Kimmel, still acting as arbiter of what the Army should and should not be told, had failed to send a copy to Short.[13]

6. Tokyo orders its diplomats to destroy their codes and code machines. On December 3, Naval intelligence in Washington sent Kimmel not one, but *two* messages, saying that Tokyo was ordering Japanese diplomats around the world to destroy their codes and code machines. I have quoted them earlier, but it is wise to review them at this point.

The first message read:

> OPNAV, For action to: CINCAF, CINPAC [Kimmel], COM 14, COM 16, Dec 3, 1941
>
> Highly reliable information has been received that categoric and urgent instructions were sent yesterday to Japanese Diplomatic and Consular Posts at Hong Kong, Singapore, Batavia, Manila, Washington, and London to destroy most of their codes and ciphers at once and to burn all other important, confidential and secret documents.[14]

---

[13] Ibid., p. 152.
[14] Committee Exhibit 37, p. 40; PHA Report, p. 100.

The second message carried an even greater implication that war was imminent. It read:

OPNAV, For action to: CINCAF, COM 16, December 3, 1941 For information to: CINPAC [Kimmel], COM 14, COPEC

Circular Twenty Four Forty Four from Tokyo one December ordered London, Hong Kong, Singapore and Manila to *destroy Purple machine.* Batavia *machine* already sent to Tokyo. December second Washington Also Directed *Destroy Purple,* All But One Copy Of Other Systems, And All Secret Documents. British Admiralty London Today Reports Embassy London Has Complied.[15] (Emphasis added)

Given that four days before the outbreak of war, Kimmel was told that the enemy was destroying not only its codes, but also its *code machines,* an act that would occur only if the Japanese were on the very brink of hostilities, one would have thought that Kimmel would confer with Short about the matter.

The record shows that he did not, however.

Getting Kimmel to admit this in cross-examination was like pulling teeth. In his appearance before the Navy Court of Inquiry, Kimmel grudgingly admitted that he had received the messages from Washington, but withheld them from Short.[16]

Q: Can you recall, Admiral, whether or not you communicated the substance of these dispatches, Exhibits 21 and 22, relative to the destruction of codes, to the Commanding General of the Hawaiian Department prior to the Japanese attack on December 7?

A: I did not myself direct that these dispatches be delivered to him. If he states he did not see them, I presume he is correct.[17]

For his part, Short testified that he never received any information about these messages from Kimmel or his counterparts.

[15] Committee Exhibit 37, p. 41; PHA Report, p. 100.
[16] PHH, 36/135–137.
[17] Navy Court of Inquiry, 32/252–253.

Mr. Kaufman: Did you receive any information from
the Navy that they had been advised that the Japanese consular posts at Hong Kong and Singapore, and other places,
were ordered to destroy their codes?

General Short: I did not.

Mr. Kaufman: You received no such information from
the Navy at all?

General Short: No, sir.[18]

Short was adamant that such information would have been of the
greatest, action-producing importance in deciding which type of war
alert he ordered.

Earlier, he had told the Roberts Commission: "The one thing that
would have affected me more than the other matter was the fact
that they had ordered their *code machines* destroyed, because to us that
means just one thing—that they are going into an entirely new phase
and that they want to be perfectly sure that the code will not be broken
for a minimum time, say of three or four days. . . ."[19] (Emphasis
added)

As an independent investigator, I concluded that Kimmel's failure
to confer with Short about these messages was a major factor and fault
in the disaster of Pearl Harbor. Again, I was gratified to find out that
the Congress agreed with me in its final report, which said:

In strange contrast with the view of code burning intelligence taken by Admiral Kimmel, virtually *all* witnesses
have agreed that this was the most significant information
received between November 27 and December 6 with respect to the imminence of war. Indeed, the overwhelming
weight of the testimony is to [the] effect that orders to
destroy codes mean from a military standpoint only one
thing: war within a very few days. It is concluded that the
failure of Admiral Kimmel to supply this information to
General Short was inexcusable. . . .[20]

I also had told Stimson that I believed Kimmel and Short had been
adequately warned by Washington that war was about to break out.

[18] PHH, 7/2997.
[19] APHB, p. 1520; PHA Report p. 130.
[20] PHA Report, pp.130–131.

Again, I was gratified that Congress agreed with my investigation, in that its final report said: "From a review of the dispatches and correspondence sent Admiral Kimmel, it is concluded that he was fully informed concerning the progressive deterioration of relations with Japan and was amply warned of the imminence of war with that nation." [21]

The question that I was not allowed to ask Kimmel in my investigation was asked for me by Congress. Why had Kimmel withheld these two messages about the destruction of codes and code machines from Short?

"I didn't consider that [as] being of vital importance when I received it," Kimmel said. [22]

The statement by itself is stunning. It shows a complete lack of understanding of the code and code machine destruction messages by Kimmel and his Fleet Intelligence Officer, Captain Layton. Nevertheless, Kimmel shouldered the blame for it, just as Marshall had done for the failures of his subordinates. But in this case, it was *Kimmel who made the decision not to show the messages to Short.* This violated the fundamental rules about how Kimmel was to exchange information with his counterpart. It was a horrific decision. And it was made with the knowledge that the two men were to have a conference later the same day.

The joint action agreement demanded that this information be exchanged. The Navy and War Departments in Washington were completely entitled to believe that the exchange would take place. But Kimmel, on his own, decided not to give Short the information that would, or should, have galvanized Short into preparing for war.

Forty-five years after the fact, Captain Layton, now a rear admiral (retired), wrote in *And I Was There* that these two messages were too important for Kimmel to have told Short about them. Layton also claimed that Naval regulations prohibited Kimmel from giving Short such highly secret information unless specifically ordered to do so. (This was the same stance Layton had taken when I took his affidavit.) As Layton put it in his book: "Kimmel was abiding by the strict regulations governing dissemination of radio intelligence and, more-

[21] Ibid., p. 100.
[22] Committee Record, p. 7477; PHA Report, p. 130.

over, was unaware that the Army had not informed Short about Purple."[23]

Layton further tried to wriggle off the hook by claiming that he had passed this information about code burning and the destruction of the code machines on to Colonel Raley. In doing so, Layton said, he was careful not to mention Purple to Raley, because that, too, would have meant breaking "our strict security regulations."

As we know from my investigation, however, Layton did not tell the truth in his book, just as he did not tell me the truth back in 1945. One must conclude from the testimony of all parties involved that Layton's book is aimed at preserving Kimmel's reputation. This was necessary because Layton also had to cover up for his own failure to advise Kimmel properly about the significance of the messages in question.

As for anything that Layton might say or write about Naval regulations' stopping Kimmel from talking to Short about the messages from Washington: It is a total falsehood.

I get no pleasure in rebutting Layton. But I do have a certain glow of satisfaction that the conclusions I drew from my investigation were correct, and that they were supported by Chief of Staff Marshall, Secretary Stimson, one of the greatest public servants in the history of America, and the final report of the Congress of the United States. The latter summed up ten million words of testimony and exhibits in accordance with my findings.

The evidence is relentless in what we have seen. All the testimony, including that of men such as Willoughby and MacArthur, points to the conclusion that Kimmel was merely following the Naval practice of hoarding secret intelligence and using it for his own purposes.

This does not excuse Kimmel for what he did. But, for the first time, it explains *why* he did it.

7. Washington orders Guam to destroy its codes. On December 4, the Navy Department informed Kimmel on a "for your information" basis, that it had instructed our base on Guam to destroy all its secret and confidential publications and other classified matter (a refined way of saying "codes"), except what was needed for immediate use. In the

---

[23] *And I Was There*, p. 250.

event of emergency, Guam was to be prepared to destroy instantly all of its classified matter.[24]

For members of the Pacific Fleet, reading such a message should have sent shivers up and down their spines. It meant that Washington believed America would quickly be involved in war and Guam might fall to the Japanese.

Once again, Kimmel did not tell Short.

8. Tell your outlying commands to destroy their codes. On December 6, the Chief of Naval Operations cabled Kimmel *for action* that, because of the mounting danger of accelerating toward war and the exposed position of the outlying islands under his command, Kimmel was authorized to order these outposts to destroy their secret and confidential documents "now or under later conditions of greater emergency."

Kimmel did not pass this information on to Short.

In fact, when he testified about the matter, Kimmel said he could not recall when he received the dispatch, before or after the attack. He thought he had not gotten it until after the attack.

He also said, "At any rate, if I did receive this before the attack, it was no more than I would have expected under the circumstances."[25]

But proof exists that this dispatch from Washington was received by Radio Honolulu at 5:54 P.M. on December 6. And, if you will recall, this was approximately the same time that Bicknell was telling Fielder and Short about the intercepted Mori conversation.

The still unanswered question, fifty years later, is why the Naval intelligence unit at Pearl Harbor didn't rush this message to Kimmel that fateful Saturday evening. Perhaps the answer can be found in Kimmel's own words: "It was no more than what I would have expected. . . ."

9. Kimmel wants his fleet at sea. On the morning of December 6, Kimmel had reviewed for himself all the intelligence before him. His first instinct was to send the fleet to sea immediately as a precautionary measure for war.

Instead of following his hunch, however, he conferred with his

---

[24] PHA Report, p. 131.
[25] Committee Record, pp. 7640, 7650.

War Plans Officer, Capt. Charles H. McMorris, and his Operations Officer (who doubled as Assistant Chief of Staff), Capt. W. S. DeLany. Kimmel also met with Vice Adm. William S. Pye. As a result of this committee work, Kimmel changed his mind and decided to keep the fleet in harbor.

But Kimmel never told Short that he was so worried about war's breaking out, he was contemplating sending the fleet to sea.

Nor did Kimmel seek Short's views on the imminence of war.

After the war, Kimmel wrote his own book, *Admiral Kimmel's Story*. In it, he claimed that Washington had not given him enough information to be prepared for war. About what he claimed Washington had failed to send him, he wrote:

> Had I learned these vital facts, and the 'Ships in Harbor' messages on November 28, it is my present conviction that I would have rejected the Navy Department's suggestion to send carriers to Wake and Midway. I would have ordered the third carrier, the *Saratoga,* back from the West Coast. I would have gone to sea with the Fleet and endeavored to keep an intercepting position at sea.[26]

It should be noted that Kimmel's retrospective viewpoint was later challenged by the man who succeeded him, Fleet Adm. Chester W. Nimitz. With a glaring, conflicting blast, Nimitz told the Bar Association of San Francisco on November 8, 1962, that: "It was God's mercy that Admiral Kimmel didn't have warning that the Japanese were about to attack Pearl Harbor. If we had been warned, our fleet would have gone out to sea, and . . . all our ships would have been destroyed one by one in deep water. . . . We would have lost the entire Pacific Fleet and eighteen to nineteen thousand men, instead of the ships and 3,300 men we did lose."

You can debate the question: Should Kimmel have gone to sea or not?

But the real question is: Why didn't Kimmel confer with Short so that when the Japanese attacked, they would be met by blazing guns instead of a peaceful Sunday's silence?

It stands to reason that the Army and the Navy had to be talking to each other about something before Pearl Harbor, but what was it?

According to the testimony of Capt. William Ward Smith, who

---

[26] Husband E. Kimmel, *Admiral Kimmel's Story,* Chicago: Henry Regnery, 1955.

was Kimmel's Chief of Staff and personal aide, in the week before Pearl Harbor, both the Army and the Navy in Hawaii were surprised to receive orders from Washington to draw up plans immediately for swapping the Marine forces on the outlying islands, like Wake, with Army troops and Army planes.

"As I remember it," Smith said, "practically the entire week before Pearl Harbor was spent with the two staffs together."

The biggest hangup was that the Army couldn't decide which fighters to send, its P-40s or P-39s.

"We told them that any planes they put on Wake would remain there for the duration, in case of war," said Smith, "because they would have to [fly] off a carrier and could not come back [they could not land on a carrier], and we had no means of putting a ship in there to bring them off, and during the discussion of this with General Short and his staff, the Commanding General of the Army Air Force [General Martin] and Admiral Pye were present, and also Admiral Wilson Brown, the War Plans Officer, the Operations Officers and, I believe, Admiral Bloch.

"Admiral Kimmel said, 'What can I expect of Army fighters on Wake?' And General Martin replied, 'We do not allow them to go more than 15 miles offshore.' That was a shock to all of us and Admiral Kimmel's reply was, 'Then they're no damn good to me.' "

The outbreak of war prevented the switch from being made, and the Marines' defense of Wake Island against overwhelming odds became one of the greatest feats of arms in military history.

It is interesting to note that the final Congressional report of this discussion between Kimmel and Short contained more of Smith's testimony, which Congress saw fit to emphasize:

> The only dispute between the Army and the Navy over that exchange was that General Short said, "If I have to man those islands, I shall have to command them." Admiral Kimmel replied, "No, that won't do. If the Army commanded one of those islands, I wouldn't be able to get a ship into one of those ports," or words to that effect, and General Short said, "Mind you, I do not want to man these islands, I think they are better manned by Marines, but if I man them, I must command them."[27]

---

[27] Hart Inquiry Record, pp. 40–41; PHA Report, p. 242.

While Smith maintained that this was the closest he had seen the two men come to arguing, I was told confidentially that Kimmel's response to Short's assertion that the Army must command Army troops wasn't "That won't do," but: *"Over my dead body!"*

10. The Navy attacks an enemy submarine. On the morning of December 7, between 6:30 and 6:45, about an hour before the Japanese attack, the U.S. destroyer *Ward* reported that it had fired on an enemy submarine at the entrance to Pearl Harbor and believed it had sunk same. The *Ward*'s report was passed on to higher Naval authorities. Both Kimmel and Bloch knew about it. (The significance of such an encounter had been predicted by Adm. Patrick Bellinger and General Marshall, in that any single submarine attack might indicate the presence of an undisclosed enemy surface force composed of fast ships accompanying a carrier.) It was the Navy's duty, primarily Bloch's, to inform Short about the attack immediately.

Neither Kimmel nor Bloch told Short about it.[28]

11. Where are the Japanese carriers? At this point in my narrative, it is important to remember that the testimony of the Navy people in Hawaii was consistent in that they did not believe Japan would attack Pearl Harbor. The Army command at Pearl Harbor agreed with them.

Yes, Kimmel and Short exchanged the "war warning" messages of November 27 sent out from Washington. But they did not sit down and discuss what they might do *jointly* to prepare a defense for the Fleet and its base.

Short testified that he conferred with Kimmel on December 1, 2 and 3. He said they talked over every phase of what they were doing.[29]

But the record shows that neither man spoke to the other from December 3 until after the Japanese attack. I believe Kimmel's violent, slap-in-the-face remark, "Over my dead body!" in respect to the Army's manning the outlying islands prevented any further discussion. Worse, neither man asked the other which stage of alert he had ordered for his own forces, whether aerial reconnaissance was being conducted, whether the Army's radar stations were manned around the

---

[28] PHA Report, pp. 138–139.
[29] Navy Court of Inquiry, pp. 242 and 251; PHA Report, p. 151.

clock, or whether the Army had supplied ammunition to its antiaircraft guns (which it had not).

So much for command by mutual cooperation, or codependency.

Both Short and Kimmel had made the wrong assumptions. As Kimmel testified to the Navy Court of Inquiry: "On November 28 . . . we arrived at the conclusion at this and succeeding conferences that the probable Japanese actions would be confined to the Far East and Thailand most probably, and Malaya, the Netherlands East Indies and the Philippines the next most probable objectives in the order named. In general, we arrived at the conclusion that no immediate activity beyond possible sabotage was to be expected in Hawaii."[30]

But what Kimmel had *not* told Short was that Navy intelligence did not know where the Japanese carriers were.

On December 1, the Japanese had changed their service radio calls for their naval forces at 2400 hours (midnight). This indicated a major step forward in the Japanese preparations for operations on a large scale. Kimmel even underlined that statement in the intelligence summary for the day.

Captain Layton, appearing before the Hewitt Investigation, testified that he and Kimmel had the following discussion on December 2:

> Captain Layton: As best I recall it, Admiral Kimmel said, "What! You don't know where the [Japanese] Carrier Division 1 and Carrier Division 2 are?" and I replied, "No, sir, I do not. I think they are in home waters [around Japan], but I do not know where they are. The rest of these units, I feel pretty confident of their location." Then Admiral Kimmel looked at me, as he sometimes would, with somewhat a stern countenance and said, "Do you mean to say that they could be rounding Diamond Head and you wouldn't know it?" or words to that effect. My reply was that, "I hope they would be sighted before now," or words to that effect.[31]

So, here we are, five days before the attack on Pearl Harbor. Kimmel knows that he doesn't know the location of the Japanese carriers. He also knows that he is not conducting the long-range re-

[30] Statement to Court of Inquiry, p. 31, PHA Report, p. 151.
[31] PHA Report, p. 135.

connaissance that he has been ordered to do by Washington. Yet, he can't bring himself to make a local phone call to Short to discuss their mutual problems.

Again, one asks: Why? A continuation of the earlier argument?

Perhaps the best answer is the one Kimmel gave the Naval Court of Inquiry when he was asked if his organization exchanged intelligence with Short:

> We did, to this extent. The Commanding General of the Hawaiian Department [Short] had his interests restricted to the defense of Hawaii and to such outlying islands as he had his forces and the ones to which he expected to send his forces. He was primarily interested in the probability of attack where his forces were stationed, and in general the information I gave to him bore upon his interests, or was confined to his interests.
>
> My own interests covered a much greater geographical area and many more factors. I tried to keep the Commanding General informed of everything that I thought would be useful to him. I did not inform the Commanding General of my proposed plans and what I expected to do in the Marshalls and other places distant from Hawaii. I saw no reason for taking the additional chance of having such information divulged by giving it to any agency who would have no part in the execution of the plan.[32]

Kimmel's statement rings with arrogance. He doesn't say that regulations prevented him from telling Short about vital intelligence matters (as Layton claimed, falsely). Kimmel simply says that he and he alone decided what Short needed to know, because he, Kimmel, knew what was best for the Army.

As we know, Kimmel even violated the Joint Defense Agreement. His hubris was, I conclude, probably the most important factor in the disaster of Pearl Harbor.

As for Short, my investigation proved that he did not understand the nature of his command. He did not comprehend his briefing by his predecessor, Herron, or the written instructions from Chief of Staff Marshall. Instead of asserting himself within the parameters of his

---

[32] Navy Court of Inquiry, p. 182; PHA Report, p. 152.

mission, he allowed Kimmel to lead him around by the nose. This was probably the second most important factor in the disaster of Pearl Harbor.

That is why I believe Kimmel and Short guilty of criminal neglect of duty.

14

"SENATOR, . . . THE PURPLE MACHINE WAS ORDERED DESTROYED"

I marked the end of my Army career as August 29, 1945, which was the day Secretary Stimson made his final report to the public. There were still some loose ends to tie up, and I worked on those while reminding Harvey Bundy about Stimson's promise to discharge me upon completion of my work.

Finally, Bundy asked me to drop by his office. "Henry," he said, "I've heard the Army has offered you a couple of choice assignments and you've turned them down."

"That's right. It's been flattering, but I'm a civilian law litigator, not an Army man. I can't wait to get back to San Francisco and pick up my law practice."

Bundy smiled. "I was sure that was the reason. You're a wonderful lawyer, Henry, and we're going to miss you around here. The Secretary was saying the other day that he was sure you had gone to Yale."

We both had a good laugh, because one of Stimson's greatest failings was that he believed only Yale could produce a good lawyer. Whenever someone did something well, he'd murmur, "Thank God for a Yale man. He's done it right." Several times, Stimson had asked me what class I'd been in at his alma mater.

"Why don't you come by tomorrow morning at ten," Bundy said. "I think the Secretary may have something to say to you. Meanwhile, you might think about packing."

I went home that evening and told Virginia of Bundy's comments. We immediately began making phone calls to California. My old law partner, Stanislaus Riley, had kept the office in good shape. In fact, he'd even built up the business while I'd been away, and he'd been urging me in his letters to hurry back. He wanted, and deserved, a vacation.

The next morning, I went to Bundy's office at the appointed hour.

Stimson looked very, very tired, but he was graciousness personified, thanking me for my work. "The Congress is going to hold a ripsnorting investigation into Pearl Harbor, Henry. I may have to ask that you give up your practice for a while and help me put our case together. I can't say when this might occur, however. Would you mind doing that?"

"Not at all, Mr. Secretary. I'd be honored. I'll be in the phone book. Just call." I didn't mean to sound flip, but I was beset by more emotion than I had expected.

"That's what I would expect a good Yale man to say," Stimson said. "Good luck on our Western frontier."

Stimson also had a couple of other surprises in store for me. The first was a set of orders relieving me from active service. The second was the news that he was putting me in for the Legion of Merit.

I was truly overwhelmed.

With the papers I held in my hand, it took only forty-eight hours for me to be reclassified and returned to civilian life. "Jesus Christ, Henry," one of my fellow officers said. "How the hell did you manage this? I've been waiting six weeks for my papers to get through Personnel."

"It was just a bit of luck," I replied. "I met someone I went to school with." I put my finger alongside my nose, winked and walked out the door.

Virginia and I packed as quickly as we could. By early September of 1945, we were settled again in San Francisco and I was preparing to defend a difficult civil suit. The morning and evening newspapers had banner headlines about the latest goings-on in Washington.

Congress ordered a full-blown investigation into Pearl Harbor.

While everyone espoused hopes that it would be nonpartisan, it was easy to see that partisan politics might override truth and justice. Even the congressmen involved acknowledged that they held little hope for impartiality.

The Committee was to be made up of ten men from the House and Senate, five from each chamber, and broken down six to four in favor of the Democrats (the Democrats knew how to use their majority, and they used it well). I had met some of the players when they testified as witnesses or were active in cases I prosecuted, such as the war profiteering trial broken open by the Truman Committee. Now Harry Truman was President, our new national leader, as the result of Roosevelt's death. I knew Sen. Homer Ferguson, a Republican from Michigan who had been most helpful as a prosecution witness when I tried the Wright Aeronautical case. As a bipartisan gesture, Truman had assigned Ferguson the job of testifying on the government's behalf.

Ferguson was solidly in the Kimmel camp and was determined to lay the blame for Pearl Harbor in Roosevelt's lap, or in Marshall's lap if Roosevelt wasn't available to hold the baby.

Three other Republicans were of the same mind: Rep. Frank B. Keefe of Wisconsin, Rep. Bertrand W. Gearhart of California and Sen. Owen Brewster of Maine. I could see a lot of controversy ahead.

It was Brewster, the Republican from Maine, who really set the fireworks alight. He had called for a Congressional investigation into Pearl Harbor from the very start. Now he claimed that Truman's order allowing any employee or member of the armed services to testify about breaking the Japanese codes before the Committee wasn't a broad enough undertaking. The news was out. For the first time, in the first week of November 1945, the public learned that we had broken the Japanese codes before Pearl Harbor. Needless to say, the Japanese government was furious to discover that we had fooled it into continuing its use of Purple as its diplomatic code after the war. I understand that some very tense meetings occurred in Tokyo and the Pentagon. But if Congress, in its infinite wisdom, wanted to make a clean breast of the matter, so be it. I believe that Congress made a terrible mistake, but that's the way a democracy works. I wouldn't want it any other way.

One morning that same week, I picked up a paper on my way to the courthouse and found myself accused of a crime. According to the minority (Republican) members of the Committee, I had coerced Colonel Bratton into changing his testimony about his activities on the night of December 6.

This was a serious charge: that I had caused Bratton to perjure himself. Further, I was supposed to have been the person whom Secretary Stimson sent out on a mission to save Marshall's reputation after the Army Board had reached its conclusions. I knew, and have proven, that those conclusions were based on tainted evidence, but they seemed all right to those who either believed in conspiracy theories or supported Kimmel and Short. The Republicans were claiming that my investigation was a fix. They further muddied the waters by charging that everyone knew that the one o'clock delivery of the fourteen-part diplomatic message meant only one thing. As Gearhart thundered: "It meant the first bomb would fall about 7 o'clock in the morning in Hawaii."[1]

I couldn't tell what Gearhart was doing. Did he know what he was talking about? It seemed unlikely. Or was he just trying to build his case against the Roosevelt administration? If it was the latter, he was doing well. But he was building a public case on lies, and that worried me. The Republican strategy appeared to be an attempt to prove that the Roosevelt administration and its top military leaders knew that the Japanese were going to attack, knew where and when the attack would occur, yet withheld the information from Kimmel and Short. If this strategy was successful, the American people were bound to vote the Democrats out of office and turn the White House over to the Republicans.

I was a Republican myself, and a fiscal conservative, too. I was furious that these Republicans would attack me and my motives. I could see that they had to do so if they were going to prove their case, but they were doing so in a cowardly fashion. (I have always called Congress a "coward's castle" because congressmen are free to make speeches that impugn people's character without fear of reprisals such as being sued for libel or slander.) Now, my fellow Republicans were challenging the integrity of my investigation and my character with blatant lies for partisan reasons.

I hoped they would call me as a witness. I'll string 'em up good, I thought.

The hearings began on Thursday, November 15, 1945, and I followed them as best I could. I bought every newspaper in town, plus

---

[1] *At Dawn We Slept,* p. 680.

all I could get from out of town. I listened to the radio news (TV wasn't around in those days), and I became fascinated by the pattern I could see developing.

The Democrats were obviously controlling the order in which witnesses were to appear. Instead of allowing Kimmel and Short to be first, the majority party was going to make sure its case could be presented before the minority members could raise their conspiracy-isolationist theories. I could agree with this as the proper way to conduct a trial, and it explained why Gearhart and Keefe had raised such a fuss before the hearings opened.

The first witness was Adm. J. O. Richardson, who had been Commander in Chief of the Pacific Fleet before Kimmel. Richardson had feuded with the President before the war about where the fleet should be based. (Richardson had wanted the fleet on the West Coast, Roosevelt wanted Hawaii.) Needless to say, the President won that discussion. Richardson was forced to find himself another command. It was apparent to me that the Republicans were hoping that Richardson would make the case that, by basing the fleet at Pearl Harbor, Roosevelt had provoked the Japanese to attack. But Richardson didn't do that. He claimed that even if the fleet had been based in Puget Sound on our West Coast, the Japanese attack would have been equally successful. This said a lot for the skill of the Japanese, and for the lack of preparedness and overconfidence of our military at the time.

Then came the testimony of our former Ambassador to Japan, Joseph C. Grew, and that of the Secretary of State, Cordell Hull, and the Under Secretary of State, Sumner Welles. The three men gave a detailed account of Japanese aggression in the Pacific region before Pearl Harbor. By the time they were through, they had seriously damaged the position of the Republican isolationists, who had difficulty understanding that the rest of the American public had been at war for four years and, in 1946, firmly believed that the Japanese and Germans were total aggressors. It seemed to me that the Republicans in the hearings could not comprehend how the world had changed since the debates that had embroiled Congress in 1939 and 1940.

The first Army man to testify was Maj. Gen. Sherman Miles, who had been Chief of the Military Intelligence Service for the Army at the time of Pearl Harbor. Confirming what he had said to me in my investigation, Miles told Congress that Short's reply to the War Department warning of November 27, 1941, was "totally inadequate." Under cross-examination, Miles was asked why more warnings hadn't been sent to Short. Miles replied: "You do not have to tell a commanding general but once that danger faces him."[2]

Next to take the stand was Maj. Gen. Leonard T. Gerow, who had been Chief of War Plans at the time of Pearl Harbor. Again, Gerow's testimony conformed to what he had told me during my investigation. He was sorry that he hadn't dug more deeply into Short's inadequate reply to the warning message of November 27. But Gerow said that he never thought a commander as experienced as Short would fail to "take some reconnaissance and other defensive measures" after having received a warning such as the one that had been sent to Hawaii. If Gerow had investigated Short's reply, he might have discovered that Short had failed to obey the directive signed by Chief of Staff Marshall. But the Committee ignored the fact that Short had improperly reversed the status of the alerts for his command and had then tried after Pearl Harbor to conceal that.

Gerow concluded by saying that if there had been any failure on the part of War Plans to inquire into Short's reply, "the responsibility must rest on the War Plans Division, and I accept that responsibility as Chief of War Plans Division."[3]

Once again, Gerow did not beg the issue. Nor did he say that his assistant, Colonel Bundy, had failed to do his job. Gerow accepted the blame. Some reporters praised him for his courage. Others said that he was merely trying to protect Marshall. I knew that he was being true to himself and his code of conduct.

Next to testify was General Marshall. He, too, accepted some of the blame for Pearl Harbor, because when he saw Short's reply to the warning of November 27, he failed to understand the inadequacy of the message and correct it. "That was my opportunity to intervene, which I did not do," Marshall said.[4]

The comment won Marshall many admirers. Indeed, the Army seemed to be doing well in acknowledging individual errors. Meanwhile, the Committee pressed Marshall about where he had been on the evening of December 6, 1941. Like his counterpart in the Navy, Admiral Stark, Marshall said he didn't remember. This was what he had also told me, and I will deal with the matter later on. They dug into the Winds Code without learning anything new. They broke the story of how Marshall had asked Republican presidential candidate Dewey not

---

[2] PHA Report, pp. 879, 901.
[3] Ibid., pp. 1019, 1031, 1033, 1036.
[4] Ibid., p. 1141.

to reveal the news about how we had cracked the Japanese codes that I spoke of earlier.

The Republican minority kept Marshall under cross-examination from December 8 through December 13. They grilled the General about my investigation. He told them his superior, Henry L. Stimson, then Secretary of War, appointed and directed me as his special investigator. They also tried to get him to agree that the blame for prewar belligerence should be borne by President Roosevelt. In this, they failed.

Marshall wasn't the best witness for himself. I believed he was trying to avoid questions about the news that he had just been chosen as President Truman's special envoy to seek peace between the Chinese Nationalists and the Chinese Communists, a task that was preordained to fail and became one of the great phony issues of the McCarthy era. I also felt that Marshall was trying to avoid opening up lines of questioning that would have compromised the intelligence operations of our British allies. They had broken the German Enigma codes, and this stunning fact was kept secret for another quarter-century. Most importantly, Marshall deflected the Committee's wrath by sticking to basics.

Now it became the Navy's turn to testify. Rear Adm. Theodore S. Wilkinson, who had been the head of Naval intelligence at the time of Pearl Harbor, took the stand. He, too, acknowledged that he had made some errors. He was sorry that he had not understood the importance of the "bomb plot" messages and had not attributed to them the significance they deserved in hindsight.

He never believed, however, that it "would be appropriate" for him to warn Kimmel about the possibility of a surprise air raid, because he was sure that "an approaching force would be detected before it got into attack range."[5] This was a strong shot at Kimmel, for the head of Naval intelligence was really saying that he knew Kimmel had been ordered to conduct reconnaissance but had failed to do so.

I could see that the inquiry was doing tremendous damage to Kimmel and Short. If I had this case before a jury, with testimony such as this, I think I could have gotten a conviction.

Strangely enough, I don't believe Kimmel and Short really understood what was happening to them, even though they were attending the hearings as witnesses, waiting to testify. But from such quirks

[5] Ibid., pp. 1728–1735, 1756–1757.

that arise in trials, outcomes are made and decided: all too often against the person who, prior to taking the stand to defend himself, could not admit that he was wrong.

The former head of the Navy's War Plans Division, Rear Adm. Richmond Kelly Turner, began his testimony on December 19. Turner's task had included the preparation of strategic estimates for the Navy. He said that Kimmel had not understood the war warning message of November 27 and had failed to take up the defensive deployment that had been ordered in the message.

Meanwhile, Turner acknowledged that there had been confusion within the Navy Department, including differences of opinion about what the Japanese might or might not do. He also acknowledged that he had not checked with his chief of intelligence before misstating to the Chief of Naval Operations, Stark, that Kimmel was receiving Magic decrypts.

Despite all this, however, Turner was unequivocal in his belief that Kimmel had been given adequate warning of a Japanese attack and had failed to act in accordance with his orders, which were to assume a defensive stature based on a "war warning."[6]

The Committee recessed for Christmas. I believe it was Turner's testimony that proved to be the last straw for Short's health. After hearing Turner say that he personally had questioned Short's inadequate reply to the November 27 warning, but had not said anything to the Army about it because he believed the Army would handle the matter, Short came down with pneumonia and was rushed to Walter Reed Hospital.

On December 31, Admiral Stark took the stand. As former Chief of Naval Operations, he said that he thought his letters and official dispatches to Kimmel were "sufficient" to have kept Kimmel "informed on the important military and political developments in the Pacific as we knew them" and that Kimmel "had received adequate information and directives to be on guard."[7]

Stark didn't want to criticize his good friend, Kimmel, but in telling Kimmel "what to do," Stark didn't think he had to explain how Kimmel should do it. In other words, Stark believed Kimmel should have sent his planes out on reconnaissance and coordinated with the Army to protect Hawaii. "I certainly would have had my planes out,"

---

[6] Ibid., pp. 1991–2001.
[7] Ibid., p. 2133.

Stark said when asked what he would have done if he had been in Kimmel's place.[8]

Stark also said that the Hawaiian commands, meaning both the Army and the Navy, "did not obey the instructions." This helped explain why the Japanese attack had been a surprise.

I needn't have been a trial lawyer to realize that the testimony against Short and Kimmel had already tightened the nooses around their necks, but I wondered if the Committee would exact the ultimate penalty. I was beginning to sense that other factors might be coming into play.

It became evident when Kimmel testified, and he did so with true authority and power, that he laid all the blame for Pearl Harbor on Washington's failure to tell him where and when the Japanese would strike. He was adamant that the "so-called 'war warning' dispatch of November 27 did not warn the Pacific Fleet of an attack in the Hawaiian Area."[9] His list of grievances against Washington continued full blast. Nothing, but nothing, was his own fault, not even a minute error in judgement.

In brief, Kimmel's strategy was to point his finger at other people and testify that everything was their fault. He would take no prisoners in making his assertions, because to equivocate even slightly and make the tiniest admission of guilt would lead to his downfall. To me, his self-assurance and chutzpah were unbelievable.

As his cross-examination continued, I wondered why the Committee members weren't making use of my report. Why weren't they zinging Kimmel about his failures to communicate with Short, or to make sure the Army had its radar working and its antiaircraft guns ready to fire? The few questions that were asked in this regard were, I thought, poorly phrased and not pressed home, and they received no adequate answers. In fact, the Republicans gave Kimmel a free ride compared with the grilling they had given Marshall.

More or less the same thing happened when Short testified. Looking frail after his illness, he took the stand and attacked his superiors in Washington for not having given him chapter and verse about when and where the Japanese would attack. He also criticized the Navy for not having carried out reconnaissance, meaning that he believed the Navy had had everything under control. Short did not seem to under-

---

[8] Ibid., pp. 2441–2445, 2450, 2451.
[9] Ibid., p. 2498.

stand that he, too, had been responsible for cooperating with the Navy, and that the Navy wasn't solely responsible for originating this cooperation. I thought his testimony showed that, as a commanding general, Short left a great deal to be desired.

Once again, no one questioned Short the way I would have: Why didn't you pay attention to the code destruction reports made to you by your own intelligence officers? Why did you ignore the intelligence produced by your own men, and then say that word from Washington about the same matters would have spurred you to a higher status of alert? The questions that could have been asked on the basis of the affidavits in my report were most unending.

As I pondered the matter, I came to realize that the Committee might have already made up its mind about Kimmel and Short. The Committee might intend to treat them in the same way as had the Army and Navy. Officers superior to Kimmel and Short had acknowledged that they made errors. Yet, Kimmel and Short insisted before the Committee that they had done nothing wrong and were, indeed, victims of the failures of their superiors, and the Committee might accept these excuses. There could be only one reason for this: The Committee Republicans still had other fish to fry.

One of them was me.

As I recall, it was around the end of January 1946 that I received notification that I would be asked to testify.

At about the same time, I heard from Stimson's office that the Secretary was in very poor health. He had suffered a severe heart attack before Christmas and was still so ill that he would not be able to appear before Congress. He would answer questions submitted to him in writing, however. I was asked if I could come to New York to help.

I said I would.

Stimson had assigned one of the best lawyers in his firm, Allen T. Klots, to work with me. He was a truly gifted writer, as well as having a keen legal mind.

What Stimson wanted us to do was answer the questions posed by Senator Ferguson and then write his final statement about Pearl Harbor for Congress. There were 176 questions. We replied that Stimson couldn't answer questions phrased in such an accusatory manner, and Ferguson backed off. (Later, Ferguson submitted a list of sixty-one supplementary questions, which were answered for the record.)

The most important thing for me, however, was the knowledge that Stimson still believed that his original report to the public, which had been based on my investigation, was 100 percent correct. Buoyed by the Secretary's faith in me, I set off to do battle with the Congressional sharpshooters.

One of the first things I realized after being sworn in was that many members of the Committee had not read my report. I thought that, because my report was still classified Top Secret, and the Committee had only two copies of it, it might have been difficult for these busy lawmakers to sign one out, study it and return it. In fact, on the evening after my first bit of testimony, I was asked to stay behind to help the Committee staff integrate my exhibits with their own. For, as you will see, my exhibits were in many cases better and more complete than what the numerous and expert Committee staff had assembled. Later, I would learn there were more sinister reasons why some Committee members hadn't seen my report.

In trying to grill me, the Committee at first didn't realize that I knew as much as or more than they did, or that I was totally unafraid of them. I was only around forty. I was a trial lawyer—a civilian and a Republican—and not a regular member of the military. They couldn't intimidate me, even the waspish Ferguson and Brewster. It took a little time for them to understand this fact of life, or that I had no personal ambition to achieve in the Army.

Almost the very first question I was asked concerned the allegation that I had tried to change the testimony of some of the witnesses I had interviewed.

I was pleased to hit this pitch out of the ball park. In fact, the Committee seemed surprised to learn, for the first time, that the two original reports of the Army Pearl Harbor Board were based on perjured evidence designed to protect the knowledge that we had cracked the Japanese codes. Nor was the Committee happy to hear that the Navy had denied the Army Board access to the Navy's so-called Hart Report. I explained that this had been the reason why Secretary Stimson, who also happened to be a staunch, dedicated Republican, had asked me to make my investigation, because "somebody should go, to General Miles, to General Gerow, and all the people who had testified before us at a time when they were under compulsion not to reveal the details of Magic, and ask them all about Magic.''[10]

---

[10] Proceedings of Joint Committee, p. 4304.

The Democratic majority of the Committee quickly understood that this meant the reports of the Army Board, upon which the minority Republican members depended so heavily for their case against Marshall and Roosevelt, were false. If the Army Board conclusions were wrong, any hypothesis built by the isolationists was automatically false. I could sense real consternation on the parts of Brewster, Ferguson, Keefe and Gearhart as I laid out their problems for them.

It was Senator Scott W. Lucas of Illinois who broke trail for me in proving that my investigation was fair.

I told Lucas I wouldn't have conducted the investigation if it had been slanted.

"I have always been a Republican, sir," I said. "Now, Colonel Stimson is a Republican. The impression I had of Secretary Stimson was that he was a man who certainly under no stretch of the imagination would, at this point in his career, have been a party to any such performance."[11] And then I added: "I was not a War Department 'Yes Man' . . ."

I also pointed out that one newspaper had asked: "Why did they send a lowly Major all over the world to get this testimony when this lowly Major had all his Army career ahead of him?"[12]

I said that when I had read this article, I, " 'the lowly Major,' was back in San Francisco practicing law. (The article also said) I was a Reserve Officer. I at no time was ever a Reserve Officer [as John Toland improperly identified me in the first edition of his best-selling book, *Infamy*]."

Lucas appeared satisfied with my remarks, and Representative Gearhart then took up the cudgel about my having slanted my investigation. He referred to a "very nice letter I have from you" pointing out that he was the source of the allegations against me and that they were untrue.

"Could you have mixed me up with some other person who is a member of this Committee?" asked Gearhart.

"The San Francisco *Chronicle* and *Call* and *Daily News* carried your name with the accusation which . . . Senator Lucas mentioned," I said. "The impression I had was that you thought I had gone around the world with a great big club in my hand and by force and duress had forced these people to sign statements."

---

[11] Ibid., p. 4309.
[12] Ibid.

Gearhart replied that he was not conscious of ever having mentioned my name.

"Well, I have the clippings, Mr. Gearhart," I replied.[13]

With that salvo taking out his waterline, Gearhart withdrew from further questioning, his face reddened by frustration.

Senator Ferguson then tried to slip a fast ball past me. He was a large man, with a mane of white hair through which he ran his fingers time and again while he jumped around and up and down in his chair. If he could have controlled these nervous habits, he would have been a much better interrogator.

He wanted to show that I had overstepped my orders for my investigation and that I should not "find any facts or go into any facts as far as the Navy was concerned."[14]

The Senator was mistaken. I pointed out to him: "Whenever [my investigation] pertained to the Army and went into the Navy, I was to go there and I did go there, and I was to enter on it and I did enter on it."[15] That was why I had been given permission by the Navy to take affidavits from men such as Rochefort, Layton, Holmes and all the others listed in my report. As I explained: "The Army had a great deal more investigating [to do], Senator, than the Navy, for the reason that the Navy had this super-duper stuff and the Army did not have it."[16]

Ferguson had to agree that the Navy had not shared intelligence with the Army, but I could see that it caused him some agitation. Now he shifted the attack to prove his theory that there had been a secret agreement between Roosevelt and the British, Dutch and Chinese to the effect that America would fight on their side if Japan attacked any one of them.

I replied that there had seemed to be a unanimous opinion on the part of the Americans, British, Chinese and Dutch that they had mutual objectives and that all of them would be overrun if the Axis nations were allowed to conquer them one by one. But, as General Marshall had testified, there was no binding contract or treaty saying America would go to war if the British or the Dutch were attacked in the Pacific. (The Chinese had been under attack and invasion by the Japanese for a number of years, and we hadn't gone to their aid.) My brief had been to investigate Pearl Harbor. That had been done. Now, if the Com-

---

[13] Ibid., p. 4310.
[14] Ibid., p. 4312.
[15] Ibid.
[16] Ibid., p. 4313.

mittee wished to investigate alleged secret understandings between Roosevelt and other nations, that would be up to Congress. All I could say was that I knew of no secret agreement on the matter, and neither did General Marshall.

The most important analysis of the ABCD Bloc was the view of Army intelligence that if Japan attacked one member of the Bloc, then an attack could be expected on every member. That was the analysis provided General Short by his assistant G-2, Colonel Bicknell, on November 29, 1941. Since it was obvious from Magic, from the British Secret Intelligence Service reports to Hawaii and from eyewitness reports that the Japanese were sending invasion forces into the South Pacific, apparently to attack the British and Dutch colonies, America should have been prepared for an attack, too. (The fact of the matter is that the Japanese attacked America first, so the question of our going to the aid of the British or Dutch became moot.)

Ferguson didn't like my reply, so we had some lawyerlike scrapping between us. I reminded him that he had been "one of my best witnesses" when we had worked on a bipartisan basis on Air Force derelictions during the war. Now, I said, I found it difficult to believe that Ferguson wanted me to say that Roosevelt "would violate the Constitution in declaring war or taking steps without going to the Congress."[17] My implication was obvious. If the Senator was going to make such a charge, he'd have to do so without any evidence from me to substantiate it. Rather than look foolish, Ferguson backed away from the issue.

Ferguson returned to the attack, however, challenging the testimony I had gotten from Colonel Bratton in Paris about his having lied to the Army Board about the delivery of the first thirteen parts of the diplomatic message to Col. Walter Bedell Smith for transmittal to Marshall on the evening of December 6, 1941.

This was, I believe, the most important item on Ferguson's agenda. If he could disprove Bratton's testimony to me, he could then say that the Army Board's findings were accurate, which would allow him to pin the blame for Pearl Harbor on Marshall. Slowly and grudgingly, I got Ferguson to understand that Bratton's testimony to me was correct. Bratton had misled the Army Board. Colonel Dusenbury had failed to deliver the decrypts on the evening of December 6, because he didn't realize their importance and didn't want to wake anyone. In

[17] Ibid., p. 4324.

one of the more unusual twists of the hearings, the Committee later called upon Bratton to confirm my statement, which he did, but it never called Dusenbury, which was sloppy procedure. I believe the Committee was afraid of what Dusenbury might say, a comment I'll explain later.

I then turned the tables on Ferguson. If he could try to use Bratton against me, I could really use Bratton against Ferguson. I said: "Senator, Colonel Bratton and Henry Clausen agree that the most important information that came into the War Department was information that the Jap consuls and their diplomatic representatives were burning their codes. That spells war in any man's language, and we do not need that long, self-serving, hocus-pocus 14-part message to know it."

Ferguson made a sarcastic comment about my being one of those officers who believed war was imminent when Washington learned the Japanese were burning their codes and "war, in effect, would be on in any moment."

"Yes, sir. It was imminent," I said.

Ferguson fell into the trap. "All right," he said. "Now, did you try to find out why an alert was not sent out on those codes?"[18]

I had him! Suddenly I knew that Ferguson hadn't read my report. I carefully replied that an alert had been sent by Bratton to Colonel Fielder, who said he had never received it, although Colonel Bicknell had seen it on Fielder's desk and taken action on it himself. This was the famous missing cable number 519.

Ferguson knew he couldn't close the lid on this Pandora's box he had opened, so he plowed through the issue and learned about the two warning messages of December 3 that had been in the Navy's hands at Pearl Harbor, on Commander Rochefort's desk, to be exact, which was where Ferguson wished the hearings hadn't gone.

In this manner, I was able to introduce the conflicting testimony given to me by Rochefort and Fielder. That set Ferguson back a step or two. Still, he plunged on. We discussed the two warning messages about the destruction of the Japanese codes that Washington had sent to Hawaii, and I asked: "Did not one of these refer, Senator, to the destruction by [the Japanese Embassy in] Washington of the Purple machine?"

"Not that I know of," replied Ferguson. "I do not think the words 'Purple machine' were mentioned in any that I have seen."

"You see, 'Purple machine' means an awful lot," I said.

---

[18] Ibid., p. 4328.

"I appreciate that," said Ferguson. "If these messages had said 'Destroy the Purple machine,' that is a different question."[19]

After I got counsel to give me the Committee's copy of my report, I looked up the appropriate page.

"Senator, as I understood it, the Purple machine was ordered destroyed," I said. "I am reading here from the affidavit of Capt. Thomas A. Huckins, which I took at Pearl Harbor. He is in the Navy, and I wanted to see just what dispatches they had gotten from Washington."

"But that was never sent to Kimmel and Short, was it?" Ferguson asked.

"It certainly was," I replied. I had him stone cold dead.[20]

I walked Ferguson through the evidence proving that Hawaii had been warned by the British Secret Intelligence Service on December 3 that war was going to break out between Japan, Britain and America, but not Russia. I also explained that on December 3 the Navy Department had warned Kimmel that the Japanese had ordered their embassy in Washington to destroy its Purple machine and its codes, with the exception of one system. Furthermore, Tokyo had sent the same order to London, Hong Kong, Singapore and Manila. Washington had advised Kimmel about that, too.

As I continued my presentation, I could sense a feeling of electricity going around the room. For the first time, the Committee had a witness who could pinpoint exactly when warnings had been sent to Pearl Harbor, prove they were adequate and show that Kimmel and Short had failed to heed them.

It was getting late in the day.

Senator Lucas broke in, saying: "There has been information brought before this committee that I didn't know anything about. Probably that is my fault, sir, because I haven't been able to read, sir, all of your affidavits." He complimented me on "the tremendous amount of information" I had brought before the Committee.

He then told me how I was going to spend most of the night. He wanted me to help Committee counsel integrate the complete traffic that "was received from November up to December 7 by Admiral Kimmel [and staff], or by General Short [and staff]."[21]

Lucas's next comment outlined the Committee's problem as he saw it.

[19] Ibid., p. 4332.
[20] Ibid.
[21] Ibid., p. 4339.

"We have had the testimony of very few witnesses in this hearing who were in Hawaii, outside of General Short," said Lucas. "I think he is the only witness who has testified here from Hawaii on the Army's responsibility at Pearl Harbor." Lucas also said that my testimony had raised questions in his mind that needed further exploration.

I was surprised when Senator Ferguson agreed. He, too, wanted me to tie all the decrypts together, including those I had gotten in Hawaii from British Intelligence. Suddenly, he became the bipartisan Senator I used to know when he looked at me and said: "The question is to find out what traffic went into Hawaii and was there in the hands of any subordinate of General Short or Admiral Kimmel."

"You won't think I am trying to put the blame on Hawaii if I do that?" I asked.

"All we want are the facts," said Ferguson.

"All right, sir."

The Committee adjourned for the evening. I had a lot of work to do, but there was joy in my heart. I had been able to refocus the Committee onto what I believed were the four important questions with which I had begun my investigation:
- What had Washington known?
- What had Washington done about it?
- What had the Hawaiian commands known?
- What had they done about it?

Perhaps something constructive could come out of this, after all.

Col. R. F. Bratton testified falsely to the Army Pearl Harbor Board about his actions on the night of December 6. By so doing he nearly destroyed Marshall. However, Clausen discovered the truth, which Bratton confirmed before Congress, including his perjury.

Col. O. K. Sadtler was a sad, burned-out witness, who over the years reversed himself a number of times. But he testified to Clausen that he "did not see any execute message" of the Winds Code, nor did he know of such a message being received by the War Department.

NAVAL MESSAGE   NAVY DEPARTMENT

		MESSAGE PRECEDENCE
PHONE EXTENSION NUMBER	ADDRESSEES	
FROM OPNAV	CINCAF CINCPAC	PRIORITY
		ROUTINE
RELEASED BY INGERSOLL		DEFERRED
DATE NOV 27 1941		
TOR CODEROOM	CINCLANT SPENAVO	PRIORITY
DECODED BY		ROUTINE
		DEFERRED
PARAPHRASED BY SHALL		4544-16

FOR ACTION — INFORMATION

INDICATE BY ASTERISK ADDRESSEES FOR WHICH MAIL DELIVERY IS SATISFACTORY

272337 CR 0921

UNLESS OTHERWISE DESIGNATED THIS DISPATCH WILL BE TRANSMITTED WITH DEFERRED PRECEDENCE.
ORIGINATOR FILL IN DATE AND TIME FOR DEFERRED AND MAIL DELIVERY

DATE   TIME   GCT

TEXT   NO

THIS DISPATCH IS TO BE CONSIDERED A WAR WARNING. NEGOTIATIONS WITH JAPAN LOOKING XMXXB TOWARD STABILIZATION OF CONDITIONS IN

THE PACIFIC HAVE CEASED AND AN AGGRESSIVE MOVE BY JAPAN IS EXPECTED WITHIN THE NEXT FEW DAYS. THE NUMBER AND EQUIPMENT OF

JAP TROOPS AND THE ORGANIZATION OF NAVAL TASK FORCES INDICATES AN AMPHIBIOUS EXPEDITION AGAINST EITHER THE PHILIPPINES OR KRA

PENINSULA OR POSSIBLY BORNEO. EXECUTE AN APPROPRIATE DEFENSIVE DEPLOYMENT PREPARATORY TO CARRYING OUT THE TASKS ASSIGNED IN

WPL46X INFORM DISTRICT AND ARMY AUTHORITIES. A SIMILAR WARNING IS BEING SENT BY WAR DEPARTMENT. SPENAVO INFORM BRITISH. CON-

TINENTAL DISTRICT GUAM SAMOA DIRECTED TAKE APPROPRIATE MEASURES AGAINST SABOTAGE.

12....ORIGINATOR   RECORD COPY TO WPD WARDEPT...   CNO

NOV 28 '41 PM   FILE(88)

4544-16

IN

WPD. WDGS

MAKE ORIGINAL ONLY, DELIVER TO COMMUNICATION WATCH OFFICER IN PERSON

SECRET

SEE ART 76(4)
NAV REGS

This was the Navy's "war warning" sent to Kimmel beside the cable of the same date saying that negotiations with Japan "appear to be terminated." It was this message that Kimmel ordered Layton to deliver personally to Short, but which Layton failed to do.

STANDARD FORM No. 14A
APPROVED BY THE
MARCH 10, 1926

RADIOGRAM

TELEGRAM

OFFICIAL BUSINESS—GOVERNMENT RATES

FROM: WAR DEPARTMENT

BUREAU AGO

AG 381 (11-27-41)MC-E

ehb - 1712

PRIORITY

NOVEMBER 27, 1941.

SECRET

COMMANDING GENERAL, HAWAIIAN DEPARTMENT,

FORT SHAFTER, T.H.

472

Auth: T. A. G.

Initials

Date. NOV 27 1941

NEGOTIATIONS WITH JAPAN APPEAR TO BE TERMINATED TO ALL

PRACTICAL PURPOSES WITH ONLY THE BAREST POSSIBILITIES THAT THE JAPANESE

GOVERNMENT MIGHT COME BACK AND OFFER TO CONTINUE PERIOD JAPANESE FUTURE

ACTION UNPREDICTABLE BUT HOSTILE ACTION POSSIBLE AT ANY MOMENT PERIOD

IF HOSTILITIES CANNOT COMMA REPEAT CANNOT COMMA BE AVOIDED THE UNITED

STATES DESIRES THAT JAPAN COMMIT THE FIRST OVERT ACT PERIOD THIS POLICY

SHOULD NOT COMMA REPEAT NOT COMMA BE CONSTRUED AS RESTRICTING YOU TO A

COURSE OF ACTION THAT MIGHT JEOPARDIZE YOUR DEFENSE PERIOD PRIOR TO HOSTILE

JAPANESE ACTION YOU ARE DIRECTED TO UNDERTAKE SUCH RECONNAISSANCE AND OTHER

MEASURES AS YOU DEEM NECESSARY BUT THESE MEASURES SHOULD BE CARRIED OUT SO

AS NOT COMMA REPEAT NOT COMMA TO ALARM CIVIL POPULATION OR DISCLOSE INTENT

PERIOD REPORT MEASURES TAKEN PERIOD SHOULD HOSTILITIES OCCUR YOU WILL CARRY

OUT THE TASKS ASSIGNED IN RAINBOW FIVE SO FAR AS THEY PERTAIN TO JAPAN PERIOD

LIMIT DISSEMINATION OF THIS HIGHLY SECRET INFORMATION TO MINIMUM ESSENTIAL

OFFICERS

MARSHALL

WAR DEPARTMENT MESSAGE CENTER: PLEASE SEND SAME RADIOGRAM TO:

COMMANDING GENERAL, CARIBBEAN DEFENSE COMMAND,
QUARRY HEIGHTS, C.Z.

ADJUTANT GENERAL.

This original should be returned to The AGO upon completion of action in order that same may become permanent record in AGO files.

See note on page 2 of basic memo. ehb

Secretary Stimson personally worked on this message in conjunction with Secretary Hull and President Roosevelt. Stimson wanted to explain in detail to Short what was going on in Washington. Not recognizing the message's significance, Short called it ambiguous and failed to prepare for hostile action.

General Marshall (seated, center) with his General Staff. (Left to right) Gerow (War Plans), Wheeler (Supply), Miles (Intelligence), Arnold (Air Corps), Marshall, Haislip (Personnel), Twaddle (Plans & Training), Bryden (Administration). Missing: Moore (Department Chief of Staff). Marshall and Miles admitted to Clausen their roles in misleading the Army Pearl Harbor Board.

Admiral Kimmel (front row, center) and his U.S. Fleet Staff pose beneath the sixteen-inch guns of the flagship *Pennsylvania* (BB-38), which was damaged in the Japanese attack on Pearl Harbor. (U.S. NAVAL INSTITUTE COLLECTION)

Battleship row at Pearl Harbor after the attack with capital ships settling on the bottom.

Secretary Stimson agreed with Clausen that the exchange of information, and consultation, between the Navy and the Army at Pearl Harbor was "inadequate." He wrote: "It was the rule that all such information should be exchanged. . . ." Also, as a sentinel, Short "failed in his mission."

Rear Adm. R. K. Turner, while head of the senior War Plans Division, tried to take over Intelligence, too, without adequate understanding of the job. He assumed and perceived without knowing, mistakenly believing Pearl Harbor was getting Purple information without asking if it was true or not. Rochefort said Turner had no use for intelligence in 1941.

Lt. Gen. W. C. Short didn't want the command in Hawaii and failed to study what his task entailed. He failed to follow Washington's orders to liaise with the Navy, to conduct reconnaissance, or to use his radar, and he failed to alert his forces against attack.

Adm. H. E. Kimmel withheld vital intelligence from his co-commander, Short. Kimmel was inflexible in his convictions and expressions. He would not liaise with the Army about its state of readiness. If he had done so, he might have been a great hero.

15 ‖ "THEY JUST QUIT"

I remember that evening in the Old Senate Office Building (it's called "Old" because another one has been built, which is called "New"). I worked until long after midnight, making sure the Army Signals Intelligence Service numbers on my exhibits corresponded to the numbers the Committee had assigned various decrypts, and making sure that the language in them conformed. I got to bed around two-thirty and was back in the hearing room the next morning before ten.

It would be late that afternoon before I had finished answering the single question Senator Lucas had asked the previous day.

I first explained to the Committee that I had checked all three recipients of British Secret Intelligence Service messages in Hawaii. They were Mayfield of the Navy, Shivers of the FBI and Bicknell of the Army. In some cases, the messages went only to Mayfield, and they carried the notation "Captain Mayfield only." In other cases, copies were distributed to all three men. I obtained nearly two hundred of these British intelligence messages that were retained by Hawaii and *never* sent to Washington. A summary of them was incorporated in my

Exhibit 6.[1] I believe this was the first time the Committee understood that Hawaii had intelligence sources that were exclusively its own, and it caused them real consternation.

I was able to read into the record in this way the affidavits I had obtained from men such as Bicknell. I slipped the camel's nose under the tent, so to speak, because it gave me the opportunity to introduce my documentary proof that the Navy had not played straight up with the Army. Furthermore, I was able to explain to Senator Lucas that the Army and the Navy had been collaborating before 1941 to obtain the cables sent from the local RCA cable office in Hawaii to Tokyo by the Japanese Consul, and to break the code in which they had been sent and received.

This, of course, upset Representative Keefe. He was carrying his own torch. He did not want my affidavits introduced as evidence, because they conflicted with his preconceived notion of events.

Fortunately, Keefe was put down by Representative Murphy, who pointed out that if the Committee followed the wishes of Keefe, "we will know nothing about Pearl Harbor."[2] Both Murphy and Senator George were forceful in saying that the Committee had called only *one* witness to date from the Army who had been at Pearl Harbor. That was Short. What they wanted now was to hear more about what had gone on in the Army's Hawaiian command. In response to this request, I was able to introduce the affidavit of Colonel Fielder, which really put the cat among the pigeons.

This meant that Bicknell, who did not possess the necessary security clearances, was identified as having seen a number of Top Secret messages. Moreover, it proved false Captain Layton's claim that he had given information to Colonel Raley; he either hadn't done so or had rendered the information useless by failing to reveal the importance of its source.

I also introduced the messages that had been intercepted from the Japanese Consul but were not translated by the Navy at Pearl Harbor until after the attack. (These were the messages requesting information about the fleet's movements at Pearl Harbor and whether it was protected by barrage balloons or torpedo nets.[3]

The members of the Committee could not recall the facts of the matter, and Ferguson asked me to make interpretations for the Com-

---

[1] See appendix, pp. 410–414 for exact headings.
[2] Proceedings of Joint Committee, p. 4354.
[3] See appendix, SIS 25877 and 25874, p. 314.

mittee. To avoid that hot potato, I replied: "Senator, I am saying the [Fielder] affidavit says what it says. . . . I am not going to put my impression on the language."[4]

In other words, I could lead the Congressional horse to water, but I mustn't make it drink. If the Committee foundered, or made the wrong evaluation on the basis of my opinion, all my work would have been negated.

This led to the operations of Theo H. Davies and Co., one of the five largest business operations in the Islands, and the British warning to Hawaii of December 3 that said: "Our considered opinion concludes that Japan envisages early hostilities with Britain and the United States."[5]

Then came the fact that the Navy had been tapping the telephones of the Japanese consulate for twenty-two months but quit on December 2 because Captain Mayfield "got peeved."[6] There was more consternation among the Committee when the members realized exactly what my affidavit from Donald Woodrum really meant.

> Senator Lucas: So the Navy just turned the work over to the FBI?
> Colonel Clausen: No, they did not turn it over. They just quit.
> Senator Lucas: They just quit and let the FBI handle it?
> Colonel Clausen: No, they didn't do that. They did not tell the FBI. They just quit and said nothing.
> The Vice-Chairman: They just quit, period, then?
> Colonel Clausen: Period.
> Mr. Gearhart: And if the FBI had known that the Navy had withdrawn, they would have extended their taps to cover the other parts of the consulates?
> Colonel Clausen: Yes, sir.[7]

Over the objections of Representative Keefe, the Committee allowed me to put into evidence the affidavits of Generals MacArthur, Sutherland and Willoughby.

Now the charge was made public that the Navy had, throughout

[4] Proceedings of Joint Committee, p. 4363.
[5] Ibid., p. 4359.
[6] Ibid., p. 4368.
[7] Ibid., p. 4369.

the course of the war in the Pacific, withheld vital intelligence from the Army.

When Senator Ferguson asked (rather pointedly, I thought) if this had been referred to in any report by Stimson or the Army's Judge Advocate General, I replied that Stimson had said in his final report that the Hawaiian command of the Army and Washington were not operating "in the highest degree of efficiency." In effect, what Stimson was saying was that, with regard to intelligence, and especially the ships-in-harbor reports, the information should have been analyzed "by a man with more analytical and imaginative insight to see the possibility of an attack on Pearl Harbor."[8]

Watching the faces of the Committee members, I could see that a seed had been planted in their minds. Whether it would come to fruition, I could not tell. But I began to sense that some members, at least, were getting the idea that something had been wrong with our overall intelligence system before Pearl Harbor.

Washington knew this; Pearl Harbor knew that. Kimmel perceived something else, and Short's staff had additional information. It was Admiral Stark, I believe, who put it rather well when he said: "We never had time to think." The situation was compounded within the Navy, for example, by the fact that its Washington offices were so crowded that when two top Navy people had to discuss matters of code-breaking intelligence, they had to step outside their offices and talk in the corridor.

To me, the question now was whether the Committee would pick up the leads I had given it.

Meanwhile, the hearings lapsed into partisan arguments.

Senator Ferguson, who consistently contended that the commanders at Hawaii had been kept in the dark about the Magic codes broken by Washington, jumped on me for not going to Short for his testimony. Ferguson said I should have asked Short if he had received the information that the affidavits I had collected said he possessed.

One of my reasons for not doing so, I explained, was that I was sure "Congress was going to conduct its own investigation."

"Oh," said Ferguson.

"So far as I was concerned," I replied, noting that some wind seemed to have gone out of Ferguson's sails, "I mean I was willing to do anything that would be required, but with the end of the Japanese War and the opportunity of Congress to confront General Short with

---

[8] Ibid., p. 4381.

whatever it wanted and to go into the matter, it would seem to me that the entire matter could be taken up at that time."[9]

Of course, the Committee had not, when he had appeared before them, grilled Short about these matters. Nor would they now. Nor would they grill Kimmel. So Ferguson let the matter drop, and tried to beat on me for exceeding my brief by questioning various Navy personnel. Why, for example, had I interrogated Commander Rochefort?

I explained that Rochefort had testified before the Army Pearl Harbor Board and had never given the Board any information on Magic. Nor had the Board asked him about Magic, because, I assumed, the Board didn't know the details of Magic at the time.

It was then that Senator Lucas came to my assistance with a neat bit of legal logic that threw another roadblock before Ferguson.

Lucas pointed out that what I was testifying to was documentary proof that had been taken from the files in Hawaii. As he put it: "Documentary proof speaks for itself." Therefore, it wouldn't be necessary to cross-examine Short or Kimmel about it.

Okay, I thought. I have one member of the Committee on my side.

A short time later, I sensed another member was coming over to my side in the argument.

Representative Murphy asked if he could see my Summary exhibit of Far Eastern documents. I replied that I had a copy. It had been Exhibit A before the Army Pearl Harbor Board. Murphy said that was good news, because, of the two copies of the Summary that had been furnished earlier to the Committee, one had been held by Senator Ferguson since October 25, and the other had been held by Representative Gearhart since November 17.

What Murphy was saying, in the polite manner congressmen use in speaking with each other, was that Gearhart and Ferguson had been blocking the other Committee members from seeing this section of my report. Why? Because they believed it would be harmful to their isolationist-revisionist cause. Gentlemen, I thought, the time has come. You can no longer shield Kimmel and Short by keeping my entire investigation from being read by your colleagues. Stop playing petty party politics, and turn over this evidence to the other members of the Committee.

It took me until nearly four in the afternoon to reach the point

---

[9] Ibid., p. 4411.

where I had finished answering the single question posed to me by Lucas the day before. Now, the opposition was going to counterattack.

Ferguson was first. His premise was that I had conducted my investigation because Secretary Stimson had been dissatisfied with the findings of the Army Board. He also believed that Stimson was trying to protect Marshall from the criticism in the Board's report. He didn't believe my investigation had been necessary; he was dissatisfied that I had been appointed to do the job.

I pointed out that he was wrong on all counts. As to why I had been appointed to do the job, I said: "I can only apologize for being a major . . . and I have to apologize for being my age . . . I do not delude myself. They selected me [for the job] because I was the fellow they could spare the most."[10]

By now, it was five in the afternoon. Ferguson was so set to nail me against the wall that a special evening session was scheduled. The Committee broke for dinner. I went to my hotel and lay down on the bed, trying to figure out what they were going to ask me next.

My guess proved right. Ferguson came charging back, accusing me of favoring Marshall over Short. But he kept stumbling over his questions. He was especially put off when I pointed out to him that the Army Board had questioned Short *after* the Board had officially learned about Magic, and that I had determined from my investigation that the intelligence unit in Short's command had adequately advised Short and his staff about the problems of Japanese aggression against America, Great Britain, the Netherlands and China in the Pacific.

Finally, Ferguson acknowledged that the work of the Army Board had been of a questionable nature because it had not fully investigated the implications of Magic. Then he tried to turn this around, saying it had destroyed my investigation, too.

I pointed out that this wasn't true, telling him to "go back to your Public [Law] 339. You told Stimson to investigate—first, you extended the statute of limitations. Then [you] ask Col. Stimson and Mr. Forrestal to conduct several investigations. In other words, each department conduct its own and that is the reason you should not put any invidious implication upon my not going into the Army, or the Navy going into the Army, because you put in there the word 'several.' Now it would have been better, I think, if you had all amalgamated and called everybody up and had sort of an adversary proceeding. . . . The

---

[10] Ibid., pp. 4420, 4421.

thing that Colonel Stimson had in mind was to comply with your Public, 339, and he could not court-martial Kimmel, he doesn't have any jurisdiction over Kimmel. . . ."

Ferguson did not appreciate hearing this fact. He then attacked me for not having grilled Secretary Stimson.

To this I replied: "You mean I should investigate the investigator. That would be like the grand jury investigating the grand jury. You told him [Stimson] to do the job. If you wanted somebody else to investigate Stimson you should have said so in the law."[11]

Ferguson became incensed. He realized I had him cold. Congress had ordered Stimson to conduct an investigation. I was Stimson's investigator. We had done exactly what Congress ordered. What angered Ferguson was that my investigation produced answers that did not agree with his preconceived notions.

I told Ferguson: "[Stimson] was complying with your Public [Law], 339, and you did not say in there how he should do it. You did not say that he should not take affidavits, or that he should take affidavits."

Said Ferguson, "No."

I continued. "You did not say that he should appoint a board, or not appoint a board, and if you wanted him to have three high-ranking generals you should have said so."

Ferguson said that no one would have thought that Stimson would start out with three generals investigating as a board and then switch to the Assistant Recorder of the board to complete the investigation.

"You are misconceiving, sir," I replied. "The Board finished its job. They were glad to be gone, and they made their report. It would have been all right with Henry C. Clausen if [Stimson] had picked somebody else."

Ferguson asked when I had first learned of the fourteen-part Japanese message.

I told him that it had not been until the last week the Board had been in session. In fact, the Board had "been so afraid to touch it that it delegated General Russell as custodian of the material and he alone had the combination of the safe in which it was kept." Furthermore, the two Recorders of the Court, of which I was one, were never given the documents to handle because of their high security classification.

Ferguson didn't have any more rocks to throw. But now he lobbed

---

[11] Ibid., p. 4428.

in a question. If people had testified to the Army Board and had failed to testify fully, why shouldn't their later testimony be discounted?

I replied: "Senator, it is very unfair to take the testimony of a man who has not been authorized to reveal Magic information and say that he testified so and so before so and so. . . . If those subjects are such that they cannot testify fully before the Boards . . . you must make allowance for the fact that they were bound by oath not to reveal it to a soul. . . . Now, you cannot say that when he is under oath not to reveal things, like General Miles, that he did not tell the truth. You cannot gag him on one hand and say, 'Oh, you did not say that to the Board.' "[12]

Now, if you ever want to upset a Senator, all you have to do is to contradict him, or say that there is information that Congress cannot have because of security regulations.

Ferguson hit the roof. He could not comprehend that these men had sworn to tell the truth before various investigating bodies, but, at the same time, were bound by a higher oath not to reveal anything about Magic. (As I said earlier in my narrative, I had a feeling of déjà vu when I read the testimony of Richard Helms about the CIA's operations some forty years later; Congress will never believe that it shouldn't have access to every secret in government. On the other hand, as I have witnessed it over the years, could Congress keep a secret if it knew one?)

This took us into the instructions that had been given to General Miles about how he was to testify before the Army Pearl Harbor Board. You will recall that Miles had told me that the Chief of Staff, Marshall, did not want him to talk about Magic.

Ferguson wouldn't touch this issue with a barge pole. It was too hot. Thus, he never attacked Marshall where he was most vulnerable. Instead, he moved on to my affidavit from General MacArthur. This worried him because MacArthur had testified that, as far as he had been concerned, the dispatches he received from the War Department gave him ample and complete information to warrant his alerting his command for war. Ferguson did not believe MacArthur's statement. It would have been politically inconvenient for him to do, so he tried to get me to say that other factors were more responsible for MacArthur's preparedness than the War Department's dispatches, as compared with Short's being asleep at the switch.

---

[12] Ibid., p. 4431.

With some exasperation, I said: "If you are alerted for war, you are alerted for war whether you get a thousand alerts or not. . . . I knew I was not investigating MacArthur; I was not investigating the Philippine Islands. . . . I did know there was a great deal of Japanese activity, military activity in the Mandates, the Philippines, all over. That is the reason, of course, why the basic mistake was made of thinking the Japs were going to strike in the South. It is not a question of knowing the Japs were going to strike, but where."[13]

Ferguson paused. I waited. I prayed his next question would be bipartisan. It was, thank the Lord, for Ferguson asked if I had reached any conclusion from the affidavits I had taken from MacArthur, Willoughby and Sutherland. In effect, Ferguson opened the doors to admit the most basic findings of my investigation.

I fudged my answer somewhat at the start, saying that I had a "hazy curbstone opinion" that the Navy at Manila had shortchanged the Army about intelligence in that the Navy had not given the Army all the intelligence available.

Once Ferguson and I had agreed on what the term "short-changed" meant, Ferguson asked if the claim was being made that the Navy had been shortchanging the Army before Pearl Harbor, as far as intelligence was concerned. This meant Magic in particular.

"That is what General Willoughby says in his affidavit," I replied. "He said it existed down to the time of the Philippine campaign; after the reconquest of the Philippines, and for that reason he wanted an integrated, one overall agency to handle this stuff, so you do not in the future have one service monopolizing the information to the detriment of the other, and neither one may be knowing what the other is doing."

Ferguson picked up on this immediately. He asked that I expand my statement.

"If I have a basket of Magic here," I explained, "and I am the Navy, and you are the Army over there, then I would pick these up and determine in my mind what would affect you."

"You would give me what you wanted to give me?" asked Ferguson.

"I would give you what I wanted to give you and obviously that would be wrong," I said. "Because I, as a Navy man, would not know what the military implications may be to you."

[13] Ibid., p. 4437.

Suddenly, we had established an unusual colloquy. Both of us understood the importance of this magic moment about Magic; both of us understood the message we were delivering.

Ferguson wanted to know if the same ''shortchanging'' occurred in Washington.

''I think there was far more cordial and freer exchange, but the same thing applies, Senator,'' I said. ''For the sake of the country, it should be known that there was evidently some jealousy between the services, and this existed prior to Pearl Harbor.''

''You mean it existed in Washington, Hawaii and the Philippines?'' asked Ferguson.

''That is what I understand,'' I said. ''In other words, what a ludicrous situation is presented if you have a fleet intelligence officer, Captain Layton, saying he gave information to Colonel Raley but would not tell Raley where it came from! How could Colonel Raley know how to evaluate it?''

''That is what I was going to get at for many days in this hearing here in Washington,'' said Ferguson.

''If I can make one single contribution to this case,'' I said, ''and if anything came out of this hearing, it would be that you pursue the idea of having one agency and let that be coordinated on a business basis, so you do not have monopolistic agencies trying to hide the information for themselves.''

''All right,'' Ferguson said, reiterating that the intelligence shortchanging existed in at least three places: Washington, Manila and Pearl Harbor. ''Did you find any supervising head who was able, in any of the services, to really evaluate the intelligence so that it could be used by the United States?''

''Now you've hit the nail right on the head,'' I replied. ''If one thing more should be done, it is this: You ought to train people to look at this stuff and be able to read it, just like lawyers can pick up a case in a short time; you can do that by training people. You cannot do it by going through normal communications and so forth. . . .''

Said Ferguson: ''I am talking about an overall head that really coordinated the various officers in the Philippines, the Hawaiian Islands and in Washington?''

''Of course not,'' I said. ''Then you would not have had the ludicrous situation of Admiral Turner saying that he thought Hawaii was getting this stuff based on what Admiral Noyes told him. What a silly thing that is! What kind of a set up is that?''

''That is what I am trying to find out here,'' Ferguson said.

"I did not find any such thing," I said again, "and I hope the future sees a different picture. Otherwise, we are liable to have Pearl Harbor all over again."[14]

I could see that my remarks had struck home. Ferguson asked me a series of rather inconsequential questions and then returned to the subject. He wanted to know what Pearl Harbor had possessed in terms of decrypting equipment. He seemed shaken when I pointed out, again, that the Navy did not have equipment in Hawaii capable of breaking the diplomatic Purple code.

As for what other facilities the Navy had at Pearl Harbor, I pointed out that the Army was "solely at the mercy of the Navy" when it came to getting code-breaking intelligence. The Navy, claiming its communications were more secure than the Army's, had limited what the Army in Washington could send to its Hawaiian command in terms of advisories based on Magic. And while the Navy was supposed to keep Short and his staff fully advised about intelligence received from Washington, Colonel Fielder had sworn to me that if he had asked the Navy for such information, it would have been refused him.

Meanwhile, the Navy was doing things in a sub-rosa fashion, like tapping the phones of the Japanese Consul's home and office, and the phone of the Japanese steamship line, then, when it became frightened, cutting off the taps without telling anyone.

Ferguson asked if I had found that the Navy had been giving the Army all the intelligence it had obtained in Hawaii.

"Well, as I size it up," I said, "the Navy was not doing it. It just comes down to that."

Ferguson was looking for a closer, a kicker for the story, as a journalist would say. Suddenly, we were back in the Philippines with General Willoughby.

"Here is a man fighting the war in the Philippines," I said, "when I was there, with guns booming, and he at that time is having this vexing problem of trying to get the information from the Navy when the war was going on!"

How long after Pearl Harbor was Willoughby having these problems, Ferguson asked.

In May 1945, I replied, or some four and one-half years after the Japanese attacked Pearl Harbor.[15]

Ferguson said he had no more questions.

---

[14] Ibid., pp. 4437–4439.
[15] Ibid., p. 4441.

I was delighted to be finished with Ferguson and hoped I might have changed his point of view. I knew he had fully understood the implications of what I had told him.

Now, I had another hostile congressman after my scalp.

Representative Keefe was bound and determined to prove that my investigation was prejudiced from its inception. He wanted to prove that Stimson had sent me on my mission to save Marshall's reputation from the stinging criticism of the Army Board.

We went around the mulberry bush for some time on the matter, and I finally let him have it.

"Mr. Keefe," I said, "I at no time went out with any preconceived idea to slant any investigation. I would not have been a party to it. Mr. Stimson would not have authorized it. You assumed, in your questions, that I was some kind of stooge sent out by the War Department."

"Well, now," Keefe said, retracting his charges. "You are jumping at conclusions."

"I am glad to hear you say that," I said. Still, battle was joined.[16]

Keefe seemed to be marching to his own drummer. He could not grasp the fact that the secrecy surrounding Magic had caused serious problems for the Army Board, to say nothing about the way Marshall had handled the issue of Magic in a secret session before the general officers of the Board, and that testimony about Magic had been denied the Board. It wasn't difficult to figure out that Keefe was madder than hell at me, for I was the person who found the evidence that Marshall was not guilty of the charges the Army Board had made against him. I was the guy who rained on Keefe's parade.

It was now twenty minutes after ten at night. The Committee was worn out. So was I. The hearing recessed until the next morning.

When the hearing resumed, Senator Lucas began the questioning, which gave me something of a breather. He helped rebut Keefe's charges by stating the groundwork for my investigation as being the Army Board's meeting for three months without having had the chance to question any witnesses about Magic. Furthermore, when the witnesses came close to the issue of Magic, they had squirmed and danced their way out of trouble.

[16] Ibid., p. 4451.

I said that this was true, that "my experience as a trial lawyer led me to see these various witnesses as they testified; and there seemed to be, in two instances, at least . . . as though they were on the brink of something and could not say something. . . ."[17]

That's why it was necessary, in the words of the Judge Advocate General, "to complete the picture and, in fairness to other personnel," to follow the leads I thought necessary to complete my investigation.[18]

This led to the question as to who had more power and authority concerning my investigation or any other war matters: Stimson or the Army Board?

I pointed out that the Secretary of War had the power and authority, not the Army Board. It was the Secretary whom Congress empowered under Public Law 339 to conduct the investigation into Pearl Harbor. I also again pointed out: "There was no form prescribed by that law as to how the investigation would be conducted."[19]

The fact that Stimson chose me, like himself a former U.S. Attorney skilled as a trial lawyer, to be his investigator was perfectly legal and correct. If I questioned fifteen people who had testified before the Army Board, located another thirty-five new witnesses (who, as it turned out, never testified before any other investigation, including that of Congress) and presented their sworn testimony to the Secretary of War to enable him to reach a decision about the guilt or innocence of certain parties involved in Pearl Harbor, that, too, was perfectly legal and proper.[20]

Now, Lucas introduced the real reason for Keefe's petulance about my testimony. He read into the record Keefe's statement on the floor of the House dated November 6, 1945, about how "Colonel Clausen went to Colonel Bratton along with all the other witnesses and browbeat him into signing an affidavit a year later in which his testimony is subject to some change." Keefe had declared, "I want to talk to Colonel Bratton."

"Now, that is a pretty serious charge against you, Colonel Clausen," Lucas said.

I replied that "I considered it so . . . when it is not true and correct. . . . I treated every single person whom I interviewed with as much fairness as I knew how. I certainly did not conduct an inquisi-

[17] Ibid., p. 4462.
[18] Ibid.
[19] Ibid., p. 4463.
[20] Ibid., p. 4472.

tion. I went to them and, in all cases where I could, showed them what other people had said about the subject. Now, one example, General Fielder. . . . There had also been testimony about the Navy giving the Army all [of the Navy's] information. That immediately put General Fielder on the spot and in order to be fair to him I took him with me to Guam and there confronted him with Captain Layton, who was the fleet [intelligence] man and who had the information of this super-duper code-cracking, and Captain Layton said he did not give it to General Fielder. Now, that is the kind of investigation I tried to conduct.''

I could see Keefe, Gearhart and Ferguson squirming in their seats. Under the Committee rules, they couldn't say anything at the moment, but I knew they were going to come after me hammer and tongs when their time came.

Meanwhile, Lucas laid another cornerstone for the reason Bratton had changed his story to me. Lucas asked: ''What I specifically want to know is whether or not you browbeat this 225-pound Colonel here [Bratton was sitting just behind me] into giving evidence that was other than what he considered at that time the truth?''

''No, sir,'' I said.

''Did you browbeat him into signing this affidavit?''

''No, sir.''

''Since I have seen the Colonel here, I would not want to attempt to browbeat him into anything,'' said Lucas.[21]

Later on in the hearings, Lucas questioned Bratton on this issue. ''Were you ever mistreated by Clausen in the way of being browbeaten into signing this [your] affidavit? Lucas asked Bratton.

''Not in any manner whatsoever, sir,'' Bratton testified to Lucas. ''My relations with Colonel Clausen were cordial in every respect.''[22]

In continuing his questions to me, however, Lucas went on to say that I had testified to things that took place in Hawaii ''which, frankly, I was amazed and startled at. I confess that I had not had time to read your report . . . but I cannot see how this Committee can conclude this hearing without calling a couple of witnesses from Hawaii. We have been investigating Washington all this time.''

I thought this was quite an admission for a senator to make. Not only did he acknowledge that he had not read my report, but he was

---

[21] Ibid., pp. 4464–4465.
[22] Ibid., p. 4535.

saying that, given my testimony, he was now of the opinion that the Congressional investigation was improperly focusing on what had happened in Washington. I was making some real headway, after all.[23]

This brought us back to the issue of the Navy's having tapped the phones of the Japanese Consul in Honolulu.

Lucas placed in evidence the testimony of Captain Mayfield (now an admiral) before the Hewitt Investigation. Mayfield had been cross-examined by Sonnett and said that nothing of military significance had been obtained by tapping the Consul's phones. He also explained that he had stopped the phone taps, "since the interceptions to that date had revealed nothing of particular value," and a conflict was perceived with the FBI's tap on the Consul's phone.

Sonnett had then asked Mayfield if he recalled the transcript of the Mori conversation that FBI Agent Shivers had intercepted. Mayfield said that Shivers had brought it to him on the afternoon of December 6 and that it was never brought to the attention of Kimmel. Mayfield did not know if the matter had been brought to Short's attention.

It had been, of course, by Bicknell, who had taken the transcript of the conversation to Fielder and Short that Saturday evening. This was the conversation in which Short could not see anything suspicious even though it appeared to be in a code based on the flowers in bloom in Hawaii at that time. The answer to Tokyo's question had been that the "flowers in bloom were the fewest out of the whole year, but that hibiscus and poinsettias were in bloom."

In his testimony, Mayfield acknowledged that he thought this language was strange, but it was not until after the Japanese attack that he "heard or read something to the effect that such a code may have been in existence."

Lucas asked whether, during my investigation, I had learned if anyone in the Army or the Navy knew about the existence of such a code.

"You remember, Senator," I replied, "[Bicknell] said he had been trained under General Knowland . . . [who was] G-2 in the European War [World War I], and he always instructed his men that no matter how insignificant the detail might appear, the information might have some important bearing. Colonel Bicknell was especially alarmed because of the use of those two words, poinsettias and hibiscus, and he testified before the [Army] Board that the next morning when the

---

[23] Ibid., pp. 4464–4465.

attack was going on he stood on the veranda of his home, repeating automatically to himself, as the Japs were dropping bombs on the ships, 'poinsettias and hibiscus.' ''

The hearing room was silent for several moments when I finished this statement. Then, Representative Gearhart came to the attack.

He probed around a bit, asking if I had been given a free hand to conduct my investigation. I said that was true. He next asked about the Winds Code messages. He could not understand why I had spent so much time investigating them.

I told him that I agreed with him that the Winds Code had been overemphasized. But I had to follow up the leads in Captain Safford's testimony before the Hart Inquiry, because he was asserting ''that all the Japanese intentions were known on December 6. Well, that would imply that you even knew that Pearl Harbor was the attack target. . . . That is one reason why it [the Winds Code] is magnified out of all proportion.''

It is interesting to note that Safford tried to aid Kimmel in the years after the attack by saying that the execute message for the Winds Code had been intercepted. But no one could verify his claim. The other dramatic part of Safford's statement was whether the so-called execute message had been mislaid, whether somebody swiped it or whether it had been destroyed. I couldn't find evidence that a Winds Code execute message had *ever* been received by Washington. I told Gearhart: ''The 'Winds Code' set-up, and the query and implement message, is magnified out of proportion to all the aspects of this tragedy.''

Then, Gearhart got down to brass tacks. ''The greatest mystery of all of these Pearl Harbor investigations,'' he said, ''is the mystery of where the Chief of Staff of the Army was, and where the Chief of Naval Operations of the Navy was, on the night of December 6.''

It was obvious what Gearhart was after: Marshall's scalp. In particular, Gearhart was focusing on the report of the Army Board, which criticized Marshall because, as the Board put it: *''He [Marshall] failed in his relations with the Hawaiian Department in the following particulars—to get to General Short on the evening of December 6th and the early morning of December 7th the critical information indicating an almost complete break with Japan, though there was ample time to have accomplished this.''* (Emphasis added)

Said Gearhart: ''That is the finding and the conclusion and the indictment, if you please, of the Army Board itself, and that ties in with General Marshall and Magic as closely as any two ideas could be associated.''

I couldn't believe Gearhart could be so obtuse.

Even Keefe had understood that Marshall had not been given the fourteen-part diplomatic message on the night of December 6, as Colonel Bratton had claimed. But Gearhart could not comprehend that Bratton had lied to the Army Board. Nor could he understand the significance of the fact that General Miles had seen the first thirteen parts of the fourteen-part message while dining with his counterpart, the head of Naval intelligence, that same evening, yet neither man had done anything about it. Nor could Gearhart understand why Marshall could not remember where he had been that fateful evening. (Some members of Congress had gone so far as to accuse Marshall of having been to the movies with a WAC, although the Women's Army Corps was not then in existence.) Nor could Gearhart comprehend how the office of the Chief of Staff or other officers functioned.

He thought Marshall should be on duty twenty-four hours a day.

I pointed out that this obligation still allowed Marshall to sleep. The office of the Chief of Staff is open twenty-four hours a day, and Marshall could be contacted at any time, I said, just like our California Supreme Court.

"That is right," said Gearhart.

"But I bet the justices go out to play golf on Sundays once in a while," I said.

"Answer my question," said Gearhart with asperity. "It means you must be in touch with your office, in touch with your command, for the full 24 hours of the day, doesn't it?"[24]

I pointed out to Gearhart that that was the reason Marshall had a staff, and the staff had testified that there were procedures that could be followed to reach Marshall at any place, at any time. Then I figured out how I could stop Gearhart in his tracks.

"Mr. Gearhart," I said, waving my hand over my report and the exhibits, "I think you will find through here plenty of evidence that, according to the procedure then in operation, if it became necessary to see the Chief of Staff the night of December 6, he could be seen. . . . Let's prove the negative. I don't know of anybody that tried to see the Chief of Staff on the night of December 6 and could not find him."[25]

---

[24] Ibid., p. 4475.
[25] Ibid., p. 4477.

You know, when you hit a man with a good punch, you can see his eyes glaze over. That's how Gearhart looked as he tried to recover.

"Well, maybe there will be some testimony that they were trying to deliver to him. . . ."

I pointed out that Colonel Bratton had testified that he gave the thirteen parts to Colonel Dusenbury for delivery to Marshall at his quarters when Dusenbury went home. Furthermore, Dusenbury had testified to me that he had *not* delivered the material to Marshall's quarters. In reality, Dusenbury didn't deliver the material to anyone until nine hours later the following morning, Sunday, December 7. (It is also interesting to note that Congress never asked Dusenbury to testify before the Committee. In other words, Congress accepted my affidavit.)

Gearhart tried to keep punching on the Marshall question, but the best he could do was ask: "The mystery still remains—the big mystery of the Pearl Harbor investigation after 5 years of investigation. How do you account for that?"

"Well, you want me to answer your opinion," I said. "I can't very well argue with you. I mean, it's not my function. I am here as a witness. But I don't agree. In other words, I don't think that is the big mystery of Pearl Harbor at all.

"*The big mystery—there are some big highlights.*

"*Query: What information did Washington have?*

"*Query: What did Washington do about it?*

"*Query: What did Hawaii do about it?*

"*I mean, those are the basic, big questions.*" (Emphasis added)

Still, Gearhart tried to contend that Marshall's whereabouts were more important than anything else. Give a congressman a chance to expound on a conspiracy theory, and you've got trouble. Gearhart was bound and determined to prove his belief that Marshall had gone to ground so that the Japanese attack on Pearl Harbor would be a surprise success. He didn't seem to realize that if the Japanese had attacked and been repulsed, the result would have been the same: America would have gone to war, anyway.

The Congressman kept wriggling, trying to get off the hook on which he had impaled himself. I had to admire him for trying as hard as he did.

Finally, I said: "Mr. Gearhart, if you and I were in Fresno trying a damage action involving automobiles, we would be following, according to the judges, the rules of the road. We would be squaring our proof to certain rules, certain standards.

"Now, in assessing responsibility against Army officers, you just can't discard the rules of the military. You have to consider the military rules. They are contained in books. There is nothing secret about the functions of the staff officers and what they are supposed to do. Your proof here, or in any other case involving the military, must be by the standards of the military. . . ." I pointed out that even if everyone knew where Marshall was on "the night of 6 December, he still didn't get the 13 parts [of the diplomatic message]. And his G-2, the man supposed to be charged with certain aspects and obligations, just like the Chief of Staff, he did know [about the message]."[26]

Still, Gearhart went on to say that both Marshall and Stark were missing on the night of December 6. The fact was that Stark, who had said originally that he also couldn't recall where he was, had remembered later that he went to the theater that night. After President Roosevelt had read the thirteen parts of the fourteen-part message and had declared, "This means war!" he tried to call Stark, but did not want him paged at the theater. The two men did talk later that night, after Stark came home. Meanwhile, Secretary Knox called Stimson and Hull to set up a conference at the State Department for ten o'clock the next morning. But Roosevelt *never* tried to call Marshall.

Dusenbury's failure on December 6 to deliver the messages to Marshall kept the one man unalerted who, I believe, would have taken immediate action upon learning of the impending crisis. To paraphrase the words of President Kennedy, there's always some poor fellow who never gets the word. In the case of Pearl Harbor, it was Marshall, the most important man in town.

As I say, Gearhart didn't give up easily, but he gave up in the end. A Republican, Gearhart broke ranks with his fellow minority members when the Committee reached its final conclusions. He voted against Kimmel and Short, against the Roosevelt-Marshall conspiracy mob, and I am sure my testimony and my report were major factors in his change of heart.

That still left me facing the remaining members of the Committee.

Murphy of Pennsylvania indicated that he agreed with me. He drove home the point that Marshall had told the Committee he believed he was in his own home on the evening of December 6, and the

---

[26] Ibid., p. 4481.

Committee had heard "not a single word of evidence in this record that the General was not at home that night."[27]

I agreed, and said again that during my investigation, I hadn't been able to find anyone who had brought the thirteen-part or fourteen-part message to Marshall on the night of December 6.

Murphy did ask a very important question: Who had seen the reply that Short made to the warning message Marshall had sent on November 27?

The answer was, of course, Gerow, Marshall and Secretary Stimson. Both Gerow and Marshall had accepted the blame for not having been more alert to Short's failure to provide an adequate reply. The explanation for this error may well have been that each of the commands in Manila, Panama and California had sent lengthy, detailed replies that gave all the background of their readiness to repel an attack, so Short's brief message slipped by. But historians will never know for sure, because Colonel Bundy, who had been responsible for the Far East messages at the time, was killed before he could be questioned on the matter.

I didn't have much time to think about all this, however, because Senator Ferguson began throwing his beanballs again.

First, he wanted to know whether or not the so-called pilot message of December 6, the one alerting Washington that a fourteen-part message would be sent by Tokyo, had been seen by Bratton, Gerow or anyone else.

I could only reply that I had tried to check out who had seen what, and when they had seen it, but everyone had testified that the Magic intercepts as distributed, and all receipts signed for them at the time, had been destroyed. That had been the SOP, the standard operating procedure. In retrospect, the SOP might have been improperly set up, but there was nothing that could be done about it after the fact.

Ferguson kept trying to break me about Bratton's having lied to the Army Board.

When the Senator found he could not do this, he switched targets. He next wanted to know what the policies of the War Department had been. I had to reply that the scope of my investigation did not apply to matters of analytical military nature. Furthermore, the policies of the War Department were set by Secretary Stimson, the man for whom I worked. In other words, if Ferguson had questions or arguments about

[27] Ibid., p. 4483.

policy, he should direct them to the man who made the policy, not to me.

Surprisingly, Ferguson gave up at this point. Now, it was Representative Keefe's turn for a parting shot. He read into the record the affidavit from Dusenbury and made a great point about how Dusenbury had said that he had "received all 14 parts of the Japanese diplomatic message at about 12 that night. Thereupon, I left and went home. I returned the next morning and began the distribution of this intercept consisting of the 14 parts."[28]

The most important part of the message for Keefe was the fact that Dusenbury had testified that the message had been sent to the Army by the Navy. *Therefore, the Navy had known around midnight, and before the Army, that the Japanese were breaking off diplomatic relations.*

Keefe was concerned because there were great and glaring inconsistencies in various testimonies about the timing of the receipt of the fourteen-part message.

I had to agree that he was correct.

Keefe then brought up the biggest contradiction to date, which was that, according to the Navy, the fourteenth part of the diplomatic message had not come in, "or did not start coming in, until 5 o'clock in the morning and was finally decoded and translated about 7:15 on the morning of the 7th."[29]

What Keefe was trying to do was to show that my affidavit from Dusenbury was flawed, because of conflicting testimony by the Navy about its not having received the fourteenth part until early in the morning of December 7.

I replied that when I questioned Dusenbury, and he had been one of my very first witnesses, I had not known what the testimony of the Navy might be. I don't believe the Navy had even broached the subject at the time. Dusenbury had been on his way to a new posting at Chungking when I first talked to him. He was available now to testify before the Committee. But, as I said earlier, the Committee never called him. If Keefe was trying to imply that I was wrong in not having cross-examined Dusenbury about the discrepancy in timing, I can only say that Keefe and the Committee were guilty of an even worse failure, because they never tracked down the matter, or the man. (Nor did they

[28] Ibid., p. 4493.
[29] Ibid., p. 4495.

question Colonel Rowlett, whose affidavit to me supported Dusenbury's statement that the fourteenth part was in hand around midnight.)

Senator Brewster of Maine was the last Committee member to take a shot at me. A Republican, he was pro-Kimmel to a fault and anti-Roosevelt in every bone in his body. Of course, the first thing he tried to do was get me to criticize the Committee's work.

That wouldn't do. I saw through his blustering. Instead, I said that the Committee had done a very fine thing. Congress could investigate Pearl Harbor better than anyone else.

"I also think," I said, "that the basic recommendation that can come from this Committee is a fine one if you make it that never again shall Magic, this information, be monopolized by one service or the other service, but have it distributed by one agency on an overall basis."[30]

Brewster disliked my implied criticism of the Navy and Kimmel. It showed when he began questioning me about the report of the Army Board, which had chastised Marshall. I pointed out—again, since Brewster had not been present during my earlier testimony—that the Army Board had not known about Magic until the last week of its existence, and therefore its findings were tragically flawed.

Brewster replied that he didn't care when the Board had found out about Magic.

His mind was already made up. I could tell that. So he attacked me as hanging my investigation on a "slender peg" and tried to discredit the work I had done.

Murphy came to my rescue, however. He read into the record a statement that Brewster had given to the Chicago *Tribune* only five days earlier.

"Much of the responsibility for the Pearl Harbor disaster must rest upon the late President Roosevelt and figures in his administration who sought strenuously to fasten the blame on Kimmel and Short," Brewster reportedly told the *Tribune*.

Brewster didn't like having this read into the record, but he said, "I think that statement I made is a very fair one."[31]

He then went after Marshall's keeping the Army Board from getting information about Magic. Fair comment, I thought. He refused to accept Bratton's change in testimony, or the fact that Dusenbury had

[30] Ibid., p. 4499.
[31] Ibid., p. 4502.

sworn that he had not delivered the diplomatic messages to Marshall on the night of December 6. He criticized me and my report in general, but I don't think his bluster scored any points with the other members of the Committee.

My testimony had ended.

The Committee broke for lunch at 12:40 on the afternoon of February 14, 1946. I couldn't tell what the final effect of my testimony would be, but as I left the hearing room, I said a silent prayer asking the good Lord to let my message get through: We had to get our methods of gathering and disseminating intelligence squared away. The military could never be trusted to do the job for themselves. A new, independent, impartial intelligence agency would have to be created.

I also wondered whether the Committee would vote its findings along purely partisan lines. If this were to happen, the question of who was to blame for Pearl Harbor would never be laid to rest. Would the isolationists, the anti-Roosevelt faction, force through their beliefs that our President had been involved in a conspiracy that allowed the Japanese to attack Pearl Harbor? Or would cooler heads prevail?

The facts were on the table. Now it was up to the Congressional jury to decide.

16 ‖ FINAL JUDGEMENT

With Congress behind me, I checked with Allen Klots in New York to see if I could help. Stimson was still very ill. He had indeed given his country every measure of strength he possessed. Now he could do no more. In my previous talk with the Secretary, he had entrusted to me for delivery from the Pentagon to his law office the personal diary he had kept during the war. I promised that I would not read it, and I didn't. On arrival at Stimson's office, I met with Klots and another partner, whose name, I believe, was Putnam. They decided that the safest place for this priceless war recollection would be in what they called a ''client's box,'' which I assumed would be like a safe deposit box in their office vault. I turned the diary over to them, and we began work on Stimson's final statement to Congress.

Klots was magnificent in all this. He introduced excerpts from Stimson's diary into the record. For the first time, the public was given access to the Secretary's most personal thoughts about the events leading up to war, especially the warning messages of November 27 to Short and Kimmel.

As his diary showed, Stimson had telephoned Secretary of State

Hull early on the morning of November 27 to find out what had been Hull's final words with the Japanese. Hull told Stimson that the talks with Tokyo had been broken off. The matter was now in the hands of the Army and the Navy. Stimson then called Roosevelt and learned that what Hull had said was true. Stimson knew that the Japanese were sending an expeditionary force of thirty to fifty ships along the China coast south of Formosa. Thus, Stimson was pleased that Hull had made a strong statement to the Japanese about the situation. The Japanese, of course, were quick to say that Hull's statement was an ultimatum. Stimson believed, however, that "no impartial reading of this document can characterize it" as such.

Later in the morning, Stimson and General Arnold discussed sending a reconnaissance flight over the Marshall Islands to see if Japanese forces were massing there.

General Marshall was not in Washington. He was attending Army maneuvers in the South. (I have always believed that Marshall should not have left Washington at that time, but the Chief of Staff believed the maneuvers were of extreme importance, and history shows they were.) This meant that when Secretary of the Navy Knox and the Chief of Naval Operations, Stark, came to the War Department later in the morning to confer with Stimson and Gerow, they did not have Marshall's counsel. Both Stark and Gerow were hoping that the military could be given more time to prepare for war. A memorandum had been drawn up for the President's approval on the matter. The military agreed, however, that action would have to be taken if the Japanese attacked American, British or Dutch territory, or if Japan moved her forces into that strategic isthmus known as the Malay Peninsula.

The conference discussed the types of warning messages that might be sent to the American commanders in the various theaters. Stimson believed another warning should be sent. He had discussed the matter with Roosevelt, and the President had approved the idea of a final alert, "namely, that they should be on the *qui vive* for any attack, and explaining the exact situation." Because Marshall was unavailable, Stimson involved himself with the drafting of the message. To make sure it was accurate, he called Hull again to get "his exact statement as to the status of the negotiations, which was then incorporated into the first sentence of the message." Stimson personally inserted in the second sentence of the dispatch the words: "*but hostile action possible at any moment.*" (Emphasis added)

As far as Stimson was concerned, this message "presented with the utmost precision the situation with which we were all confronted and in the light of which all our commanding officers, as well as ourselves, had to govern our conduct.'' In other words, if there was going to be a war, Japan would have to strike first.

I have always thought that the criticism of the wording of Stimson's message has been overplayed by both the military and the isolationist critics. Apparently, the isolationists could not comprehend the thoughtfulness with which Stimson explained to our commanders in the field just how difficult our negotiations with Japan had become, and that they should be on the alert for ''hostile action.'' As for the military commanders in Hawaii, their failure to comprehend indicates that the only language they would have understood would have been a message like ''drop your buns and grab your guns.''

Now, the reader can see why I contend that, had Short and Kimmel known that the ''war warning'' message had been sent with the approval of the President, with information supplied by the Secretary of State and written by the Secretary of War himself, they never would have criticized it the way they did. The military is very careful about biting the hand that feeds it. I doubt that Short, or Kimmel, would have bitten the hand of his civilian masters if he had known who was taking such care to feed him the information that ''hostile action [is] possible at any moment.''[1]

As far as Stimson's final statement was concerned, although he might have been in extremely fragile health, the Secretary didn't waver from his original report based on my investigation. If anything, because of Klots' wonderful writing style and other contributions, the prose in Stimson's statement to Congress was even stronger than before. He castigated Short and Kimmel for failing to employ reconnaissance to defend Pearl Harbor and for failing to communicate with each other in the days leading up to the Japanese attack.

We stayed away from the issue of the Navy's hoarding of intelligence, however. After much discussion, including whether we should criticize the Navy, the Secretary believed that I had presented the case as well as I could before the Committee. Now it was up to Congress to act.

As for General Short, Stimson's report concluded: ''The outpost commander is like a sentinel on duty. His fundamental duties are clear and concise. He must assume that the enemy will attack at his partic-

---

[1]Proceedings of Joint Committee, pp. 5422–5424.

ular post . . . at the time and in the way in which it will be most difficult to defeat him. It is not the duty of the outpost commander to speculate or rely on the possibilities of the enemy attacking some other outpost instead of his own. It is his duty to meet him at his post at any time and to make the best possible fight that can be made against him with the weapons with which he has been supplied. . . . [No other factors] in my opinion alter in any material degree the responsibility of General Short for the complete absence of a real alert, which he had been directed to take in the message of November 27, and for the placing of his defense in a more helpless position than it was before the alert message was sent out. After all, *he was the man upon whom the country had a right to rely for the defense of Hawaii, and he had been sufficiently warned.''* (Emphasis added)

I believe that Stimson's statement has withstood the test of time. I have always been proud to have been associated on a personal level with one of the finest men I have ever known. We had a farewell phone conversation after his statement had been through a final typing, and I knew I was saying a permanent good-bye. Stimson was still suffering the effects of his heart attack, and he had not yet recovered sufficiently to begin working on his autobiography, *On Active Service in Peace and War,* with McGeorge Bundy, the son of my colleague Harvey Bundy. Stimson was to linger in poor health for four more years. He died in 1950, and I felt that America had lost one of the greatest men who had ever served in government.

We delivered Stimson's report to Congress in early March 1946, and I went back to San Francisco to my practice.

The full Committee met and discussed until July 15, but it had cut back deeply on the number of witnesses it would call from Hawaii. The Republican minority had forced the Committee to probe far more deeply into what had happened in Washington than what had occurred in Hawaii. I believe the Democrats on the Committee were just too tired to investigate any further.

The Committee released its report on July 20, and the headline news was that Kimmel and Short had been found not guilty of dereliction of duty, but guilty of errors of judgement. Reading the news stories carefully, I could see that the Committee had been faced with the same problems in making judgements as had I in working for Stimson.

If you add up the votes of the ten-man ''Congressional jury,'' you find that the vote split eight to two, which means that two Republicans deserted the superisolationists, Brewster and Ferguson (who filed a minority view). Most important was that in their minority report, Brewster and Ferguson agreed with the majority that Kimmel and Short shared in "the failure to perform the responsibilities in Hawaii."[2] This judgement by Kimmel's supporters was a real blow to the Republicans. They lost the issue they believed would win them the presidency in the 1948 election.

In its majority report, the Committee reached twelve conclusions about Pearl Harbor. There were seven specific charges listed against Kimmel and Short. In brief, the two men were charged with the failure:

(1) To discharge their responsibilities in light of warnings received from Washington or from other information they possessed, and in light of the principle of command by mutual cooperation;

(2) To integrate and coordinate their facilities for defense;

(3) To liaise with each other and to exchange fully all intelligence;

(4) To maintain effective reconnaissance (which included the failure to use radar);

(5) To establish a state of readiness in the Army and Navy capable of meeting all possible attacks;

(6) To employ the facilities in their possession to properly repel a Japanese attack;

(7) To appreciate the significance of intelligence and other information available to them.

These were the items upon which the headline and editorial writers of the day fixed their attention. So did the majority of historians who have focused on the two issues: Were Short and Kimmel guilty and properly relieved of command, or were Roosevelt and his administration guilty of conspiring to force Japan to attack? To me, the newspapers and historians have missed the real meanings of the Committee report.

Let me explain.

Congress writes its reports in ways that baffle the ordinary citizen. It doesn't say that this official or that official is guilty of a criminal act. Instead, Congress points out the evidence it has uncovered and says that it hopes the appropriate agencies involved will take the necessary action, as it did with the case I prosecuted during the war when the Truman Committee uncovered criminal activities in aircraft engine procurement. By reporting this way, Congress maintains the separation

---

[2]PHA Report, p. 573.

of powers. It doesn't intrude upon other agencies, such as the Department of Justice or the Department of State. Congress says we have found facts, fellows, and it's up to you to apply them and correct the situation.

Thus, as I read the twelve conclusions reached by Congress, my heart jumped when I saw that, at the end of the list, the Committee had come to grips with the problems of intelligence I had investigated. Aside from its findings on Kimmel and Short, the Committee determined that both the Intelligence and the War Plans Divisions of the Army *and* the Navy were "deficient." Furthermore, both the War *and* the Navy Departments were not "sufficiently alerted" on the eve of Pearl Harbor.

Now, these words are fairly innocuous. They don't give the headline writer much of a peg on which to hang a banner. Nor do they give the editorial writer much room for a feisty opinion piece. But to myself, I said, "Oh, boy. Something wonderful is going on here."

What has been generally ignored are the two sections of the report that take professionals like me to the heart of the matter. This is where you find the blockbuster comments. The first section is titled, simply, "Recommendations." The second is called "Supervisory, Administrative and Organizational Deficiencies in our Military and Naval Establishments Revealed by the Pearl Harbor Investigation."

Let me demonstrate how a prosecutor such as myself uses this material.

Back in 1946, I wasn't able to devote myself exclusively to these matters. I had several difficult trials to conduct. The newspapers, having finished with the long-running story of the verdicts on Kimmel and Short, weren't digging any deeper into the matter.

It was about a year after the Committee had made its final report that Virginia, the children and I returned home to San Francisco from a weekend in Los Altos to find a large, dirty gray sack propped against our front door.

Our son, Don, was the first to identify it as being the property of the U.S. Mail. Meanwhile, our daughter, Flo, warned him away from it, saying it might be a bomb.

I couldn't imagine what it was. I approached the sack cautiously, after waving Virginia and the kids off to what I thought might be a safe distance. Sure enough, it was a mail sack, a very full sack, addressed to me.

I carefully undid the metal clip that crimped together the cords at the neck of the sack and slowly worked the top of the sack open. Inside were a mass of books printed on very thin paper with gray-brown jackets.

I couldn't believe it. I now had every volume of the proceedings of the Pearl Harbor Hearings before Congress, some 9,754 printed pages of testimony, with the attendant 469 exhibits. My investigation had been given its own volume, number 35.

I have never been able to figure out who sent me these priceless volumes. Knowing how scarce they are, I have always kept them in a special place, as if I were protecting the Holy Grail. Over the years, I have taken out one volume after another and carefully gone over the *ten million* words they contain, looking at the evidence they hold not as a historian would, but as a Federal prosecutor would.

In doing this, I will focus now on the recommendations made by Congress, and on the twenty-five areas of deficiency found by the Committee (fourteen of which dealt with intelligence matters raised by my own investigation). I will also add my own assessment of the guilt of the parties involved.

If what I propose seems time-consuming, please bear with me. There is logic to my method. We're now going to plug the hole in the doughnut, and I believe my final judgement will put an end to the questions and doubts about Pearl Harbor that have existed for half a century.

You will recall that throughout my investigation, I found the problem of codependency between the operations of the Army and Navy at Hawaii to be unworkable.

The very first thing Congress recommended was "that immediate action be taken to assure that *unity of command* is imposed at all joint military and naval outposts." (Emphasis added)

In other words, Congress determined that the way the Army and the Navy had split up the commands at Pearl Harbor was totally un-workable in real-life terms. The concept of mutual dependency, or codependency, was to be abolished. Only "unity of command," or command by a single person, would be acceptable in the future. Yet, it took until 1991 for the military to stop their internal squabbles over this issue. Operation Desert Storm was the first military operation conducted with multiservice troops under the concept of *unity of command,* and it resulted in a great victory.

In the second recommendation, Congress called for a complete integration of the Army and Navy intelligence agencies. Let me quote this point in full, as you must read the exact wording to understand how zesty I found this morsel of wisdom. The recommendation reads:

> That there be a complete integration of Army and Navy intelligence agencies in order to avoid the pitfalls of divided responsibilities which experience has made so abundantly apparent; that upon effecting unified intelligence, officers be selected to intelligence work who possess the background, penchant and capacity for such work; and that they be maintained in the work for an extended period of time in order that they may become steeped in the ramifications and refinements of their field and employ this reservoir of knowledge in evaluating material received. The assignment of an officer having an aptitude for such work should not impede his progress nor affect his promotions. Efficient intelligence services are just as essential in time of peace as in war, and this branch of our armed services must always be accorded the important role which it deserves.

As the man remarked, I couldn't have said it better myself. If such an intelligence agency had been in existence in 1941 and staffed with qualified people as recommended, we wouldn't have suffered Pearl Harbor.

Yes, something beneficial did come from this recommendation. President Truman created the National Security Agency (NSA), which is the most secret arm of our government today and employs some thirty thousand people who specialize in electronic intelligence. The historians at the NSA have told me that mine was the first public testimony advocating the creation of their intelligence service. If this is true, and I believe it is, I am proud to have been of service.

The third recommendation made by Congress called for an overhaul of the Communications Act of 1934. This would allow legislation to protect our intelligence secrets, such as Magic, while allowing us to eavesdrop legally on our nation's suspected enemies. In other words, if this legislation had been amended before Pearl Harbor, Captain Mayfield would not have thought he had to remove the telephone taps on the Japanese consulate in Honolulu, or worry about intercepting the Consul's coded messages to Tokyo at the local cable office, which was against the law at the time.

The fifth recommendation (there is no need to discuss the fourth) was that the military branches of our government give serious consideration to the other twenty-five deficiencies that Congress had found.

In other words, Congress was telling the military to make fundamental changes in its operations.

The first deficiency landed squarely on the Navy. Congress found that Adm. Richmond K. Turner, as head of the most important department of the Navy, the War Plans Division, had improperly attempted to assume control of evaluating intelligence, because he had the job of issuing operational orders. This meant that there had been a feud between Turner and Adm. Theodore S. Wilkinson, the head of the Intelligence Division. It got out of control in the days before Pearl Harbor. Congress was sure, and I still am, that Turner's grab for intelligence turf severely damaged the effectiveness of Naval intelligence in those crucial days.

This was one of the reasons Admiral Layton wrote *And I Was There*. As I have said earlier, however, Layton shows the one-dimensional character of his work by using this argument to exonerate Kimmel's actions, as well as his own. (I will discuss this later in greater detail.)

As for what happened in Hawaii, Congress said that there was a "marked failure" to allocate responsibility. Adm. Claude C. Bloch, for example, the Commandant of the Fourteenth Naval District, didn't know whom Kimmel would hold responsible if planes were unready or unable to fly. The Navy pyramided one command onto another to the extent that Adm. Patrick N. L. Bellinger commanded nothing and reported to no one.

As Congress pointed out, "Operational and intelligence work requires centralization of authority and clear-cut allocation of responsibility."

The next deficiency Congress found concerned the tragic theme that can be seen throughout the testimony about Pearl Harbor, wherein an individual would say, "I thought he was alerted," or "I took it for granted he would understand." This concerned not only Kimmel's relationship with Short and vice versa, but also Kimmel's failure to understand Washington's dispatches of December 3 and 6, in which he was told that the Japanese embassies and consulates around the world—including in Washington—were destroying their codes and code machines.

Congress agreed with the testimony it had heard that an enemy's destruction of codes (which includes code machines) meant "war in any man's language."

Kimmel did not interpret these messages in the same way. Neither did his Fleet Intelligence Officer, Capt. (later Adm.) Edwin T. Layton.

(As you can see, this is where Layton's argument that the blame for Pearl Harbor falls primarily upon the feud between Turner and Wilkinson loses its punch.) The truth is that Layton failed to give his boss the proper analysis of these messages—that they meant immediate conflict.

As a result of this mix-up between Kimmel and Washington, Congress said that the people in Washington who send such dispatches should no longer assume that the message will be properly interpreted by the commander in the field. Therefore, an intelligence update should be accompanied by the best estimate of the significance of the intelligence.

As I read the exact wording of the deficiency as Congress found it in 1946, I cannot help thinking of how it relates to the problems of our international business community today, or the complaints of Gen. Norman Schwarzkopf about the intelligence supplied to his Operation Desert Storm. As Congress put it, "Supervisory officials cannot safely take anything for granted in the alerting of subordinates."

I would add: It is continually demonstrated that the military and civilian worlds are different and separate. This accounts for confusion in drafting and reading communications. It furthers the mistakes made in distinguishing between cause and effect. I remember General Marshall's discounting to me the value of one general officer who, he said, "could not trace cause and effect."

The next two deficiencies were aimed primarily at Kimmel. I believe, however, that they could be aptly considered penalties to be equally assessed against both the Navy and the Army.

For example, Congress found that the Chief of Naval Operations, Stark, had been wrong in his assumptions when he hesitated about sending the one-o'clock alert message on the morning of December 7 because he believed his outposts were alerted and he did not want to confuse them. Kimmel was not alerted, nor was Short, although General Marshall tried to get the word to Hawaii the moment he learned of the fourteen-part diplomatic message about the breaking off of relations between Japan and America.

You will recall that there were several other instances in the Army before December 7 in which subordinates wanted to send clarifying information to Hawaii, but were overruled by superior officers who believed Short was adequately informed.

As Congress put it: When in doubt, get the word out. No ifs, ands or buts.

As for the delegation of authority, Congress said that the administration by Kimmel and Short of their respective commands was "the epitome of worthy plans and purposes which were never implemented."

This is a damning charge against the abilities of the two commanders. As Congress put it so rightly, "The job of an administrator is only half completed upon the issuance of an order; it is discharged when he determines the order has been executed."

When you think about it, that line should be writ large in every book about business management. It doesn't do any good to issue an order from an air-conditioned executive suite if the guys who are sweating their guts out on the factory floor don't obey it.

This point was driven home by another fault, which Congress summed up as follows: "Official orders must be followed with closest supervision." This was aimed at the Army, and at the failure of the War Plans Division to ascertain for itself whether Short had ordered the proper stage of alert after receiving the warning message of November 27.

As for the state of alertness in Hawaii, Congress pointed out, rightly, that had Japan attacked on November 28, she would have been just as successful as she was on December 7. Why? Because "the Hawaiian commands were at no time properly alert."

Wow! I thought. I'd hate to have that assessment made on my service jacket when it came time for annual review.

The next deficiency Congress uncovered dealt with the failure of the War and Navy Departments to be sufficiently geared up for action on the evening of December 6. We knew that the Japanese reply to America's note of November 26, which had prompted Stimson to send a final warning message to Short on November 27, was being transmitted on the afternoon of December 6. Subordinates were not prepared to relay the contents of the Japanese reply to either Marshall or Stark. Other prominent military officials, such as the heads of Naval intelligence and Army intelligence, were dining together and read the material. Possibly because they were enjoying themselves at the time, they failed to comprehend the significance of the messages, to demand follow-up material or to try to contact anyone else in their respective services.

The same could be said of Kimmel when he made his sarcastic remark: "Do you mean to say they could be rounding Diamond Head?" referring to the fact that his Fleet Intelligence Officer didn't know where the Japanese carriers were. Similarly, it could also be said of Short's comment that the Mori message was nothing to be worried about.

Congress really hit the nail on the head when it said, "The people are entitled to expect greater vigilance and alertness from their Army and Navy—whether in war or in peace."

In the next deficiency, Congress started coming to grips with my hypothesis that the entire *system* for the coordination and evaluation of intelligence was flawed. The Committee accepted my conclusions to a certain degree, but it contended that "no amount of coordination and no system . . . [can] compensate for lack of imagination and alertness." To which I suggest, one should add "common sense" and "competence." The Committee then said from a review of the investigation in its entirety, however, that there is "substantial evidence . . . to conclude that the system of handling intelligence was seriously at fault and the security of the Nation can be insured only through continuity of service and centralization of responsibility in those charged with handling intelligence." That's a big one for me, I thought.

Put it another way: Intelligence was not appreciated by the peacetime Army or Navy before Pearl Harbor. It was a chore, a tour of unpleasant duty that was either a dead end for one's career or a punishment.

The military was guilty of not seeking out men for intelligence who possessed "the background, capacity and penchant for such work." Above all, the military was criticized for failing to promote its intelligence specialists.

The results of this could be seen in what happened when Short chose Fielder instead of Bicknell to serve as his Intelligence Officer, or when Turner tried to take control of Naval intelligence. Our intelligence specialists were forced to accept relatively low grades and pay scales, while less qualified officers were promoted on the basis of having commanded a ship or battalion. The man who can create a code-breaking machine, however, or who can decipher the enemy's codes and read the enemy's intentions, is worth far more to his nation than any mere admiral or general.

Once a code is broken, the question becomes one of properly distributing and using the information assembled by the code breaker. The British had evolved a fairly workable system by 1941, but we had not yet begun to deal with the problem.

Another matter in which Congress found the military deficient was that the superior attitudes worn by its officials had been "fatal." This was as true in Washington as it was in Hawaii. But the Committee was really aiming its biggest guns at Kimmel. He failed to understand the meaning of the "war warning" of November 27 and "chose to implement an order which manifestly he did not understand . . . without seeking advice from the Navy Department."

As Congress saw it, "There should never be any hesitancy in asking for clarification of instructions or in seeking advice on matters that are in doubt."

The Committee touched on intelligence yet again, making the statement that there is no substitute for imagination and resourcefulness on the part of supervisory and intelligence officials. As the Committee saw Pearl Harbor from its position, which gave it a bird's-eye view of the situation, *both* Washington and Hawaii possessed "unusually significant and vital intelligence." But there wasn't enough awareness in either place of what the intelligence meant, nor was it given analysis or imaginative interpretation. As far as the Committee was concerned, this was caused by the failure of both the military and our diplomats to vest in "intelligence work the important and significant role which it deserves."

Considering what Congress had said earlier about giving partial credence to my beliefs about the failures in the intelligence system, I thought this deficiency Congress found cemented the fact that our overall system didn't work. Period.

I think every student of management could profit from reading the deficiencies at Pearl Harbor that Congress listed. They make a wonderful case study. Not only do they cover the problems of communicating with subordinates and overseas managers, but the truisms Congress espoused are the foundation stone for corporate—or military—survival.

For example:

"Communications must be characterized by clarity, forthrightness, and appropriateness." I'd put this another way: What can be misunderstood will be misunderstood.

"There is great danger in careless paraphrase of information received. . . ."

"Procedures must be sufficiently flexible to meet exigencies of unusual situations."

"There is great danger of being blinded by the self-evident."

"Officials should at all times give subordinates the benefit of significant information."

"An official who neglects to familiarize himself in detail with his organization should forfeit his responsibility." Boy, oh, boy. Doesn't that throw the hook into Short, especially with my discovery that he preferred to read a novel instead of the detailed briefing book his predecessor prepared for him.

"Failure can be avoided in the long run only by preparation for any eventuality."

"Personal or official jealousy will wreck any organization." In other words, Congress believed that if Kimmel and Short had been as worried about protecting their garrisons on Wake and Midway Islands as they were about their prerogatives, they would have been more concerned about defending the Hawaiian Islands, a point I made earlier.

"Personal friendship . . . should never be accepted in lieu of a liaison or confused therewith where the latter is necessary to the proper functioning of two or more agencies." The Committee thought it very "human" that Short and Kimmel tried to testify that their personal friendship demonstrated a close relationship between the two men and their commands. I hadn't been fooled by this, and in the end, neither was Congress. As the Committee put it: "They played golf together, they dined together—but they did not get together on official business . . . to effect coordination and integration of their efforts." If Congress didn't want to carry this issue any further, so be it, but in my book, what the Committee described is nothing less than dereliction of duty.

"No considerations should be permitted as excuse for failure to perform an essential task," said Congress. I recall that cadets at West Point and midshipmen at Annapolis, when cited for infractions of the rules, are taught to say, "No excuse, sir!" Both Short and Kimmel were charged with protecting the fleet at Pearl Harbor. Both men forgot their cadet training when it came to the question of why Pearl Harbor wasn't alert against a surprise attack. As the Congress said, "No excuse or explanation can justify or temper the failure to discharge this responsibility which superseded and surpassed all others."

In closing out its list of deficiencies, the Committee returned once again to intelligence. It found that the dissemination of information derived from Magic was seriously flawed. The *fact* that we had broken the Japanese codes was more important to the military mind of the time than the *information* we gained from the decrypts. The situation was so ludicrous that Gen. Hayes A. Kramer testified that as the head of the Army's G-2 Intelligence Branch in Washington, he was never given access to Magic, yet his subordinate, Colonel Bratton, was running the all-important program to disseminate Magic without supervision. Meanwhile, at Pearl Harbor, the Army had no one in its intelligence operations who was cleared for Top Secret Magic material, which made a mockery of the concept of mutual cooperation for the defense of the fleet.

Lastly, the Committee was dreadfully concerned about the fact that there was no way to determine who had seen which Magic signal or when. Since no records were kept about this vital information, superior officers could duck the issue of having seen this message or that, or charge their subordinates with failing to show it to them.

I said it more succinctly: The system didn't work.

Now that I have given the answers to the four primary questions about what Washington and Hawaii knew before the attack and what each did about it, the time has come to summarize the guilt of the parties involved.

The proximate cause or guilt for the disaster at Pearl Harbor was an unworkable system of military intelligence, including the fact that the Navy withheld from the Army vital intelligence information that called for Army action.

In turn, this can be translated into guilt that can be charged against individuals. I shall list these people in terms of their culpability, based on a scale of zero to ten, with ten being the high end of the scale.

10. *Lt. Gen. Walter C. Short:* His was the primary duty and task of defending the fleet and Hawaii from attack. He didn't want the command. He failed to study what the task entailed before he took command. He failed to alert his forces to the probability of a surprise Japanese attack. He failed to follow Washington's orders to conduct reconnaissance before the attack. He failed to communicate with his counterpart, Admiral Kimmel, and determine the Navy's state of readiness before the attack. If Short's fighter planes and antiaircraft guns had fired on the first Japanese plane they saw, or the second one, Short would have been a hero even if a large number of the fleet's ships were sunk. As it was, his planes were on the ground and the ammunition for his antiaircraft guns was locked away. It took nearly four hours for his command to get ready to fight.

10. *Admiral Husband E. Kimmel:* As the Commander in Chief of the U.S. Pacific Fleet, he also would have been a hero if he had gone to sea with his ships and been ready to fight. As it was, he withheld vital intelligence information not only from Short, but from his own command. (When Admiral Newton sailed from Pearl Harbor with some of the fleet's most important ships in Task Force 3, for example, Kimmel failed to tell Newton that Washington had sent Kimmel a "war warning" on November 27.) Kimmel also knew from two dispatches from Washington on December 3 that the Japanese were destroying their codes and code machines. He failed to tell Short. Nor did he ask Washington for clarification of what Washington really knew or what Washington wanted him to do. So, Kimmel is off in left field, all by himself, saying that the intelligence he received either wasn't important or wasn't given to him.

He was a man who was inflexible in his convictions and expressions. He believed that what he assumed was correct. He would not liaise with the Army about its state of readiness. Take, for example, the items I quoted earlier proving that Kimmel did not play fair and square with Short. It does no good to say, "Oh, Short's subordinate had that information." That is not exchanging information. That is partially exchanging information. Kimmel was required to give Short the identical information that the Office of Naval Intelligence in Washington gave Kimmel. The obligation was for one commander to confer and exchange information with his fellow commander. That was the only way the two commands could survive in an era of mutual dependency. Thus, Short became one of the first victims of the Navy's practice of hoarding secret information.

If Kimmel had given Short the information that Short needed to jolt him into ordering an alert against an air attack, then Kimmel would have been the bigger hero of the two.

If I were prosecuting this case, I would ask the jury one question: Knowing the intelligence Kimmel and Short possessed, and knowing what they did with it, when combined with the rule of common sense based on the Joint Action Agreement for defending Hawaii, were the actions taken by Short and Kimmel correct?

I believe today, now that the partisan political dust has settled, no jury would declare these men innocent. They were obviously guilty.

As for those individuals who should be charged with *contributory negligence,* I list the following, grading their degree of guilt on the same scale as above.

9. *Col. Carlisle Clyde Dusenbury,* Assistant in the Far East Section of Army G-2 (Intelligence) in Washington: You will recall that Dusenbury swore in his affidavit to me that he had all fourteen parts of the fourteen-part Japanese diplomatic message in his possession around midnight of December 6, 1941. (I will speak of this again.) Dusenbury had been ordered to deliver this latest Magic material to General Marshall at his quarters when Dusenbury went home for the night. He did not do so.

I believe that had Marshall received that night the fourteen-part message, in which it was made clear that diplomatic relations between Washington and Tokyo were going to be broken off, he would have sent a special alert to Short in time to blunt or repel the Japanese attack. As it stood, Dusenbury lost approximately nine crucial hours of this warning time.

8. *Lt. Col. Kendall J. Fielder,* G-2 (Intelligence) of the Hawaiian Department: Fielder represented all that was wrong with the Army's intelligence system. As I pointed out earlier, he was an infantry officer. Although a graduate of West Point, he had no intelligence training. He was not cleared for Top Secret, Magic-type information. He was chosen for his job because of his social graces—golfing skills, a smiling demeanor and magic shows—not for his military intelligence skills. He required that his subordinates do the major portion of his work. He shunned responsibility; he failed to find out what was really going on in the intelligence world within the Hawaiian Army and Navy commands. His was a sorry list of qualifications. As one result, Short paid the supreme price.

8. *Lt. Col. George W. Bicknell,* Assistant G-2 for the Hawaiian Department: When I first talked to Bicknell, I thought well of him. It wasn't until I carefully studied the record and placed one item of evidence alongside the other that Bicknell's failures became apparent. Trained in intelligence during World War I, Bicknell was recalled to duty as a reserve officer and had been shunted aside when Short appointed Fielder to be Bicknell's boss. Yet, it was Bicknell whom the Navy and FBI trusted with secret information, because he was a true intelligence officer. Working against him, however, was the fact that he dealt with, but was *not* cleared for, Top Secret, Magic-type intelligence. Thus, the system placed Bicknell in an untenable position.

Bicknell could have absolved himself. He could have saved the day at Pearl Harbor.

He had been able to get Rochefort to show him on December 3 at least one of two all-important warnings from Naval intelligence in Washington advising Kimmel that the Japanese embassies and consulates around the world, including in Washington, were burning their codes and, by implication, executing the so-called Winds Code orders by destroying their code machines.

Bicknell had every reason in the world to rush to Short with this priceless, earthshaking dispatch. I can only speculate as to why he didn't. He knew that Rochefort had broken security regulations in showing him this Magic information. He also knew that he could get into serious trouble if he revealed the source of his information, which he had been tapping for some time. Instead, Bicknell chose to wait three days and reveal this information in a watered-down form at the weekly staff conference, where he masked its importance by reducing the source to dull routine.

Unfortunately, one can only speculate about what would have happened if Bicknell had seen the second warning message of December 3 to Kimmel: the one that said Tokyo had ordered its embassies to destroy their Purple code machines. Would this have spurred Bicknell into making a supreme effort to alert Short?

Bicknell's attempt to redeem himself by going to Short and Fielder with the Mori telephone intercept on the evening of Saturday, December 6, becomes something of an afterthought, because he raised the wrong alarm about code words such as "hibiscus" and "poinsettias," something he could understand but they could not comprehend. Again, he had the opportunity to tell all; again, he failed to do so.

8. *Capt. Edwin T. Layton,* Fleet Intelligence Officer, Pacific Fleet: It's odd. When you look at the list of Kimmel's staff as drawn up by Congress, Layton's name is missing. His name is also missing from the table of organization for the Fourteenth Naval District in Hawaii. Perhaps it was the Navy's way of saying that the Pacific Fleet did not have an intelligence officer. Yet, Layton was there. He even called his book *And I Was There.* In it, he claimed that internal feuding in the Navy Department in Washington was responsible for Pearl Harbor. As it turned out, this was only partially true. What Layton really did and didn't do illustrates the slippery nature of the intelligence specialist: He suckered the Army.

Layton failed to follow Kimmel's direct order to personally deliver the "war warning" message of November 27 to General Short.

Layton also tried to pull a snow job on me during my investigation.

He claimed that he passed vital intelligence information to Fielder in the best traditions of military cooperation. When I brought Fielder with me to Guam, Layton met him with a big grin, saying, "Wooch! [Fielder's nickname] Glad to see you, Wooch." But in his affidavit to me, Layton had to admit that he never had any professional contact with Fielder.

According to the rules of the Joint Action Agreement and the concept of codependency, Layton was required to keep Fielder abreast of intelligence matters. And if Layton was worried that Fielder did not have the proper security clearance for this information, he should have asked Washington how to handle it. He might have suggested liaison with Bicknell. (That might have made the system more workable.)

Layton should not have pretended that Col. Edward W. Raley, who was in charge of intelligence for the Hawaiian Air Force, was Fielder's surrogate. Nor should he have divulged to Raley intelligence information based on Magic without telling him its proper source.

When the Navy Department warned Kimmel on December 3 that the Japanese were burning their codes and destroying their Purple code machines, Kimmel called Layton to his office to find out what Purple was. Layton didn't know. He had to ask a young officer fresh from Washington to find out that Purple was the supersecret Japanese electronic code machine, the most priceless item of Japanese intelligence in existence.

Layton should have known the implications of the December 3 warnings: War was imminent and unavoidable. Layton failed to communicate this point to Kimmel.

Like Kimmel, Layton would never acknowledge that he had made a mistake.

Nor did he, in giving me his affidavit, ever mention that a single thing was wrong with the overall intelligence system. He waited until 1985 to make these charges, after he had safely retired with the rank of rear admiral.

Now, if the information in the warnings of December 3 was as unimportant as Kimmel claimed, then there was no reason to deny it to the Army. But Layton claimed it was so important that he was prohibited by regulations from giving it to the Army. The Fleet Intelligence Officer wants it both ways. Then, he said, he violated this very prohibition by giving information based on Purple to Colonel Raley, which Raley denied. (Raley said he would have passed it on to Short if he had known it was based on Purple.)

So, you see, there is no truth to Layton's claim that he was prohibited from passing intelligence to the Army. As General Marshall and Secretary Stimson pointed out in their testimony, Kimmel and Short, with reference to their respective commands, were dependent upon each other to share *all* intelligence. It never happened. Layton has hidden behind Kimmel's epaulettes ever since.

8. *Rear Adm. Richmond K. Turner,* head of the Navy's War Plans Division in Washington: To understand the contributory negligence of Kelly Turner, one must comprehend that, in the Navy's table of organization, the War Plans Division was the most senior, or dominant, division. Turner was not a man willing to play second fiddle to anyone, including his boss, the Chief of Naval Operations, Adm. Harold R. Stark, who was nicknamed "Betty."

It was Congress that uncovered the problems within the Navy Department. Turner believed that he should be the one to interpret Naval intelligence, since he was sending out the orders to the Navy commanders overseas. This destroyed the efficiency of Rear Adm. Theodore S. Wilkinson and his Intelligence Division. It also kept Capt. Arthur H. McCollum of the Far Eastern Section of the Intelligence Division uninformed of the instructions sent to the fleet based on intelligence matters.

In brief, if Turner had not tried to seize control of the Navy Department while head of the War Plans Division, there is every chance that the Navy would have been better run.

Turner also suffered from what I call the "Navy mind fix." He assumed and perceived without knowing. He was too arrogant to ask, "Is this true?" He believed Kimmel was getting Purple intelligence when Kimmel neither had a Purple machine nor knew anything about Purple. He also believed that Wilkinson was keeping Kimmel supplied with Purple information, which was not the case.

If Turner had found out that Kimmel was not getting Purple, it would have been easy to build another Purple machine and send it to the Pacific Fleet. A simple question, if asked, answered and acted upon, would have gone far to prevent Pearl Harbor.

7. *Capt. L. F. Safford,* head of the Security (Intelligence) Section of the Navy Department's Communications Division: As I said earlier,

Safford was a strange duck. He was in overall charge of the Navy's hyperactive code-breaking activities in Washington. He testified that he was pretty sure that something was going to pop on the weekend of December 6–7, 1941, but he went home early that Saturday afternoon. He claimed he was totally worn out. He was in his pajamas, having breakfast in the early afternoon (Washington time) on Sunday when he heard that the Japanese had attacked Pearl Harbor. His immediate reaction was that someone in a high place had blown the call. He never came to grips with the fact that if he had remained on duty, knowing and suspecting what he did, he could have prevented the call from being blown.

7. *Capt. Irving H. Mayfield,* Intelligence Officer, Fourteenth Naval District, Hawaii: He broke the law to illegally tap the telephones of the Japanese consulate in Hawaii for some twenty-two months. Then, in a fit of pique, he broke off the taps without telling anyone so that surveillance could be continued in the five crucial days before Pearl Harbor. I believe that if the taps had been continued, there might have been yet another opportunity to avoid Pearl Harbor.

7. *Col. Rufus S. Bratton,* Chief of the Far Eastern Section of G-2 (Intelligence) in Washington: Bratton failed to assure that his deputy (Dusenbury) followed his orders to deliver the crucial fourteen-part Japanese decrypt to Marshall on the night of December 6. For his part, Bratton believed the material to be so important that he rushed the first thirteen parts of it to the office of the Secretary of State. But then he went home to bed!

Later, he misled the Army Pearl Harbor Board when he lied about what he had really done that night. His false testimony wounded Marshall a second time, nearly mortally. In so doing, he lost his chance for a general's star. But I discovered, and Bratton candidly confirmed, the truth of what happened, including his perjury. Moreover, at the Congressional hearing, he conceded my conduct was fair and judicial, blowing out of the water Messrs. Ferguson, Keefe, Gearhart and Brewster.

6. *Comdr. Joseph J. Rochefort,* Chief of the Communications Security (Intelligence) Unit, Fourteenth Naval District, Hawaii: It became known on December 3 that the Japanese Consul in Hawaii had destroyed all but one of Japan's code systems. Rochefort failed to realize the significance of the fact that the Japanese consulate in Hawaii could communicate with Tokyo via only this commercial cable system, which he was capable of cracking. He failed to relay the importance of this development to Layton. He also failed to exert maximum effort to crack this traffic. If he had done so, Rochefort would have discovered, as was found out after the attack, that Pearl Harbor had been classified as a target.

6. *Brig. Gen. Leonard T. Gerow:* As head of the Army's War Plans Division, Gerow bore the responsibility for allowing Short's ambiguous reply about the improper state of alert for the Hawaiian command to slip through the safety net unchecked.

6. *Lt. Comdr. Alwin D. Kramer* (on loan from the Far Eastern Section, Intelligence Division) of the Translation Section of the Navy's Communications Division in Washington: Kramer worked under Safford's direction. What was more important, however, was that Kramer had the job in the Navy similar to Dusenbury's and Bratton's in the Army. There was only one Kramer, however, which meant that there was a horrific chance that something might go wrong if he was not available to deliver material to Admiral Stark or President Roosevelt. The President of the United States had designated the Navy to bring him the Magic decrypts. The Navy foolishly designated only one man to do the job: Kramer.

I believe you can begin to see the problem that has bothered me for years: What happened when Kramer was home asleep?

On the evening of December 6, 1941, Kramer made his rounds and delivered, he claimed, the first thirteen parts of the fourteen-part diplomatic message to the White House. His wife drove the car for him that evening. He finished his last delivery to top-ranking Naval officers and, he claimed, checked in at his office. There was nothing else in the hopper. He claimed he left orders with the watch officer that he was to be called if any important messages related to the fourteen-part message came in or if a message was intercepted saying when the fourteen-part message was to be delivered. Kramer then went home to bed.

At the first minute past midnight of December 6, or 00:01 hours December 7, the responsibility to handle Magic traffic fell to the Navy. That was how the crazy system worked: the Army was responsible for Magic on the even-numbered days, the Navy on odd-numbered days.

So, here we were: The Navy was responsible for handling the

decrypts, and the only man in the Navy responsible for translating them was home in bed!

Kramer testified later that he could have been in the office within fifteen minutes if the watch officer had called him. As we know, the messages he had been expecting came in while he was at home. It was understood that the message that told the Japanese diplomats to inform the Americans at one P.M. on Sunday was decrypted at around three (Washington time) Sunday morning. It would have taken Kramer only two minutes to translate. Thus, the Navy possessed the news that diplomatic relations would be broken by Japan, and that our State Department was to be told of this at one o'clock the next afternoon, while Kramer and the rest of Washington slept.

I contend, however, given the testimony I received from Dusenbury, which has never been challenged, that the Army received from the Navy at around midnight (Washington time) the fourteenth part of the diplomatic message with the news that diplomatic relations with Japan would be ruptured. I contend that Kramer knew this fourteenth part was in hand, too. But Kramer was so worn out that he could not bring himself to make the rounds one more time after midnight with the news. (Nor could he ask his wife to drive him around town again.) Besides, he had to be present and correct the next morning to confer with his superiors.

Congress never investigated this adequately. The Committee never questioned Dusenbury, or Rowlett, or Mary J. Dunning, which means that the affidavit Dusenbury gave me must be accepted as true. The Committee never cross-examined Kramer about the conflict between his testimony and that of Dusenbury. Why? Because when the Committee got to this particular issue, its work became sloppy. Besides, no one wanted to prove that the way the Army and Navy had divvied up the distribution of Magic intelligence was more like a comic opera than good intelligence work.

After the Army refused for reasons of security to send the Japanese decrypts to the White House, Roosevelt specifically designated the Navy to provide him with Magic. The Navy failed to do so at a crucial moment in history. Now, the analogy between the failure of the Navy to deliver an important document to the head of state and the Navy's reluctance to divulge intelligence to the Army may seem tenuous, but it isn't.

That is why I conclude my list of those who bore contributory negligence for Pearl Harbor as follows:

5. *President Franklin D. Roosevelt:* I cannot walk away from my investigation and say that Roosevelt was innocent in the matter of Pearl Harbor.

I didn't find any evidence that would have linked him to a conspiracy to force Japan to attack Pearl Harbor. Nor can I accuse him of having more knowledge of what might happen at Pearl Harbor than other people possessed. After all, there were a number of others who read the first thirteen parts of the fourteen-part diplomatic message around midnight on December 6, 1941. Among them were Secretary of State Hull, Secretary of the Navy Knox, Chief of Naval Operations Stark, and the intelligence chiefs of the Navy and the Army, Admiral Wilkinson and General Miles. None of them foresaw what Roosevelt did when he read the message and told his assistant, Harry Hopkins, "This means war!"

The question of contributory negligence on the part of the President comes down to what Roosevelt did, or did not do, after making that momentous statement some sixteen hours before the Japanese attacked.

His men were looking for leadership at a crucial moment. He did not provide it. Roosevelt made a number of telephone calls after he read the message. But he never phoned the one man he should have called: Marshall.

Roosevelt's instincts were correct. War *was* coming. It was a situation somewhat analogous to what Kimmel experienced on December 6, when he thought he should take his fleet to sea, but allowed himself to be talked out of the decision.

Roosevelt knew what the Japanese message meant, but instead of telling his subordinates that war was coming, getting them out of bed that night to work and find out what the next Japanese decrypts might say, Roosevelt demurred. He put everything on hold until a meeting could be convened the next morning at ten.

He didn't know the meeting, held in accordance with regular business hours, would be too late. He didn't know the Japanese were going to attack Pearl Harbor. He didn't know Kimmel and Short weren't ready to defend themselves.

Like the others who had access to Magic, Roosevelt thought he had time, when, in truth, time had run out.

The Commander in Chief of the Armed Forces failed to take prompt and effective action to bring his subordinates together to achieve a decision about what should be done. Thus, it is only fair that

Roosevelt share the guilt with the other members of the military who have been named in this account.

Which gets me to another point.

One of the reasons to assign guilt to individuals for the disaster at Pearl Harbor is that the frailties of individuals and institutions are more understandable in such a context.

When I was a prosecutor, I never enjoyed winning a case and sending someone to jail. I felt sorry for the convict-to-be. I felt even sorrier for the members of his family, who suffered their loved one's perceived guilt even though they were innocent.

But by looking at the individuals and the deeds they did or did not commit as relates to Pearl Harbor, one comes to grips with the ultimate question: Did the system in which these people were embroiled work properly?

In the case of how Magic was handled before Pearl Harbor, the intelligence system, beset by human frailty, did not work.

President Roosevelt loved the Navy. He would never have allowed his precious ships and men to be sent to the bottom. That was not in his character. But Roosevelt favored the Navy over the Army. He chose the Navy over the Army to bring him the Magic decrypts. By so doing, he gave the Navy too much power in the intelligence field.

We're talking about a real-life situation, real human nature, not a sociology course. Roosevelt made a conscious decision to pat the Navy on the head, and the Navy turned around and bit him.

Thus, our President became the ultimate victim of Pearl Harbor.

If Commander Kramer had slept in his office the night of December 6, 1941, as hospital interns take catnaps while working hundred-hour weeks, then Roosevelt might have received that night the all-important fourteenth part of the diplomatic message, plus the following dispatch that came in between one and three A.M. December 7, saying it was to be handed to the American government at one P.M. Sunday. This would have given ample time to forestall the disaster that befell Pearl Harbor.

Before you, the reader, make up your own mind about the guilt or innocence of the people named in this book, let me raise two final matters.

After Pearl Harbor, Kimmel and Short were relieved of command. They never again served on active duty. All the others named in this narrative, including those to whom I have assigned guilt, continued on active duty throughout the war. They served their nation well, many with true distinction. The fact that our judicial system allowed this continuing service to happen speaks well of it. The fact that we learned from Pearl Harbor, and created an independent National Security Agency to prevent similar disasters from occurring in the future, also speaks well of our democratic system of government.

The trick will be to ensure that our intelligence operations work properly in the future.

‖ APPENDIX

EXHIBIT B

CLAUSEN INVESTIGATION EXHIBIT NO. 7

Investigation by Lt. Colonel Henry C. Clausen, JAGD, for the Secretary of War
Supplementary to Proceedings of the Army Pearl Harbor Board

(NOTE: THESE WERE THE ITEMS CLAUSEN CARRIED IN HIS BOMB POUCH.)

a. The first two documents are notes of two intercepts dated 6 December 1941 of radio messages from the Japanese Consul at Honolulu to Tokyo which were not included in Top Secret Exhibit ''B'' before the Army Pearl Harbor Board.

b. The documents following those mentioned in **a** above are the intercepts which comprise Top Secret Exhibit ''B'' before the Army Pearl Harbor Board.

Certain of these have been initialed by witnesses before me and are referred to in their affidavits.

NOTE: THE PAGES THAT FOLLOW CONTAIN OFFICIAL DOCUMENTS. THE PUBLISHER HAS ATTEMPTED TO REPRODUCE THE ORIGINAL LANGUAGE AS ACCURATELY AS POSSIBLE.

TOP SECRET

From: Hon.
To: Tokyo
Dec. 6, 41
PA-KY
#253 release p5 ------123a.

1. On American continent in Oct. Army began training barrage balloon troops at Camp Davis, N.C. 400,500 balloons considering use in defense of Hawaii & Panama. So far as Hawaii concerned though investigations made, they have not set up mooring equipment, nor have they selected troops to man them. No training for maintenance balloons. No signs barrage balloon equipment. "In addition, it is difficult to imagine that they have actually any limits to barrage balloon defense." I imagine that in all probability there is considerable opportunity left to take advantage of a surprise attack against these places.

In my opinion battleships do not have torpedo nets. Details not known; will report results of investigation.

Army 7178 25877 2a Trans 12/8/41 (2-TT)

TOP SECRET

From: Hon
To: Tokyo
Dec. 6, 41
PA-K2
#254

1. On evening 5th, among battleships which entered port—one sub tender. The following ships observed at anchor on 6th.

9 battleships, 3 light cruisers, 3 sub tenders, 17 destroyers, in addition 4 light cruisers, 2 destroyers lying at docks (heavy cruisers & airplane carriers all left.)

2. "It appears that no air reconnaissance is being conducted by the fleet air arm."

Army 7179 25874 trans 12/8/42 3 a.

From: Tokyo (Toyoda)
To: Honolulu
September 24, 41
J-19
#83
    Strictly secret.

Henceforth, we would like to have you make reports concerning vessels along the following lines insofar as possible.

1. The waters (of Pearl Harbor) are to be divided roughly into five sub-areas. (We have no objection to your abbreviating as much as you like.)

Area A. Waters between Ford Island and the Arsenal.

Area B. Waters adjacent to the Island south and west of Ford Island. (This area is on the opposite side of the Island from Area A.)

Area C. East Loch.

Area D. Middle Loch.

Area E. West Loch and the communicating water routes.

2. With regard to warships and aircraft carriers, we would like to have you report on those at anchor, (these are not so important) tied up at wharfs, buoys and in docks. (Designate types and classes briefly. If possible we would like to have you make mention of the fact when there are two or more vessels along side the same wharf.)

260 SECRET Trans. 10-9-41 (S)

From: Washington (Nomura)
To: Tokyo
October 14, 1941
Purple
#943 (Part 1 of 2)[1] (To be handled in Government Code)

I had an interview with Rear Admiral TURNER. If I sum up what he told me, it is this:

"What the United States wants is not just a pretense but a definite promise. Should a conference of the leaders of the two governments be held without a definite preliminary agreement, and should, in the meantime, an advance be made into Siberia, the President would be placed in a terrible predicament. Japan speaks of peace in the Pacific and talks as if she can decide matters independently, and so it would seem to me that Japan could set aside most of her obligations toward the Three-Power Alliance. As to the question of withdrawing or stationing troops, since it is impossible to withdraw troops all at

[1] For part 2 see SIS #23516

once, it would seem that a detailed agreement could be arranged between Japan and China for a gradual withdrawal."

He speculated on the various difficulties which Japan had to face internally. It seems that this opinion of his has also been given to the Secretary of State.

ARMY 5854 23570 SECRET Trans. 10/16/41 (2)

From: Washington (Nomura)
To: Tokyo
October 14, 41
Purple
#943 (Part 2 of 2)[2]

He said that should the Russo-German war suddenly end and should Germany offer Great Britain peace, it would after all be a German peace and England would not now accept it. Now, this man is a responsible fellow in an important position and I take it that this is the view of the Navy. On the other hand, HOOVER and his following consider that should Moscow make a separate peace with Berlin and should Berlin then turn to London with generous peace terms, this whole fray would end with unimaginable quickness. CASTLE[3] told me that HUGH GIBSON feels the same way and that Japan, too, should be on the alert for this possibility. This, however, I take to be a minority view entertained by the Isolationists. MOORE[4] reports that Secretary HULL told Senator THOMAS that he is proceeding patiently with the Japanese-American negotiations, but he hopes that Japan will not mistake this for a sign of weakness on America's part, and that no answer had arrived to the memo of October 2nd. KIPLINGER[5] reports that there is a very good basis for rumors of a cessation of hostilities between Russia and Germany and that the chances for war between Japan and the United States are fifty-fifty.

ARMY 5854 23516 SECRET Trans. 10-15-41 (7)

From: Tokyo (Toyoda)
To: Washington
October 16, 1941
Purple (CA)
#671

Although I have been requested by both the German and Italian Ambassadors in Tokyo to give them confidential information on the Japanese-

---

[2] Part 1 of 2 not available.
[3] Former U.S. Ambassador to Japan.
[4] American legal adviser to Japanese Embassy in Washington.
[5] A Washington newspaper correspondent.

American negotiations, I have, in consideration of the nature of the negotiations, been declining to do so. However, early this month, following the German attacks on American merchant ships and the consequent (revival?) of the movement for the revision of the Neutrality Act, the German authorities demanded that the Japanese Government submit to the American Government a message to the effect that the Japanese Government observes that if the ROOSEVELT Administration continues to attack the Axis Powers increasingly, a belligerent situation would inevitably arise between Germany and Italy on the one hand and the United States on the other, and this would provide the reasons for the convocation of the duties envisioned in the Three Power agreement and might lead Japan to join immediately the war in opposition to the United States. We have not, as yet, submitted this message because, in view of the Japanese-American negotiations, we found it necessary to consider carefully the proper timing as well as wording of the message. The German authorities have been repeatedly making the same request and there are reasons which do not permit this matter to be postponed any longer. While Japan on the one hand finds it necessary to do something in the way of carrying out the duties placed upon her by the Three Power Alliance she had concluded with Germany, on the other hand, she is desirous of making a success of the Japanese-American negotiations. Under the circumstances, we can do no other than to warn the United States at an appropriate moment in such words as are given in my separate wire and as would not affect the Japanese-American negotiations in one way or another. This message is a secret between me and you.

(Separate Wire)

The Imperial Japanese Government has repeatedly affirmed to the American Government that the aim of the Tripartite Pact is to contribute toward the prevention of a further extension of the European war. Should, however, the recent tension in the German-American relations suffer aggravation, there would arise a distinct danger of a war between the two powers, a state of affairs over which Japan, as a signatory to the Tripartite Pact, naturally cannot help entertain a deep concern. Accordingly, in its sincere desire that not only the German-American relations will cease further deterioration but the prevailing tension will also be alleviated as quickly as possible, the Japanese Government is now requesting the earnest consideration of the American Government.

ARMY 5901 23631 Secret

From: Washington (Nomura)
To: Tokyo
October 22, 1941
Purple (CA)

I have already wired you something about my present psychology. I am sure that I, too, should go out with the former cabinet. I know that for some time the Secretary of State has known how sincere your humble servant is, yet how little influence I have in Japan. I am ashamed to say that it has come to my ears that this is the case. There are some Americans who trust this poor novice and who say that things will get better for me, but alas, their encouragement is not enough. Among my confreres here in the United States there are also some who feel the same way, but, alas, they are all poor deluded souls. As for Your Excellency's instructions, WAKASUGI can carry them out fully. Nor do I imagine that you all have any objections. I don't want to be the bones of a dead horse. I don't want to continue this hypocritical existence, deceiving other people. No, don't think I am trying to flee from the field of battle, but as a man of honor this is the only way that is open for me to tread. Please send me your permission to return to Japan. Most humbly do I beseech your forgiveness if I have injured your dignity and I prostrate myself before you in the depth of my rudeness.

ARMY 6017 23859 Secret Trans. 10-23-41 (7)

From: Tokyo
To: Washington
5 November 1941
(Purple - CA)
#736

(Of utmost secrecy)

Because of various circumstances, it is absolutely necessary that all arrangements for the signing of this agreement be completed by the 25th of this month. I realize that this is a difficult order, but under the circumstances it is an unavoidable one. Please understand this thoroughly and tackle the problem of saving the Japanese-U.S. relations from falling into a chaotic condition. Do so with great determination and with unstinted effort, I beg of you.

This information is to be kept strictly to yourself only.

JD-1: 6254 Secret (D) Navy Trans. 11-5-41 (S-TT)

From: Tokyo
To: Hongkong
November 14, 1941
Purple
Cir. #2319 (To be handled in Government Code)
            (Strictly secret outside the Department)

Though the Imperial Government hopes for great things from the Japan-American negotiations, they do not permit optimism for the future. Should the negotiations collapse, the international situation in which the Empire will find herself will be one of tremendous crisis. Accompanying this, the Empire's foreign policy as it has been decided by the cabinet, insofar as it pertains to China, is:

a. We will completely destroy British and American power in China.

b. We will take over all enemy concessions and enemy important rights and interests (customs and minerals, etc.) in China.

c. We will take over all rights and interests owned by enemy powers, even though they might have connections with the new Chinese government, should it become necessary.

In realizing these steps in China, we will avoid, insofar as possible, exhausting our veteran troops. Thus we will cope with a world war on a long-time scale. Should our reserves for total war and our future military strength wane, we have decided to reinforce them from the whole Far Eastern area. This has become the whole fundamental policy of the Empire. Therefore, in consideration of the desirability to lighten our personal and material load, we will encourage the activities of important Chinese in their efforts in the occupied (2) territories insofar as is possible. Japan and China, working in cooperation, will take over military bases. Thus, operating wherever possible, we will realize peace throughout the entire Far East. At the same time, we place great importance upon the acquisition of materials (especially from the unoccupied areas). In order to do this, all in the cabinet have concurred, in view of the necessity, in a reasonable relaxation of the various restrictions now in force (after you have duly realized the critical situation which has brought the above decisions into being you will, of course, wait for instructions from home before carrying them out).

In connection with the above, we have the precedent of the freezing legislation. We are writing you this particularly for your information alone. Please keep absolutely quiet the existence of these decisions and the fact that they have been transmitted to you.

This message is directed to Nanso,[6] Hokudai,[6] Shanghai, Tientsin, Hsinkow, Canton, and Hongkong. Hokudai[6] will transmit to Kalgan and

---

[6] Kana spelling.

Taiyuan. Tsingtao will transmit to Tsinan. Canton will transmit to Amov.
25322
JD 6801 Secret Trans. 11/26/41 (NR)

From: Tokyo (Togo)
To: Washington (Riyoji)
15 November 1941
(J-19)
#111

As relations between Japan and the United States are most critical, make
your "ships in harbor report" irregular, but at a rate of twice a week. Although you already are no doubt aware, please take extra care to maintain
secrecy.
JD-1: 6991 Secret (Y) Navy Trans. 12-3-41 (S)

From: Tokyo
To: Washington
November 16, 1941
Purple (Ca) (Urgent)

For your Honor's own information:
1. I have read your #1090,[7] and you may be sure that you have all my
gratitude for the efforts you have put forth, but the fate of our Empire hangs
by the slender thread of a few days, so please fight harder than you ever did
before.
2. What you say in the last paragraph of your message is, of course, so, and
I have given it already the fullest consideration, but I have only to refer you
to the fundamental policy laid down in my #725.[8] Will you please try to
realize what that means. In your opinion we ought to wait and see what turn
the war takes and remain patient. However, I am awfully sorry to say that the
situation renders this out of the question. I set the deadline for the solution of
these negotiations in my #736,[9] and there will be no change. Please try to
understand that. You see how short the time is; therefore, do not allow the

---

[7] See JD-: 6553 in which NOMURA gives his views on the general situation. Part 3 not available.
[8] SIS #24330 in which TOGO says that conditions both within and without the Japanese Empire
will not permit any further delay in reaching a settlement with the United States.
[9] SIS #24373 in which TOGO says it is absolutely necessary that all arrangements for the signing
of these agreements be completed by the 25th of this month.

United States to sidetrack us and delay the negotiations any further. Press them for a solution on the basis of our proposals, and do your best to bring about an immediate solution.

Army 24878 JD-1: 6638 Secret Trans. 11/17/41

From: Tokyo (Togo)
To: Honolulu
November 18, 1941
J-19
#113

Please report on the following areas as to vessels anchored therein: Area "N", Pearl Harbor, Manila Bay,[10] and the areas adjacent thereto. (Make your investigation with great secrecy.)

Army 25773 7063 Secret Trans 12/5/41 (S)

From: Honolulu (Kita)
To: Tokyo
November 18, 1941
J-19
#222

1. The warships at anchor in the Harbor on the 15th were as I told you in my #219[11] on that day.

Area A[12]—A battleship of the Oklahoma class entered and one tanker left port.

Area C[13]—3 warships of the heavy cruiser class were at anchor.

2. On the 17th the Saratoga was not in the harbor. The carrier, Enterprise, or some other vessel was in Area C. Two heavy cruisers of the Chicago class, one of the Pensacola class were tied up at docks "KS". 4 merchant vessels were at anchor in area D.[14]

3. At 10:00 A.M. on the morning of the 17th, 8 destroyers were observed entering the Harbor. Their course was as follows: In a single file at a distance of 1,000 meters apart at a speed of 3 knots per hour, they moved into Pearl

[10] Probably means Mamala Bay.
[11] Available in ME code dated November 14. Code under study.
[12] Waters between Ford Island and the Arsenal.
[13] East Loch.
[14] Middle Loch.

Harbor. From the entrance of the Harbor through Area B to the buoys in Area C, to which they were moored, they changed course 5 times each time roughly 30 degrees. The elapsed time was one hour, however, one of these destroyers entered Area A after passing the water reservoir on the Eastern side.

Relayed to ----.

Army 25817 7111 Secret Trans. 12/6/41

From: Tokyo
To: Washington
19 November 1941
(J19)
Circular #2353

Regarding the broadcast of a special message in an emergency.

In case of emergency (danger of cutting of our diplomatic relations) and the cutting off of international communications, the following warning will be added in the middle of the daily Japanese language short wave news broadcast:

(1) In case of a Japan-U.S. relations in danger HIGASHI NO KAZEAME (EAST WIND RAIN)

(2) Japan–U.S.S.R. relations: KITANOKAZE KUMORI (NORTH WIND CLOUDY)

(3) Japan-British relations: NISHI NO KAZE HARE (WEST WIND CLEAR)

This signal will be given in the middle and at the end as a weather forecast and each sentence will be repeated twice. When this is heard, please destroy all code papers, etc. This is as yet to be a completely secret arrangement.

Forward as urgent intelligence.

See Supplementary Information File

(Voice broadcasts)

SIS 25432 JD-1: 6875 Secret Navy Trans. 11-28-41

From: Tokyo
To: Washington
19 November 1941
(J19)
Circular #2354

When diplomatic relations are becoming dangerous we will add the following at the beginning and end of our general *intelligence* broadcasts:

(1) If it is Japan U.S. relations *"HIGASHI"*
(2) Japan Russia relations *"KITA"*
(3) Japan British relations; (including Thai, Malaya, and NEI) *"NISHI"*
The above will be repeated five times and repeated five times at beginning and end.

Relay to Rio de Janeiro, B.A., Mexico City, and San Francisco.
SIS-25392 JD-1: 6850 Secret Navy Trans. 11-26-41

From: Tokyo
To: Washington
19 November 1941
(Purple-CA)

Re my #797[15]

The condition outlined by them namely "After the peaceful policies of Japan have been made more definite" we imagine would naturally have reference to the question of the three-power treaty. It does not mean merely that Japan will withdraw her troops from Southern Indo-China, and that then the U.S. will go back to conditions prior to the freezing act. It leaves the way open for the U.S. to bring up rather complicated terms.

On the other hand, the internal situation in our country is such that it would be difficult for us to handle it if we withdraw from Southern French Indo-China, merely on assurances that conditions prior to this freezing act will be restored. It would be necessary to have a proposed solution that would come up to the B[16] proposal. With the situation as urgent as it is now, it is of utmost importance that you play your hand for the amelioration of the situation, to the extent of the proposal in your message, then to push on for an understanding.

The Ambassador did not arrange this with us beforehand, but made the proposal contained in your message for the purpose of meeting the tense situation existing within the nation, but this can only result in delay and failure in the negotiations. The Ambassador, therefore, having received our revised instructions, (after reading our #797,[15] #800[17] and #8001[18]) will please present our B proposal of the Imperial Government, and no further concessions can be made.

If the U.S. consent to this cannot be secured, the negotiations will have to be broken off; therefore, with the above well in mind put forth your very best efforts.

---

[15] JD-1: 6657.
[16] JD-1: 6250, with additional paragraphs 5, 6, 7 in JD-1: 6528.
[17] JD-1: 6660
[18] JD-1: 6661

We note what you say in your #1133[19] and, #1134[19], but, in these negotiations consent can be given only within the scope of the instructions of this office. We would emphasize this.

S.I.S. #25040
JD-1: 6658
(F) Navy Trans. 11-20-41

From: Tokyo
To: Washington
November 22, 1941
Purple CA (Urgent)
#812

To both you Ambassadors.

It is awfully hard for us to consider changing the date we set in my #736.[20] You should know this however, I know you are working hard. Stick to our fixed policy and do your very best. Spare no efforts and try to bring about the solution we desire. There are reasons beyond your ability to guess why we wanted to settle Japanese-American relations by the 25th, but if within the next three or four days you can finish your conversations with the Americans; if the signing can be completed by the 29th (let me write it out for you— twenty-ninth); if the pertinent notes can be exchanged; if we can get an understanding with Great Britain and the Netherlands; and in short if everything can be finished, we have decided to wait until that date. This time we mean it, that the deadline absolutely cannot be changed. After that things are automatically going to happen. Please take this into your careful consideration and work harder than you ever have before. This, for the present, is for the information of you two Ambassadors alone.

From: Tokyo
To: Washington
November 26, 1941
Purple
#836. To be handled in Government Code.

The situation is momentarily becoming more tense and telegrams take too long. Therefore, will you cut down the substance of your reports of negoti-

---

[19] Not yet available.
[20] See JD #6254. Tokyo wires Washington that because of the various circumstances it is absolutely necessary that arrangements for the signing of the agreement be completed by the 25th of this month.

ations to the minimum and, on occasion, call up Chief YAMAMOTO of the American Bureau on the telephone and make your report to him. At that time we will use the following code:

Japanese	*English*
Sangoku Joyaku Mondai	(Three-Power Treaty question)
Nyuu Yooku	(New York)
Taignu Mondai	(The question of non-discriminatory treatment)
Shikago	(Chicago)
Shina Mondai	(The China question)
Sanfuranshisuko	(San Francisco)
Soori	(Premier)
Itoo Kun	(Mr. Itoo)
Gaimudaijin	(Foreign Minister)
Date Kun	(Mr. Date)
Rikugun	(The Army)
Tokugawa Kun	(Mr. Tokugawa)
Kaigun	(The Navy)
Maeda Kun	(Mr. Maeda)
Nichi-bei kooshoo	(Japan-American negotiations)
Endan	(Marriage proposal)
Daitooryoo	(President)
Kimiko San	(Miss Kimiko)
Haru	(Hull)
Fumeko San	(Miss Fumeko)
Kokunaijoosei	(Internal situation)
Shoobai	(Trade)
Jooho Suru	(To yield)
Yama Wo Uru	(To sell the mountain)
Jooho Sezu	(Not to yield)
Yama Wo Urenu	(Not to sell the mountain)
Keisei Kyuuten Suru	(Situation taking critical turn)
Kodomo Gaumarero	(The child is born)

For your information, telephone addresses other than our Home Office are as follows:

Bureau Chief YAMAMOTO	Setagaya 4617
Section Chief KASE	Yotsuya 4793
The Minister's residence	Ginza 3614
The Vice-Minister's residence	Ginza 1022

From: Washington
To: Tokyo
November 26, 1941
Purple. (Extremely urgent)
#1180. (Part 1 of 2)
　　From NOMURA and KURUSU.

　　As we have wired you several times, there is hardly any possibility of having them consider our "B" proposal in toto. On the other hand, if we let the situation remain tense as it is now, sorry as we are to say so, the negotiations will inevitably be ruptured, if indeed they may not already be called so. Our failure and humiliation are complete. We might suggest one thing for saving the situation. Although we have grave misgivings, we might propose, first, that President ROOSEVELT wire you that for the sake of posterity he hopes that Japan and the United States will cooperate for the maintenance of peace in the Pacific (just as soon as you wire us what you think of this, we will negotiate for this sort of an arrangement with all we have in us), and that you in return reply with a cordial message thereby not only clearing the atmosphere, but also gaining a little time. Considering the possibility that England and the United States are scheming to bring the Netherlands Indies under their protection through military occupation, in order to forestall this, I think we should propose the establishment of neutral nations, including French Indo-China, Netherlands India and Thai. (As you know, last September President ROOSEVELT proposed the neutrality of French Indo-China and Thai.)

From: Washington
To: Tokyo
November 26, 1941
Purple (Extremely urgent)
#1180. (Part 2 of 2)[21]

　　We suppose that the rupture of the present negotiations does not necessarily mean war between Japan and the United States, but after we break off, as we said, the military occupation of Netherlands India is to be expected of England and the United States. Then we would attack them and a clash with them would be inevitable. Now, the question is whether or not Germany would feel duty bound by the third article of the treaty to help us. We doubt if she would. Again, you must remember that the Sino-Japanese incident would have to wait until the end of this world war before it could possibly be settled.
　　In this telegram we are expressing the last personal opinions we will have

[21] SIS #25444 (Part 1 of 2)

to express, so will Your Excellency please be good enough at least to show it to the Minister of the Navy, if only to him; then we hope that you will wire us back instantly.

From: Washington (Nomura)
To: Tokyo
November 26, 1941
Purple. (Extremely urgent)
#1190. (Part 2 of 2)[22]
    To be handled in Government Code.

The United States is using the excuse that she is at present negotiating with the various competent countries. In view of the fact that she will propagandize that we are continuing these negotiations only with the view of preparing for our expected moves, should we, during the course of these conversations, deliberately enter into our scheduled operations, there is great danger that the responsibility for the rupture of negotiations will be cast upon us. There have been times in the past when she could have considered discontinuing conversations because of our invasion of French Indo-China. Now, should we, without clarifying our intentions, force a rupture in our negotiations and suddenly enter upon independent operations, there is great fear that she may use such a thing as that as counter-propaganda against us. They might consider doing the same thing insofar as our plans for Thai are concerned. Nevertheless, such a thing as the clarification of our intention is a strict military secret; consequently, I think that it might be the better plan, dependent of course on the opinions of the Government, that the current negotiations be clearly and irrevocably concluded either through an announcement to the American Embassy in Tokyo or by a declaration for internal and external consumptions. I would like, if such a course is followed, to make representations here at the same time.

    Furthermore, in view of the fact that there are considerations of convenience having to do with my interview with the President, should there be anything that you would want me to say at that time, please wire me back at once.

[22] SIS #25444 (Part 1 of 2)

From: Washington
To: Tokyo
26 November 1941 (1946 to 1953 EST)
(Telephone Code)[23]
Transpacific Telephone
To Kumaicho Yamamoto[24] from Kurusu:

Kurusu: "I have made all efforts, but they *will not yield.*[25] I sent a cable expressing my opinions to the Foreign Minister this morning. The situation is just like that. Otherwise there is no means of accomplishing it. I shall cable you now. Already," he interrupted himself, "you have a general understanding I imagine. Accordingly, I do not know how things will turn out regarding my meeting with the President. Hull is not making much progress it seems."

Apparently referring to the above mentioned cable he continued: "If that method can be worked out I shall work night and day on it. But there is no other means we can use. It is very regrettable."

Yamamoto: "The situation in Tokyo is extremely critical also." After thanking Kurusu for his efforts he continued: "The proposition sent to the Foreign Minister is extremely difficult."

Kurusu: "I believe it is of no avail."

Yamamoto reiterated his opinion regarding its difficulty.

Kurusu: "I rather imagine you had expected this outcome."

Yamamoto: "Yes, I had expected it, but wished to exert every effort up to the final moment in the hope that something might be accomplished."

Kuruso: "I am unable to make any movement (i.e. progress?) at all. Something will have to be done to get out of this situation."

From: Tokyo
To: Washington
November 28, 1941
Purple. (CA)
#844
　　Re your #1189[26]

Well, you two Ambassadors have exerted superhuman efforts but, in spite of this, the United States has gone ahead and presented this humiliating proposal. This was quite unexpected and extremely regrettable. The Imperial Government can by no means use it as a basis for negotiations. Therefore,

[23] See JD-1: 6841, (SIS #25344), of this date.
[24] Head of American Division of Japanese Foreign Office.
[25] Interpretation is doubtful as yet. The interceptor read this as "Sore . . . kesa" (that . . . this morning) and translated it as "It is now . . . ." with a distinct pause before and after this phrase. However, the telephone code was not available to him. Verification will follow receipt of record.
[26] SIS #25441, #25442.

with a report of the views of the Imperial Government on this American proposal which I will send you in two or three days, the negotiations will be de facto ruptured. This is inevitable. However, I do not wish you to give the impression that the negotiations are broken off. Merely say to them that you are awaiting instructions and that, although the opinions of your Government are not yet clear to you, to your own way of thinking the Imperial Government has always made just claims and has borne great sacrifices for the sake of peace in the Pacific. Say that we have always demonstrated a long-suffering and conciliatory attitude, but that, on the other hand, the United States has been unbending, making it impossible for Japan to establish negotiations. Since things have come to this pass, I contacted the man you told me to in your #1180[27] and he said that under the present circumstances what you suggest is entirely unsuitable. From now on do the best you can.

From: Tokyo
To: Honolulu
29 November 1941
(J19)
#122

We have been receiving reports from you on ship movements, but in the future will you also report even when there are no movements.
JD-1: 7086 Secret (Y) Navy Trans. 12-5-41 (2)

From: Tokyo
To: Washington
29 November 1941
(Purple-CA)
#857
Re my #844[28]

We wish you would make one more attempt verbally along the following lines:
The United States government has (always?) taken a fair and judicial position and has formulated its policies after full consideration of the claims of both sides.
However, the Imperial Government is at a loss to understand why it has

[27] SIS #25435, #25436. The man is the Navy Minister.
[28] JD-1: 6898 (SIS 25445) dated 28 Nov., in which Tokyo's first reaction to the new U.S. proposals castigates them as humiliating. When Japan sends a reply in 2 or 3 days giving its views on them the negotiations will be 'de facto' ruptured. However, do not give the impression that negotiations are broken off.

now taken the attitude that the new proposals we have made cannot be made the basis of discussion, but instead has made new proposals which ignore actual conditions in East Asia and would greatly injure the prestige of the Imperial Government.

With such a change of front in their attitude toward the China problem, what has become of the basic objectives that the U.S. government has made the basis of our negotiations during these seven months? On these points we would request careful self-reflection on the part of the United States government.

(In carrying out this instruction, please be careful that this does not lead to anything like a breaking off of negotiations.)

JD-1: 6921 Secret (F) Navy trans. 30 Nov. 1941 (S-TT)

From: Washington
To: Tokyo
30 November 1941 (2230 to 2238 EST)
Telephone Code

TransPacific Radio Telephone

NOTE: Following is a preliminary, condensed version of conversation between Ambassador Kurusu and the Japanese Foreign Office American division Chief Yamamoto on Sunday night.

Kurusu: "It is all arranged for us to meet Hull tomorrow. We received a short one from you, didn't we? Well, we will meet him in regard to that. There is a longer one coming isn't there? In any case, we are going to see him about the short one." (i.e. telegram. The longer one is probably Tokyo's reply to Mr. Hull's proposals.)

Yamamoto: "Yes. I see."

Kurusu: "The President is returning tomorrow. He is hurrying home."

Y: "Is there any special significance to this?"

K: "The newspapers have made much of the Premier's speech, and it is having strong repercussions here."

Y: "Is that so?"

K: "Yes. It was a drastic statement he made. The newspapers carried large headlines over it; and the President seems to be returning because of it. There no doubt are other reasons, but this is the reason the newspapers are giving."

(Pause)

"Unless greater caution is exercised in speeches by the Premier and others, it puts us in a very difficult position. All of you over there must watch out about these ill-advised statements. Please tell Mr. Tani."

Y: "We are being careful."

K: "We here are doing our best, but these reports are seized upon by the correspondents and the worst features enlarged upon. Please caution the Premier, the Foreign Minister and others. Tell the Foreign Minister that we had expected to hear something different, some good word, but instead we get this.'' (i.e. Premier's speech.)

JD-1: 6922 Secret (M) Navy trans. 30 Nov. 1941 (R-5) 25497

(After a pause, Kurusu continues, using voice code.)

K: ''What about the internal situation?'' (In Japan)

Y: ''No particular—(one or two words faded out)—.''

K: ''Are the Japanese-American negotiations to continue?''

Y: ''Yes.''

K: ''You were very urgent about them before, weren't you; but now you want them to stretch out. We will need your help. Both the Premier and the Foreign Minister will need to change the tone of their speeches. ! ! ! Do you understand? Please all use more discretion.''

Y: ''When will you see them. The 2nd?''

K: ''Let's see . . . this is Sunday midnight here. Tomorrow morning at ten. That will be Monday morning here.''

(Pause)

''Actually the real problem we are up against is the effects of happenings in the South. You understand don't you?''

Y: ''Yes. Yes. How long will it be before the President gets back?''

K: ''I don't know exactly. According to news reports he started at 4:00 this afternoon. He should be here tomorrow morning sometime.''

Y: ''Well then—Goodbye.''

JD-1: 6922 Secret (M) Navy Trans. 30 Nov. 1941 (R-5) 25497

From: Tokyo
To: Berlin
November 30, 1941
Purple (CA)
#985. (Part 1 of 3)[29]
   Re my Circular #2387.[30]

1. The conversations begun between Tokyo and Washington last April during the administration of the former cabinet, in spite of the sincere efforts of the Imperial Government, now stand ruptured—broken. (I am sending you an outline of developments in separate message #986[31]) In the face of this, our Empire faces a grave situation and must act with determination. Will Your

[29] Part 2 not available. For Part 3 see SIS #25553.
[30] Not available.
[31] See SIS #25554 and 25555.

Honor, therefore, immediately interview Chancellor HITLER and Foreign Minister RIBBENTROP and confidentially communicate to them a summary of the developments. Say to them that lately England and the United States have taken a provocative attitude, both of them. Say that they are planning to move military forces into various places in East Asia and that we will inevitably have to counter by also moving troops. Say very secretly to them that there is extreme danger that war may suddenly break out between the Anglo-Saxon nations and Japan through some clash of arms and add that the time of the breaking out of this war may come quicker than anyone dreams.

25552 JD 6943 Secret Trans 12-1-41 (NR)

From: Tokyo
To: Berlin
November 30, 1941
Purple. (CA).
#985. (Part 3 of 3)

4. If, when you tell them this, the Germans and Italians question you about our attitude toward the Soviets, say that we have already clarified our attitude toward the Russians in our statement of last July. Say that by our present moves southward we do not mean to relax our pressure against the Soviets or that if Russia joins hands tighter with England and the United States and resists us with hostilities, we are ready to turn upon her with all our might; however, right now it is to our advantage to stress the south and for the time being we would prefer to refrain from any direct moves in the north.

5. This message is important from a strategic point of view and must under all circumstances be held in the most absolute secrecy. This goes without saying. Therefore, will you please impress upon the Germans and Italians how important secrecy is.

6. As for Italy, after our Ambassador in Berlin has communicated this to the Germans, he will transmit a suitable translation to Premier MUSSOLINI and Foreign Minister CIANO. As soon as the date is set for a conference with the Germans and Italians, please let me know.

Will you please send this message also to Rome, together with the separate message.

25553 Secret Trans. 12-1-41 (NR)

From: Tokyo
To: Berlin
November 30, 1941
Purple
#986 (Strictly Secret) (To be handled in Government Code) (Part 1 of 2)
(Secret outside the Department)

1. Japan-American negotiations were commenced in the middle of April of this year. Over a period of half a year they have been continued. Within that period the Imperial Government adamantly stuck to the Tri-Partite Alliance as the cornerstone of its national policy regardless of the vicissitudes of the international situation. In the adjustment of diplomatic relations between Japan and the United States, she has based her hopes for a solution definitely within the scope of that alliance. With the intent of restraining the United States from participating in the war, she boldly assumed the attitude of carrying through these negotiations.

2. Therefore, the present cabinet, in line with your message, with the view of defending the Empire's existence and integrity on a just and equitable basis, has continued the negotiations carried on in the past. However, their views and ours on the question of the evacuation of troops, upon which the negotiations rested (they demanded the evacuation of Imperial troops from China and French Indo-China), were completely in opposition to each other.

Judging from the course of the negotiations that have been going on, we first came to loggerheads when the United States, in keeping with its traditional ideological tendency of managing international relations, re-emphasized her fundamental reliance upon this traditional policy in the conversations carried on between the United States and England in the Atlantic Ocean. The motive of the United States in all this was brought out by her desire to prevent the establishment of a new order by Japan, Germany and Italy in Europe and the Far East, that is to say, the aims of the Tri-Partite Alliance. As long as the Empire of Japan was in alliance with Germany and Italy, there could be no maintenance of friendly relations between Japan and the United States was the stand they took. From this point of view, they began to demonstrate a tendency to demand the divorce of the Imperial Government from the Tri-Partite Alliance. This was brought out at the last meeting. That is to say that it has only been in the negotiations of the last few days that it has become gradually more and more clear that the Imperial Government could no longer continue negotiations with the United States. It became clear, too, that a continuation of negotiations would inevitably be detrimental to our cause.

ARMY 6944 25554 SECRET TRANS. 12/1/41 (NR)

79716—46—Ex. 148—43

From: Tokyo
To: Berlin
November 30, 1941
Purple.
#986. (Part 2 of 2)

3. The proposal presented by the United States on the 26th made this attitude of theirs clearer than ever. In it there is one insulting clause which says that no matter what treaty either party enters into with a third power it will not be interpreted as having any bearing upon the basic object of this treaty, namely the maintenance of peace in the Pacific. This means specifically the Three-Power Pact. It means that in case the United States enters the European war at any time, the Japanese Empire will not be allowed to give assistance to Germany and Italy. It is clearly a trick. This clause alone, let alone others, makes it impossible to find any basis in the American proposal for negotiations. What is more, before the United States brought forth this plan, they conferred with England, Australia, the Netherlands, and China— they do so repeatedly. Therefore, it is clear that the United States is now in collusion with those nations and has decided to regard Japan, along with Germany and Italy, as an enemy.
ARMY 6944 25555 SECRET Trans 12-1-41 (NR)

From: Washington
To: Tokyo
1 December 1941
(Purple)
#1227

Indications are that the United States desires to continue the negotiations even if it is necessary to go beyond their stands on the so-called basic principles. However, if we keep quibbling on the critical points and continue to get stuck in the middle as we have been in the past, it is impossible to expect any further developments. If it is impossible from the broad political viewpoint, to conduct a leaders' meeting at this time, would it not be possible to arrange a conference between persons in whom the leaders have complete confidence, (for example, Vice President Wallace or Hopkins from the United States and the former Premier Konoye, who is on friendly terms with the President, or Adviser to the Imperial Privy Council Ishii). The meeting could be arranged for some midway point, such as Honolulu. High army and navy officers should accompany these representatives. Have them make one final effort to reach some agreement, using as the basis of their discussions the latest proposals submitted by each.

We feel that this last effort may facilitate the final decision as to war or peace.

We realize of course that an attempt to have President Roosevelt and former Premier Konoye meet, failed. Bearing in mind the reaction to that in our nation, it may be to our interest to first ascertain the U.S. attitude regarding this possibility. Moreover, since we have no guarantee either of success or failure of the objectives even if the meeting is held, careful consideration should first be given this matter.

We feel, however, that to surmount the crisis with which we are face to face, it is not wasting our efforts to pursue every path open to us. It is our opinion that it would be most effective to feel out and ascertain the U.S. attitude regarding this matter, in the name of the Japanese Government. However, if this procedure does not seem practical to you in view of some internal conditions, then how would it be if I were to bring up the subject as purely of my own origin and in that manner feel out their attitude. Then, if they seem receptive to it the government could make the official proposal.

Please advise me of your opinions on this matter.

25727 JD-1: 7055 SECRET (D) Navy Trans 12-4-41 (1)

From: Tokyo.
To: Washington.
1 December 1941
(Purple)
Circular #2436

When you are faced with the necessity of destroying codes, get in touch with the Naval Attache's office there and make use of chemicals they have on hand for this purpose. The Attache should have been advised by the Navy Ministry regarding this.

25545 JD-1: 6939 (D) Navy Trans. 12-1-41 (S-TT)

From: Tokyo
To: London
1 December 1941
(Purple)
Circular #2443

Please discontinue the use of your code machine and dispose of it immediately.

In regard to the disposition of the machine please be very careful to carry out the instructions you have received regarding this. Pay particular attention to taking apart and breaking up the important parts of the machine.

As soon as you have received this telegram wire the one word SETUJU in plain language and as soon as you have carried out the instructions wire the one word HASSO in plain language.

Also at this time you will of course burn the machine codes and YU GO No. 26 of my telegram. (The rules for the use of the machine between the head office and the Ambassador resident in England.)

(NOTE: THIS MESSAGE CARRIED A NOTATION ON THE BOTTOM AS A RESULT OF MY AFFIDAVIT OF CAPTAIN LAYTON SAYING:

Message not seen but—British reported that Japs had destroyed their purple machine in London, 26 April 1945. [signed] E. J. Layton.)

25787 JD-1: 7091 Secret (H) Navy Trans. 12-5-41 (L)

From: Tokyo
To: Hsinking
1 December 1941
(Purple)
#893

------ In the event that Manchuria participates in the war ------- in view of various circumstances it is our policy to cause Manchuria to participate in the war in which event Manchuria will take the same steps toward England and America that this country will take in case war breaks out.

A summary follows:

1. American and British consular officials and offices will not be recognized as having special rights. Their business will be stopped (the sending of code telegrams and the use of short wave radio will be forbidden). However it is desired that the treatment accorded them after the suspension of business be comparable to that which Japan accords to consular officials of enemy countries resident in Japan.

2. The treatment accorded to British and American public property, private property, and to the citizens themselves shall be comparable to that accorded by Japan.

3. British and American requests to third powers to look after their consular offices and interests will not be recognized.

However the legal administrative steps taken by Manchoukuo shall conform to the provisions of the Japanese-Soviet neutrality pact. Great care shall be exercised not to antagonize Russia.

Codes Manchoukuo, etc.

JD-1: 7092 SIS 25783 Secret (H) Navy Trans. 12-4-41 (5-AR)

From: Tokyo
To: Washington
1 December 1941
(Purple-CA)
#865

Re my #857[32]
1. The date set in my message #812[33] has come and gone, and the situation continues to be increasingly critical. However, to prevent the United States from becoming unduly suspicious we have been advising the press and others that though there are some wide differences between Japan and the United States, the negotiations are continuing. (The above is only for your information.)

2. We have decided to withhold submitting the note to the U.S. Ambassador to Tokyo as suggested by you at the end of your message #1124[34]. Please make the necessary representations at your end only.

3. There are reports here that the President's sudden return to the capital is an effect of Premier Tojo's statement. We have an idea that the President did so because of his concern over the critical Far Eastern situation. Please make investigations into this matter.

JD-1: 6983 Secret (D) Navy Trans. 12-1-41 (S-TT)

Completed Translation

From: Washington
To: Tokyo
December 2, 1941
Purple
#1232 (Part 1 of 2)

Re my #1231
Today, the 2nd Ambassador KURUSU and I had an interview with Under-Secretary of State WELLES. At that time, prefacing his statement by saying that it was at the direct instruction of the President of the United States, he turned over to us the substance of my separate wire #1233[35]. Thereupon we said: "Since we haven't been informed even to the slightest degree concerning the troops in French Indo-China, we will transmit the gist of your repre-

[32] JD-1: 6921.
[33] JD-1: 6710.
[34] Not available.
[35] Not available.

sentations directly to our Home Government. In all probability they never considered that such a thing as this could possibly be an upshot of their proposals of November 20th." The Under-Secretary then said: "I want you to know that the stand the United States takes is that she opposes aggression in any and all parts of the world." Thereupon we replied: "The United States and other countries have pyramided economic pressure upon economic pressure upon us Japanese. (I made the statement that economic warfare was even worse than forceful aggression.) We haven't the time to argue the pros and cons of this question or the rights and wrongs. The people of Japan are faced with economic pressure, and I want you to know that we have but the choice between submission to this pressure or breaking the chains that it invokes.[36] We want you to realize this as well as the situation in which all Japanese find themselves as the result of the four-year incident in China; the President recently expressed cognizance of the latter situation.

[*1*] From: Washington (Nomura)
To: Tokyo
December 2, 1941.
Purple.
#1232. (Part 2 of 2)

Furthermore, I would have you know that in replying to the recent American proposals, the Imperial Government is giving the most profound consideration to this important question which has to do with our national destiny. Under-Secretary of State WELLES said: "I am well aware of that." I continued: "We cannot overemphasize the fact that, insofar as Japan is concerned, it is virtually impossible for her to accept the new American proposals as they now stand. Our proposals proffered on the 21st of June and the proposals of September 25th, representing our greatest conciliations based on the previous proposal, still stand. In spite of the fact that the agreement of both sides was in the offing, it has come to naught. At this late juncture to give a thoughtful consideration to the new proposals certainly will not make for a smooth and speedy settlement of the negotiations. Recently, we promised to evacuate our troops from French Indo-China in the event of a settlement of the Sino-Japanese Incident and the establishment of a just peace in the Far East. In anticipating the settlement of fundamental questions, the question of the representations of this date would naturally dissolve." The Under-Secretary assiduously heard us out and then said: "The American proposals of the 26th were brought about by the necessity to clarify the position of the United States

[36] Original translation incomplete from this point on. Trans. 12/3/41.

because of the internal situation here." [2] Then he continued: "In regard to the opinions you have expressed, I will make it a point immediately to confer with the Secretary."

I got the impression from the manner in which he spoke that he hoped Japan in her reply to the American proposals of the 26th would leave this much room.

Judging by my interview with Secretary of State HULL on the 1st and my conversations of today, it is clear that the United States, too, is anxious to peacefully conclude the current difficult situation. I am convinced that they would like to bring about a speedy settlement. Therefore, please bear well in mind this fact in your considerations of our reply to the new American proposals and to my separate wire #1233[37].

25660 ARMY Trans. 12-3-41 (7)

From: Tokyo (Togo)
To: Washington
December 2, 1941.
Purple.
#867 (Strictly Secret)

(CORRECTED TRANSLATION)

1. Among the telegraphic codes with which your office is equipped burn all but those now used with the machine and one copy each of "O" code (Oite) and abbreviating code (L). (Burn also the various other codes which you have in your custody.)

2. Stop at once using one code machine unit and destroy it completely.

3. When you have finished this, wire me back the one word "haruna."

4. At the time and in the manner you deem most proper dispose of all files of messages coming and going and all other secret documents.

5. Burn all the codes which Telegraphic official KOSAKA brought you. (Hence, the necessity of getting in contact with Mexico mentioned in my #890[38] is no longer recognized.)

#25640 Translated 12-3-41 (X) Corrected 12-4-41

---

[37] Not available.
[38] SIS #25550 in which Tokyo wires Washington advising them to have KOSAKA return to Japan on the Tatsuta Maru which sails on the 28th. If this makes it impossible for KOSAKA to make his trip to Mexico, make some other arrangements with regard to KOSAKA's business in Mexico.

From: Tokyo (Togo)
To: Honolulu
December 2, 1941
J-19
#123 (Secret outside the department)

In view of the present situation, the presence in port of warships, airplane carriers, and cruisers is of utmost importance. Hereafter, to the utmost of your ability, let me know day by day. Wire me in each case whether or not there are any observation balloons above Pearl Harbor or if there are any indications that they will be sent up. Also advise me whether or not the warships are provided with anti-mine nets.
NOTE: This message was received here on December 23.
ARMY 8007 27065 (Japanese) Trans. 12/30/41 (5)

From: Washington
To: Tokyo
3 December 1941
(Purple)
#1223

Judging from all indications, we feel that some joint military action between Great Britain and the United States, with or without a declaration of war, is a definite certainty in the event of an occupation of Thailand.
25785 JD-1: 7098 (D) Navy Trans. 12-5-41 (7)

From: Berlin
To: Tokyo
December 4, 1941.
Purple (CA)
#1410

In case of evacuation by the members of our Embassy in London, I would like to arrange to have Secretary Matsui of that office and three others (URABE and KOJIMA and one other) from among the higher officials and two other officials (UEHARA and YUWASAKI) stay here. Please do your best to this end.
ARMY 25807 JD-7134 Trans. 12-5-41 (W)

From: Washington
To: Tokyo
5 December 1941
(Purple)
#1268 Re your #867[39]

From Councillor of Embassy Iguchi to the Chief of the Communication
Section:

We have completed destruction of codes, but since the U.S.-Japanese
negotiations are still continuing I request your approval of our desire to delay
for a while yet the destruction of the one code machine.

25836 JD-1: 7136 (M) Navy Trans. 12-6-41 (S-TT)

From: Tokyo
To: Washington
December 6, 1941
Purple
#901 Re my #844[40]

1. The Government has deliberated deeply on the American proposal of the
26th of November and as a result we have drawn up a memorandum for the
United States contained in my separate message #902 (in English).

2. This separate message is a very long one. I will sent it in fourteen parts
and I imagine you will receive it tomorrow. However, I am not sure. The
situation is extremely delicate, and when you receive it I want you please to
keep it secret for the time being.

3. Concerning the time of presenting this memorandum to the United
States, I will wire you in a separate message. However, I want you in the
meantime to put it in nicely drafted form and make every preparation to
present it to the Americans just as soon as you receive instructions.

ARMY 7149 25838 Secret Trans 12-6-41 (S)

---

[39] (Dated 2 December) JD-1: 7017 (SIS #25640): Directs Washington to destroy all copies of
codes except one copy of certain ones, and also destroy one code machine.
[40] See SIS #25445 in which Tokyo wires Washington that the Imperial Government cannot
accept the United States proposal and, therefore, with a report of the views of the Imperial
Government which will be sent in two or three days, the negotiations will be de facto ruptured.
Until then, however, Washington is not to give the impression that negotiations are broken off.

From: Washington
To: Tokyo
December 6, 1941
Purple (Urgent)
#1272

In addition to carrying on frontal negotiations with the President and HULL, we also worked directly and indirectly through Cabinet members having close relations with the President and through individuals equally influential (because of its delicate bearing upon the State Department, please keep this point strictly secret). Up until this moment we have the following to report:

(1) On the 4th those engaged in Plan "A" dined with the President and advised him against a Japanese-American war and urged him to do the "introducing" at once between Japan and China. However, the President did not make known what he had in mind. According to these men, this attitude of the President is his usual attitude. Recently, when the President discussed matters with LEWIS and settled the strike question, I understand that he did so on the advice of these individuals.

(2) Those carrying on Plan "B" included all of our proposal of November 20th into that of September 25th and after incorporating those sections in the United States' proposal of November 26th which are either innocuous or advantageous to us ------------ (MESSAGE INCOMPLETE) -------------.

ARMY 25846 7176 Secret Trans. 12/7/41 (2T)

From: Tokyo
To: Washington
December 6, 1941
Purple
#902 (Part 1 of 14) Separate telegram

MEMORANDUM

1. The Government of Japan, prompted by a genuine desire to come to an amicable understanding with the Government of the United States in order that the two countries by their joint efforts may secure the peace of the Pacific area and thereby contribute toward the realization of world peace, has continued negotiations with utmost sincerity since April last with the Government of the United States regarding the adjustment and advancement of Japanese-American relations and the stabilization of the Pacific area.

The Japanese Government has the honor to state frankly its views concerning the claims the American Government has persistently maintained as well as the measures the United States and Great Britain have taken toward Japan during these eight months.

2. It is the immutable policy of the Japanese Government to insure the

stability of East Asia and to promote world peace, and thereby to enable all nations to find each BOAMPYBR place in the world.

Ever since the China Affair broke out owing to the failure on the part of China to comprehend Japan's true intentions, the Japanese Government has striven for the restoration of peace and it has consistently exerted its best efforts to prevent the extension of war-like disturbances. It was also to that end that in September last year Japan concluded the Tri Partite Pact with Germany and Italy.

JD-1: 7143 Secret Navy Trans. 12-6-41 (S) 25843

From: Tokyo
To: Washington
December 6, 1941
Purple
#902 (Part 2 of 14)

However, both the United States and Great Britain have resorted to every possible measure to assist the Chungking regime so as to obstruct the establishment of a general peace between Japan and China, interfering with Japan's constructive endeavours toward the stabilization of East Asia, exerting pressure on The Netherlands East Indies, or menacing French Indo-China, they have attempted to frustrate Japan's aspiration to realize the ideal of common prosperity in cooperation with these regions. Furthermore, when Japan in accordance with its protocol with France took measures of joint defense of French Indo-China, both American and British governments willfully misinterpreted it as a threat to their own possession and inducing the Netherlands government to follow suit, they enforced the assets freezing order, thus severing economic relations with Japan. While manifesting thus an obviously hostile attitude, these countries have strengthened their military preparations perfecting an encirclement of Japan, and have brought about a situation which endangers the very existence of the empire.

JD-1: 7143 Secret Navy Trans. 12-6-41 (S) 25843

From: Tokyo
To: Washington
December 6, 1941
Purple
#902 (Part 3 of 14)

Nevertheless, to facilitate a speedy settlement, the Premier of Japan proposed in August last, to meet the President of the United States for a discussion of important problems between the two countries covering the entire

Pacific area. However, while accepting in principle the Japanese proposal, insisted that the meeting should take place after an agreement of view had been reached on fundamental—(75 letters garbled) —The Japanese government submitted a proposal based on the formula proposed by the American government, taking fully into consideration past American claims and also incorporating Japanese views. Repeated discussions proved of no avail in producing readily an agreement of view. The present cabinet, therefore, submitted a revised proposal, moderating still further the Japanese claims regarding the principal points of difficulty in the negotiation and endeavored strenuously to reach a settlement. But the American government, adhering steadfastly to its original proposal, failed to display in the slightest degree a spirit of conciliation. The negotiation made no progress.

JD-1: 7143 Secret Navy Trans. 12-6-41 (S) 25843

From: Tokyo
To: Washington
December 6, 1941
Purple
#902 (Part 4 of 14)

Thereupon, the Japanese Government, with a view to doing its utmost for averting a crisis in Japanese-American relations, submitted on November 20th still another proposal in order to arrive at an equitable solution of the more essential and urgent questions which, simplifying its previous proposal, stipulated the following points:

(1) The Governments of Japan and the United States undertake not to dispatch armed forces into any of the regions, excepting French Indo-China, in the Southeastern Asia and the Southern-Pacific area.

(2) Both Governments shall cooperate with a view to securing the acquisition in the Netherlands East Indies of those goods and commodities of which the two countries are in need.

(3) Both Governments mutually undertake to restore commercial relations to those prevailing prior to the freezing of assets.

The Government of the United States shall supply Japan the required quantity of oil.

(4) The Government of the United States undertakes not to resort to measures and actions prejudicial to the endeavours for the restoration of general peace between Japan and China.

(5) The Japanese Government undertakes to withdraw troops now stationed in French Indo-China upon either the restoration of peace between Japan and China or the establishment of an equitable peace in the Pacific area; and it is prepared to remove the Japanese troops in the southern part

of French Indo-China to the northern part upon the conclusion of the present agreement.

JD-1: 7143 Secret Navy Trans. 12-6-41 (S) 25843

From: Tokyo
To: Washington
December 6, 1941
Purple
#902 (Part 5 of 14)

As regards China, the Japanese Government, while expressing its readiness to accept the offer of the President of the United States to act as "Introducer" of peace between Japan and China as was previously suggested, asked for an undertaking on the part of the United States to do nothing prejudicial to the restoration of Sino-Japanese peace when the two parties have commenced direct negotiations.

The American government not only rejected to above-mentioned new proposal, but made known its intention to continue its aid to Chiang Kai-Shek; and in spite of its suggestion mentioned above, withdrew the offer of the President to act as the so-called "Introducer" of peace between Japan and China, pleading that time was not yet ripe for it. Finally, on November 26th, in an attitude to impose upon the Japanese government those principles it has persistently maintained, the American government made a proposal totally ignoring Japanese claims, which is a source of profound regret to the Japanese Government.

JD-1: 7143 Secret Navy Trans. 12-6-41 (S) 25843

From: Tokyo
To: Washington
December 6, 1941
Purple
#902 (Part 6 of 14)

4. From the beginning of the present negotiation, the Japanese Government has always maintained an attitude of fairness and moderation, and did its best to reach a settlement, for which it made all possible concessions often in spite of great difficulties.

As for the China question which constituted an important subject of the negotiation, the Japanese Government showed a most conciliatory attitude.

As for the principle of Non-Discrimination in International Commerce, advocated by the American Government, the Japanese Government expressed its desire to see the said principle applied throughout the world, and declared that along with the actual practice of this principle in the world, the Japanese

Government would endeavour to apply the same in the Pacific area, including China, and made it clear that Japan had no intention of excluding from China economic activities of third powers pursued on an equitable basis.

Furthermore, as regards the question of withdrawing troops from French Indo-China, the Japanese government even volunteered, as mentioned above, to carry out an immediate evacuation of troops from Southern French Indo-China as a measure of easing the situation.

JD-1: 7143 Secret Navy Trans. 12-6-41 (S) 25843

From: Tokyo
To: Washington
December 6, 1941
Purple
#902 (Part 7 of 14)

It is presumed that the spirit of conciliation exhibited to the utmost degree by the Japanese Government in all these matters is fully appreciated by the American government.

On the other hand, the American government, always holding fast to theories in disregard to realities, and refusing to yield an inch on its impractical principles, caused undue delays in the negotiation. It is difficult to understand this attitude of the American government and the Japanese government desires to call the attention of the American government especially to the following points:

1. The American government advocates in the name of world peace those principles favorable to it and urges upon the Japanese government the acceptance thereof. The peace of the world may be brought about only by discovering a mutually acceptable formula through recognition of the reality of the situation and mutual appreciation of one another's position. An attitude such as ignores realities and imposes one's selfish views upon others will scarcely serve the purpose of facilitating the consummation of negotiations.

7143 Secret 25843

From: Tokyo
To: Washington
December 6, 1941
Purple
#902 (Part 8 of 14)

Of the various principles put forth by the American government as a basis of the Japanese-American agreement, there are some which the Japanese government is ready to accept on principle, but in view of the world's actual conditions, it seems only a Utopian ideal, on the part of the American government, to attempt to force their immediate adoption.

Again, the proposal to conclude a multilateral non-aggression pact between Japan, the United States, Great Britain, China, the Soviet Union, the Netherlands and Thailand, which is patterned after the old concept of collective security, is far removed from the realities of East Asia.

(2) The American proposal contains a stipulation which states: "Both governments will agree that no agreement, which either has concluded with any third powers, shall be interpreted by it in such a way as to conflict with the fundamental purpose of this agreement, the establishment and preservation of peace throughout the Pacific area." It is presumed that the above provision has been proposed with a view to restrain Japan from fulfilling its obligations under the Tripartite Pact when the United States participates in the war in Europe, and, as such, it cannot be accepted by the Japanese Government.

JD-1: 7143 Secret Navy Trans. 12-6-41 (S) 25843

From: Tokyo
To: Washington
December 6, 1941
Purple
#902 (Part 9 of 14)

The American Government, obsessed with its own views and opinions, may be said to be scheming for the extension of the war. While it seeks, on the one hand, to secure its rear by stabilizing the Pacific area, it is engaged, on the other hand, in aiding Great Britain and preparing to attack, in the name of self-defense, Germany and Italy two powers that are striving to establish a new order in Europe. Such a policy is totally at variance with the many principles upon which the American Government proposes to found the stability of the Pacific area through peaceful means.

3. Whereas the American Government, under the principles it rigidly upholds, objects to settling international issues through military pressure, it is exercising in conjunction with Great Britain and other nations pressure by economic power. Recourse to such pressure as a means of dealing with international relations should be condemned as it is at times more inhuman than military pressure.

JD-1: 7143 Navy Trans. 12-6-41 (S) 25843

From: Tokyo
To: Washington
December 6, 1941
Purple
#902 (Part 10 of 14)

4. It is impossible not to reach the conclusion that the American Government desires to maintain and strengthen, in collusion with Great Britain and other powers, its dominant position it has hitherto occupied not only in China but in other areas of East Asia. It is a fact of history that one countr---(45 letters garbled or missing)---been compelled to observe the status quo under the Anglo-American policy of imperialistic exploitation and to sacrifice the ----es to the prosperity of the two nations. The Japanese Government cannot tolerate the perpetuation of such a situation since it directly runs counter to Japan's fundamental policy to enable all nations to enjoy each its proper place in the world.

JD-1: 7143 Navy Trans. 12-6-41 (S) 25843

From: Tokyo
To: Washington
December 6, 1941
Purple
#902 (Part 11 of 14)

The stipulation proposed by the American Government relative to French Indo-China is a good exemplification of the above-mentioned American policy. That six countries,—Japan, the United States, Great Britain, The Netherlands, China and Thailand,—excepting France, should undertake among themselves to respect the territorial integrity and sovereignty of French Indo-China and equality of treatment in trade and commerce would be tantamount to placing that territory under the joint guarantee of the governments of those six countries. Apart from the fact that such a proposal totally ignores the position of France, it is unacceptable to the Japanese government in that such an arrangement cannot but be considered as an extension to French Indo-China of a system similar to the n---- (50 letters missing) ---sible for the present predicament of East Asia.

JD-1: 7143 Secret Navy Trans. 12-6-41 (S) 25843

From: Tokyo
To: Washington
December 6, 1941
Purple
#902 (Part 12 of 14)

5. All the items demanded of Japan by the American government regarding China such as wholesale evacuation of troops or unconditional application of the principle of Non-Discrimination in International Commerce ignore the actual conditions of China, and are calculated to destroy Japan's position as the stabilizing factor of East Asia. The attitude of the American government demanding Japan not to support militarily, politically or economically any regime other than the regime at Chungking, disregarding thereby the existence of the Nanking government, shatters the very basis of the present negotiation. This demand of the American government falling, as it does, in line with its above-mentioned refusal to cease from aiding the Chungking regime, demonstrates clearly the intention of the American government to obstruct the restoration of normal relations between Japan and China and the return of peace to East Asia.

JD-1: 7143 Secret Navy Trans. 12-6-41 (S) 25843

From: Tokyo
To: Washington
December 6, 1941
Purple
#902 (Part 13 of 14)

5. In brief, the American proposal contains certain acceptable items such as those concerning commerce, including the conclusion of a trade agreement, mutual removal of the freezing restrictions, and stabilization of the Yen and Dollar exchange, or the abolition of extra-territorial rights in China. On the other hand, however, the proposal in question ignores Japan's sacrifices in the four years of the China Affair, menaces the empire's existence itself and disparages its honor and prestige. Therefore, viewed in its entirety, the Japanese government regrets that it cannot accept the proposal as a basis of negotiation.

6. The Japanese Government, in its desire for an early conclusion of the negotiation, proposed that simultaneously with the conclusion of the Japanese-American negotiation, agreements be signed with Great Britain and other interested countries. The proposal was accepted by the American government. However, since the American government has made the proposal of November 26th as a result of frequent consultations with Great Britain, Australia,

The Netherlands and Chungking, ANDND[41] presumably by catering to the wishes of the Chungking regime on the questions of CHTUAL CYLOKMMTT[42] be concluded that all these countries are at one with the United States in ignoring Japan's position.

JD-1: 7143 Secret Navy Trans. 12-6-41 (S) 25843

From: Tokyo
To: Washington
7 December 1941
(Purple-Eng)
#902 (Part 14 of 14)

(NOTE: IN THE FORWARDING INSTRUCTIONS TO THE RADIO STATION HANDLING THIS PART APPEARED THE PLAIN ENGLISH PHRASE "VERY IMPORTANT.")

7. Obviously it is the intention of the American Government to conspire with Great Britain and other countries to obstruct Japan's efforts toward the establishment of peace through the creation of a New Order in East Asian, and especially to preserve Anglo-American rights and interests by keeping Japan and China at war. This intention has been revealed clearly during the course of the present negotiations. Thus, the earnest hope of the Japanese Government to adjust Japanese-American relations and to preserve and promote the peace of the Pacific through cooperation with the American Government has finally been lost.

The Japanese Government regrets to have to notify hereby the American Government that in view of the attitude of the American Government it cannot but consider that it is impossible to reach an agreement through further negotiations.

JD-1: 7143 Secret (M) Navy Trans. 7 Dec. 1941
(S-TT) 25843

(NOTE: THE TIME THE ENTIRE MESSAGE #25843 WAS TRANSLATED AND AVAILABLE FOR DISTRIBUTION IN WASHINGTON HAS BEEN THE SUBJECT OF CONTROVERSY FOR FIFTY YEARS. ARMY WITNESSES CLAIM THEY HAD COPIES OF THE ENTIRE FOURTEEN-PART MESSAGE AROUND MIDNIGHT DECEMBER 6. IT WAS THE ENTIRE 25843 SERIES OF MESSAGES THAT COLONEL DUSENBURY FAILED TO DELIVER TO GENERAL MARSHALL THAT NIGHT.)

[41] Probably "and as."
[42] Probably "China, can but."

From: Tokyo (Togo)
To: Honolulu
December 6, 1941
PA-K2
#128

Please wire immediately re the latter part of my #123[43] the movements of the fleet subsequent to the fourth.
ARMY 7381 26158 Secret (Japanese) Trans. 12/12/41 (5)

From: Tokyo
To: Washington
December 7, 1941
Purple (Urgent—Very Important)
#907. To be handled in government code.

Re my #902[44]
Will the Ambassador please submit to the United States Government (if possible to the Secretary of State) our reply to the United States at 1:00 p.m. on the 7th, your time.
ARMY 7145 25850 Secret Trans. 12/7/41 (S)

From: Tokyo
To: Washington
December 7, 1941
Purple (Extremely Urgent)
#910

After deciphering part 14 of my #902[45] and also #907[46], #908[47], and #909[48], please destroy at once the remaining cipher machine and all machine codes. Dispose in like manner also secret documents.
25854 Trans. 12/7/41 (S)

[43] Not available.
[44] JD-1: 7143—text of Japanese reply.
[45] SIS #25843—text of reply.
[46] SIS #25850.
[47] SIS #25853.
[48] SIS #25858.

From. Budapest
To: Tokyo
December 7, 1941
LA
#104

Re my #103[49]
On the 6th, the American Minister presented to the Government of this country a British Government communique to the effect that a state of war would break out on the 7th.

ARMY 25866 7184 SECRET Trans. 12/7/41 (2)

---

[49] Relayed to Berlin.

CLAUSEN INVESTIGATION EXHIBIT NO. 8

Investigation by Lt. Colonel Henry C. Clausen, JAGD, for the Secretary of War Supplementary to Proceedings of the Army Pearl Harbor Board

The following documents comprise intercepts obtained by Colonel Clausen from British sources (i.e., Bletchley Park).

They consist of 41 documents extending over the period 21 November 1941 to 22 December 1941.

MOST SECRET

To be kept under lock and key: never to be removed from the office.

Japanese Consul, Singapore, Requests Issue of Code Words

No. 097975
Date: 21st November 1941

From: Japanese Consul-General, SINGAPORE
To: Foreign Minister, TOKYO
No.: 717
Date: 17th November 1941.

Immediate:

Some day the British authorities will prohibit the use of cypher telegrams by this office. To prepare for this eventuality please draw up secret code words and send them by Consul-General OKAMOTO as diplomatic correspondence. Please include in this secret code, words necessary for military intelligence, evacuation of residents, the closing down of this office, etc. Please see the Naval Secret Code which I have received recently.

Director. F.O. (3). F.I.D. Admiralty. Colonial Office. M.I.5.

Japanese Code Phrases for Broadcasting in Event of Emergency.

No. 09127
Date: 25th November 1941

From: The Foreign Minister. TOKYO
To: The Japanese Chargé. LONDON.
No: 2363 Circular
Date: 19th November, 1941

To be treated as Chef de Mission Cypher.

The international situation is tense and we cannot tell when the worst may happen. In such an event, communications between the Empire and the enemy countries will immediately cease. Therefore when our diplomatic relations are on the point of being severed, we shall broadcast, as the weather report, the following phrases in the middle and at the end of the news in Japanese in our overseas broadcast service:

(1) If Japanese–American relations are in question: "Higashi no kaze ame" (Easterly wind, rain).

(2) If JAPAN and the SOVIET are concerned: "Kita no kaze kumori" (Northerly wind, cloudy).

(3) In the case of JAPAN and BRITAIN (including the invasion of THAILAND or an attack on MALAYA): "Nishi no kaze hare" (Westerly wind, fine).

The appropriate phrase will each time be broadcast twice in a resolute voice and you should act accordingly [group corrupt: destroy by fire] codes documents etc.

The above is to be treated as strictly confidential.

From: The Japanese Chargé
To: The Foreign Minister, TOKYO.
No: 700 Urgent of 21st November 1941.
Reference your circular telegram No. 2353. (above).

Director. F.O. (3). F.I.D. Admiralty. War Office (3). India Office (2). Colonial Office. Air Ministry. M.I.5.

Sir E. BRIDGES
Dominions Office.

Japanese Foreign Office View of Conversations With America

No: 998151
Date: 25th November 1941

From: The Foreign Minister, TOKYO
To: The Japanese Diplomatic Representatives, ANGORA, &c.
No: 2364 Circular.
Date: 20th November 1941.

Confidential.

1. Since the formation of the new Cabinet the Government has started a conference in daily contact with Imperial Headquarters and has been able to debate a fundamental national policy to cope with the pressing situation of the day. At the morning session on the 5th instant, a decision was taken on the policy to be adopted for adjusting Japanese–American diplomatic relations.

2. The Japanese–American negotiations are to be pursued by considering the adjustment of diplomatic relations on an equitable basis. These have been in progress since the 7th, but there is a considerable difference of opinion between the two parties, and in view of the progress made so far there is some doubt as to whether a compromise will be reached. For our part, we are doing our utmost to reach a compromise, but we cannot make any further concessions, and the outlook is not bright. Should the negotiations break down, that part of the situation in which the Japanese Empire is involved will be critical.

The foregoing is for your exclusive information.

This telegram is addressed to BERNE, ANGORA and VLADIVOSTOK.

BERNE will repeat to VICHY, MADRID, LISBON, STOCKHOLM, HELSINGFORS and PRETORIA.

ANGORA will repeat to BUCHAREST, SOFIA and BUDAPEST.

TOGO.

Director (3) P.O. (3). P.I.D. Admiralty. War Office (3). Air Ministry. Sir E. Bridges.

At this post there is nothing for it but to use the Navy's wireless. Details have been telegraphed by the Naval Attaché to the Admiralty. Please refer to them and make the necessary arrangements.

Japanese Broadcasts: Reception in Rome.

No: 098232
Date: 27th November 1941

From: The Japanese Ambassador, ROME.
To: The Foreign Minister, TOKYO.
No: 740
Date: 20th November 1941

In regard to the general news broadcasts, not only JUO but JAP (which was changed on the 20th) were generally impossible to receive. This was due to unstable weather conditions at this time of year which made the note weak, in addition to which there was much interference from miscellaneous noises.

In view of the recent international situation the demand for [group corrupt: ? news ? information] is steadily increasing. We foresee no difficulty about reception arrangements at this end but in present weather conditions good reception will not be possible on one wavelength only. It is essential that simultaneous broadcasts be sent on two or three wavelengths. I understand that the recently changed DOMEI broadcasts in English have begun simultaneous broadcasts, and I ask that every effort be made for these simultaneous broadcasts to be carried out.

For your information I will, till further notice, telegraph reception efficiency every three days.

                                            HORIKIRI.
Director. F.O. (3). P.I.D. M.I.5.

Japanese Cypher Machines: Security Measures.

No. 098313
Date: 29th November 1941

From: The Foreign Minister, TOKYO.
To: BERNE, WASHINGTON, etc.
No: 2398 (Circular telegram).
Date: 25th November 1941

Most Secret:
Recently our cypher machines (the printing portion of "A" and the shift key of "B") have been designated as a State Secret. Any leakage of information connected therewith will incur the application of the National Defense Peace Preservation Law. As regards the machine in your keeping, you are strictly enjoined to take every precaution for safe and secret custody.

On the right hand side of the number plate affixed to the printing portion and shift key, please write the words "Kokka Kimitsu" [State Secret] in red enamel.

This telegram is to be relayed, as the Foreign Minister's instructions, in the following manner: From WASHINGTON to MEXICO, RIO DE JANEIRO and BUENOS AIRES. By cable.

BERNE to LONDON, VICHY, BERLIN, ROME and ANGORA. By cable.

VICHY to MADRID. By safe hand.

HANOI to SAIGON. By safe hand.

Director. F.O. (3). M.I.5.

Japanese Ambassador, Hanoi, Asks for Instruction in Event of Emergency.

No: 098400

Date: 1st December 1941.

From: Japanese [? Ambassador] HANOI.

To: Foreign Minister, TOKYO.

No: 118.

Date: 26th November, 1941.

[In Chef de Mission cypher recyphered on the machine].

(Secret.)

To judge from what I hear from the Military, the American answer reached us [? on the 24th]. If this is so the Cabinet Council will no doubt finally reach a decision in a day or two and determine whether it is to be peace or war. If Japanese–American negotiations are to be held we shall of course take in hand progressively the various undertakings previously planned; but if the negotiations break down, as preparations for military operations are nearing completion, an advance would be possible within ten days or so. In that event considerable modifications would be necessary in the programme of undertakings to be carried out under our present policy, and it will be necessary to initiate measures and negotiations in keeping with our military operations. What causes me most concern and [? anxiety] is whether, in the event of an outbreak of hostilities, it is the policy of the Government and Imperial Headquarters to carry on military operations leaving the status of the Government of INDOCHINA as it is at present, and on this point I require to be informed in advance: and not only so but I want to make necessary preparations with all speed. If, therefore, you have any views on the development of the Japanese–American negotiations and the prospects I alluded to I beg that you will telegraph them at once. Moreover, while it goes without saying that secrecy must be preserved, nevertheless, according to newspaper reports, AMERICA has been consulting with BRITAIN, AUSTRALIA, the NETHERLANDS and the Chinese in WASHINGTON, and these Governments are aware of the purport of the Japanese–American negotiations. And what is more, the Military here, as the result of comings and goings between here and TOKYO, are aware of the nature of your instructions and of the ins and outs of the negotiations: in fact I have the impression that the only people who are left in the dark are Foreign Office officials. Seeing that the situation is as tense as is indicated in your circular telegram No. 2383 [our No. 098127], should be glad to receive your instructions on these points as soon as possible, either by telegram, messenger or some other method.

Director (3). F.O. (3). P.I.O. Admiralty War Office (3). India Office (2). Colonial Office. Air Ministry. M.I.B. Major Morton. Sir E. Bridges. Dominions Office.

From: Foreign Minister, Tokyo.
To: Japanese [? Ambassador], HANOI.
No: 93 of 26th November, 1941.
(Also in Chef de Mission cypher recyphered).
Reference your No. 118 (above).

My circular telegram *No. 2414 gives the course of the Japanese–American negotiations and my circular telegram *No. 2416 tells of their present continuation. Even in the event of the worst happening the Imperial Government has not taken any special decision to make a change in the status of the Government of INDO-CHINA. You may therefore take it that for the present our policy is to maintain the status quo. Please do your best on this understanding.

Repeated to Paris and Berlin.

TOGO.

[Dept. Note *Not yet decyphered].

Japan and the Axis: Plans in Event of Breakdown of Washington Conversations

No: 098413.
Date: 1st December, 1941.
From: Foreign Minister, TOKYO.
To: Japanese Ambassadors, BERLIN and ROME.
No: 2387 Circular.
Date: 24th November, 1941.

[Very corrupt text. In Chef de Mission cypher recyphered on the machine].

For your own information only.

The Japanese–American negotiations [?] are [seem to be] approaching their final stage . . . [two lines corrupt]. In the event of the breakdown of the negotiations we shall be face to face with a rupture of relations with BRITAIN and AMERICA, and the necessity is likely to arise for the sudden tightening up of the relations which have hitherto prevailed for cooperation between JAPAN, GERMANY and ITALY. My idea is that [? you] should then propose [two groups] action to be taken: but [two groups] I shall ask Your Excellency to be active during this month. It is possible that circumstances may necessitate your having a special interview with Führer HITLER (Premier MUSSOLINI), so please bear this in mind. [Two groups] until you approach them you should refrain absolutely from saying anything to the Germans (Italians). This for your information and in haste.

At the moment the time is not ripe for a detailed report on the Japanese–American negotiations. Please note, however, that we have taken every precaution to obviate any obstacle to the maintenance of the Three Power Pact.

This telegram is addressed to BERLIN and ROME.

TOGO.

Director (3). F.O. (3). P.I.D. Admiralty. War Office (3). India Office (2). Colonial Office. Air Ministry. Sir E. Bridges. Dominions Office.

Japanese Communications by Naval Wireless in Event of Emergency

No. 098414.
Date: 1st December, 1941.
From: Japanese Chargé, London.
To: Foreign Minister, Tokyo.
No: 778.
Date: 29th November, 1941.

In the present circumstances it may happen that the despatch and delivery of telegrams may be purposely delayed or completely held up and that we shall not be able to depend on the reliability of communications. I therefore request you to take steps to [? make simultaneous use of] the Naval wireless, as in my No. 760 [our No. 098127].

[Dept: Note: Cyphered in "X" and recyphered on the machine.]

Director. F.O. (3). P.I.D. Admiralty. War Office (3). India Office (2). Colonial Office. Air Ministry. M.I.5. Sir E. Bridges. Dominions Office.

Japanese Plans: Instructions to Ambassador at Berlin

BJ/35.
No: 098452.
Date: 2nd December, 1941.
From: Foreign Minister, TOKYO.
To: Japanese Ambassador, BERLIN.
No: 935 Very urgent.
Date: 30th November, 1941.
[In Chef de Mission cypher recyphered on the machine].

Reference my circular telegram No. 2387. [Our No. 098413]

1. The Japanese–American negotiations begun in April of this year under the former Cabinet have now reached a stage at which a breakdown is inevitable, in spite of the sincere efforts of the Imperial Government. The Empire, faced with this situation, has to take the most serious decisions. You should therefore see Führer HITLER and Foreign Minister RIBBENTROP at once and give them an outline of developments in confidence. At the same time you should tell them in confidence that the attitude of BRITAIN and AMERICA has recently been provocative and they have continued to move troops into all parts of Eastern ASIA. To meet this we too have been compelled to move troops, and it is greatly to be feared that an armed collision will occur and we shall find ourselves in a state of war with BRITAIN and AMERICA. You should add that this may happen sooner than is expected.

[Here Part II is missing. It will be sent in later if received].

4. If when you make this communication questions are asked by the Germans and Italians as to our attitude towards RUSSIA, you should tell them that our attitude towards the SOVIET is as explained to them on 2nd July of this year, that we will of course not relax our restraint on the SOVIET as the result of our action in the south; but that if the SOVIET, acting in cooperation with BRITAIN and AMERICA, take hostile action against us, we are prepared to resist it resolutely; that it is on the South, however, that we lay most emphasis, and that we propose to refrain from deliberately taking positive action in the North.

5. As all this concerns our plan of campaign it of course requires the utmost secrecy, and you should make a point of impressing this strongly on the Germans and Italians.

6. With regard to telling the Italians, immediately after our Ambassador in BERLIN has told the Germans, Premier MUSSOLINI and Foreign Minister CIANO should be informed. As soon as the dates for the German and Italian interviews are fixed please telegraph.

Please repeat to Rome as my instructions.

TOGO.

Director (3). F.O. (3). P.I.D. Admiralty. War Office (3). India Office (2) Colonial Office. Air Ministry. Sir E. Bridges. Dominions Office.

Japanese orders for destruction of cypher machine in London Embassy

Date: 3rd December, 1941.
No: 698509

From: Foreign Minister, TOKYO
To: Japanese Ambassador, LONDON.
No: [? 2443] Circular.
Date: 1st December, 1941.
Secret and Urgent.

Please take steps for the immediate disuse of the cypher machine at your Embassy.

With regard to the steps to be taken, these should conform to the instructions sent previously. Please exercise the greatest care and, in particular, with regard to the methods of dismantling and breaking up the essential parts, carry them out strictly in accordance with instructions.

On receipt of this, please telegraph immediately the one word "SETSUJU"* (Received) en clair, and, having carried out these instructions, telegraph the word "HASSO"* (Despatched) also en clair.

With regard to the cypher connected with the machine, you are, of course, also to burn your copy No. 26 of the YU code (machine code) (the settings for use on the machine for communication between this Department and the Embassy in LONDON).

79716 -- 46 -- Ex. 148 -- 44

(Dept. Note: *These messages received, dated 2nd December, 1941.)
Director (3). F.C. (3). P.I.D. Admiralty. War Office (3). India Office (2). Colonial Office. Air Ministry. M.I.5. Sir E. Bridges. Dominion Office.

Japanese-Thai Relations: Japanese Ambassador, Berlin, Care Thai Minister

No: 698525.
Date: 4th December, 1941.
From: Japanese Ambassador, BERLIN.
To: Foreign Minister, TOKYO.
No: 1347
Date: 20th November, 1941

I received a visit from the Thai Minister on the 20th. He opened his remarks by saying that he was also a soldier and would like to have a frank talk with me as between men who had known each other for many years. He then referred to a recent crop of rumours to the effect that JAPAN was to invade THAILAND, and to reports of large Japanese troop concentrations on the Thai frontier of French INDO-CHINA, and asked point blank whether there was any truth in them or not. I replied that I had had no news from my home Government on these matters but that my own belief was that JAPAN's actions toward all Far Eastern races were aimed at applying the principle of live-and-let-live, the fact being that in cases such as that of the recent arbitration between THAILAND and French INDO-CHINA JAPAN had done her utmost for THAILAND for this very reason and would never invade THAILAND for the purpose of aggression. But the facts were that GREAT BRITAIN and AMERICA had set up the so-called ABCD front in opposition to JAPAN's establishment of a New Order, finally threatening the existence even of JAPAN herself. JAPAN of course would be compelled to continue her course brushing this aside, and that she wished to attain this and by peaceful means was obvious from the mere fact of her having sent Mr. KURUSU to AMERICA. However if the worst came to the worst and it was unavoidable, JAPAN would have to take the necessary steps for her own existence—not that there would be any question of this happening if THAILAND soon understood JAPAN's ultimate purpose and displayed an attitude of cooperation with JAPAN; she would have to invade THAILAND only if that country should blindly follow the lead of GREAT BRITAIN and AMERICA and take up an attitude of opposition.

The Minister interposed by describing the position in which THAILAND was placed and by stating emphatically that THAILAND would never oppose JAPAN as an Anglo-American cat's-paw.

When suggesting his visit the Minister said that he wished to see me urgently, and OMMINISI's view that he probably came on instructions from his home Government.

The Germans are also extremely interested in Thai problems and I should be glad if you would inform me at once as to the latest situation.

Director (3). F.O. (3). P.I. Admiralty. War Office (3). India Office (2). Colonial Office. Air Ministry. M.I.5. Sir E. Bridges. Dominions Office.

Japanese Chargé, London, Submits Plans for Withdrawal of Embassy, etc. Staffs

Date: 4th December, 1941.
No: 098539.

From: The Japanese Chargé d'Affaires, LONDON.
To: The Foreign Minister, TOKYO.
No: 781.
Date: 1st December, 1941.

It is feared that in the event of the situation becoming critical the exchange of telegrams may become impossible. I therefore submit the following points for your consideration and request instructions.

1. In view of conditions at this post, countries suitable for protecting our interests after the withdrawal of this Embassy are BRAZIL or SWITZERLAND. I suggest that the matter be discussed in TOKYO with the country concerned, so that instructions may be sent by that Government to its Ambassador (Minister) in LONDON.

2. Is there any objection to burning the consular exequaturs at present held in custody, viz: LIVERPOOL, DUBLIN, RANGOON, BOMBAY, CALCUTTA, BATAVIA, MACASSAR and VANCOUVER?

3. The stipulations for withdrawal of the Embassy etc. staffs and of resident Japanese should be made with the British on a strictly reciprocal basis. If this could be done it would be necessary to effect the exchange at a stipulated place, each side providing a ship. An agreement would have to be drawn up regarding the dates of departure, etc. to prevent anything going amiss.

(In the case of GERMANY the exchange took place in HOLLAND, in ITALY's case it was LISBON. If hostages are taken there is the danger that our nationals will not be able to leave the country.) The evacuees to be exchanged are:

1st party: Embassy and Consular staff
2nd party: Newspaper correspondents

3rd party: Japanese Staff of banks and companies who were sent out from JAPAN (the 2nd and 3rd parties are not necessarily in order of precedence). Exchange for each party will be arranged separately. As a principle I do not wish to include employees locally engaged and Japanese residing here of their own wish. Concerning the above negotiations should be undertaken both here and in TOKYO and, if necessary, instructions can be given via the countries who will protect our interests.

In round figures the number of persons is:

(a) Officials—34 (including the Chargé d'Affaires, secretaries, military and naval attachés, advisory consuls, telegraphic attachés, chancellors, special employees and their families).

(b) Newspaper correspondents—6.

(c) Bank and Company employees—30.

Director (3). F.O. (13). F.I.D. Admiralty. War Office (3). India Office (2). Colonial Office. Air Ministry. M.I.S. Sir R. Hopkins. M.E.W. (2). Sir E. Bridges. Dominions Office.

Japanese Orders for Destruction of Cyphers etc. in Washington Embassy

> Date: 4th December, 1941.
> No: 098540
> BJ/87

From: Foreign Minister, TOKYO.
To: Japanese Ambassador, WASHINGTON.
No: 867 Secret.
Date: 2nd December, 1941.
  [Dept: Note: Compare our No. 098509].

Of all telegraphic cyphers with which your Embassy is provided you are to burn all (including the cyphers of other Ministers in your charge) except one copy each of the machine cypher now in use, cypher "O" and cypher "L".

2. You are also to discard* one complete cypher machine.

3. As soon as this is done you should telegraph one word "HARUNO".

4. You should deal with files of in and out telegrams and other secret documents in an approporate and suitable manner at your discretion.

5. The cyphers brought by Cypher Officer KOSAKA [? should all be burnt]. (Consequently the need to get in touch with MEXICO referred to in my telegram No. 860 [not received] [last word corrupt]).

  [Dept: Note: *The word used, "haiki", can mean "cease to use", "abolish", "discard". It is not the normal word for "destroy"].

Director (3). F.O. (3). P.I.D. Admiralty. War Office (3). India Office (2). Colonial Office. War Ministry. M.I.5. Sir E. Bridges. Dominions Office.

Japanese Ambassador, Berlin, Reports Ribbentrop's Statement on
German War Plans

No: 098541
Date: 4th December, 1941.

From: Japanese Ambassador, BERLIN.
To: Foreign Minister, TOKYO.
No: 1393.
Date: 29th November, 1941.
(Chef de Mission Cypher).

I was to have had an evening meeting yesterday, the 28th, with RIBBENTROP
at his request, but he suddenly asked me to postpone it, and it was ten at night
before we met.

The reason for the postponement was that GOERING and leading Government and Forces personalities met at the Fuehrer's official residence and
held an important conference lasting for many hours. Now that the objects
of the Russian campaign have for the most part been achieved, and the
results of interviews with the Premiers and Foreign Ministers of the European countries collated, they discussed the direction and policy of next
year's campaign, and I have no doubt that at this conference JAPAN's action
was also discussed.

1. First of all RIBBENTROP again asked if I had received any news about the
Japanese–American negotiations. I replied that I had not yet received any
official news. RIBBENTROP said JAPAN must not lose this opportunity of achieving the establishment of the New Order in East ASIA, and never had there been
a time when close cooperation between the three Allies was more imperative.
If JAPAN hesitated and GERMANY carried through the New Order in EUROPE
alone, BRITAIN and AMERICA would turn the brunt of their attack against
JAPAN. He insisted that, as the Fuehrer had said that day, the existence of
JAPAN and GERMANY on the one hand and of AMERICA on the other was
fundamentally incompatible, and the Germans were in receipt of reports that,
owing to the stiff attitude of the Americans, there was practically no possibility of the Japanese–American negotiations being successful. If this was so,
and if JAPAN determined on war against BRITAIN and AMERICA, not only would
this be to the common advantage of JAPAN and GERMANY, but he believed it
would be to JAPAN's advantage also.

I said I know nothing of JAPAN's plans and therefore could not answer; but
I asked whether His Excellency really thought a state of war would arise
between GERMANY and AMERICA. He replied that Roosevelt was diseased, and
there was no knowing what he would do.

Considering that hitherto RIBBENTROP has always answered that AMERICA
would avoid war, and in view of recent speeches by HITLER and RIBBENTROP,
it seems to me that GERMANY's attitude towards AMERICA is gradually stiff-

ening, and that she has reached the stage where she would not shun even war with AMERICA.

2. I enquired about the future of the war against RUSSIA. RIBBENTROP replied that the Fuehrer had said that it was now his inflexible determination to sweep away and crush the SOVIET once and for all. The most important military operations had been concluded, and a large part of the army would be withdraw to GERMANY. They would, however, continue operations in the CAUCASUS, and next Spring with a part of it they would make an attack on and beyond the URALS and chase STALIN into SIBERIA. I asked when approximately this was to be, and he said it was intended that the attack should start in about May of next year.

I next observed that I gathered from what he said that they were quite determined on attacking the SOVIET, and the thing I should like done as soon as possible was the creation of air communications between MANCHURIA and GERMANY. He replied that the Germans had been thinking of this for some time past, and he thought that next Summer it would not be impossible to fly in one hop from somewhere near the URALS to MANCHURIA.

3. I asked about plans for an attack on BRITAIN. He said that before the landing in BRITAIN they would chase British influence clean out of the NEAR EAST, AFRICA, GIBRALTAR and the MEDITERRANEAN. I gather from this statement by RIBBENTROP that they attach even more importance than before to this area. I asked if they intended to carry on without, attacking the BRITISH ISLES. RIBBENTROP said that GERMANY was of course making preparations for this: but according to reports reaching GERMANY the internal situation in BRITAIN was not any too good. For instance the split in the Conservative Party, the lack of confidence in CHURCHILL and the revolutionary ideas of BEVIN, the Labour leader, were making internal conditions quite difficult. There were of course some people who did not believe this: but the Fuehrer believed that conditions in BRITAIN were bad and thought that as a result of GERMANY's future operations, even, it might be, without an invasion, BRITAIN would be beaten.

In any case, however, GERMANY for her part had no intention whatever of making peace with ENGLAND, and the plan was to drive British influence out of EUROPE entirely. After the War, therefore, BRITAIN would be left absolutely powerless, and although the BRITISH ISLES would remain, all other British territory would be split up into three under GERMANY, ITALY and JAPAN. In AFRICA, GERMANY would, generally speaking, be satisfied with her old colonies and would give a great part to ITALY. It was, he said, to obtaining (group corrupt) that GERMANY attached the most importance.

4. Remarking in conclusion that the very satisfactory progress of the War under Germany leadership was fully recognised and that GERMANY naturally had to extend the area of operations by regarding as enemies not only BRITAIN but also countries under British influence and those helping BRITAIN, I asked him when he thought the War would end. To this he replied that, although he hoped it would be brought to a conclusion in the course of next year, it might possibly continue till the following year.

He also said that if JAPAN were to go to war with AMERICA, GERMANY would, of course, join in immediately, and HITLER's intention was that there should be absolutely no question of GERMANY making a separate peace with ENGLAND.

At the end of this talk RIBBENTROP asked that the substance of it should be kept strictly secret, so please pay special attention to its handling.

This telegram has been given to the Naval and Military Attachés and to Vice-Admiral NOMURA and Major-General ABE. Please have it shown to the Army and Navy.

OSHIMA.

Director (3). F.O. (3). P.I.D. Admiralty. War Office (3). India Office (2). Colonial Office. Air Ministry. M.I.5. Sir E. Bridges. Dominions Office.

Japanese Instructions Regarding Cypher Machines and Codes

BJ/88.
No.: 098563
Date: 5th December, 1941.

From: Foreign Minister. TOKYO.
To: Japanese (? Ambassador), HANOI, etc.
No: 2444 Circular. Secret.
Date: 1st December, 1941.

Instructions have been sent to LONDON, HONGKONG, SINGAPORE and MANILA to discard the cypher machine, and BATAVIA's machine has been returned to JAPAN.

Notwithstanding my circular telegram No. 2447 (see below), WASHINGTON is retaining its machine and machine code.

BERNE to repeat to VICHY, BERLIN, ROME and NAGORA. WASHINGTON to repeat to BRAZIL, ARGENTINA and MEXICO.

From: Foreign Minister, TOKYO.
To: Japanese Ambassador, ROME etc.
No: 2447 Circular of 2nd December, 1941.

Instructions have been sent to the following to burn all telegraphic codes except one copy each of OITE and L:

North AMERICA (including HONOLULU, CANADA, PANAMA, (one group corrupt), South Seas (including one group: ? Portuguese) TIMOR), SINGORA, CHIENMAI, British possessions (including Embassy in LONDON), and Dutch possessions.

TOGO.

Director (3). F.O. (3). P.I.D. Admiralty. War Office (3). India Office (2). Colonial Office. Air Ministry. M.I.5. Sir E. Bridges. Dominions Office.

Japanese Orders for Destruction of Cyphers etc.

BJ/89.
No: 098577
Date: 5th December, 1941.

From: Foreign Minister, TOKYO.
To: Japanese Consul, MOMBASA [and other posts unspecified].
No: 2446. Circular.
Date: 2nd December, 1941.
(Secret).

Immediately on receipt of this telegram you are to carry out the following instructions with the greatest care and as inconspicuously as possible.

(A) Burn all cyphers except one copy each of "O" and "L". As soon as you have done this immediately telegraph the one word HARUNA en clair.

(B) Burn all files of in and out telegrams and all secret and confidential documents.

These are precautions envisaging an emergency, and you should therefore redouble [rest of text corrupt: ? precautions in the discharge of your duties].

Director (3). F.O. (3) P.I.D. Admiralty. War Office (3). India Office (2). Colonial Office. Air Ministry. M.I.5. Sir E. Bridges. Dominions Office.

Japanese Code Words for Telegraphing to Notify Critical Condition of Situation.

No: 098602.
Date: 6th December, 1941.

From: The Foreign Minister, TOKYO.
To: The Japanese Representatives, LONDON, etc.
No: 2409 Circular.
Date: 27th November, 1941.
To be treated as Chef de Mission Cypher.

The following is the method of telegraphing secret code words to notify the critical condition of the situation.

Using the names on the first column a plain language text will be made up on some ordinary subject. The second column will contain the information which it is desired to send. (Example:

"Collision between the Japanese and Soviet Armies" will appear in the text under date [? 15th] as "Junior Secretaries HIJIKATA and KUBOTA are ordered for duty at your post. STOP").

Further telegrams sent by this method will all end with the word "STOP" to distinguish them from other communications. The word "OWARI" [— "end"] will therefore not be used.

Arimura:	cypher communications prohibited.
Asai:	communicate by wireless broadcast.
Asakura:	listen carefully for wireless communication by broadcast.
Asikaga:	jamming by overseas broadcasts reception impossible.
Azuma:	pressure on JAPAN becoming greater.
Edoguti:	prepare for evacuation.
Hanabusa:	evacuation preparations made.
Hanazono:	proceed with preparations for requesting suitable foreign envoy (consulate) to protect Japanese interests.
Hatakeyama:	diplomatic relations severed between Japan and . . .
Hattori:	relations between JAPAN and . . . are extremely critical.
Hijikata:	collision between Japanese and . . . armies.
Hosino:	JAPAN is engaged with . . . on the whole front.
Ibaragi:	telegraph time at which rupture of diplomatic relations between JAPAN and country to which you are accredited anticipated.
Inagaki:	has telegram been received on the matter of . . .?
Ishikawa:	telegram received on the matter of . . .
Kashiwagi:	positive action has begun against . . .
Kobayakawa:	stop granting Japanese entry and transit visas to . . . nationals.
Kodama:	Japan.
Komiyama:	China.
Koyanagi:	Great Britain.

Kubota:	U.S.S.R.
Kuribara:	France.
Kusunoki:	Germany.
Matsutani:	Italy.
Minami:	United States of America.
Miwata:	Canada.
Miyazaki:	Mexico.
Morokoshi:	[? Brazil].
Motizuki:	Panama.
Nagamine:	Argentine.
Nakazato:	Thailand.
Nango:	England and America.
Teigi:	Dutch East Indies.
Ogawa:	Burma.
Okamoto:	Malaya.
Okumura:	Australia.
Onizuka:	Union of [? South Africa].
Nodera:	enemy country.
Otani:	[? the individual in question].
Onishi:	year.
Sibuya:	next year.
Simanaka:	this year.
Sakakibara:	month.
Sigeno I:	[? day].
San Zyo:	time.
Itiro:	one.
Nisaku:	2
Santaro:	3
Yoiti:	4
Goro:	5
[? Ma] Sa	
Roku:	6
Simetaro:	7
Yasokiti:	8
Hisamatu:	9
Atumi:	0 (zero).

TOGO.

Director (3). F.O. (3). P.I.D. Admiralty. War Office (3). India Office (2). Colonial Office. Air Ministry. M.I.5. Sir E. Bridges. Dominions Office.

From: Foreign Minister, TOKYO.
To: Japanese Consul-General, Singapore [and other posts unspecified].
No: 2461 Circular of 3rd December, 1941.
Secret:

Duplicates of secret code words (including those for use in broadcasting*) are to be kept until the last moment. If anyone has already burnt them he should inform me by telegram and they will be telegraphed again.

TOGO.

[Dept: Note: *These are presumably those given in our No. 098127].

Japanese Orders for Destruction of Cyphers, etc.

BJ/90
No: 098603
Date: 6th December, 1941.

From: Foreign Minister, TOKYO.
To: Japanese Ambassador, LONDON.
No: 2445 Circular. (Secret).
Date: 2nd December, 1941.

Please take the following action without delay and see to it that no word of it leaks to outsiders.

1. Except for one copy each of the O, E, H, P, G, and L codes and the Character Code, all telegraphic codes (including the cypher books for inter-communications between the Ministries of Foreign Affairs, War, and Marine) to be burnt.

2. When this has been done, the one word "HARUNA" to be telegraphed.

3. The files of all incoming and outgoing telegrams and all other confidential documents to be burnt.

4. Taking all possible care not to arouse outside suspicion, all secret documents to be treated in the same way.

As these are precautions envisaging an emergency, you should communicate this to no one but members of your staff and you should redouble your attention to your duties and maintain your calmness and self-respect.

Director (3). F.O. (3). P.I.D. Admiralty. War Office (3). India Office (2). Colonial Office. Air Ministry. M.I.5. Sir E. Bridges. Dominions Office.

From: Japanese Chargé, London.
To: Foreign Minister, Tokyo.
No: 790 of 3rd December, 1941.

HARUNA [see paragraph 2 of telegram above].

Japanese code words for telegraphic to notify critical condition of situation

No: 098604
Date: 6th December, 1941.

From: The Foreign Minister, TOKYO.
To: The Japanese Representatives, LONDON, etc.
No: 2421 Circular.
Date: 29th November, 1941.

Additions to list given in my circular No. 2409 [our No. 098602].
(To be treated as Chef de Mission Cypher).

Kasima:	Have residents been interned?
Kanoo:	All residents are safe.
Kikuti:	All residents have been interned.
Katuno:	Some residents have been interned.
Kawasimo:	General Information. Wave-length changed to . . . k/cs from . . . [month] . . . [day].
Kakao:	General Information. Sensitivity bad; please change wave-length.
Tujikita:	General Information. Please change to shorter wave-length.
Tabuse:	General Information. Please change to longer wave-length.
Saitoo:	General Information. Time of broadcast changing on . . . [day] from . . . [time] to . . . [time].
Isezaki:	Hundred.
Wanami:	Thousand.
Yasu [?RYO]:	0,000.
Uno:	00,000.
Itimata:	000,000.

Director (3). F.O. (3). P.I.D. Admiralty. War Office (3). India Office (2). Colonial Office. War Ministry. M.I.5. Sir E. Bridges. Dominions Office.

Japanese code words for telegraphing to notify critical condition of situation

No: 098608
Date: 6th December, 1941.

From: Foreign Minister, TOKYO.
To: Japanese Ambassador, RIO etc.
No: 2432. Circular.
Date: 29th November, 1941.

As the following additions have been made for use in connection with your area only, please add them to the list already sent to you. (See our Nos. 098602 and 098604).

Asahima:	The supplying of fuel to Japanese ships putting into Port has been stopped from . . . (date).
Date:	Please telegraph what quantity of . . . can be bought.
Kawahara:	It is thought that about . . . tons of . . . can be bought.
Niwaii Quiti:	Purchase of . . . impossible.
Makamuta:	Negotiations for purchase of . . . in progress.
Mukakata:	(?Please) communicate via . . . (name of country.)
Kazama:	Communications (? to be carried out) via diplomatic mission in . . . (name of country).
Tokusima:	Japanese ship due . . . (name of country) on . . . (month) . . . (day).

Director (3). F.O. (3). P.I.D. Admiralty. War Office (3). India Office (2). Colonial Office. War Ministry. M.I.5. Sir E. Bridges. Dominions Office.

Takemouti:	Can a Japanese ship visit . . . (name of country).
Tonagi:	Japanese ship can be sent to . . . (name of country).
Takagi:	Metal.
Sawamura:	Lead.
Hasumi:	Mercury.
Iwasaki:	Coal.
Mikokata:	Diamonds for industrial use.
Iyami:	Platinum.
Kada:	Copper.

Makagawa:	Carat.
Makhata:	PERU.
Masuko:	CHILE.
Hakada:	COLOMBIA.
Takekaka:	(? URUGUAY).
Simazu:	(? PARAGUAY).
Ihazawa:	VENEZUELA.
Fujikaka:	SAN (?DOMINGO).
Hasimoto:	(?ECUADOR).
Simeo:	HAVANA.
Taii Ki:	(? RIO).
Tokawa:	(? BOLIVIA).
Hasegawa:	River PLATE.
Iri—Ine:	SANTOS.
Ksomoto:	(Bauru, sic. ? PAULO).
Bappu:	CURITIBA.
Tekamatu:	(? BELEM).
Suatugu:	BUENOS AIRES.
Suzuki:	SANTIAGO.
Yamato:	LIMA.
Uskgawa:	BOGOTA.
Hara:	CARACAS.
Isono:	?
Fukamati:	ASUNCION.

Japanese—American negotiations account sent to Japanese Ambassador, Berlin.

No: 098633.
Date: 7th December, 1941.

From: Foreign Minister, TOKYO.
To: Japanese Ambassador, BERLIN.
No. 986.
Date: 30th November, 1941.

(Dept. Note: First paragraph missing).

2. The present Cabinet has therefore continued the negotiations (with AMERICA) hitherto on an equitable basis though at the same time exercising every care to safeguard JAPAN's authority and existence.

Amongst the most knotty points in these negotiations has been the conflict in the respective opinions regarding the question of withdrawing troops from CHINA and INDO-CHINA (was demanded) etc., but to judge by circumstances in the negotiations hitherto, the fundamental obstacle has been the traditional policy of AMERICA with regard to the conduct of international relations, that is to say her adherence to the same fundamental principles as were expressed in the recent Anglo-American talks at sea (? i.e., the Atlantic Charter). In short, AMERICA's real intention is to veto and obstruct the establishment of the New Order in EUROPE and ASIA by JAPAN, GERMANY, and ITALY (i.e. the purpose of the Tripartite Pact), their view being that Japanese-American relations cannot be maintained on a friendly basis so long as JAPAN makes common cause with GERMANY and ITALY, and, acting on this view, they have to all intents and purposes demanded JAPAN's renunciation of the Tripartite Pact. This has brought the negotiations to their final stage, and, as the talks of the last few days have made this matter still more clear, JAPAN has been compelled to realize that to continue the negotiations any longer cannot be expected to serve any useful purpose.

3. Again, the proposals presented by the American Government on the 26th made the above attitude even clearer, the clause affecting the Tripartite Pact being worded: "It is agreed that any treaty which either of the two Governments may have concluded with a third country shall not be construed as conflicting with the principles of this treaty, in other words, with the maintenance of peace in all regions of the PACIFIC . . ." It is apparent that this was planned with the object of restricting the interpretation of JAPAN's obligations under the Tripartite Pact, and thereby making JAPAN refrain from giving support to GERMANY and ITALY in the event of American participation in the (group corrupt.!European) war, and to judge this by clause alone it has been realized that, quite apart from all other questions, it would be impossible for the American proposals to be made (group corrupt: ! the subject of) negotiations. Moreover the fact is that the American Government held constant discussions with GREAT BRITAIN, CHINA, AUSTRALIA, and the Dutch before presenting their proposals, and hence it can be seen that AMERICA is at present (? acting in common) with these countries and regards JAPAN as an enemy together with GERMANY and ITALY.

Director (3). F.O. (3). P.I.D. Admiralty. War Office (3). India Office (2). Colonial Office. Air Ministry. Major Norton. Sir E. Bridges. Dominions Office.

Japanese Ambassador, Rome, reports interview with Mussolini

No: 098650
Date: 7th December, 1941.

From: Japanese Ambassador, ROME.
To: Foreign Minister, TOKYO.
Date: 3rd December, 1941.
(Chef de Mission cypher recyphered on the machine).
Reference your No. 988 to BERLIN (our No. 098452).

Accompanied by ANDO I saw the Duce, MUSSOLINI (CIANO also was present) at 11 a.m. on the 3rd. I first gave him an outline of the Japanese–American negotiations as set forth in your No. 988 to BERLIN (our No. 098633). MUS-SOLINI said he had been following the negotiations from their inception until to-day with the greatest attention, and my communication had caused him no surprise. There was no doubt that the present situation was the natural result of the (? obstinacy) of the American Government and of President ROOSEVELT's policy of intervention. The plutocrats of AMERICA aimed at the economic exploitation of Eastern ASIA for their own benefit, and wanted to detach JAPAN from the Axis and intervene in the European war. He had always known from the beginning that JAPAN, who was faithful and loyal, would not respond to such an attitude on AMERICA's part, negotiations or no negotiations. As I and my predecessor knew, he was a whole-hearted sup-porter of JAPAN's fundamental policy for the establishment of a New Order in East ASIA, and as it was in the past, so it was in the present and would be in the future. He firmly believed that JAPAN, as a natural right, would be the leader of Great East ASIA.

Director (3). F.O. (3). P.I.D. Admiralty. War Office (3). India Office (2). Colonial Office. Air Ministry. Major Norton. Sir E. Bridges. Dominions Office.

I then spoke on the lines of your telegram under reference ([This passage in brackets is not clear. The sense seems to be: "With regard to paragraph 3 of your telegram, it was to be done as one copy between our Ambassador in BERLIN and RIBBENTROP and talks of some sort were in progress. I should like him to ask the German Ambassador about it."]). With regard to paragraph 2 in your telegram MUSSOLINI said that if war broke out ITALY would give military support to the best of her power; that is to say she would do her best to keep the British Navy in the MEDITERRANEAN. Moreover GERMANY and ITALY together had recently established an air blockade and were trying to put further pressure on Britain in the MEDITERRANEAN. Also with regard to [? 2 ? 3], he was ready to sign to-day. I therefore asked further with regard to 2 if ITALY would do this at once if JAPAN declared war on BRITAIN and AMERICA. He replied that in accordance with the Three Power Pact naturally she would.

As, however, it would be necessary to do it simultaneously with GERMANY, they would have to go through the formality of consulting with GERMANY. With regard to 3, I submitted the [one group] translation in your telegram No. 237 [not received], and asked which procedure he preferred, a single copy or separate copies. He replied that it should be done simultaneously with GER-MANY, but he did not mind what form it took. If it were possible a single copy would give a greater impression of strength. He would at once consult MACK-ENSEN on this point.

At this meeting MUSSOLINI asked me questions about the Russian question, and I therefore did not refer to it.

Repeated to BERLIN.

HORIKIRI.

Japan and the Axis, Proposed Three-Power Pact

No: 098651
Date: 7th December, 1941.

From: The Japanese Ambassador, ROME.
To: The Foreign Minister, TOKYO.
No: 782.
Date: 5th December, 1941.

Reference my telegram No. 775. [Not received].

Accompanied by ARDO I had an interview with Foreign Minister CIANO on the 5th at his request.

CIANO showed me the Italian text of the draft of a Three-Power Pact to which GERMANY and ITALY have agreed. (BERLIN will have telegraphed this to you, I imagine), regarding participation in the war and not making an independent armistice or independent peace. He said that if the Japanese would agree to this it could be signed at any time. The procedure could be arranged by conversations between BERLIN and TOKYO and then all parties could sign. Repeated by telegram to BERLIN.

Director (3). F.O. (3). P.I.D. Admiralty. War Office (3). India Office (2). Colonial Office. Air Ministry. M.I.5. Sir E. Bridges. Dominions Office.

Japanese Foreign Minister's View of Washington Conversations

No: 098671.
Date: 8th December 1941

From: Foreign Minister, TOKYO.
To: Japanese Ambassador, BERLIN, etc.
No: 2416 Circular.
Date: 28th November, 1941.
[Dept: Note: Very corrupt text].
(Chef de Mission cypher).

With regard to the Japanese–American negotiations, the counter proposal made by the the Americans on the 27th ignores the position of Japan and cannot be considered for a moment. It seems, therefore, that there is nothing for it but to discontinue the negotiations. The situation is that it is impossible to guarantee that within a few days from now there will be no [? change in] the relations of JAPAN with BRITAIN and AMERICA.

This is for your personal information only.

                              TOGO.

Director (3). F.O. (3). P.I.D.

Japanese Broadcasting

No: 098673
Date: 8th December 1941.

From: The Japanese Ambassador, RIO DE JANEIRO
To: The Foreign Minister, TOKYO.
No: 482.
Date: 30th November, 1941.

Recently at this post, we have been testing general news reception.

At present it is quite impossible [group corrupt: ? to hear] the 10:30 p.m. Tokyo time, broadcast and, for the time being, please note that we are only listening to JVJ's [group corrupt: ? JZJ's] broadcast directed to American states at 6:30 p.m. Tokyo time. The same, I understand, applies to Argentina.

Actually, reception conditions here are considered best between 4 a.m. and 6 a.m. Tokyo time, and I consider it would be most advantageous to use this period for South American broadcasts. Two wave-lengths [of frequencies] between 10 and 15 megacycles [group corrupt: ? are suggested].

Director. F.O. (3). P.I.D. M.I.5.

Japanese Ambassador, Bangkok, Wishes to Burn Codes

No: 098674
Date: 8th December 1941

From: The Japanese Ambassador, BANGKOK.
To: The Foreign Minister, TOKYO.
No: 883.
Date: 30th November, 1941.

In view of the state of emergency, I should like to burn all telegraphic codes except those set out below. Please wire at once whether you have any objection.

YO, KA < OITE, TO, TSU, FUJI, X. [Group corrupt]. MATSU with No. 1 rules for use, directions for using "B" machine (KO-OTSU [(a) - (b)]) and the machine code—one of each of the above.

L, YAKKO [—NU] —two of each.

Further, I should like to burn all shipping codes, naval codes and codes for use between the three Ministries. Please negotiate with the Departments concerned and telegraph instructions.

Director (3). F.O. (3). P.I.D. Admiralty. War Office (3). India Office (2). Colonial Office. Air Ministry. M.I.5. Sir E. Bridges. Dominions Office.

Japan and the Axis: Proposed Three-Power Pact.

No: 098693
Date: 8th December 1941

From: Japanese Ambassador, BERLIN.
To: Foreign Minister, TOKYO.
No: 1416
Date: 5th December, 1941.
  [Dept: Note: See our No. 088851].
  (Chef de Mission Cypher).
  Reference my No. 1407 [not received].

I called on RIBBENTROP at his request at 3 a.m. on the 5th. he made a formal reply that they accepted the two points put forward by us. My following telegram gives the draft Treaty which he gave me in this connection.

OSHIMA

No: 1417 of 5th December, 1941.
(Chef de Mission Cypher).

(1. The last part of the Agreement is in the same form as the Three Power Treaty.
2. The place of signature is BERLIN.)
[Dept: Note: Translation follows at end of text].
Director (3). F.O. (3). P.I.D. Admiralty. War Office (3). India Office (2). Colonial Office. Air Ministry. M.I.5. Sir E. Bridges. Dominions Office.
(Part of German text in original illegible.)

Artikel 1.
Falls zwischen Deutschland und Italien einersits und den Verinigten Staaten con Amerika andererseits der Kriegszustand einritt, wird sich Japan sofort auch seinerseits als im Kriegszustand mit den Vereinigten Staaten befindlich betrachten und diesen Krieg mit allem ihm zur Verfügung stehenden Machtmittein führen.

Artikel 2.
Deutschland, Italien und Japan verpflichten sich, im Falle eines gemäss Artikel 1 dieses Abkommens von den drei Mächten geminsam gegen die Verienigten Staaten von Amerika geführten Krieges ohne volles [gegen] seitiges Einverständnis keinen Waffenstillstand oder Frieden mit den Vereinigten Staaten zu schliessen.
Sie übernemen die gleiche Verpflichtung auch hinsichtlich eines Waffenstillstands oder Friedens mit England für den Fall, das zwischen Japn und Egland der Kriegzustand eintritt.

Artikel 3.
Die drei Regierungen sind darüber einig, dass dieses Abkommen auf das strengste gehim gehalten wird. Sie werden jedoch die von ihnen in Artikel 2 übernommene Verpflichtung in einer noch zu verabrenden Form bekanntgeben, sobald sich Deutschland, Italien und Japan gemeinsam im Kriegzustand mit den Vereinigten Staaten von Amerika oder England oder mit diesen beiden Mächen befinden.

Artikel 4.
Dieses Abkommen tritt sofort mit seiner Unterzeichnung in Kraft und bleibt ebenso lange wie der am 27. September 1940 abgeschlossene Dreimächtpakt in Geltung.

OSHIMA.

Translation

In view of the increasingly obvious desire of the UNITED STATES and EN-GLAND to bring to naught a just New Order with all the armed forces at their disposal and to cut off the means of existence of the German, Italian and Japanese peoples, the German Government, the Italian Government and the Japanese Government have, in order to ward off these grave threats to the existence of their peoples, jointly resolved on the following:

Article (1).

Should a state of war arise between JAPAN and the UNITED STATES, GER-MANY and ITALY for their part shall also consider themselves to be at war with the UNITED STATES, and shall conduct this war with all the armed forces at her disposal.

Article (2).

GERMANY, ITALY and JAPAN bind themselves in the event of a war waged jointly by the Three Powers against the UNITED STATES according to Article (1) of this Treaty, not to conclude any armistice or peace with the UNITED STATES without full mutual agreement.

They undertake a similar obligation regarding an armistice or peace with ENGLAND, should a state of war arise between JAPAN and ENGLAND.

Article (3).

The three Governments are in full agreement that this agreement shall be kept most strictly secret. They shall, however, announce in a form yet to be decided, the undertakings assumed in Article (2), as soon as GERMANY, ITALY and JAPAN find themselves jointly at war with the UNITED STATES of AMERICA or with ENGLAND or with both these Powers.

Article (4).

This agreement comes into force immediately on signature and remains in force as long as the Three Power Pact concluded on 27th September 1940.

Japanese Notification of "Extremely Critical" Relations with Great
Britain and United States

> BJ/91
> No: 098694
> Date: 8th December 1941

From: Foreign Minister, TOKYO.
To: Japanese Embassy, LONDON, etc.
No. 2494 Circular.
Date: 7th December, 1941

Relations between JAPAN and GREAT BRITAIN and the UNITED STATES are
extremely critical.

JAPANESE FOREIGN MINISTER.

[Dept. Note: This telegram was sent in plain language with the special code
words inserted given in our No. 098602. It was despatched from TOKYO at
1150 hours OMT on 7th December 1941, i.e. Japan time 8:50 p.m. on 7th
December 1941].

Director (3). F.O. (3). P.I.D. Admiralty. War Office (3). India Office (2).
Colonial Office. Air Ministry. M.I.S. Sir E. Bridges. Dominions Office.

Japan and the Axis: Proposed Three-Power Pact.

> No: 098696
> Date: 8th December 1941

From: The Foreign Minister, TOKYO.
To: The Japanese Ambassador, BERLIN.
No: 1004. Most immediate.
Date: 7th December, 1941.
[Dept: Note: In Chef de Mission cypher recyphered on the machine].

Reference your Nos. 1418 and 1419 [these telegrams were received in
corrupt and fragmentary form. The former appears to deal with Russian
supplies and the latter with the draft treaty].

We are in complete agreement with GERMANY's counter-proposals. Accordingly there is no objection to initialling right away and formally signing
as soon as the [group corrupt: ? necessary] procedure has been completed.
However, the situation may take a sudden turn and we cannot tell whether a
[group corrupt] collision may not occur in the interval before the formal
signing is performed. Thus, supposing we initial now, it must be understood
that for the actual signing, the text proposed by Germany may not apply to the

existing circumstances [for example, clauses like No. 1 will be unnecessary if GERMANY and ITALY join in the war without delay).

[Two groups] I wish you to see RIBBENTROP immediately and explain the above particulars confidentially to him. Also make clear that it is the expectation of the Imperial Government that if war breaks out between JAPAN and AMERICA before the formal signature of the agreement, GERMANY and ITALY will immediately participate.

Director (3). F.O. (3). P.L.D. Admiralty. War Office (3). India Office (2). Colonial Office. Air Ministry. M.I.S. Sir E. Bridges. Dominions Office.

As regards the text of the agreement, [group corrupt: ? please negotiate] only for the stipulation concerning the non-conclusion of a separate peace. Respecting GERMANY, please refer to the text in my No. 997 (not received). Further, discuss with GERMANY whether the formal signing should be made public after GERMANY and ITALY have joined in the war and telegraph the reply.

Please repeat to ROME.

Far Eastern War: Question of German and Italian Participation

RJ/92.
No: 098722
Date: 9th December 1941

From: Japanese Ambassador, BERLIN.
To: Foreign Minister, TOKYO.
No: 1432. Most immediate.
Date: 7th December, 1941.
(Chef de Mission cypher).

At 11 p.m. to-day, the 7th, I received a radio report that hostilities had broken out betwen JAPAN and AMERICA, and at once called RIBBENTROP. He said that from reports which he too had received he thought this was true, and that, therefore, although he had not yet secured HITLER's sanction, the immediate participation in the war by GERMANY and ITALY was a matter of course. The secret agreement had in consequence already become ----- ? -----, and [? they had decided] to drop it * * * [a portion is lost here] * * * Form of German and Italian participation. RIBBENTROP said he would discuss with me to-morrow, the 8th, about the time of publication of this declaration and so on.

RIBBENTROP rang up CIANO then and there and notified him of the foregoing.

Director (23). F.O. (3). P.I.D. Admiralty. War Office (3). India Office (2). Colonial Office. Air Ministry. Sir E. Bridges. Dominions Office.

Far Eastern War: Text of Japanese-German-Italian Agreement

BJ/98
No: 098760
Date: 10th December 1941

From: The Japanese Ambassador, BERLIN.
To: The Foreign Minister, TOKYO.
No. 1440. Most immediate.
Date: 8th December, 1941.
To be treated as Chef de Mission Cypher.

Reference my No. 1432. (Our no 088722).
The text of the agreement, after consultation with GERMANY, is given below. An explanation follows in my separate telegram.

In dem unerschütterlichen Entschluss, die Waffen nicht niederzulegen, bis der gemainsame Krieg gegen die Vereinigten Staaten von Amerika und England zum erfolgreichen Ende geführt worden ist, haben sich die Deutsch Regierung, die Italienische Regierung und die Japanische Regierung über folgende Bestimungen geeinigt:

Artikel 1.—Deutschland, Italien und Japan werden den ihnen von der Verienigten Staaten von Amerika und England aufgezwungenen Krieg mit allen ihnen zu Geboted stehenden Machmittelm gemeinsam bis zum siegreichen Ende führen.

Artikel 2.—Deutschland, Italien, und Japan verpflichten sich, ohne volles gegen seitiges Enverständnis weder mit den Vereinigten Staaten von Amerika not mit England Waffenstillstand oder Frieden zu schliessen.

Director (3). F.O. (3). P.I.D. Admiralty War Office (3). India Office (2). Colonial Office. Air Ministry. Sir E. Bridges. Dominions Office.

Artikel 3.—Deutschland, Italien und Japan werden nack siegreicher Beendigung des Krieges zum Zwecke der Herbeiführung einer gerechten Neuordnung auf das engste zusammenarbeiten.

Artikel 4.—Dieses Abkommen tritt sofort mit seiner Unterzichnung in Kraft.

Zu Urkunde dessen haben die Unterzeichneten, von ihren Regierungen gehörig. bevollmächtigt, dieses Abkommen unterzeichnet und mit ihren Siegelm versehen.

Ausgefertigt in dreifacher Urschrift in deutscher, intalienischer und japanischer Sprache, in Berlin am . . . Dezember 1941 in 20ten Jahre der Faschistischen Ära—entsprechend dem Tage des 12ten Monats des 16ten Jahres der Ära Syowa.

No. 1441 of 8th December, 1941.

With reference to my telegram No. 1440 [see above].

From 5 p.m. to-day myself, RIBBENTROP, KASE, USHIDA, and GAUSS put our heads together on this matter of the declaration of the non-conclusion of a separate peace with a view to imparting to this declaration the loftiest possible significance, and produced the text of the agreement contained in my telegram under reference. This goes beyond the adoption of our proposal in regard to a promise of nonconclusion of a separate peace (Clause II) to the following extent:

(a) The Three Powers' firm intention to fight together against Anglo-American aggression until final victory is expressed in Clause II.

(b) Cooperation with a view to the establishment of a new order after the war is promised in Clause III.

Thereby the significance of this war is elucidated, while at the same time Clause III has an advantage from the point of view of obtaining German and Italian cooperation when the Great East Asia co-prosperity sphere is established after the war, this, I believe, being in accord with the views of the Japanese Government. I hope therefore that the above text will be adopted unless there are any serious objections, and that the formalities for signature may be completed promptly. I would add that in the meantime the Germans have notified me that the Italian Government is in complete agreement with this proposal.

2. Ribbentrop said that he would like the publication of this agreement to take place on the 10th and immediately afterwards hoped to stage a big demonstration. He was unable at the moment to say what kind of demonstration this would be but it was sure to be something distinctly favourable to JAPAN, and he was most anxious that signature should be on the 10th. I therefore told him that this could not be undertaken in view of formalities in JAPAN, but as it is likely to be helpful to us if we play our part in falling in with GERMANY's intention I would suggest that you push on with the formalities as fast as possible with a view to prompt signature. Should signature on the 10th not be possible please reply immediately by telegram on what date it can be accomplished.

3. Just as this very talk was in progress RIBBENTROP received the Imperial Headquarters report of the victory in which the American battleships were sunk, and was greatly delighted and praised highly the daring of our Navy.

No: 1442 of 8th December, 1941.
Most immediate. Secret.
Reference my No. 1440. [See above].

As the matter is urgent, I have tentatively compiled the Japanese text given below. If you have no objections I should like to take this as the (Japanese) text of the agreement. Please telegraph your reply at once.

The Japanese Government, the German Government and the Italian Government with the inflexible determination not to lay down their arms in the joint war against the UNITED STATES and the BRITISH EMPIRE until final victory is achieved have made the following agreement.

1. JAPAN, GERMANY and ITALY will conjointly prosecute the war forced upon them by the UNITED STATES and the BRITISH EMPIRE with all the means at their disposal until victory is attained.

2. JAPAN, GERMANY and ITALY, except by mutual consent, undertake not to conclude a separate [Dept. Note: the Japanese word used means literally "arbitrary" "self-willed"] armistice and/or peace with the UNITED STATES and the BRITISH EMPIRE or with either of them.

3. JAPAN, GERMANY and ITALY, after victory is attained, will cooperate closely in the establishment of an equitable New Order.

5. This agreement will come into force simultaneously with its signature. In witness whereof, the undermentioned, having received competent authority from their respective countries, have set their seals this — day of the 12th month of the 16th year of the Showa Bra Era i.e. — December 1941 or the — day of December of the 20th year of the Fascist Era, in BERLIN, the said agreement having been drawn up in Japanese, German and Italian.

Japanese Instructions to Embassy, Rio, etc. to burn cyphers, etc.

BJ/97
No: 098786
Date: 10th December 1941

From: Foreign Minister, TOKYO.
To: Japanese Ambassador, Rio de Janeiro, etc.
No. 2318 Circular.
Date: 8th December, 1941.

Immediate and Confidential

1. On receipt of this telegram, please burn the following, leaving one copy of each, NU, CITE, TSU, L and X. Depending on the situation, it will also be all right to burn the remaining codes, but please keep TSU as long as possible and leave CITE and L to the last.

2. Please leave one copy each of HIMOKI and the Machine Code in current use following the rules for use between our Embassy in England (sic) and us—only MEXICO does not possess these). But if in view of the situation you wish at any time to destroy them please telegraph me.

3. With regard to the files of my telegrams and other secret documents please watch developments and adopt suitable means of destroying them.

4. In the event of your completing the above, telegraph me the one word JURYO. If you have destroyed TSU the word SHOTI, if CITE and L have been destroyed the word ANZEN.

5. If you have in your care telegraphic codes of other Posts please destroy them all.

Director (3). F.O. (3). P.I.D. Admiralty. War Office (3). India Office (2). Colonial Office. Air Ministry. Sir E. Bridges. Dominions Office. M.I.5.

Japanese Codes to be Destroyed at Bangkok

No: 098831
Date: 11th December, 1941.

From: Foreign Minister, TOKYO.
To: Japanese Ambassador, BANGKOK.
No: 881. Confidential.
Date: 2nd December, 1941.

In reply to your telegram No. 863. [Our No. 098674]. I agree with your request, to which there is no objection. But please transfer one copy of OITZ to SINGORA for safe keeping. Please destroy the codes for use between the active Ministries; also all the naval code books. The codes remaining after consultation with the posts concerned and the cypher machine[s] please deposit in the special safe. Please be sure that this is carried out.

Director (3). F.O. (3). P.I.D. Admiralty. War Office (3). India Office (2). Colonial Office. Air Ministry. M.I.5. Sir E. Bridges. Dominions Office.

Japanese Broadcasting: Reception in Bangkok

No: 098801
Date: 11th December, 1941.

From: The Japanese Ambassador, BANGKOK.
To: The Foreign Minister, TOKYO.
No: 902
Date: 4th December, 1941.

At 10:30 p.m. J.A.P.'s selectivity is gradually improving.
We look for broadcasts at this hour and also for JUP at 6:30 p.m.
Director (3). F.O. (3). P.I.D. Admiralty. War Office (3). India Office (2).
Colonial Office. Air Ministry. M.I.5. Dominions Office.

Japanese Consul, Dublin, Reports—Destruction of Cyphers

No: 098831
Date: 12th December 1941

From: The Japanese Vice-Consul, DUBLIN.
To: The Foreign Minister, TOKYO.
Date: 7th December, 1941. 1040 hours.
                          *HARUNA
                    Japanese Consul.

[Dept. Note: *See paragraph 2 of TOKYO circular telegram No. 2445 of 2nd
December, 1941, our No. 098803].
    Director. F.O. (3). Dominions Office.
                    79716—46—Ex. 148—45

Japanese Vice-Consul, Ouritiba, Reports—Destruction of Cyphers, etc.

No: 098832
Date: 12th December 1941.

From: The Japanese Vice-Consul, OURITIBA.
To: The Foreign Minister, TOKYO.
Date: 10th December, 1941. 2040 hours.
                          *JURYO,
                    Komine.

[Dept. Note: *See Tokyo circular telegram No. 2318 of 8th December,
1941. paragraph 4, our No. 098786].
    Director. F.O. (3). M.I.5.

Japan and the Axis: Signature of Treaty

> BJ/101.
> No: 098833
> Date: 12th December, 1941

From: The Japanese Ambassador, BERLIN.
To: The Foreign Minister, TOKYO.
No. 1451.
Date: 10th December, 1941.
   (Dept: Note: See our No. 098760, BJ/98).
   Reference your telegram No. 1013. (Not received).

I have received the whole of the Japanese text. I called on the Foreign Minister at noon to-day, 10th, and arranged for signature on the 11th at 1100 hours Berlin time and for publication at 1600 hours. Accordingly please publish at 2300 hours in JAPAN.

                OSHIMA.

Director (-). F.O. (3). P.I.D. Admiralty. War Office (3). India Office (2). Colonial Office. ---- Ministry. Sir E. Bridges. Dominions Office.

Japanese Ambassador, Berlin, Authorized to Sign Three-Power Treaty

> No: 098846
> Date: 12th December, 1941.

From: Foreign Minister, TOKYO.
To: Japanese Ambassador, BERLIN.
No: 1016.
Date: 10th December, 1941.
   (Dept: Note: See our No. 098760).
   Most immediate.
   To be treated as Chef de Mission cypher.
   My telegram No. 1013. (Not received).

For your information, the following is a translation into German of the document giving you the power and authority to sign:

   (Übersetzung).
   TOKYO, den . . . Dezember des schzehnten Jahres von Showa.
   (Amtliches Insiegel).
   Der Minister des Auswärtigen Amtes, Shigenori TOGO.
   An den Ausserorderntlichen und Bevollmächtigt—Botschafter in BERLIN, Herrn OSHIMA.

Seine Majestät de kaiser haben nachdem die Beratung des kaisserlichen geheimen Staatrates abgeschlossen ist, mit dem heutigan Datum den

Abschluss

Director.

F.--. (3).

P.I.D.

Abschluss des Abkommens zwischen JAPAN, DEUTSCHLAND und ITALIEN zu bewilligen geruht.

Sie sind bevollmächtigt, das oben genannte Abkommen zu unterzeichen und zu siegelu.

(Translation of German given below is as follows: —

(Translation).

TOKYO, the —th December, in the 16th year of the Showa Era.

(Official Seal).

Foreign Minister Shigenori TOGO,

To Mr. OSHIMA, Ambassador Extraordinary and Minister Plenipotentiary at BERLIN.

The advice of the Imperial Privy Council, His Majesty the Emperor is pleased to agree to the conclusion of a Pact, dated to-day, between JAPAN, GERMANY and ITALY.

(You are empowered to sign and seal the aforesaid Pact).

Japan and the Axis: Text of Three-Power Treaty

Date: 12th December, 1941.

From: The Foreign Minister, TOKYO.

To: The Japanese Ambassador, BERLIN.

No:

Date: 9th December, 1941.

To be treated as Chef de Mission cypher.

At 9:00 p.m. to-day the German Ambassador called on me and we had a second interview when he submitted the new draft of the text. You will already have received this, I expect.

In regard to this text I said that this involved the 1st paragraph of Article 3 of the Three-Power Treaty, and suggested the removal of Article 3. At the same time, I said, if GERMANY stuck to the retention of this Article, after the words "an equitable New Order" in that same Article should be added "in the Three-Power Treaty concluded on 27th September, 1940".

The Japanese text is given in my immediately following telegram. (See below.)

[The remainder of the telegram gives instructions for telegraphing the texts in the three languages to enable the formalities in JAPAN to be concluded. See Dept. Note: at the end of TOKYO–BERLIN no. 1011 of 9th December, 1941. (See below)].

TOGO.

Director (3).
F.O. (3).
P.I.D.
Admiralty.
War Office (3).
India Office (2). [Continued overleaf]
Colonial Office.
Air Ministry.
Sir E. Bridges.
Dominion Office.

No. 1011 of the 9th December, 1941.
Reference my immediately preceding telegram No. 1010. (See above).
(To be treated as Chef de Mission cypher).
Pact between JAPAN, GERMANY, and ITALY.

In the inflexible resolve not to lay down their arms till the joint war against the UNITED STATES and ENGLAND has been successfully concluded, the Japanese, German, and Italian Governments have jointly agreed as follows:

Article 1.

JAPAN, GERMANY, and ITALY will fight together with all the resources at their command until victory is achieved over the UNITED STATES and ENGLAND.

Article 2.

JAPAN, GERMANY, and ITALY undertake not to make a separate armistice or separate peace with the UNITED STATES or ENGLAND without full mutual understanding.

Article 3.

JAPAN, GERMANY, and ITALY will after the victorious conclusion of the war collaborate closely in establishing an equitable new Order in the spirit of the Three-Power Treaty signed on 27th September, 1940.

Article 4.

This pact shall come into force at the time of signature.

As witness whereof the undermentioned plenipotentiaries etc.

Signed in triplicate in Japanese, German and Italian at BERLIN (dates).

TOGO.

(Dept. Note: The German and Italian versions of the above were cabled to TOKYO from BERLIN as Nos. 1450 and 1453 respectively, dated 10th December, 1941.)Most Secret.

Japanese Broadcasts of General Information Reports.

No. 098971

Date: 16th December, 1941.

From: Foreign Minister, TOKYO.

To: Japanese Ambassador, ANGORA, etc.

No: 2548 Circular. Secret.

Date: 11th December, 1941.

From 10:30 p.m. 11th December, general information reports will be sent on the 9450 wavelength [? with the call sign] JUO.

TOGO.

Director

P.O. (3).

P.I.D.

Admiralty.

War Office (3).

Air Ministry. M.I.5.

Sir E. Bridges.

Japanese Naval Plans in South Atlantic and Pacific.

No. 099199

Date: 22nd December, 1941.

From: Foreign Minister, TOKYO.

To: Japanese Ambassador, Buenos Aires.

No. 288.

Date: 9th December, 1941.

[The first part of this telegram recounts the events that led up to the outbreak of war from the Japanese point of view—Japanese patience and A.B.C.D. encirclement. Part II follows].

2. The Imperial Japanese forces, however, right at the outset and in one heavy attack, have achieved to following: two battleships sunk, four severely damaged, four heavy cruisers severely damaged (three are confirmed), one aircraft-carrier sunk and over one hundred aircraft destroyed. It may be said that the main strength of the American Pacific Fleet has been practically annihilated.

From now on the Imperial (Japanese) Navy will be able to extend the scope of its (? activities) little by little to the South Atlantic and South Pacific and it is clear at least that we shall obtain command of the seas in the South Pacific before long. Even, therefore, if economic intercourse between JAPAN and the South American States bordering the Pacific be cut off for the time being, it will not be long before communication is restored. Not only so, but intercourse with ARGENTINA and BRAZIL by merchant ships in convoy will be urged upon these two countries, while sea communication with BRITAIN, AMERICA, and Latin AMERICA will, on the other hand, be severed (? shortly) by the Imperial (Japanese) Navy.

Director (3).
F.O. (3). (Dept. Note: Part III of this telegram missing.)
P.I.D.
Admiralty.
War Office (3).
India Office (2).
Colonial Office.
Air Ministry.
M.E.W. (2)
Sir E. Bridges.
Dominions Office.

(PHH 35/114)

EXHIBIT D

INVESTIGATION BY LT. COLONEL HENRY C. CLAUSEN, JAGD FOR THE SECRETARY OF WAR

Supplemental to Proceedings of the Army Pearl Harbor Board

1. Memorandum for Mr. Bundy, 17 February 1945, concerning investigation of Major Clausen, supplementary to Army Pearl Harbor Board.

2. Memorandum for Mr. Bundy, 3 March 1945, concerning investigation of Major Clausen, supplementary to Army Pearl Harbor Board.

3. Receipt from the District Intelligence Office 14ND of designated material, 19 April 1945.

4. List of Photostated copies of C.I.D. files furnished to Lt. Colonel Clausen, 19 April 1945.

5. Memorandum for Mr. Bundy, 23 May 1945, concerning investigation of Lt. Colonel Clausen supplementary to Army Pearl Harbor Board. **6.** Memorandum for Mr. Bundy, 1 August 1945, fourth progress report of Colonel Clausen's investigation supplementary to Army Pearl Harbor Board.

7. Memorandum for Mr. Bundy, 12 September 1945, fifth progress report of Colonel Clausen's investigation supplementary to Army Pearl Harbor Board.

(PHH 35/114 [247])

WAR DEPARTMENT,
Washington, 12 September 1945

Memorandum for Mr. Bundy.

Subject: Fifth progress report of Lt. Colonel Clausen's investigations supplementary to Army Pearl Harbor Board.

1. Since 1 August 1945 I have concluded the investigations of the following:

   a. Army Personnel interviewed:
     General George C. Marshall
     Major General Charles D. Herron
     Major General Sherman Miles
     Colonel Otis K. Sadtler
     Colonel George W. Bicknell
     Colonel Rex W. Minckler

       Colonel Harold Doud
       Colonel Harold G. Hayes
       Lt. Colonel Frank B. Rowlett

b. British Army personnel interviewed:
       Colonel Gerald Wilkinson

c. Civilians interviewed:
       Miss Mary J. Dunning
       Miss Louise Prather

d. Related conferences:
       Mr. Harvey H. Bundy
       Major General Myron C. Cramer
       Commodore Inglis, ONI
       Brig. General Carter W. Clarke
       Brig. General Thomas North
       Colonel Ernest W. Gibson
[248]   Colonel William J. Hughes
       Lieutenant John F. Baecher, USN
       Mr. John F. Sonnett
       Mr. A. T. Klots

e. Affidavit evidence obtained:
       General George C. Marshall
       Major General Sherman Miles
       Major General Charles D. Herron
       Colonel Otis K. Sadtler
       Colonel Rex W. Minckler
       Lt. Colonel Frank B. Rowlett
       Captain Howard W. Martin
       Miss Mary J. Dunning
       Miss Louise Prather

> Henry C. Clausen,
> HENRY C. CLAUSEN,
> Lt. Colonel, JAGD

(PHH 35/115 [249])

> WAR DEPARTMENT,
> Washington, 1 August 1945.

Memorandum for Mr. Bundy.
Subject: Fourth Progress Report of Colonel Clausen's Investigation Supplementary to Army Pearl Harbor Board.

1. Activities Reported: Investigations at Blandford, Blenchley Park, London, England; Cannes, Marseille, Paris, Versailles, France; Casserta, Italy; Berlin, Frankfurt on Main, Potsdam, Germany; and Washington D.C., were conducted during 15 May to 1 August 1945.

    a. Army Personnel Interviewed:
        Lt. General Leonard T. Gerow
        Lt. General W. B. Smith
        Maj. General John R. Deane
        Brig. General Thomas J. Betts
        Colonel George W. Bicknell
        Colonel Rufus S. Bratton
        Colonel Warren J. Clear
        Colonel Robert E. Schukraft
        Major Louis Stone
    b. British Navy Personnel Interviewed:
        Captain Edward Hastings
    c. Civilians Interviewed:
        Dr. Stanley Hornbeck
        George W. Renchard
        John F. Stone
    d. Related Conferences:
        Harvey H. Bundy
        General Thomas T. Handy
        Maj. General Myron C. Cramer
        Maj. General Otto Nelson
        Brig. General Carter Clarke
[250]   Brig. General Thomas North
        Brig. General G. Bryan Conrad
        Brig. General Marion Van Voorst
        Colonel C. W. Christenberry
        Colonel R. W. Hauenstein
        Colonel F. W. Hilles
        Captain Wm. T. Carnahan
        Captain Edmund H. Kellogg
        John F. Sonnett
        Admiral Henry K. Hewitt
    e. Affidavit Evidence Obtained:
        Lt. General Leonard T. Gerow
        Lt. General W. B. Smith
        Maj. General John R. Deane
        Colonel George W. Bicknell
        Colonel Rufus S. Bratton
        Colonel Robert E. Schukraft

George W. Renchard

John F. Stone

Brig. Gen. Thomas J. Betts

f. Documentary Evidence Obtained:

British radio intelligence material

2. Significant Features of Additional Evidence Developed:

(a) Colonel Bratton's Testimony Before APHB: Colonel Bratton admitted to me that his testimony given to the APHB was incorrect on some very important subjects, and should be revised accordingly. These changes include the following points:

1. He previously testified that the top secret radio intelligence material, contained in Top Secret Exhibit "B", had been delivered to the President, the Secretary of War, the Secretary of state, the Chief of Staff, the Assistant Chief of Staff, W.P.D., and the Assistant Chief of Staff, G-2.

But, in his affidavit to me made when his memory was more refreshed, he admitted that he could not recall with any degree of accuracy, and that there were no records to show who delivered what to whom during the period in question.

[251] **2.** He previously testified that he personally delivered the top secret radio intelligence material to the officers concerned.

In his affidavit to me, however, he admitted that in addition to himself, deliveries were made by Major or Lt. Colonel Dusenbury, Major Moore and Lieutenant Schindel.

3. He previously testified that on the evening of 6 December 1941 he delivered to the Office of the Chief of Staff, the Assistant Chief of Staff, G-2, the Assistant Chief of Staff, W.P.D., and the office of the Secretary of State, the thirteen parts of the fourteen part Japanese reply to the settlement conditions which the Secretary of State had given the Japs on 26 November 1941. He had also testified that he put the thirteen parts of this message on the desk of the Chief of Staff. He had further testified that on 6 December 1941 he had given sets of the thirteen parts to Lt. General W. B. Smith for the Chief of Staff, to Brig. General Gailey for Lt. General Gerow, and to Maj. General Miles, as G-2, and that it was his recollection that these officers received these sets that night. He had also testified that on 6 December 1941 he discussed the thirteen part message with General Miles.

But in his affidavit to me he admitted that the only set of the thirteen parts message he delivered on 6 December 1941 was to the duty officer of the Secretary of State; that the sets for the Secretary of War, the Assistant Chief of Staff, G-2, the Assistant Chief of Staff, W.P.D., were not delivered the night of 6 December 1941; that these sets were not given the night of 6 December 1941 to General Smith, General Gerow or General Miles; that he could not recall having discussed the message with General Miles on 6 December 1941; that he did not know how the set for the Chief of Staff came into his possession, although he claimed that he had asked Colonel Dusenbury to deliver it on 6 December 1941 to the home of the Chief of Staff. Colonel Dusenbury admitted in his affidavit to me that he received the messages on 6 December 1941, but that he did not deliver any until after 9:00 A.M. on the morning of 7 December 1941.

[252] **4.** He previously testified that on the morning of 7 December 1941 he arrived at his office about 7:00 or 8:00 A.M. and telephoned the home of the Chief of Staff at about 9:00 A.M., and that the Chief of Staff arrived at his office at 11:25 A.M.

In his affidavit to me, he fixed the time at which the Chief of Staff was in his office on 7 December 1941 as being between 10:30 and 11:30 A.M.

The affidavit of Maj. General Deane fixed the time at which Colonel Bratton arrived at his office on 7 December 1941 as between 9:00 and 9:30 A.M., which also agrees more nearly with the recollection of Colonel Dusenbury.

Affidavits mentioned in previous reports, as well as the new affidavits of Generals Gerow, Smith, Deane, and Messrs. Stone and Renchard, tend to support the revised testimony of Colonel Bratton.

(b) ''Winds Code'' Message: Investigations at British sources failed to reveal that the British ever intercepted an implementation message. Apparently, the evidence to date of the existence of such an implementation depends primarily on the recollection of certain Navy witnesses, and among whom there is a conflict. Colonel Schukraft claimed to have seen an implementation in a form different from that testified to by the Navy witnesses. On this subject it should be recalled that the action to be taken by the Jap Consular and diplomatic agents on receipt of an implementing message, namely, destruction of codes, actually was ordered by Tokyo in a radio which was intercepted about 4 December 1941. As I previously reported, this information was given to Short prior to 7 December 1941, according to his G-2 and Assistant G-2. Short testified before the Navy Court of Inquiry, however, that he did not get this information, and that to him it would have been the only important part of the message which the Chief of Staff sent him by radio on 7 December 1941. Assuming that the recollections of Short's two members of his Staff are correct, then Short had received prior to 7 December 1941 the ultimate in available information according to his own statement of what should have been given him for a different alert than that which he had ordered on 27 November 1941.

[253] **(c)** Sufficiency of War Department Warnings to Short: General Gerow in his affidavit to me sets forth detailed reasons why in his opinion the overseas commanders were given adequate information of impending events. Also, why the radio intelligence messages were not sent to the commanders. In this regard, testimony should be recalled to the effect that, for security reasons, the Army was restricted by the Navy from sending these messages,

and that representatives of the Navy had stated that the Navy unit at Honolulu was getting the messages from their own facilities.

(d) Conflicts in Testimony: Many of the points heretofore in doubt and hereinbefore mentioned have been sufficiently developed to reach appropriate conclusions. A number of conflicts remain, however, which it is planned to resolve by completion of the investigation.

3. Progress and Objectives: The investigation will be concluded by exploration of the remaining leads and the making of a final and comprehensive report. This will involve:

(a) Interviews with Generals Marshall, Herron and Miles, Colonels Bicknell, Doud, Minckler and Sadtler, Major Bash, Messrs. Roberts, Hoover, Friedman, and Wilkinson, and Misses Adams, Cave, and Prather.

(b) Examinations of the testimony given Admiral Hewitt by Admiral Mayfield, Captain McCollum, Commanders Kramer and Mason, and other Navy witnesses if necessary; the engagement book of former Secretary of State Hull; the statement by General Smith; and the recent G-2 examination involving Mr. Friedman, resulting from Navy disclosures.

(c) It is recommended that, for security reasons, the Secretary of War direct all witnesses heretofore and hereafter examined by me to send or give me forthwith, for filing with the records of this investigation, any copies of affidavits made before me and any incidental and related notes or papers which may be in their possession or under their control, they to advise me in writing that this has been done or that there are no such records, and that they be advised that these records will be available in the War Department in the event access thereto is ever required.

> Henry C. Clausen
> HENRY C. CLAUSEN
> Lt. Colonel, JAGD

(PHH 35/117 [254]

> WAR DEPARTMENT
> Washington, 23 May 1945

Memorandum for Mr. Bundy:
Subject: Investigation of Colonel Clausen
  Supplementary to Army Pearl Harbor Board.

1. Activities Reported: Investigations at Honolulu, Guam, Saipan, Leyte, and Luzon were conducted during the period 26 March to 12 May, 1945.

a. Army Personnel Interviewed:
General Douglas MacArthur
Lt. Gen. Richard K. Sutherland
Maj. Gen. C. A. Willoughby
Maj. Gen. Spencer B. Aiken
Maj. Gen. C. L. Ruffner
Brig. Gen. Kendall J. Fielder
Brig. Gen. C.A. Powell
Brig. Gen. J. J. Twitty
Brig. Gen. M. W. Marston
Colonel O. N. Thompson
Lt. Col. Byron N. Muerlott
Major H. H. Henderson
Major Maresh
Chief Warrant Officer Louis R. Lane
b. Navy Personnel Interviewed:
Captain E. T. Layton
Captain Harper
Captain W. J. Holmes
Captain T. A. Huckins
Commander J. S. Holtwick, Jr.
Commander Burr
Commander Carr
Lieut. Donald Woodrum, Jr.
Chief Ships Clerk Theodore Emanuel
[255] **c.** Civilians Interviewed:
D. R. Dawson
Robert L. Shivers
Harry L. Dawson
John E. Russell
d. Related Conferences:
General Richardson
Admiral Nimitz
Admiral McMorris
Admiral Towers
Mr. H. H. Bundy
Gen. Carter W. Clarke
Gen. Myron C. Cramer
Commander John F. Sonnett
e. Affidavits and Statements Obtained
General Douglas MacArthur
Lt. Gen. Richard K. Sutherland
Maj. Gen. C. A. Willoughby

Brig. Gen. Kendall J. Fielder
Brig. C. A. Powell
Brig. Gen. M. W. Marston
Colonel O. N. Thompson
Lt. Col. Byron N. Muerlott
Chief Warrant Officer Louis R. Lane
Captain E. T. Layton
Captain W. J. Holmes
Captain T. A. Huckins
Commander J. S. Holtwick, Jr.
Lieut. Donald Woodrum, Jr.
Chief Ships Clerk Theodore Emanuel
Mr. John E. Russell
Mr. Robert L. Shivers

f. Documentary Evidence Obtained:

1. British intelligence mateiral (SIS) consisting of more than 200 reports from Gerald Wilkinson at Manila to Honolulu, from July 1941 to and including December 1941.

2. Files of the Hawaiian Department, G-2, Army Contact Office. These are set forth on the attached receipt dated 19 April 1945.

[256] **3.** Navy District Intelligence Office files, set forth on the attached receipt dated 19 April 1945.

4. Files of the Hawaiian Department, AG. These include photostats of file copies of pertinent communications received before 7 December 1941.

5. FBI records of telephone intercepts and British SIS reports.

2. Significant Features of Additional Evidence Developed:

a. *Short's Defenses:* Assumption that Navy knew the whereabouts of the Jap fleet: Actually, as could have been ascertained from plots prepared by Captain Holmes, USN, and daily Communication Intelligence Summaries prepared by Captain Rochefort (see affidavit of Captain Huckins), the Navy did not have such information.

Claim that War Department acquiesced in reply of Short to radio of 27 November 1941 signed "Marshall", and thereafter did not give him additional information: The reply of Short also stated "liaison with Navy." Attention is invited to new evidence of items of intelligence possessed or available to Short.

Claim that a more effective alert would have interfered with training and would have alarmed the civilian population: Evidence shows there was no civilian alarm when the Herron all-out alert of 1940 was ordered and Short did not order the radar into 24 hours operation and did not order any visual lookouts or sound detectors against a possible air attack (See notes on Navy court testimony).

b. *Intelligence and Information available to Short:* Short and his G-2 testified in effect that they were almost wholly dependent on the War Department for information and that they actually received very little. New evidence indicates that the Hawaiian Department received a great deal more military and diplomatic information than has been previously developed. For example, the British SIS reports (See Russell and Shivers affidavits), the intercepts of telephone conversations in and out of the Jap Consulate (See Emanuel, Shivers and Woodrum affidavits), information from the Navy District Intelligence Office and the Fleet Intelligence Officer (See files and affidavit of Captain Layton). Much material was gathered from observers, travellers, and Washington sources, and evaluated and disseminated by the Army contact office. [257] Various papers dealing with this intelligence were initialed by Short. For example, see the Inter-Staff Routing Slip, 11 September 1941, concerning information from the Tokyo Naval Attaché as to Japan's intentions; the Slip, 6 November 1941; the War Department Military Attaché Report, 3 November 1941; the Special Intelligence Report, 17 October 1941; the memo of Colonel Bicknell, 21 November 1941; the War Department G-2 Report, June 1941, regarding the lurking of small submarines in Hawaiian waters preparatory to attacks on Pearl Harbor; the War Department G-2 Report, 28 August 1941, of a warning by one George Paisn; the Contact Office Report and Estimate, 25 October 1941; the report 19 June 1941 of Japanese books.

A detailed study of the foregoing and other items of intelligence, in relation to testimony adduced before the Army Pearl Harbor Board, will be made on completion of the investigation.

Incidentally, a special investigation by Colonel H. S. Burwell, AC, 9 July 1941, reported to General Short many deficiencies of his Command. Among other things, the report set forth that the attitude of mind in the Hawaiian Department, the Hawaiian Air Force and Hickam Field was deficient as to "the immediate need for positive preparations to prevent the success of planned and ordered sabotage," and further "it is found that a considerable portion of the Command do not see the mental picture of the interplay of relations now existing between inter-continental theatres of war and our local sphere of action." The report further stated that the Command was not alert to:

"(a) The possibility at any time of an overt naval retaliation on our part to an overt hostile act either near or far away. * * *

"(d) Or, an abrupt conflict with Japan over America's proposed aid to Russia."

The report found the cause for this attitude of mind was, among other things, traceable:

"(1) To the ingrained habits of peace-time.

"(2) To the carefree sense of easy control born in the isolation of a tropical island garrisoned by large forces. * * *

"(4) To the relative inattention accorded in peace-time to intelligence functions as compared to that given to operations and supply functions. * * *

[258] "(11) To the lower priority accorded intelligence in consequent of the above first needs. * * *

"(14) To the loss of aggressive initiative implicit in a purely defensive waiting attitude.

"(15) To the fact that no serious evidence of factual record exists, from which to induce the proof that a critical need at present exists for a critical concern for the future."

The reported concluded:

"(a) That the measurable degree of sinking morale is due to a feeling of instability, bias or lack of confidence in the general set-up, not to the effects of subversive activities within the command; although such a condition naturally provides a more fertile breeding grounds for hostile proclivities."

Under Appreciations, the report stated:

"(a) Appreciation is expressed for the advice of Lieutenant Colonel Bicknell, Assistant G-2, Hawaiian Department, and of Mr. Shivers, Federal Bureau of Investigation."

c. *Imminence of War with Japan:* Short testified that if this had been known to him he would have ordered a different alert. The affidavit of Fielder and the documentary evidence mentioned shows that Short was so informed. For instance, see the estimates dates 17 October 1941 and 25 October 1941 by Colonel Bicknell, initialed by Short; the memo of Bicknell, dated 21 November 1941; and the speeches of Short and Kimmel, reported in the Honolulu Star-Bulletin, 18 September 1941, a copy of which is attached.

d. *"Winds Code" Message:* Contrary to Short's testimony and the findings of the Army Pearl Harbor Board, this information was given the Army at Honolulu. See the affidavit of Shivers, verifying that of Colonel Bicknell. It should be noted that in the documentary evidence is a translation of the Jap Consul's desk pad. He had written thereon several wave lengths of Jap broadcasts on the date the Winds Code was broadcast. No evidence was found, however, that the code was implemented (see statement of Holtwick), other than the 3 December 1941 British SIS report to Honolulu, copy of which went to Colonel Bicknell, reading in part:

[259] "(C) Our considered opinion concludes that Japan envisages early hostilities with Britain and U.S. Japan does not repeat not intend to attack Russia at present but will act in South."

Significantly, the date 3 December 1941 agrees with the testimony of Captain Safford as to when he saw an implementing message to the code in similar terms.

e. *5 December 1941, War Department G-2 Message:* See affidavits of Fielder, Powell, Thompson and Lane. In view of previous statements recently obtained from Colonel Bicknell and personnel of G-2, it is a reasonable certainty that the message was received by the Army in Hawaii on 5 December 1941.

f. *Destruction by Japs of Codes:* Short denied receiving this information and claimed that he would have considered it most important, calling for a different alert order. But Fielder states in his affidavit that he gave his information to Short on 6 December 1941. See also the affidavit of Shivers, verifying that of Colonel Bicknell.

g. *Pearl Harbor as attack target:* If the Jap Consul commercial radio traffic, which was available at Hawaii to the Navy especially from the latter part of November 1941, included the reports as to ships in the harbor, then it was similar to that received at Washington. Several messages are contained in the documentary evidence above which are indicative that some such traffic was available at Hawaii before 7 December 1941. Further details are being explored in conjunction with the Navy. The availability of these messages is confirmed by the affidavits of Shivers, Marston, and testimony of Captain Rochefort.

It should be noted that Jap inquiries as to ship movements included reports at many other places, such as Manila, Seattle, etc. Also, so far as Hawaii specifically was concerned, intercepts of telephone conversations at the Jap consulate revealed that in 1940 a Jap agent was collecting information on ship movements.

Another item of intelligence which pointed to Pearl Harbor was the 3 December 1941 message from the Jap Consul at Honolulu to Tokyo, giving the visual signals devised by Otto Kuhn to report ship movements. This message falls into the category stated as requiring further exploration as to its availability before 7 December 1941.

[260] As to the Army Signal Intelligence Service activities at Hawaii, see the Powell affidavit. Two of the most vital messages, intercepted before 7 December 1941, were sent in to Washington by Hawaii. General Powell, however, states he was not aware of the contents.

In the documentary evidence mentioned there is correspondence from War Department to Hawaii in June 1941 concerning a report of the Military Attaché at Mexico City as to the Jap intentions to strike Pearl Harbor with midget submarines at the outbreak of hostilities.

h. *Jap Navy Task Force in Marshalls:* Short testified that he did not have this information. But, the contrary might well be true in view of the affidavits of Layton, Huckins and Shivers, in addition to the proof previously reported.

i. *Sufficiency of War Department warnings:* General MacArthur, who received information similar to that received by Short, stated in his affidavit, after reviewing the intercepts, that the War Department warnings were ample and complete for the purpose of alerting his Command for war.

Colonel Bicknell told Shivers the Army had been alerted when Shivers mentioned the alert he received from Hoover on 28 November 1941. (Shivers affidavit).

j. *Possible alarm to civilian population:* The affidavits of Marston and

Shivers confirm the lack of ground for Short to fear any such alarm, in view of the experience of the all-out Herron alert of 1940.

3. *Miscellaneous:* Many rumors relating to Pearl Harbor had been circulated concerning information available to General MacArthur, reports by him to Hawaii, and the War department warnings to him. These are set at rest by the affidavits of MacArthur, Sutherland and Willoughby.

4. *Wyman-Rohl investigation:* Concurrent with the foregoing, evidence was obtained at Hawaii and Leyte in exploration of certain leads.

5. *Progress and objectives:* I propose to complete the interviews of overseas witnesses by going to the ETO to develop some very important and promising leads. Those to be questioned on the Pearl Harbor phases include, among others, General Gerow, General Bedell Smith, General T. J. Betts, Colonel Rufus Bratton, Colonel Harold S. Doud, Colonel R. E. Schukraft and Colonel W. H. Tetley. This would include an investigation of new matters as well as of

[261] those items previously discussed. It is felt desirable to leave as soon as possible in order that interrogation be done before the witnesses are further scattered or are perhaps unavailable later.

Certain overseas witnesses pertinent to the Wyman-Rohl investigation would also be interviewed, thus completing the overseas phase of that investigation also.

I am keeping in touch and cooperating in a reciprocal manner with the Navy on additional investigation.

When my investigation is completed I shall make a comprehensive critique and report of all the new evidence then developed in relation to the Army Pearl Harbor Board Secret and Top Secret Reports.

Henry C. Clausen,
HENRY C. CLAUSEN,
Lt. Colonel, JAGD

(PHH 35/121 [262]

Confidential
Headquarters Central Pacific Base Command
Office of the Assistant Chief of Staff for Military
Intelligence
Counter Intelligence Division
Box 3, APO 456

In reply refer to:

19 April 1945.

Memorandum:
Subject: Photostated copies of C.I.D. files.

1. The following photostated copies of C.I.D. files were furnished to Col.
Clausen as directed by the Secretary of War and the Commanding General,
CPBC:

G-2, Hawn Dept. list Intelligence Reports prepared by Contact Office,
Honolulu, T.H.

G-2, CID memo dtd 9/12/44 re Shinto Shrines and custodial detention of
persons connected with shrines.

War Dept., Hq Army Pearl Harbor Board memo dtd 9/7/44 to CG, POA re
Documentary Evidence.

G-2, Hawn Dept report re Japan, Foreign Relations and Domestic Conditions. (2 copies) (1 Dec 1941)

Exhibit I—A Study of the Subversive Activities in the Hawaiian Islands
Before, on, and After December 7, 1941.

Exhibit II—December Seventh and Before in the Hawaiian Islands Through
the Eyes of the Press.

Hawn Dept. Summary of the Situation As of 7:30 A.M., 7 December 1941,
dtd 12/22/41.

Transcript of Trans-Pacific Telephone Call to Dr. Motokazu Mori.

Radio from War Dept. to G-2, Hawn Dept re Japanese negotiations, 11/
27/41.

Informal report re Thailand.

Army Contact Office memo dtd 8/1/41 re Asama Maru and Conditions in
Japan.

Radio from Short to AG, Wash. dtd 11/13/41.

Brief re Japanese Magazine Translation from the "Gendai", July 1941.

Army Contact Office memo dtd 5/2/41 re Comments on observations of a
missionary.

Memo for Col. Bicknell dated 8/1/41 re Local Japanese Situation During
the Period 26–31 July 1941.

Copy of radio received 11/27/41.

Inter-Staff Routing Slip re Information re Japanese Situation.

Radio from Naval Attache Tokyo to Asst Naval Attache Shanghai.

[263] Radio re speeches made by Military Naval Official urging population to unite and serve empire.

War Dept. ltr dtd 8/5/41 to G-2, Hawn Dept transmitting ltr from F.B.I. re Info on Japan's entry into war dtd 7/28/41.

Inter-Staff Routing Slip dtd Nov. 1941 re Military Attache Report No. 23 dtd 11/3/41.

G-2, H.H.D. Special Intelligence report dtd 10/17/41 re New Japanese Premier Hideki or Eiki Tojo.

Army Contact Office memo dtd 11/21/41 re Seizure and Detention Plan (Japanese).

Inter-Staff Routing Slip dtd Jan. 1942 re M.A. Report entitled "Activities of Foreigners in Country. Mexico." (Distribution list and M.A. report attached).

Inter-Staff Routing Slip dtd Feb. 1941 re Japanese Residents of T.H.— Loyalty of—ONI report dtd 1/26/42 (attached).

Ltr from Hq Second Corps Area dtd 11/28/41 re George Paish (Paisn). w/FBI report same Subject attached. (2 copies.)

M.I.D. War Dept. Summary of Information dtd 8/18/41 re French Indo-China.

M.I.D. War Dept. Summary of Information dtd 8/18/41 re Formosa.

M.A. Report dtd 8/14/41 re General Report, Countries in Pacific Area.

Inter-Staff Routing Slip dtd Aug. 1941, w/M.A. Report dtd 8/19/41 re General Report, Japan and China.

M.A. Report dtd 8/19/41 re Airports in S.W. Pacific and Australia.

M.A. Report dtd 9/10/41 re Japan and Japanese Relations.

M.A. Report dtd 9/25/41 re Thailand.

M.A. Report dtd 9/25/41 re French Indo-China.

M.A. Report dtd 10/2/41 re Japan.

M.A. Report dtd 10/23/41 re Formosa.

M.A. Report dtd 10/28/41 re Japan.

M.A. Report dtd 11/3/41 re Japan, Aerodromes and Aircraft (Continued).

M.A. Report dtd 11/18/41 re Japan, Military Agents.

Inter-Staff Routing Slip dtd Feb. 1941 w/14MD report dtd 2/9/42 re Fifth Column Activities at Pearl Harbor, Hawaii.

Cable re movements of fleet and return to Japan of members of diplomatic staff.

Inter-Staff Routing Slip w/WD Radio #628,12,12,41 re Japanese Spy Activities.

Memo dtd 12/12/41 re Dormer windowed houses in Kalama.

14ND report dtd 2/9/42 re Espionage Activities at Japanese Consulate, Honolulu.

FBI memo to ONI dtd 1/4/42 re Japanese Consulate Activities.

Ltr dtd 12/3/41 from Kita to Foreign Minister, Tokyo.

Extract from ONI report dtd 12/9/41 re Activities on Maui, Uanai & Molokai, since 7 December 1941.

[264] Report dtd 12/12/41 by R. C. Miller re Katsuro Miho.

Memo re ONI and FBI agents to Lanikai & Kalama to observe unusual activities.

Memo dtd 12.17.41 from R. A. Cooke Jr. re John Waterhouse House at Kailua.

Memo dtd 12/12/41 re Dr. Tokue Takahashi.

Extract from Army & Navy Register, 7/8/39—The Spy Game.

Four coded messages from Togo to Riyoji.

Army Contact Office memo for Col. Bicknell dtd 10/7/41 re Japanese Arrival In and Departure from Honolulu on Taiyo Maru.

M.I.D., Wash. ltr of transmittal dtd 8/28/41, w/ltr dtd 8/3/41 from George Paisn to Pres. Roosevelt re Japanese in Hawaii, Summary of Information dtd 9/30/41 re ltr, and H.H.D. ltr dtd 9/30/41 to G-2, 2nd Corps Area (reply thereto attached).

M.I.D., Wash. ltr of transmittal dtd 9/16/41, w/M.I.D. Summary of Information re Alleged exodus of Japanese.

Inter-Staff Routing Slip dtd Aug. 1941, w/ltr from Admiral Bloch to Gen. Short dtd 7/25/41.

Inter-Staff Routing Slip dtd June 1941 re Unknown Subjects, Book Entitled "Three-Power Alliance and American–Japan War" by Kinoaki Matsuo, w/note attached.

Inter-Staff Routing Slip dtd Jul 1941 re Small Japanese Submarines reported to be concealed in Shallow Water near Malokai, w/G-2, H.H.D. ltr. of transmittal dtd 7/25/41 re Activities of Foreigners in Country— Mexico.

F.B.I. report dtd 10/9/41 re Rev. Unji Hirayama.

F.B.I. report dtd 11/6/41 re Rev. Unji Hirayama.

F.B.I. ltr dtd 3/19/41 re translations made of coded & confidential material from Japanese Consulate.

Inter-Staff Routing Slip dtd 3/14/42 re Translation of a Register of Radiograms sent by Japanese Consulate, w/F.B.I. ltr. of transmittal dtd 3/13/42 and report same subject attached.

F.B.I. report to F.B.I. Wash. 3/28/42 re notes found on desk pad at Japanese Consulate.

14ND report dtd 2/14/42 re Japanese Consulate, Honolulu—Espionage Activities.

14ND report dtd 6/15/42 re Japanese Consulate, Honolulu—Espionage Activities.

14ND report dtd 2/15/43 re Japanese Consulate, Honolulu—Espionage Activities.

G-2, H.H.D. ltr of transmittal to G-2, Wash. dtd 3/7/42 re Translation of 3/7/42 and F.B.I. report dtd 3/2/42 re same subject.

Inter-Staff Routing Slip dtd 4/2/42 re Photographs of Message Register of Japanese Consulate, w/F.B.I. ltr. dtd 4/2/42 same subject.

[265] The aforementioned files were furnished to
_____ on the _____ th day of
_____ 1945.

M. H. Sheward
M. H. SHEWARD
2nd Lt., M.I.

Receipt acknowledged.

_____

[266]
FOURTEENTH NAVAL DISTRICT,
DISTRICT INTELLIGENCE OFFICE,
SIXTH FLOOR, YOUNG HOTEL,
Honolulu, Hawaii, 19 April 1945

RECEIPT FROM THE DISTRICT INTELLIGENCE OFFICE 14ND IS HEREBY ACKNOWLEDGED FOR THE FOLLOWING MATERIAL:

1. Five (5) Secret Photostats (one positive and one negative of decoded cablegrams) from the Japanese Consul General, Honolulu, to Tokyo.

Listed are the dates and numbers of the above cablegrams in date order.

DATE OF CABLEGRAM	NUMBER OF CABLEGRAM
(a) 12/3/41	#363
(b) 12/4//41	#365
(c) 12/4/41	#364
(d) 12/5/41	#221
(e) 12/5/41	#368
(f) 12/6/41	#369

2. One SECRET PHOTOSTAT of copies of four (4) cablegrams all dated 11/27/41, to the following Addressees:

(a) SHAGRO, San Francisco

(b) Dr. HOLMES, 45 Young Hotel, Honolulu

(c) GROWSUMIDA, Honolulu

(d) SHOKIN, Honolulu

3. One SECRET PHOTOSTAT of copies of four (4) cablegrams all dated 11/25/41, to the following addressees.

(a) Rev. Hiro HIGUCHI, Waipahu Community Church, Waipahu, Oahu, T.H.

(b) AMERICAN CONSUL, Papeete

(c) Y. WATANABE, Box 511, Wailuku, Maui, T.H.

(d) SHOKIN, Honolulu

4. One SECRET PHOTOSTAT of copy of coded and decoded cablegram dated 11/19/41, addressed to Inosuke HACHIYAE.

5. Four (4) Confidential 14ND, NNI-119 reports on JAPANESE CONSULATE, HONOLULU—Espionage Activities, dated as follows:

(a) 9 February 1942

(b) 14 February 1942

(c) 15 February 1942

(d) 15 February 1943

6. One PHOTOSTAT (positive and negative) of each of the following SECRET intercepts:

(a) 1-540; 11/30/41 & 12/1/41

(b) NYK-38; 12/2/41

(c) 6-1; 10/11/41

(NOTE: THE FOLLOWING ITEMS ARE BRITISH SECRET INTELLIGENCE SERVICE REPORTS FURNISHED BY THE BRITISH TO PEARL HARBOR THAT COLONEL CLAUSEN DISCOVERED IN HAWAII.)

[267] **7.** One Photostat (Positive and Negative) of the following: (Page numbers indicate DIO file page.)

(1) Wilkinson report dated 18 October 1941—(No. DIO file page number.)

(2) Wilkinson report dated 10/6/41, pg. 174.

(3) Wilkinson report dated 9/16/41, pg. 173.

(4) Wilkinson report dated 10/22/41, pg. 172.

(5) Wilkinson report dated 10/17/41, pg. 171.

(6) Cable received from Wellington, 11/25/41, regard Pacific Raider Intelligence, pg. 168A.

(7) Memo for the files, dated 12/3/41, in reference to Wilkinson report dated 10/6/41, pg. 168.

(8) Wilkinson report, not dated, pg. 166.

(9) Wilkinson report, not dated, pg. 162.

(10) Confidential letter to DNI from Com14, dated 10/14/41, Ser. #0965916, Subj.: "Transmission of Correspondence between British Intelligence Agent in Manila (16th Naval District) and District Intelligence Officer, 14th Naval District. (British Agent in Manila—Information received from), pgs. 160–159.

(11) Wilkinson report dated 9/3/41, pg. 158.

(12) Wilkinson report dated 10/14/41, pg. 157.

(13) Wilkinson report dated 10/14/41, pg. 156.

(14) Wilkinson report dated 10/14/41, pg. 155.

(15) Wilkinson report dated 10/13/41, pg. 154.

(16) Wilkinson report dated 10/13/41, pg. 153.

(17) Wilkinson report dated 10/11/41, pg. 152.

(18) Wilkinson report dated 10/2/41, pg. 151.

(19) Wilkinson report dated 9/29/41, pg. 150.

(20) Wilkinson report dated 9/25/41, pg. 149.

(21) Wilkinson report dated 9/26/41, pgs. 147–148.

(22) Wilkinson report dated 9/24/41, pg. 145.

(23) Wilkinson report dated 9/25/41, pg. 144.

(24) Wilkinson report dated 9/23/41, pgs. 142–143.

(25) Wilkinson report dated 9/14/41, pg. 140.

(26) Wilkinson report dated 9/10/41, pg. 139.

(27) Wilkinson report dated 8/28/41, pg. 134.

(28) Wilkinson report dated 8/25/41, pg. 133.

(29) Wilkinson report dated 8/23/41, pg. 132.

(30) Wilkinson report dated 8/21/41, pg. 131.

(31) Memo by T. W. Joyce, dated 11/5/41. (Notes & Comments), pg. 130.

(32) Wilkinson report dated 10/4/41, pg. 129.

(33) 14ND card #1536, dated 9/23/41, Subj.: "Shanghai French Concession—Japanese designs on", pg. 121.

(34) 14ND card #1534, dated 9/23/41, Subj.: "Thai-Japanese Activities in", pg. 120.

[268] (35) 14ND card #1535, dated 9/23/41, Subj.: "Formosa-Heito Airdrome", pg. 120.

(36) 14nd card #1533, dated 9/31/41, Subj.: "Japan—General Intelligence", pg. 118.

(37) 14ND card #1531, dated 9/23/41, Subj.: "Japanese Fleet Organization", pg. 118.

(38) 14ND card #1532, dated 9/23/41, Subj.: Indo-China–Japanese Moves in", pg. 118.

(39) 14ND card #1528, dated 9/23/41, Subj.: "Japan—Ordnance Production", pg. 117.

(40) 14ND card #1530, dated 9/23/41, Subj.: "Far East Exports to Germany", pg. 117.

(41) 14ND card #1526, dated 9/23/41, Subj.: China Blockade—Smuggling", pg. 116.

(42) 14ND card #1527, dated 9/23/41, Subj.: "Formosa—Coastal Defenses", pg. 116.

(43) 14ND card #1525, dated 9/23/41, Subj.: "Formosa (Takao)—General Military Intelligence", pg. 115.

(44) 14ND card #1523, dated 9/23/41, Subj.: "Formosa—Conscription", pg. 114.

(45) 14ND card #1524, dated 9/23/41, Subj.: "Formosa—Troop Movements", pg. 114.

(46) 14ND card #1520, dated 9/23/41, Subj.: "Japanese—Troop Movements", pg. 113.

(47) 14ND card #1521, dated 9/23/41, Subj.: "Japanese—Troop Movements", pg. 113.

(48) 14ND card #1522, dated 9/23/41, Subj.: "Formosa—Supplies", pg. 113.

(49) 14ND card #1518, dated 9/23/41, Subj.: "Manchuria—Travel Restrictions", pg. 112.

(50) 14ND card #1519, dated 9/23/41, Subj.: "Manchuria—Censorship", pg. 112.

(51) 14ND card #1516, dated 9/23/41, Subj.: "Manchuria—Mobilization", pg. 111.

(52) 14ND card #1517, dated 9/23/41, Subj.: "Manchuria—Construction", pg. 111.

(53) 14ND card #1482, dated 9/12/41, Subj.: "Hongkong—Prospective Disorders", pg. 97.

(54) 14ND card #1468, dated 9/9/41, Subj.: "Japanese Foreign Policy", pg. 95.

(55) 14ND card #1470, dated 9/9/41, Subj.; "Japanese-Siamese Relations", pg. 95.

(56) 14ND card #1466, dated 9/9/41, Subj.: "Manchuria—Japanese Troop Movements", pg. 94.

(57) 14ND card #1467, dated 9/9/41, Subj.: "Japanese Foreign Policy", pg. 94.

(58) 14ND card #1465, dated 9/9/41, Subj.: "Manchuria—Railways, Buildings, etc.", pg. 93.

[269] (59) 14ND card #1463, dated 9/9/41, Subj.: "Shanghai French Concession—Japanese Designs On", pg. 92.

(60) 14ND card #1456, dated 9/9/41, Subj.: "Formosa—Japanese Airplane Movements", pg. 90.

(61) 14ND card #1457, dated 9/9/41, Subj.: "Formosa—Japanese Troop

Movements'', pg. 90.

(62) 14NR card #1453, dated 9/9/41, Subj.: "Japanese Naval Ordnance'', pg. 89.

(63) 14ND card #1454, dated 9/9/41, Subj.: "Japanese Factory'', pg. 89.

(64) 14ND card #1455, dated 9/9/41, Subj.: "Japanese Troops in Indo China'', pg. 89.

(65) 14ND card #1450, dated 9/9/41, Subj.: "Japanese Troop Movement'', pg. 88.

(66) 14ND card #1451, dated 9/9/41, Subj.: "Japanese Naval Construction'', pg. 88.

(67) 14ND card #1452, dated 9/9/41, Subj.: "Japanese Naval Construction'', pg. 88.

(68) 14ND card # (?), dated 9/9/41, Subj.: "Japanese Aircraft Factory'', pg. 87.

(69) 14ND card #1448, dated 9/9/41, Subj.: "Spratley Island—Japanese Construction'', pg. 87.

(70) 14ND card #1449, dated 9/9/41, Subj.: "German Raiders in Pacific'', pg. 87.

(71) 14ND card #1444, dated 9/9/41, Subj.: "Japan—Kobe Navy Yard'', pg. 86.

(72) 14ND card #1445, dated 9/9/41, Subj.: "Japanese Submarine Construction'', pg. 86.

(73) 14ND card #1446, dated 9/9/41, Subj.: "Japanese Aerial Bomb Factory'', pg. 86.

(74) 14ND card #1442, dated 9/9/41, Subj.: "Japanese National Policy'', pg. 85.

(75) 14ND card #1443, dated 9/9/41, Subj.: "Japan—Airdrome at Kamakura'', pg. 85.

(76) 14ND card #1440, dated 9/9/41, Subj.: "Japan—General Military and Naval Information'', pg. 84.

(77) 14ND card #1441, dated 9/9/41, Subj.: "Japan—Underground Airdrome at Takarazuka'', pg. 84.

(78) 14ND card #1438, dated 9/9/41, Subj.: "Japanese National Policy'', pg. 83.

(79) 14ND card #1439, dated 9/9/41, Subj.: "Philippine—Japanese Propaganda In'', pg. 83.

(80) 14ND card #1435, dated 9/9/41, Subj.: "Dutch East Indies—Japanese Propaganda In'', pg. 82.

(81) 14ND card #1436, dated 9/9/41, Subj.: "Saigon'', pg. 82.

[270] **(82)** 14ND card #1437, dated 9/9/41, Subj.: "Philippines—Japanese Business In'', pg. 82.

(83) 14ND card #1434, dated 9/9/41, Subj.: "Japanese National Policy'', pg. 81.

(84) 14ND card #1433, dated 9/9/41, Subj.: "Anti-American Measures by Japanese in Occupied China", pg. 80.

(85) 14ND card #1431, dated 9/9/41, Subj.: "Indo-China", pg. 79.

(86) 14ND card #1432, dated 9/9/41, Subj.: "Formosa", pg. 79.

(87) Conf. Ltr. to DNI from DIO, 14ND, dated 9/20/41, Subj.: "British Secret Agent in Manila, exchange of information with", pg. 78.

(88) Extract #61 for Honolulu, dated 8/8/41, pg. 79.

(89) Extract #59 for Honolulu, dated 8/10/41, pg. 69.

(90) Extract #57 for Honolulu, dated 8/19/41, pg. 67.

(91) Extract #54 for Honolulu, dated 8/19/41, pg. 64.

(92) Extract #52 for Honolulu, dated 8/21/41, pg. 61.

(93) Extract #35 for Honolulu, dated 8/18/41, pg. 42.

(94) Extract #33 for Honolulu, dated 8/16/41, pg. 40.

(95) Extract #27 for Honolulu, dated 8/12/41, pg. 34.

(96) 14ND card #1420, dated 9/2/41, Subj.: "Japanese Repatriation", pg. 30.

(97) 14ND card #1421, dated 9/2/41, Subj.: "HULL, Amos Tyler, Jr.", pg. 30.

(98) 14ND card #1417, dated 9/2/41, Subj.: "DAKAR—Military Exercises in", pg. 29.

(99) 14ND card #1418, dated 9/2/41, Subj.: "DAKAR—Attitude of Natives", pg. 29.

(100) 14ND card #1419, dated 9/2/41, Subj.: "MOROCCO—Outgoing visas from", pg. 29.

(101) Conf. Ltr. to Hd. of Domestic Intell. Branch, ONI, from DIO 14ND, dated 8/22/41, Subj.: "British Secret Agent in Manila; information received from", pgs. 26–27.

(102) Extract #24, Subj.: "HULL, Amos Tyler", pg. 21.

(103) Extract #20, dated 8/1/41, Subj: "German S/S RAMSES", pg. 19.

(104) 14ND card #1333, dated 8/15/41, Subj.: "JAPANESE MILITARY ARMOR", pg. 14.

(105) Japan Military Body Armour, pg. 13.

(106) 14ND card #1334, dated (?), Subj.: "Japanese Industrial Management", pg. 12.

(107) Extract from letter from Manila, dated 7/12/41, pg. 10.

(108) Factual Information regarding Japanese Professions, pgs. 7–9.

(109) Extract #9 for Honolulu, dated 7/3/41, pg. 6.

(110) Extract #10 for Honolulu, dated 7/2/41, pg. 5.

(111) Extract #11 for Honolulu, dated 7/2/41, pg. 4.

[271]   **(112)** Extract #12 for Honolulu, dated (?), pg. 3.

(113) Extract #13 for Honolulu, dated (?), pg. 2.

(114) Extract #14 for Honolulu, dated (?), pg. 1.

B. One (1) Photostat (Positive and Negative) of each of pages 1, 3 and 5 of a copy of a broadcast from Station JZI (9535 Kc), dated 12/8/41 (Japanese time).

Henry C. Clausen,
Lt. Col., JAGD; US Army

FOR ARMY PEARL HARBOR BOARD

(PHH 35/127 [272])

[272]

WAR DEPARTMENT
Washington, 3 March 1945

Memorandum for Mr. Bundy:
Subject: Investigation of Major Clausen,
Supplementary to Army Pearl Harbor Board.

1. Activities reported: Report is made of my investigation for the Secretary of War, supplementary to proceedings of the Army Pearl Harbor Board, during the period 17 February–3 March 1945, as follows:

a. Army personnel interviewed as leads:
Major Edward B. Anderson, T.C.
Colonel George W. Bicknell, M.I.
General Robert H. Dunlop, A.G.
Colonel Edward F. French, S.C.
Colonel Clarence G. Jensen, A.C.
Lt. Ann Long, S.C.
Miss Margaret McKenney, G-2
Colonel Frank B. Rowlett, S.C.
Mr. Smith, S.C.
General Ralph C. Smith, G-2

b. Navy personnel interviewed as leads:
Captain Joseph J. Rochefort

c. Affidavits obtained:
Major Anderson
Colonel Bicknell
General Dunlop
Colonel Jensen
Miss McKenney
Captain Rochefort
Miss Ross
Lt. Colonel Rowlett
General Smith

[273]   **d.** Conferences additional to foregoing:
          Mr. Harvey H. Bundy
          General Carter W. Clarke, G-2
          General Myron C. Cramer, JAGD
          Mrs. Foley, OPD
          Commander John F. Sonnett, USN

   2. *Significant features of additional evidence developed:*

   a. *"Winds" code message:* General Short contended and the Army Pearl Harbor Board concluded that no information concerning this intelligence was available to General Short in the Hawaiian Department. For example, General Short stated in a letter to the Secretary of War: "Such information was not made available to me in the exercise of my command in the Hawaiian Islands." But it now appears probable that before 7 December 1941, both his G-2, Colonel Fielder, and his Assistant G-2, Colonel Bicknell, received information of the "Winds" code, and that his Assistant G-2 took action for the purpose of intercepting an execution message. If it is a fact that General Short did have available in his Hawaiian Department the information from the Navy as to intercepts of the "Winds" code message, this confirms the impression of General Marshall and Admiral Turner.

   b. *Destruction by Japanese of codes:* General Short also contended that this information was not available to him. He attached more importance to this than almost any other intelligence. He testified before the Navy Court of Inquiry that had he received this information he would not have been led to attach much importance to not alarming the civilian population. In response to a question as to whether he would have gone into a different alert if he had received by telephone the 7 December 1941 message from General Marshall, he testified:

> "I think I would because one thing struck me very forcibly in there, about the destruction of the code machines. *The other matter wouldn't have made much of an impression on me.* But when you destroy your codes or code machines, you are going into an entirely new phase. I would have had this advantage also: I could have asked him the significance to him. But leaving that out, the code machine would have been very significant, *the destruction of the code machine would have been very significant to me.* I would have been very much more alarmed about that than the other matter. * * * I would have taken the destruction of the code machines very seriously."

It now appears probable that both General Short's G-2 and his Assistant G-2 were informed before 7 December 1941 of the destruction by the Japanese of their secret codes and papers at Washington, London,

[274] Hongkong, Singapore, Manila and elsewhere, and his Assistant G-2 saw the Navy Department message which so informed the Navy at Pearl Harbor. It will be recalled that this Assistant G-2 reported to Short's staff on the morning of 6 December 1941 that the Japanese Consuls were destroying their secret papers. He, also, in the late afternoon of 6 December 1941, brought to the attention of General Short and his G-2 the fact that the FBI had intercepted a telephone message between a Japanese agent in Honolulu and a purported newspaper correspondent in Tokyo referring to the fleet, sailors, searchlights, aircraft, weather conditions, "hibiscus" and "poinsettias" in the Hawaiian Islands. This information was not given to the War Department. It should be observed that the "Winds" code was to be implemented by a false weather broadcast as a signal for the Japanese Consuls and diplomatic agents to destroy codes and papers. Hence, knowledge of the "Winds" code arrangement, coupled with later information that the Japanese were destroying their codes and papers, would indicate that the "Winds" code had been implemented. Colonel Bratton sent the 5 December 1941 warning wire to the Hawaiian Department because he had received information of the destruction by the Japanese of their codes. This was an inferential notice of implementation of the "Winds" code. Since it now appears probable, subject to additional investigation, that Short's G-2 and his Assistant G-2 knew of the "Winds" message and of the destruction by the Japanese of their codes, it follows that there may have been available in the Hawaiian Department the same information possessed by the War Department.

C. *Inquiries and Reports on Ships in Pearl Harbor:* These were perhaps the most telling indications of the Japanese intentions. Two, which were very suspicious, dated 2 and 6 December 1941, were intercepted or received by the Army Signal Corps at Honolulu and mailed to Washington. The message dated 2 December 1941 was not received at Washington until 23 December 1941. Translations of these were therefore not available in time to be of any use as a forewarning to Washington. Inquiry will be made at Honolulu as to all the circumstances, and whether anyone in the Hawaiian Department had prior knowledge of the tenor of these or similar messages. In this connection, I have discovered evidence that more than a week before 7 December 1941 the Navy arranged to receive and did receive copies of some commercial cables from the Japanese Consul at Honolulu to Tokyo, which tied into the radio intercepts. Some were decrypted and translated before 7 December. Others, supposed to be the more suspicious ones, were not decrypted and translated until later. Copies of these are supposed to be at Honolulu. Short's Assistant G-2 was aware before 7 December 1941 that the Navy had made arrangements for receiving these copies.

d. *5 December 1941 message from G-2, War Department:* Colonel Fielder denied receiving this message. But now it appears probable that it was sent by Washington and received in Honolulu on 5 December 1941. The importance of this fact is that it was the War Department method of informing the Hawaiian Department of the "Magic" messages.

[275]   **e.** *Alarm to civilian population:* General Short contended that this caution had been urged upon him by the War Department and was one of his reasons for his No. 1 alert. It now appears that General Short did not inquire of his staff, and ascertain in the experience of those on duty in 1940, as to what effect the Herron alert of 1940 had on the civilian population. Had he done so, he would have learned that the Herron all-out alert did not materially alarm the civilian population.

   f. *Standing Operating Procedure of 5 November 1941:* General Short testified that the War Department had this in Washington when he sent his reply to the 27 November 1941 message from General Marshall. It now appears that the Standing Operating Procedure was not received in Washington until March 1942, and hence the War Department cannot be charged with prior knowledge thereof.

   3. *Miscellaneous items:* Several administrative matters pertaining to the Army Pearl Harbor Board have been coordinated.

   4. *Wyman-Rohl activities:* Several administrative matters pertaining to the Army Pearl Harbor Board have been coordinated.

   5. *Progress and objectives:* I shall develop some very important and promising leads in Hawaii and elsewhere when the studies in Washington have been completed, which is expected to be within the next two weeks.

Henry C. Clausen,
HENRY C. CLAUSEN,
Major, JAGD

(PHH 35/129 [276])

HEADQUARTERS, ARMY SERVICE FORCES
OFFICE OF THE JUDGE ADVOCATE GENERAL
Washington 25, D.C., 17 February 1945

Memorandum for Mr. Bundy:
Subject: Investigation of Major Clausen,
Supplementary to
   Army Pearl Harbor Board.

   1. *Activities reported:* During the period 3–17 February 1945, in pursuance of directives, I conducted for the Secretary of War investigations at Washington, D.C., supplementary to the proceedings of the Army Pearl Harbor Board, as follows:

a. Army personnel interviewed as leads:
General Carter W. Clarke, G-2
Colonel Carlisle Clyde Dusenbury, G-2
General Charles K. Gailey, Jr., OPD
General Thomas T. Handy, D.C.S.
General Thomas North, OPD
Colonel Moses W. Pettigrew, G-2
Colonel Frank B. Rowlett, S.C.
Colonel Eric H. F. Svensson, G-2
Miss Margaret McKenney, G-2
b. Navy personnel interviewed as leads:
Captain Joseph J. Rochefort
c. Affidavits obtained:
Colonel Dusenbury
Colonel Pettigrew
Captain Rochefort (being completed)
d. Conferences:
Mr. Harvey H. Bundy
Major Henry A. Correa, IADB
General Myron C. Cramer, JAGD
Colonel William J. Hughes, Jr., JAGD
General H. I. Hodges, G.S.C.
Commander John F. Sonnett, USN
[277] **e.** Studies of Navy Court of Inquiry and Army Pearl Harbor Board records reports and exhibits.

2. *Significant features of additional evidence developed:*

a. Colonel Bratton had testified that he delivered decrypted and translated intercepts to various distributees immediately preceding 7 December 1941. Colonel Dusenbury stated in his affidavit that it was he who, almost exclusively, delivered the intercepts immediately preceding 7 December 1941.

79716-46-Ex. 148–10

b. Colonel Bratton had testified that he wrote the 5 December 1941 message from G-2, War Department to G-2, Hawaiian Department, requesting that Commander Rochefort be contacted regarding a "Winds" broadcast. Colonel Dusenbury and Colonel Pettigrew stated in affidavits that this message was written by them.

c. Colonel Bratton testified that the thirteen parts of the Japanese reply to Hull, called by some witnesses a Japanese declaration of war, intercepted 6 December 1941, were delivered to him by the usual distributees on the evening of 6 December 1941. Colonel Dusenbury stated in an affidavit that he was on duty and waited that night for the receipt of the parts of this message and that when about half of it had come in, Colonel Bratton left for his home. Colonel Dusenbury further stated that none of the parts were delivered that night and that he, Colonel Dusenbury, delivered them the following morning, 7 December 1941.

d. Colonel Bratton testified that the Japanese message to deliver the Japanese reply to Hull at 1 p.m. on 7 December 1941, was received by him between 8:30 and 9 a.m. on 7 December 1941, and that he then called the home of the Chief of Staff. Colonel Dusenbury stated in his affidavit his impression that this message was received by Colonel Bratton between 9 and 10 a.m., 7 December 1941. This confirms the recollection of the Chief of Staff as to when Colonel Bratton made the telephone call to his quarters. This latter time element is also supported by the testimony of Navy witnesses.

e. Colonel Fielder, G-2, Hawaiian Department, stated he had no recollection of receiving the 5 December 1941 message from Washington asking him to communicate with Commander Rochefort regarding the "Winds" message. He stated he did not have any knowledge of the "Winds" message. Commander Rochefort stated to me, and an affidavit to this effect has been prepared and submitted to him for execution, that since the Fall of 1941 he had very close liaison with his opposite number, Colonel Fielder; that he, Commander Rochefort, was monitoring at Hawaii for the implementation of the "Winds" message before 7 December 1941; that since this was of interest to the Army he did, before 7 December 1941, discuss with Colonel Fielder the "Winds" message as well as the destruction by the Japanese of their code and cipher machines in London and in Washington, and of secret papers in Honolulu, and any other important information of that character.

[278] **3.** *Miscellaneous items:*

I have coordinated several administrative matters pertaining to the Army Pearl Harbor Board.

Admiral Kimmel by letter dated 6 February 1945 to the Secretary of the Navy requested a copy of the record of the Navy Court of Inquiry and an examination of the record of the Army Board of Investigation. The Secretary of the Navy replied by letter dated 12 February 1945 that the request so far as the Navy Court of Inquiry is concerned should be denied because courts of inquiry and other investigative bodies are convened for the purpose of informing the convening authority or higher authority of facts attending the matter inquired into, and furthermore, that the investigation has not been completed. So far as the Army Board of Investigation is concerned, the Secretary stated that this is a matter over which the Navy Department has no authority.

4. *Wyman-Rohl activities:*

In conjunction with the foregoing, investigations and conferences have been conducted and held by me on phases involving Colonel Theodore Wyman, Jr. These do not pertain to responsibility for the Pearl Harbor disaster, but some of the persons to be interrogated are in the same locations as those to be questioned in connection with the foregoing unexplored leads. The

Under Secretary of War and the Judge Advocate General have directed that I conduct the appropriate additional investigation, including the development of leads suggested by the Army Pearl Harbor Board.

5. *Progress and objectives:*

It is intended to complete the examination of the Navy Board of Inquiry proceedings, to interview and confer with such other persons as are available locally, and then to gather such information elsewhere as is essential. When concluded, I shall correlate, digest, and, interpret the additional facts in relation to the Army Pearl Harbor Secret and Top Secret Reports.

Henry C. Clausen,

HENRY C. CLAUSEN,

Major, JAGD.

NOTE: ONE OF THE QUESTIONS CLAUSEN ASKED HIMSELF AT THE START OF HIS INVESTIGATION WAS: WHAT DID PEARL HARBOR KNOW ABOUT JAPANESE INTENTIONS BEFORE THE ATTACK OF DECEMBER 7, 1941? THE FOLLOWING MEMORANDUM PROVIDED THE BASE FROM WHICH CLAUSEN BEGAN HIS DETECTIVE WORK.)

INFORMATION MADE AVAILABLE TO GENERAL SHORT FROM WAR DEPARTMENT AND OTHER SOURCES OF THREAT OF WAR WITH JAPAN AND OF THREAT OF SURPRISE ATTACK BY JAPANESE ON PEARL HARBOR ARRANGED IN CHRONOLOGICAL SEQUENCE BY LT. COLONEL HENRY C. CLAUSEN, JAGD

Secretary of the Navy to the Secretary of War, letter, 24 January 1941:

> "If war eventuates with Japan, it is believed easily possible that hostilities would be initiated by a surprise attack upon the fleet or the naval base at Pearl Harbor * * *'' (Roberts Report, p. 5)

The letter continues:

> "The dangers envisaged, in their order of importance and probability, are considered to be (1) air bombing attack, (2) air torpedo-plane attack, (3) sabotage, (4) submarine attack, (5) mining, (6) bombardment by gunfire. Defense against all but the first two of these dangers appears to have been provided for satisfactorily." (APHB, Vol. 4, p. 369)

On 27 January 1941, Ambassador Grew notified the State Department that he had learned thru the Peruvian Minister in Tokyo, that Japanese sources had indicated that in event of trouble with the United States a mass attack on Pearl Harbor was planned. (APHB, Vol. 36, p. 4203)

(The telegram is quoted, APHB, Vol. 16, p. 1778)

Marshall to Short, letter, 7 February 1941:

> "* * * My impression of the Hawaiian problem has been that if no serious harm is done us during the first six hours of known

hostilities, thereafter the existing defenses would discourage an enemy against the hazard of an attack. The risk of sabotage and the risk involved in a surprise raid by air and by submarine, constitute the real perils of the situation. * * * Please keep clearly in mind in all your negotiations that our mission is to protect the base and the Naval concentration. * * *.'' (APHB 13–17)

'' * * * As I say, I don't know; I have never had explained to me, why there was apparently the cessation of fears of air attack, that seemed to be preeminent in the mind of Admiral Kimmel in February, when he wrote a letter to the Secretary of the Navy. * * *'' (APHB 50)

Secretary of War to Secretary of the Navy, letter, 7 Febraury 1941, paragraph 6:

"I am forwarding a copy of your letter and this reply to the Commanding General of the Hawaiian Department, and am directing him to cooperate with the local naval authorities in making these measures effective." (APHB, Vol. 4, p. 368)

Marshall to Short, letter, 5 March 1941, saying in part:

"I would appreciate your early review of the situation in the Hawaiian Department with regard to defense from air attack. The establishment of a satisfactory system of coordinating all means available to this end is a *matter of first priority*." (APHB Report, 101)

Re: Joint Air Operations Agreement.

"General Grunert: Now, in there there was an estimated possible enemy action, and you stated the high probability of a surprise dawn attack. Now, that was in the mind of you airmen at the time you drew up the agreement?

"General Martin: Yes, sir.

"General Grunert: Now, what was done to avoid such a surprise attack that you people thought was highly probable?

"General Martin: Well, nothing more then what I stated. The search of the area was in the hands of the Navy." (APHB, Vol. 17, p. 1823)

General Martin further testified:

" * * * The probability of that taking place was considered the best opportunity the Japanese had. * * * We felt as though it was just too much of a risk for them to take. * * * The possibilities for those things, of course, are always in our minds, but the average opinion was very vague as to there being an actual attack, as I recall it. * * *" (APHB, Vol. 17, pp. 1837–38)

Paragraph III, Addendum No. 1, Joint Air Operations Agreement:

"(a) A declaration of war might be preceded by:
    1. A surprise submarine attack on ships in the operating area.
    2. A surprise attack on Oahu including ships and installations in Pearl Harbor.
    3. A combination of these two." (APHB, Vol. 4, p. 388)

In view of this agreement, signed by Short, the following testimony was adduced:

"General Grunert: You were fully aware, then, of the possible surprise air attack?
"General Short: Oh, yes." (APHB, Vol. 4, p. 388)

General Philip Hayes testified in pertinent part as follows:

"General Frank: Do you remember whether or not they [Admiral Bellinger and General Martin] anticipated an air raid * * * as the most probable enemy action?
"General Hayes: As the most probable. And that was also the estimate of the situation of the Department. General Herron's estimate, which was still in effect, as I remember, was that the most probable line of action was an air raid some time shortly after dawn. He did not name Sunday specifically." (APHB, Vol. 3, pp. 267–8)

General Arnold testified as follows:

> " * * * As early as March 31st they had a board out in Honolulu as to what might happen in case the Japanese did attack Pearl Harbor, and that was a board signed by Martin and Bellinger in which they outlined in that report pretty nearly what actually did happen. So there is no doubt in my mind that the people in Hawaii were thinking on the subject and giving it very serious thought." (APHB, Vol. 3, p. 182)

Admiral Bellinger testified, as to the Naval Base Defense Air Force:

> " * * * Specifically, the organization was designed to function, through mutual cooperation between the Army and Navy for the defense of Pearl Harbor against air attack." (APHB, p. 1579)

> "There was a standard drill procedure to practice for such air raids as occurred." (APHB, p. 1579)

> "According to Admiral De Lany, such an air raid drill was held as late as 20 November 1941." (APHB, p. 1727)

> "Colonel Donegan said that the possibility of an air attack or an air raid on Oahu was discussed * * * many, many times, every time we had a joint Army and Navy exercise, when they came in on Navy carriers. I believed it was possible; I didn't think it was probable * * *. Frankly, I didn't expect one * * *. My reason would be that I thought their interest lay more in Asia than that they would care to jeopardize the chances, or their limited fleet, in coming to Hawaii. * * * " (APHB, Vol. 17, pp. 1961–63)

From the Adjutant General, War Department, to Commanding General, Hawaiian Department, 7 July 1941:

> "For your information. Deduction from information from numerous sources is that the Japanese Government has determined upon its future policy which is supported by all principal Japanese political and military groups. This policy is at present one of watchful waiting involving probable aggressive action against the Maritime Provinces of Russia if and when the Siberian Garrison has been materially reduced in strength and it becomes evident

that Germany will win a decisive victory in European Russia. Opinion is that Jap activity in the South will be for the present confined to seizure and development of Naval, Army and Air Bases in Indo China although an advance against the British and Dutch cannot be entirely ruled out. The neutrality pact with Russia may be abrogated. They have ordered all Jap vessels in U.S. Atlantic ports to be west of Panama Canal by first of August. Movement of Jap shipping from Japan has been suspended and additional merchant vessels are being requisitioned.'' (APHB, Vol. 1, p. 33; Vol. 26, p. 2974)

25 July 1941:

The Secretary testified that the War Department sent a warning on this date but we have been unable to locate the message. (APHB, Vol. 35, p. 4055)

Colonel Fielder, G-2, Hawaiian Department, informed the War Department on 6 September 1941:

''1. It has been noted that many of the Summaries of Information received from your office originate with Office Naval Intelligence, 14th Naval District and have already been furnished this office by the Navy.

''2. The cooperation and contact between Office Naval Intelligence, Federal Bureau of Investigation, and the Military Intelligence Division, in this Department, is most complete and all such data is received simultaneous with the dispatch of information to the respective Washington offices.

''3. Inasmuch as such advices are received in duplicate and unless there are other reasons to the contrary it is recommended that such notices from your office be discontinued in order to avoid the duplication of effort.'' (APHB, Vol. D., p. 292–3)

Chief of Naval Operations to Commander-in-Chief, Pacific Fleet, 16 October 1941:

"Japanese Cabinet resignation creates a grave situation. If a new Cabinet is formed it probably will be anti-American and strongly nationalistic. If the Konoye Cabinet remains it will operate under a new mandate which will not include rapprochement with the United States. Either way hostilities between Japan and Russia are strongly possible. Since Britain and the United States are held responsible by Japan for their present situation, there is also a possibility that Japan may attack these two powers. In view of these possibilities you will take due precautions, including such preparatory deployments as will not disclose strategic intention nor constitute provocative action against Japan." (APHB, Vol. 4, p. 279)

Short admits having received message.

War Department to Commanding General, Hawaiian Department, radiogram, 20 October 1941:

"Following War Department estimate of Japanese situation for your information. Tension between the United States and Japan remains strained but no, repeat no, abrupt change in Japanese foreign policy seems imminent."

General Marshall testified that the foregoing message was sent on 20 October 1941 (C-194) but this message is apparently the one referred to as being sent on 18 October 1941. (APHB, Vol. 28, p. 3307; Vo. 37, p. 4258; Vol. 37, p. 4264; Vol. 4, p. 412–413)

(G-2 ESTIMATE OF INTERNATIONAL (JAPANESE) SITUATION, DATED 25 OCTOBER 1941, IS AS FOLLOWS:)

"1. *Summary of Situation*. Reference paragraph 1, G-2 Estimate of the International (Japanese) Situation, 1200 Oct. 17, 1941, there have been no fundamental changes in the international situation, centering on Japan, since the time mentioned; and the estimate is still in almost complete accord with contemporary opinions of most high officials and reputable observers who are known to be in close touch with the various phases of the present fast-moving situation. However, the following general summary is considered appropriate at this time:

"a. A crisis of the first magnitude was created in the Pacific by the fall of the Third Konoye Cabinet on the 16th instant. The fall of said cabinet was allegedly precipitated by unsatisfactory progress of the rapprochement negotiations between America and Japan, and by extreme pressure from 'rightist' elements who have been clamoring for stronger ties with the Axis and more forceful opposition to the ABCD block, including Russia.

"b. An apparently imminent collapse of the Russian forces in the west, together with the loudly proclaimed German successes everywhere, tended to accentuate the cry for action on the side of the Axis to such a degree that the Konoye cabinet could no longer resist, hence resigned en bloc, and was almost immediately replaced by a new cabinet by ex–War Minister General Tojo.

"c. Ministers of the new cabinet, as well as Premier Tojo, have openly declared their intentions of stronger ties with the Axis, which automatically underscores Japan's policies with 'intensified aggression'; definitely places Japan in a camp hostile to the United States and other democracies; makes all protestations of peaceful intentions a sham or objective of suspicion; and forces America into a state of constant vigilance, but at least clarifies the situation to such an extent that we do know where we stand, what to expect, and what should be done.

"2. *Conclusions*. No change in paragraph 2 of G-2 Estimate of 17 October 1941. However, several important incidents have transpired, or are scheduled to take place, which are certain to have a profound bearing on the probable course of events in question in the near future. These are:

"a. The formation of a new Japanese 'War Cabinet', headed by ex–War Minister, General Tojo.

"b. The decision of Premier to continue his predecessor's order to permit three Japanese vessels to visit American ports for the purpose of transporting stranded Americans and Japanese nationals to their respective homelands.

"c. Premier Tojo's expressed desire to continue rapprochement negotiations with the United States.

"d. The order by the Navy Department to American vessels to avoid Asiatic ports in the north Pacific, including Shanghai.

"e. The announced decision of the American Government to abandon Vladivostok as a port of entry for war supplies to Russia, and to adopt the port of Archangel as the sole point of entry for such shipments.

"f. Announcement of Ambassador Nomura's return to Japan

for consultation with the new cabinet.

"3. *Justification for conclusions*. The following is a brief analysis and evaluation of the above, based on limited reports, and is not to be regarded as conclusive, bur rather to assist in making accurate conclusions on the general situation as subsequent events and special situations are presented:

"a. *New Cabinet*. Paragraph 1c above is the general answer. The only other noteworthy viewpoint received and considered to be worth mentioning, is that General Tojo was selected to head the new cabinet because he was the *only* man considered capable of controlling the 'extremist' army elements, and thus stave off any precipitate action until such time as the situation in Europe has become definitely clear, and until at least a decisive stage has been reached in rapprochement negotiations with the United States.

"b. *Japanese vessels to America*. The Japanese Government's decision to permit three ships to visit America for the purpose of repatriating stranded nationals of both countries, may be regarded either as a peaceful gesture or as a measure to 'clear the decks' in the Pacific with a view to future naval and military moves. It will be recalled that the Japanese were careful to remove Japanese nationals from the interior of south China before spreading military operations to that section. It is considered impracticable to remove *all* Japanese nationals from America and American territories.

"c. *Rapprochement Negotiations*. Inasmuch as the new Japanese cabinet has openly declared its intentions of stronger ties with the Axis—definitely our enemy—we can only expect Japan to make a similar use of peace negotiations as her partner, Hitler, i.e., as a means to delude and disarm her potential enemies. From a military point of view such peaceful overtures should be preceded by concrete evidence of sincerity before they can be seriously considered.

"d. *Navy Order to Clear American Ships from North Pacific*. This action on the part of the Navy seems to have been largely 'precautionary', which also appears fully justified, realizing that we are now definitely dealing with an exponent and ally of Hitler.

"e. *Abandonment of Vladivostok as a Port of Entry for Russian Supplies*.

"Two issues are here involved:

"(1) *Military*. The crucial point as to whether we will be able to continue to face Hitler across the English Channel, across the Atlantic, or on American shores, centers in the British Isles. Convoys must cross the Atlantic in order to hold the British Isles at all cost, irrespective of what happens in the Pacific. Convoys to Archangel, for the greater part of the distance, could be carried on incidental to convoys going to the British Isles. Requirements of armed escorts for the remaining distance to Archangel would probably be less than what would be required over any Pacific route. In fact, with a hostile Japanese fleet in the Pacific, any practicable route across the Pacific to Russia may have been entirely ruled out. Assuming this to be the case, the most logical step would be not to undertake a thing that would certainly have to be abandoned later.

"(2) *Diplomatic*. Inasmuch as the shipping of supplies to Russia via Vladivostok has been one of the major issues between America and Japan recently, the abandonment of said route may serve to keep the door of diplomacy open for a longer period; and, in case of an unforeseen major reverse for the Axis in Europe, might provide an open door for successful negotiations at a time when Japan desired to change her mind, seeing that further ties with the Axis are useless, and that a compromise with the democracies has become inevitable.

"f. *Nomura's report to New Cabinet*. This is considered a very normal procedure with the Japanese Government. Mr. Nomura will be expected to give a review of his efforts in Washington and perhaps the last word on the American attitude. If his previous work is still in harmony with Japan's new policy, he may return to Washington. If not, it seems fair to assume that he may not even be replaced. In case the abnormal procedure is followed, of dispatching a subordinate to Tokyo, it may be taken as an attempt to conceal the real gravity of the situation. This is not, however, a prediction.

"REMARKS: Everyone is interested in the answer to the question, When will Japan move?—a question which no one dares to predict with certainty. However, the following points are considered to be worthy of mentioning:

"a. Things which tend to indicate that a major move will not take place for approximately another month are:

"(1) The dispatch of Japanese vessels to the United States for return of stranded nationals of both countries to their respective homelands.

"(2) Ambassador Nomura's return to Japan for purpose of reporting to the new cabinet.

"(3) Repeated declarations by Japanese officials that Japan desires to continue rapprochement negotiations.

"(4) Extreme cold over Eastern Siberia makes military operations against Russia very risky before spring.

"(5) A protracted Russo-German war seems much more likely now than it did immediately prior to the assumption of office by the new cabinet, and that the 'rightists' who were crying for action against a 'collapsing' Russia, may again hesitate to take the final plunge on the side of Hitler. If the intense cold plus a tired Russian Army is able to stop the invincible legions of Hitler before Moscow (?), wisdom may dictate not to risk the matchless legions of Nippon against a rested Russian army under temperatures still lower than around Moscow.

"(6) Announcement that Cabinet leaders have requested Emperor Hirohito to convoke a special five-day session of the Imperial Diet, beginning Nov. 15, at which time, it is predicted, the government will be asked to clarify its stand on international policies, particularly with reference to former Premier Konoye's message to President Roosevelt and the progress of the Washington negotiations.

"b. In other words, it seems logical to believe that no major move will be made before the latter part of November—in any direction—with a chance that the great break, if it comes, will not occur before spring."

Those are the only G-2 estimates dealing with the Japanese situation which I have been able to find in the War Department in Hawaii. (APHB, Vol. 30, p. 3689)

The Joint Army and Navy Board Report, dated 31 October 1941, stated in paragraph 4a in pertinent part as follows:

" * * * The mission of the Army on Oahu is to defend the Pearl Harbor Naval Base against all attacks by an enemy. The contribution to be made by the Hawaiian Air Force in carrying out this mission is:

(1) to search for and destroy enemy surface craft within radius of action by bombardment aviation.

(2) to detect, intercept, and destroy enemy surface craft in the vicinity of Oahu, by pursuit aviation." (Bellinger, Vol. 15, p. 158)

Re G-2 and Probable Air Attack:

> "General Russell: General Miles, in the fall of 1941, did you
> in G-2 have sufficient data on Japanese developments in the man-
> dated islands to predicate an intelligent opinion as to the possi-
> bilities of launching convoys from there which might have
> included aircraft carriers?
>
> "General Miles: I would say that positively we knew enough to
> form an estimate that such a thing was a strong possibility, not a
> probability; that they had the means. That they would do it is
> another matter. * * *" (APHB, Vol. 2, pp. 104–5)

The Department Surgeon, General King, was "extraordinarily disappointed"
with Alert No. 1, in November 1941 (APHB, Vol. 24, p. 2700) " * * * based
upon what we had heard of the use of air in Europe it seemed to me that the
greatest amount of damage could come from an air attack * * *". (APHB,
Vol. 24, p. 2701)

General Russell: I have been furnished by the G-2 office, Hawaiian Department, two estimates of the international Japanese situation. The issuing
office was G-2, Hawaiian Department, Army Contact Office, Honolulu, Territory of Hawaii. One is dated the 17th of October, 1941, and signed by one
George W. Bicknell, Lieutenant Colonel, General Staff Corps. It shows the
distribution as follows: Chief of Staff, H.H.D., G-2, H.H.D., G-2, H.A.F.,
G-2 Schofield Barracks (3 copies), G-3 H.H.D., F.B.I. Honolulu (2 copies),
ONI Honolulu (2 copies).

(G-2 ESTIMATE OF INTERNATIONAL (JAPANESE) SITUATION,
OCTOBER 17, 1941, IS AS FOLLOWS:)

"1. *Summary of Situation*
"a. With the fall of the Third Konoye Cabinet, the 16th instant, tension
in the Pacific reached a new high. The fall of said cabinet is apparently
primarily due to a breakdown of the rapprochement negotiations between
America and Japan, and also due to extreme pressure from the rightest element in Japan as a result of German success against Russia, and also for fear
of complete encirclement of Japan by the ABCD group.
"b. The situation is generally admitted as being extremely critical, and
is still necessarily uncertain, due to the fact that the formation of the new
cabinet has not been completed and, consequently, little or no definite infor-

mation is available as to the attitude of individual members, and nothing as to what the attitude of the cabinet as a whole will be.

"c. Based upon contemporary opinions from various sources, however, it is fairly certain that Japan's basic policy, as heretofore frequently stated, will remain unchanged; and it is expected that Japan will shortly announce her decision to challenge militarily any nation or combination of nations which might oppose the execution of said policies—irrespective of what means she may choose to adopt or course she may decide to take in their achievement.

"2. *Conclusions*

"According to present indications, it is highly probable that Japan will, in the near future, take military action in new areas of the Far East. The primary reasons for such a move or moves are believed to be as follows:

"a. *Capabilities*

"1. Desperate economic conditions internally—making it perhaps preferable to risk a major foreign war rather than internal revolution.

"2. Violent opposition by the 'rightest' elements who are opposed to any appeasement of the democracies and desire more active cooperation with the Axis—for the time being.

"3. That major successes of the Axis in Europe and the potential collapse of Russian resistance, afford an unparalleled opportunity for expansion with chances of minimum resistance—that is, when the strength of the Axis is at its maximum, and the strength of the democracies not yet fully mobilized.

"4. A desire to break the so-called encirclement of the ABCD block.

"b. *Probable Moves.* The most likely moves which Japan may make in the near future, and the sequence thereof, are as follows:

"1. Attack Russia from the east.

"2. Pressure French-Indo-China and Thailand for concessions in the way of military, naval, and air bases, and guarantees of economic cooperation.

"3. Attack British possessions in the Far East.

"4. Defend against an American attack in support of the British.

"5. Attack simultaneously the ABCD block at whichever points might promise her greatest tactical, strategic and economic advantages.

"c. *Reasons Justifying These Moves.* The basis for each of the above possible moves are considered to be as follows:

"1. *Attack on Russia*

"(a) Japan's desire to extend her first line of defense as far to the west as possible as a primary defense against potential aerial attacks on the heart of Japan proper by a continental power.

"(b) To set up a buffer state between herself and Germany (assuming that Germany will eventually attempt to extend her influence and control eastward to the Pacific.)"

"(c) To secure immense quantities of much-needed raw materials known to be in Siberia.

"(d) To secure effective control over, or perhaps stamp out, communism in the Far East by striking at the root or source of the doctrine.

"(e) A possibility that an attack on Russia at this time can be undertaken with a reasonable chance of non-military intervention by the United States; and that even the British might not resort to active military action in support of Russia in the Pacific, due to the fact that both the Americans and British are preoccupied in Europe, and that neither power has any genuine desire to ever see the state of the USSR emerge sufficiently strong to again plague the democratic states with the sinister ideals of communism.

"(f) To open communications with Germany for the purpose of closer coordination and supply, in case it becomes necessary to continue the war against other Pacific powers.

"(g) To achieve a spectacular victory which is now greatly needed to revive the morale of the people and prepare them for future efforts toward the south.

"2. *Pressure French Indo-China and Thailand.*

"Pressure on French Indo-China and Thailand for concessions of military, naval or air bases, and guarantees of economic cooperation, is entirely to be expected, and this may either precede or follow, or occur simultaneously with an attack on Russia, in order to insure security in the south while her primary objective in the north is being achieved; and to afford her more and better strategic bases from which she can operate against Chungking's lines of communications in case it becomes necessary to defend herself against either or both of these powers. Also, to secure additional raw materials, food, etc.

"3. *Attack on British Possessions in the Far East.*

"Following the principle of defeating one opponent at a time—famous with her Axis partner, Hitler—it is believed that Japan, if faced with certain British military resistance to her plans, will unhesitatingly attack the British; and do so without a simultaneous attack on American possession, because of no known binding agreement between the British and Americans for joint military action against Japan, and that the American public is not yet fully prepared to support such action. However, it must be evident to the Japanese that in case of such attack on the British, they would most certainly have to fight the United States within a relatively short time.

"4. *Simultaneous Attack on the ABCD Powers.*

"While a simultaneous attack on the ABCD powers would violate the principle mentioned above, it cannot be ruled out as a possibility for the reason that if Japan considers war with the United States to be inevitable as a result of her actions against Russia, it is reasonable to believe that she may decide to strike before our naval program is completed.

"An attack on the United States could not be undertaken without almost certain involvement of the entire ABCD block, hence there remains the possibility that Japan may strike at the most opportune time, and at whatever points might gain for her the most strategic, tactical or economical advantages over her opponents.

"3. In conclusion, barring unforeseen and untoward actions, which might set off a conflict in any quarter and invite measures and countermeasures never contemplated, it is believed that the above represents the most logical major moves that Japan may take and the probable sequence thereof. This is assuming that the new cabinet will be, as generally predicted, 'strongly military' and will support the present demands of the 'rightests' elements which were largely responsible for the fall of the Third Konoye Cabinet." (APHB, Vol. 30, p. 3684)

War Department, G-2, to G-2, Hawaiian Department, 5 November 1941:

Omitting the covering letter from General Miles dated 5 November 1941, the following is a summary of information forwarded to Hawaii:

"November 3, 1941

"Subject: Information Received from the Orient.

"Summary of Information:

"The following information received from the Orient, dated August 26, 1941, is considered reliable:

"1. Mr. HIROTA, a presiding officer at directors' meeting of the Black Dragon Society, told of an order issued by War Minister TOJO (now Premier) 'to complete full preparation to meet any emergency with United States in the Pacific. All guns to be mounted in the islands of the Pacific under Japanese mandate. The full preparation to be completed in November.'

"2. HIROTA and others are said to have stated: 'War with United States would best begin in December or in February.'

"3. 'Very soon', they say, 'the Cabinet will be changed. The new Cabinet would likely start war within sixty days.'

G-2 Note: Full name of individual mentioned above is KOKI HIROTA, who is reported to be a member of the House of Peers, former Premier of Japan and Director of the Bureau of Intelligence, U.S. Section.

"Distribution:
  All Corps Areas
  All Departments
  Alaska
  FBI
  ONI
  State
  File (checked)
(pen and ink notation) Source: Dr. Cho
          Date of original paper 10-28-41
  I. B. Cognizant   (initials illegible)
                Evaluation
—of course   —of information
          X   Reliable
              Credible   X
              Questionable
              Undetermined.''
(APHB, Vol. D, pp. 289–91)

Reference is made to page 292, wherein it is stated Colonel Fielder, G-2, Hawaiian Department, informed the War Department on 6 September 1941:

''1. It has been noted that many of the Summaries of information received from your office originate with Office Naval Intelligence, 14th Naval District and have already been furnished this office by the Navy.

''2. The cooperation and contact between Office Naval Intelligence, Federal Bureau of Investigation, and the Military Intelligence Division, in this Department, is most complete and all such data is received simultaneous with the dispatch of information to the respective Washington offices.

''3. Inasmuch as such advices are received in duplicate and unless there are other reasons to the contrary it is recommended that such notices from your office be discontinued in order to avoid the duplication of effort.'' (APHB, Vol. D, p. 292–3)

Early November 1941:

Colonel George W. Bicknell, who was then Assistant G-2, Hawaiian Department, early in November 1941, in his weekly Intelligence Summary, stated from all information which had been gathered in his office in Hawaii it looked as though hostilities could be expected either by the end of November or, if not then, not until Spring. (APHB, Vol. 12, p. 1439)

See preceding 5 November 1941 notice from War Department G-2 as possible source.

November 10–12, 1941:

> Captain Edwin T. Layton, U.S.N., Fleet Intelligence Officer, U.S. Pacific Fleet, believes he informed Colonel Edwin Raley, AC, G-2, Hawaiian Air Force, who was liaison with Navy for the purpose, that Japanese troops, vessels, Naval vessels, transports, were moving South along the Pacific coast. (This information came from Naval observers in China, Naval Attache in Tokyo, Naval Attache in Chungking, and from British and other sources.) An invasion of the Kra Isthmus was indicated. (APHB, Vol. 27, pp. 3031–37–51) About this time Japanese submarines had also been detected in the vicinity of Oahu. (APHB, Vol. 27, p. 3041)

Captain Layton delivered the Naval message of 27 November 1941 to General Short's senior staff officer for delivery to General Short on 27 November 1941. (APHB, Vol. 27, p. 3041)

Chief of Naval Operations to Commander in Chief, Pacific Fleet, 24 November 1941:

> "There are very doubtful chances of a favorable outcome of negotiations with Japan. This situation coupled with statements of Nippon Government and movements of their naval and military forces indicate in our opinion that a surprise aggressive movement in any direction including an attack on the Philippines or Guam is a possibility. The Chief of Staff has seen this dispatch and concurs and requests action addresses (Cincaf, Cinap, Coms 11, 12, 13, 15) inform senior army officers their respective areas. Utmost secrecy is necessary in order not to complicate an already tense situation or precipitate Jap action. Guam will be informed in a separate dispatch."

Given Short by Layton (APHB, Vol. 27, p. 3058) with estimate.

Extract from secret cablegram, War Department to Commanding General, Hawaiian Department, 26 November 1941:

"It is desired following instructions be given pilots of two B-24's on special photo mission. Photograph Jaluit Island in the Carolina group while simultaneously making visual reconnaissance. Information is desired as to location and number of guns, aircraft, airfields, barracks, camps and naval vessels including submarines x x x before they depart Honolulu insure that both B-24's are fully supplied with ammunition for guns."

War Department to Commanding Officer, Hawaiian Department, secret, first priority message, 27 November 1941:

"Negotiations with Japanese appear to be terminated to all practical purposes with only the barest possibilities that the Japanese Government might come back and offer to continue. Japanese future action unpredictable but hostile action possible at any moment. If hostilities cannot, repeat cannot, be avoided, United States desires that Japan commit the first overt act. This policy should not, repeat not, be construed as restricting you to a course of action that might jeopardize your defense. Prior to hostile Japanese action, you are directed to undertake such reconnaissance and other measures as you deem necessary but these measures should be carried out so as not, repeat not, to alarm the civilian population or disclose intent. Report measures taken. Should hostilities occur you will carry out the tasks assigned in Rainbow 5 as far as they pertain to Japan. Limit dissemination of this highly secret information to minimum essential officers."

G-2 War Department to G-2 Hawaiian Department, 27 November 1941:

"Advise only the Commanding Officer and the Chief of Staff that it appears that the conference with the Japanese has ended in an apparent deadlock. Acts of sabotage and espionage probable. Also possible that hostilities may begin."

Cincaf and Cincpac, 27 November 1941:

"This dispatch is to be considered a war warning. Negotiations with Japan looking toward stabilization of conditions in the Pacific have ceased and an aggressive move by Japan is expected within the next few days. The number and equipment of Jap troops and the organization of naval task forces indicates an amphibious expedition against either the Philippines or the Kra Peninsula or possibly Borneo. Execute an appropriate defensive deployment preparatory to carrying out the task assigned in WPL 46X inform district and army authorities. A similar warning is being sent by the War Department. Spanavo informed British. Continental district Guam Samoa directed to take appropriate measures against sabotage." (APHB, Vol. 37, p. 4262)

Captain Layton delivered the Naval message of 27 November 1941 to General Short's senior staff officer for delivery to General Short on 27 November 1941. (APHB, Vol. 37, p. 3041)

The Adjutant General, War Department, to Commanding General, Hawaiian Department, 28 November 1941:

"114 WAR KR 189, WD Prty
    "Washn. D.C. 8:42 P Nov. 28, 1941.
"C G
"Hawn Dept Ft Shafter TH

"482 28th Critical situation demands that all precautions be taken immediately against subversive activities within field of investigative responsibility of War Department paren see paragaph three MID SC thirty dash forty five end paren stop Also desired that you initiate forthwith all additional measures necessary to provide for protection of your establishments comma property comma and equipment against sabotage comma protection of your personnel against subversive propaganda and protection of all activities against espionage stop This does not repeat not mean that any illegal measures are authorized stop Protective measures should be confined to those essential to security comma avoiding unnecessary publicity and alarm stop To insure speed of transmission identical telegrams are being sent to all air stations but this does not repeat not effect your responsibility under existing instructions." (APHB, Vol. 3, p. 170; Vol. 4, p. 293; Vol. 36, p. 4176)

CNO to CINCPAC, 29 November 1941:

Message in substance was a quotation of the 27 November message of General Marshall to the Commanding General, Hawaiian Department, together with a direction that the CINCPAC take no offensive action until Japan had committed an overt act and ordering certain action in case hostilities should occur. (APHB, Roberts printed report, p. 8)

CNO to CINAC and CINCPAC, 30 November 1941:

This was a message stating that Japan, according to indications, was about to launch an attack on the Kra Isthmus and directing the Commander-in-Chief of the Asiatic Fleet to do certain scouting but to avoid the appearance of attacking. (APHB, Roberts printed report, p. 8)

General Newspaper Articles:

Army Pearl Harbor Board, Volume 28, page 3168, sets forth the various items of importance which appeared in the Honolulu newspapers immediately preceding the attack, including the headline of 30 November 1941: "Japanese may Strike Over Week End."

War Department to Commanding General, Hawaiian Department, 1 December 1941:

This message requested an opinion relative to the possible relief of Marines on Wake Island and Midway Island so they could be made available for landing parties. (APHB, Vol. 4, p. 301)

1 December 1941:

Admiral Kimmel orally gave General Short all the intelligence information he received which would help General Short in the defense of Oahu. This included a fortnightly summary of current international situations issued by the Office of the Chief of Naval Relations, Office of Naval Intelligence, Washington, dated 1 December 1941. A portion of this reads as follows:

"The Japanese Naval Situation.
(PORTION OF FORTNIGHTLY SUMMARY OF CURRENT INTERNATIONAL SITUATIONS IS AS FOLLOWS:)

"Deployment of naval forces to the southward has indicated clearly that extensive preparations are underway for hostilities. At the same time troop transports and freighters are pouring continually down from Japan and northern China coast ports headed south, apparently for French Indo-China and Formosan ports. Present movements to the south appear to be carried out by small individual units, but the organization of an extensive task force, not definitely indicated, will probably take sharper form in the next few days. To date, this task force, under the Command of the Commander in Chief Second Fleet, appears to be subdivided into two major task groups, one gradually concentrating off the Southeast Asiatic coast, the other in the Mandates. Each constitutes a strong striking force of heavy and light cruisers, units of the Combined Air Force, destroyer and submarine squadrons. Although one division of battleships may also be assigned, the major capital ship strength remains in home waters, as well as the greatest portion of the carriers.

"The equipment being carried south is a vast assortment including landing boats in considerable numbers. Activity in the Mandates, under naval control, consists not only of large reinforcements of personnel, aircraft, munitions, but also of construction material with yard workmen, engineers, etc." (APHB, Vol. 16, p. 1769)

Colonel Fielder, G-2, Hawaiian Department, testified that he considered war imminent and that "we had knowledge of a large number of ships going down the China coast to the South, which looked as if an invasion force was taking off for Indo China or the Malay States or the Philippines or some other place. I felt that there was great danger of war, but I couldn't—I didn't—anticipate that it would be inflicted on us so suddenly." (APHB, Vol. 26, p. 2988)

Short: "He [Kimmel] gave me without any hesitancy any piece of information that he thought was of interest." (APHB, Tr. 363)

Short had been instructed to conduct some aerial reconnaissance in the Jaluit area. This was a result of information furnished by the Navy concerning Japanese forces. (See APHB, Arnold, p. 152, Gerow, p. 4259, Kimmel, p. 1808, Miles, p. 112, Truman, p. 1446, Short, p. 304; Layton affidavit in Clausen investigation.)

3 December 1941:

Mr. Robert L. Shivers, then agent-in-charge, FBI, Hawaii, intercepted a telephone message from the Japanese Consulate in Honolulu on 3 December 1941, wherein the cook at the Consulate stated the Japanese Consul General was burning and destroying all his important papers. Mr. Shivers immediately furnished this information to Colonel Bicknell, Assistant G-2, Hawaiian Department, and to Captain Mayfield, District Intelligence Officer, 14th Naval District. (APHB, Vol. 28, p. 3204)

Commander Joseph J. Rochefort, then on duty as the Combat Intelligence Officer, Honolulu, testified that he transmitted this information to Washington on 3 December 1941 and that "they told us that London and Washington were burning papers." (APHB, Vol. 15, p. 1657)

Colonel Fielder, G-2, Hawaiian Department, testified that he received this information. (APHB, Vol. 26, p. 2998)

CNO to Commander-in-Chief, Asiatic Fleet; Commander-in-Chief, Pacific Fleet; Commandant, 14th Naval District; and Commandant, 16th Naval District, 3 December 1941:

"Highly reliable information has been received that categoric and urgent instructions were sent yesterday to the Japanese diplomatic and consular posts at Hong Kong, Singapore, Batavia, Manila, Washington, and London to destroy most of their codes and ciphers at once and to burn all other important confidential and secret documents." (APHB, Vol. C, p. 183; Vol. 13, p. 1513; Vol. 4, p. 424; Vol. 24, p. 2684; Vol. D, p. 306; Vol. 26, p. 2998; Roberts Report, p. 137)

(NOTE: THE MESSAGE ABOVE IS ONLY THE *FIRST* MESSAGE WASHINGTON SENT TO ADMIRAL KIMMEL ON DECEMBER 3. IT IS IMPORTANT TO UNDERSTAND THAT A *SECOND* MESSAGE OF DECEMBER 3 IS NOT SHOWN IN TESTIMONY UNTIL THE CLAUSEN AND HEWITT INVESTIGATIONS. IT WAS THE SECOND MESSAGE THAT WARNED KIMMEL THAT TOKYO HAD SPECIFICALLY ORDERED ITS CONSULATES AND EMBASSIES AROUND THE WORLD TO DESTROY THEIR *CODE MACHINES*. ACCORDING TO EXPERT TESTIMONY, THE DESTRUCTION OF CODES AND CODE MACHINES AT THIS TIME "MEANT WAR IN ANY MAN'S LANGUAGE." YET KIMMEL FAILED TO PASS ON THIS INFORMATION TO SHORT.

LAYTON EVEN CLAIMED THAT NAVAL REGULATIONS PROHIBITED THE
PASSING OF SUCH INFORMATION TO SHORT. LAYTON'S MENDACIOUS
CLAIM, AND KIMMEL'S FAILURE TO INFORM SHORT, PROVIDES A BASIS
FOR THE CHARGES CHIEF OF STAFF MARSHALL AND SECRETARY OF
WAR STIMSON MADE THAT THE NAVY WITHHELD VITAL INFORMATION
FROM THE ARMY AT PEARL HARBOR.

THE DAMAGE OF THIS STONEWALLING IS MAGNIFIED MANY TIMES
WHEN IT IS REALIZED THAT THE INSTRUCTIONS TOKYO GAVE ITS EM-
BASSIES AND CONSULATES WERE, IN EFFECT, THE ORDERS TO CARRY
OUT THE WINDS CODE.)

ONO to Commander-in-Chief, Pacific Fleet; Commander-in-Chief, Asiatic
Fleet; Commandant, 16th Naval District; Commandant, 14th Naval District;
Naval Station, Guam; and Naval Station, Samoa, 4 December 1941:

> "042000 CSP 903, 905 and RIP 66 less changes 1 and 2
> effective immediately with indicators CONID secret and JYREC con-
> fidential available all purposes communications with Guam and
> Samoa. Guam and Samoa destroy RIP 65 plus changes to RIP 66
> immediately. Other addressees may continue to use except with
> stations mentioned." (APHB, Vol. C, p. 185; Vol. 13, p. 1514;
> Vol. D, p. 306; Roberts report 8, 138)

ONO to Guam and information copies to: Commander-in-Chief, Asiatic Fleet;
Commander-in-Chief, Pacific Fleet; Commandant, 14th Naval District; and
Commandant, 16th Naval District, 4 December 1941:

> "Guam destroy all secret and confidential publications and
> other classified matter except that essential for current purposes
> and special intelligence, retaining minimum cryptographic chan-
> nels necessary for essential communications with Commander-in-
> Chief, Asiatic; Commander-in-Chief, Pacific; Commandant, 14th;
> and Commandant, 16th Naval District; and Naval Operations. Be
> prepared to destroy instantly in event of emergency all classified
> matter you retain. Report cryptic channels retained." (APHB,
> Vol. C, p. 186)

War Department G-2 to Commanding General, Hawaiian Department, 5 December 1941:

"Contact Commander Rochefort immediately through Commandant, 14th Naval District, regarding broadcasts from Tokyo reference weather." (APHB, Vol. A, p. 38; Vol. C, pp. 283–4–308)

For testimony concerning the general knowledge of Commander Rochefort on radio intercepts, see APHB, Vol. 15, p. 1646, 1656. G-2, War Department, states in Summary, Far Eastern Documents (p. 36) that Rochefort had learned the information. (APHB, Vol. C, pp. 111, 125; Gibson, Vol. D, p. 275)

The testimony of Colonel Bratton and Colonel Sadtler and Colonel Fielder is pertinent. (APHB, Vol. A, pp. 38, 62, 67; Vol. C, p. 232; Vol. D, 281–287; Vol. 27, p. 3058)

War Department, G-2, to Hawaiian Department, G-2, 5 December 1941:

Confirmation paraphrase copy of preceding message about contacting Commander Rochefort mailed. (APHB, Vol. D, p. 282)

Intercepted Dr. Mori message, 6 December 1941:

Early in the morning of 5 December, the FBI intercepted a telephone message from Dr. Mori's home in Honolulu to a newspaper correspondent in Tokyo. The message was in Japanese and concerned flying conditions, searchlights, soldiers seen in town, the ships in Pearl Harbor and certain code words that "Poinsettias and hibiscus" were blooming in Hawaii. This message was translated into English and delivered to Short's G-2 about 4 p.m., 6 December 1941. It was conveyed to General Short and Colonel Fielder about 5:30 p.m. Both the Colonel and the General thought "the message was quite in order, that it described the situation in Hawaii as it was, and that possibly there was nothing very much to be excited about in the content of the message." (APHB, Vol. 12, pp. 1417–19)

6 December 1941:

Mr. Shivers intercepted a telephone conversation between a Japanese agent in Honolulu, Dr. Mori, and a person in Tokyo on 5 December 1941. The message had military significance and was of the utmost importance in the opinion of Mr. Shivers. Among other things, patrol planes and peculiar questions about flowers blooming were discussed. (Mr. Shivers on 6 December 1941 furnished a complete translation of the message to Colonel Bicknell, G-2, and Captain Mayfield, Navy.) (APHB, Vol. 28, p. 3205)

Colonel Bicknell was also impressed with the importance of the message and its military implications and communicated the message to General Short and Colonel Fielder on 6 December 1941. They, however, discounted the importance. (APHB, Vol. 12, p. 1417; Vol. 26, p. 2961)

Staff Announcement, 6 December 1941:

> At a meeting of General Short's staff, 6 December 1941, Colonel Bicknell, Assistant G-2, announced that he "had received information to the effect that the Japanese counsuls were burning their papers; * * * it would at least show that something was about to happen, somewhere." (APHB, Vol. 12, p. 1414)

No discussion of this report occurred at the Staff meeting. It was taken as "just a routine report". The FBI was the source of the information; Mr. Shivers, Special Agent of FBI in Honolulu called Colonel Bicknell (APHB, Vol. 12, p. 1415) The burning of papers at the Japanese consulate was unusual and not a regular occurrence. (APHB, Vol. 12, p.1416)

6 December 1941:

> Colonel Bicknell informed the Hawaiian Department Staff that the Japs were burning papers on 5 December 1941, and to him this meant that war was imminent. (APHB, Vol. 12, p. 1413)

Colonel Fielder confirmed this fact. (APHB, Vo. 26, p. 2986). He stated that it was his recollection the information came from the War Department. (APHB, Vol. 26, p. 2986)

ONO to Commander-in-Chief, Pacific Fleet, 6 December 1941:

"In view of the international situation and the exposed position of the outlying Pacific Islands you may authorize the destruction by them of secret and confidential documents now or under later conditions or greater urgency. Means of communication to support our current operations and special intelligence should, of course, be maintained until the last moment." (APHB, Vol. C, p. 189; Vol. 13, p. 1514; Vol. 3, p. 239; Vol. D, p. 306; Roberts report 8, 138)

6 December 1941 (Australian time, which is 5 December 1941, Hawaiian time):

Lt. Robert H. Odell, then Assistant Military Attache, American Legation, Melbourne, Australia, testified concerning the following secret message which was sent to the Commanding General Hawaiian Department, and Commanding General, Philippine Department:

" '1. The Netherlands Far East Command ordered execution of Plan A-2 based on their intelligence report (without confirmation here) of naval movement on Menado and/or Ambon from Palau. They offered the suggestion that the Royal Australian Air Force likewise take reciprocal action on Laha, Ambon (Amboina?), and Koepang.

" 'The R.A.A.F. accordingly acquiesced to the suggestion and in addition sent task scouting planes to Northwest Passage and Buka, and dispatched a flight of Catalina aircraft to Rabaul. Reinforcements of the Australian Army were held ready for transfer to Koepang and (Amboina) should the Dutch Command so request them.

" '2. The Netherlands Command at 8:00 A.M., 7 December reported planes to have reached Koepang, and that Australian air assistance was now deemed unnecessary. However, at 11:00 A.M. the Air Corps Chief decided to go forward with all aircraft as planned.

" '3. This message was delayed 17 hours by (?) Government (x)

" '4. Manila has been informed.'
                    Signed 'Merlo-Smith.' "
(APHB, Vol. 41, p. 4506)

The reference to Plan A-2 is significant because it fell into the Rainbow Plan (p. 4511) and which plan was the source of the Joint Hawaiian Coastal

Frontier Defense Plan of General Short, which incorporated the Alerts 1, 2, and 3. In this connection, the Navy message of 27 November 1941, is significant, in ordering the execution of defensive deployment of tasks assigned in a coordinate plan.

The quoted message to the Commanding General, Hawaiian Department, evidently was relayed to the War Department for decipherment and repeat to them. (APHB, Vol. 41, p. 4509)

7 December 1941—War Department to Commanding General, Hawaiian Department:

> "Japanese are presenting at one p.m. Eastern Standard time today what amounts to an ultimatum also they are under orders to destroy their Code machine immediately stop Just what significance the hour set may have we do not know but be on alert accordingly stop Inform naval authorities of this communication." (APHB, Vol. 24, p. 2692)

THE "WINDS CODE"

(NOTE: This is final report of Congress on the Winds Code controversy and is reprinted in full from the Report of the Joint Committee, page 469–486. Lieutenant Colonel Clausen believes this to be the most authoritative analysis ever made. No one can read this report and believe the claims made by Captain Safford.)

ESTABLISHMENT AND NATURE OF "WINDS CODE"

The "Winds code" was established and confirmed by five communications, two of which were processed by the Navy; i.e., Circulars 2353 and 2354, as follows:[1]

---

[1] Committee exhibit No. 1, pp. 154, 155.

From: Tokyo
To: Washington
19 November 1941
Circular #2353
Regarding the broadcast of a special message in an emergency.
In case of emergency (danger of cutting off our diplomatic relations), and the cutting off of international communications, the following warnings will be added in the middle of the daily Japanese-language short-wave news broadcast.

(1) In case of a Japan-U.S. relations in danger: HIGASHI NO KA-ZEAME.*
(2) Japan-U.S.S.R. relations: KITANOKAZE KUMORI.**
(3) Japan-British relations: NISHI NO KAZE HARE.***
This signal will be given in the middle and at the end as a weather forecast, and each sentence will be repeated twice. When this is heard please destroy all code papers, etc. This is as yet to be a completely secret arrangement.
Forward as urgent intelligence.
25432
JD–1: 6875   (Y) Navy Trans. 11–28–41 (S–TT)

*East wind, rain
**North wind, cloudy
***West wind, clear

From: Tokyo
To: Washington
19 November 1941
Circular #2354
When our diplomatic relations are becoming dangerous, we will add the following at the beginning and end of our general intelligence broadcasts:
(1) If it is Japan-U.S. relations, "HIGASHI".
(2) Japan-Russia relations, "KITA".
(3) Japan-British relations (including Thai, Malaya, and N. E. I.); "NISHI".
The above will be repeated five times and included at beginning and end. Relay to Rio de Janeiro, Buenos Aires, Mexico City, San Francisco.

25392
JD–1: 6850   (Y) Navy Trans. 11–26–41 (S)

By way of confirming the winds code and reflecting its nature the following dispatch, No. 281430, was received from the Commander in chief of the Asiatic Fleet.[2]

---

[2] Id., No. 142.

28 NOVEMBER 1941
FROM: CINCAF[3]
ACTION: OPNAV[4]
INFO: COMSIXTEEN CINCPAC COMFOURTEEN[5]
281430

FOLLOWING TOKYO TO NET INTERCEPT TRANSLATION RE-
CEIVED FROM SINGAPORE X IF DIPLOMATIC RELATIONS ARE ON
VERGE OF BEING SEVERED FOLLOWING WORDS REPEATED FIVE
TIMES AT BEGINNING AND END OF ORDINARY TOKYO NEWS
BROADCASTS WILL HAVE SIGNIFICANCE AS FOLLOWS X HIGASHI
HIGASHI JAPANESE AMERICAN X KITA KITA RUSSIA X NISHI
NISHI ENGLAND INCLUDING OCCUPATION OF THAI OR INVASION
OF MALAYA AND NEI XX ON JAPANESE LANGUAGE FOREIGN
NEWS BROADCASTS THE FOLLOWING SENTENCES REPEATED
TWICE IN THE MIDDLE AND TWICE AT THE END OF BROADCASTS
WILL BE USED XX AMERICA HIGASHI NO KAZE KUMORI[6] XX EN-
GLAND X NISHI NO KAZE HARE X UNQUOTE X BRITISH AND COM-
SIXTEEN MONITORING ABOVE BROADCASTS

Two further dispatches relate significantly to the winds code, the first from
Consul General Foote, our senior diplomatic representative in the Netherlands
East Indies, the second from Colonel Thorpe, our senior Army intelligence
officer in Java.[7]

TELEGRAM RECEIVED

BF
This telegram must be
closely paraphrased be-   ———— Batavia
fore being communicated   FROM   Dated December 4, 1941
to anyone. (SC)   Rec'd. 9:19 a.m.

---

[3] Commander in chief, Asiatic Fleet.
[4] Office of Naval Operations.
[5] Commandant Sixteenth Naval District; commander in chief, Pacific Fleet; commandant, Fourteenth Naval District.
[6] It is to be noted that, apparently through inadvertence in transmitting the message, the code
phrase referring to Russian has been improperly comingled with that referring to the United
States.
[7] See committee exhibit No. 142.

Secretary of State,
  Washington.
    220, December 4, 10 a.m.

War Department at Bandoeng claims intercepted and decoded following from Ministry Foreign Affairs Tokyo:

"When crisis leading to worst arises following will be broadcast at end weather reports; one east wind rain war with United States, two north wind cloudy war with Russia, three west wind clear war with Britain including attack on Thailand or Malaya and Dutch Indies. If spoken twice burn codes and secret papers."

Same re following Japanese Ambassador Bangkok to Consul General Batavia:

"When threat of crises exists following will be used five times in texts of general reports and radio broadcasts: one Higashi east America, two Kita north Russia, three Nishi west Britain with advance into Thailand and attack on Malaya and Dutch Indies."

Thorpe and Slawson cabled the above to War Department. I attach little or no importance to it and view it with some suspicion. Such have been common since 1936.

HSM   FOOTE

FROM ALUSNA BATAVIA   OPNAV   RRRRR
DATE 5 DEC 1941[8]
DECODED BY KALAIDJIAN
PARAPHRASED BY PURDY
  031030   CR0222

FROM THORPE FOR MILES WAR DEPT. CODE INTERCEPT: JAPAN WILL NOTIFY HER CONSULS OF WAR DECISION IN HER FOREIGN BROADCASTS AS WEATHER REPORT AT END. EAST WIND RAIN XXXXXX UNITED STATES: NORTH WIND CLOUDY RUSSIA: WEST WIND CLEAR ENGLAND WITH ATTACK ON THAILAND MALAY AND DUTCH EAST INDIES. WILL BE REPEATED TWICE OR MAY USE COMPASS DIRECTIONS ONLY. IN THIS CASE WORDS WILL BE INTRODUCED FIVE TIMES IN GENERAL TEXT.

(Signature illegible)

---

[8] It is to be noted that this message bears the date December 5, 1941, whereas the "number group" is 031030, indicating December 3, 1941. From evidence available (see discussion, *infra*) it appears this message was dispatched from Batavia on December 3, 1941, but was not processed in the Navy Department until December 5, 1941, inasmuch as the message was sent "deferred."

DISTRIBUTION:
WAR DEPT____ ACTION   FILES: CNO____ 20OP____ 20A____
RECORD COPY: _ 20C____ X SHOW OPDO_____
TOP SECRET   SECRET

EFFORTS TO MONITOR

The evidence is undisputed that both services extended themselves in an effort to intercept a message, in execution of the winds code, not only through their own monitoring stations but through facilities of the Federal Communications Commission as well. While only fragmentary evidence of a documentary nature is available to indicate the nature of instructions to monitor for an implementing or execute message, the Federal Communications Commission file is complete and, as indicated, there is no contention that every effort was not made to intercept an execute message.[9]

Considerations Bearing on the Possibility of a Message in Execution of the "Winds Code" Having Been Received Prior to December 7, 1941

1. Capt. L. F. Safford in a prepared statement (read before the joint committee)[10] has set forth a positive assertion that a winds execute message was received in the Navy Department *on the morning of December 4, 1941,* and has elaborated on the circumstances which serve, in his opinion, to indicate that a winds execute was dispatched and why such a message would have been dispatched from Tokyo.

Safford asserted that when he first saw the message it had already been translated by Kramer; that Kramer had underscored all three "code phrases" on the original incoming teletype sheet; and that he had written in pencil or colored crayon the free translation: "War with England (including NEI,[11] etc.); war with the U.S.; peace with Russia." Safford has persistently testified that an authentic implementing message was received.

2. Capt. A. D. Kramer testified before the committee that *on the morning of December 5* the GY Watch Officer, thought by him possibly to be Lieutenant Murray, came to the door of his office and showed him a message which he, Kramer, regarded as an implementation of the winds code; that he saw this message only briefly, relying on the evaluation of the GY watch officer as to the authenticity of the message; that he had no recollection of writing on the message but that had he written anything he positively would

---

[9] See committee record, pp. 9809, 9810.
[10] Id., at pp. 9622–9654.
[11] Netherlands East Indies.

not have used the word "war"; that he proceeded to Captain Safford's office with the GY watch officer when the message was delivered to Safford; that he never saw the message again.[12]

It should be noted that Kramer testified the message he saw was on a piece of teletype paper torn off from the machine and was not more than a line or two, possibly three lines; that in no case did the message contain some 200 words as alleged by Captain Safford in his statement.[13] Further, that the message he saw referred to only one country, which to the best of his belief was England.[14] This testimony must, of course, be considered along with Kramer's testimony before the Navy Court of Inquiry. When asked what Japanese language words were used in the execute message he saw, he replied:[15] "*Higashi No Kazeame*, I am quite certain. The literal meaning of *Higashi No Kazeame* is East Wind, Rain. That is plain Japanese language. The sense of that, however, meant strained relations or a break in relations, possibly even implying war with a nation to the eastward, the United States."

3. Admiral R. E. Ingersoll testified that during December of 1941 he was Assistant Chief of Naval Operations; that he saw "messages" which were supposed to implement the winds code, they being brought to his office; that he did not recall definitely whether he saw them prior to December 7 or thereafter; that an implementation of the code received prior to December 7, if genuine, would simply have confirmed what had already been dispatched to the Fleet regarding destruction of codes by the Japanese and would have required no action; that he thought the message he saw referred to all three countries; i. e. England, United States, and Russia.[16]

4. Col. Otis K. Sadtler, in charge of the military branch of the Army Signal Corps in December of 1941, testified that about 9 a.m. or shortly thereafter on Friday, December 5, Admiral Noyes telephoned him to the effect that the "message was in" (referring to an implementing winds message); that Noyes told him "it was the word that implied a break in relations between Japan and Great Britain"; that he went to General Miles' office, informing Miles that the "word was in"; that Miles sent for Colonel Bratton and when Bratton came in, he, Sadtler, told Bratton word had been received from Admiral Noyes to the effect that diplomatic relations between Japan and Great Britain were in danger; that Bratton asked him to verify receipt of the message; that he called Admiral Noyes again, asking him to verify the "Japanese word" and Noyes replied that he did not know any Japanese but it was the one that "meant Japan and Great Britain"; that upon reporting this information to General Miles' office he did not thereafter get in touch with Admiral Noyes concerning

---

[12] Committee record, pp. 10481 *et seq.*

[13] Id., at p. 10491.

[14] Id., at p. 10501.

[15] Navy court of inquiry (top secret) record, p. 957.

[16] Committee record, pp. 11278 *et seq.*

the message; that he never saw the message Noyes reported to him; and that insofar as he could ascertain it did "not come over", i. e. to his office or the Army.[17]

5. Col. Rufus S. Bratton, Chief of the Far Eastern Section of the Intelligence Branch of the Military Intelligence Division in December of 1941, testified that sometime around 9 or 10 a.m. on the morning of December 5 he was called to General Miles' office where Sadtler stated Noyes had just called to say "it is in" (the winds execute message); that Miles, at his suggestion, requested Sadtler to get from Noyes a copy either of the Japanese text or of the English translation so a determination could be made as to whether the message was a genuine execute or another false alarm; that he did not again see Sadtler concerning the matter; that he, Bratton, called up the Navy, talking to either Captain McCollum or Kramer to inquire if they had received a winds execute message and was advised that no such message had been received; that he contacted Army SIS[18] and was likewise advised that no execute had been received; that the Army continued to monitor for an implementing message up to and after the December 7 attack.[19]

6. Admiral Richmond K. Turner, Chief of War Plans in December of 1941, testified before the committee as follows:

> On Friday afternoon, I think it was, of December 5, Admiral Noyes called on the telephone or the interphone, I do not know which, and said "The weather message", or words to this effect, "the first weather message has come in" and I said, "What did it say?" And he said, "North wind clear." And I said, "Well, there is something wrong about that," and he said, "I think so, too", and he hung up.
>
> I never saw a draft of that, I do not know from my own knowledge where he got it from. I assumed until recently that it it was an authentic message. From what I can determine since coming back here it was something entirely different, but it was never told to me. If it had come in and had been authentic I am certain that I would have received a copy of it.

---

[17] Id., at pp. 12357–12363.
[18] Signal Intelligence Service.
[19] Committee record, pp. 12068–12077:
Colonel Bratton testified: "I can state most positively that no execute of the winds codes was ever received by me prior to the attack on Pearl Harbor. I find it hard to believe that any such execute message could get into the War Department without passing over my desk.
"It is inconceivable to me. I might have missed it but I had some assistants who were on the watch for it, and there were some people in the Army SIS who were also on the watch for it. They couldn't all have missed it. It is simply inconceivable to me that such a message could have been in the War Department without some one of us knowing about it or seeing it." Committee record, p. 12089

Turner testified that he did not see an implementation of the winds code applying to the United States.[20]

7. To complete the picture it would seem apropos to set forth the testimony of Rear Adm. Leigh Noyes at this point.

Noyes, in December of 1941, Director of Naval Communications, testified before the committee that prior to December 7, 1941, no genuine winds execute message was brought to him or to his attention by anyone in the Navy Department; that prior to the Pearl Harbor attack there were several instances when messages were brought to him which were first thought to be winds execute messages but were determined not to be genuine; that the message described by Captain Safford in his statement, if received, would not have been regarded as an authentic execute message since (1) it is alleged to have been in Morse code and not by voice (2) no provision was made for a negative expression in the winds code (3) an execute would not have been interpreted to mean war, and (4) Circular 2353 made no provision for N. E. I. as stated by Safford.

With respect to Colonel Sadtler's testimony that Noyes called him saying "The message is in," or words to that effect, Noyes stated he had no present recollection of having made such a statement although he would not say it did not occur inasmuch as he talked with the chief signal officer a number of times each day.[21]

Further, Noyes testified that he was directed to prepare a folder for the Roberts Commission but that it did not include a winds execute message and the folder in fact was supposed to contain no magic nor any reference to it; that the McCollum message,[22] to his knowledge, contained no reference to a winds execute message.[23]

---

[20] Committee record, p. 5214.

[21] In a statement submitted to the committee under date of February 25, 1946, in amplification of his testimony, Admiral Noyes said: "In reading over my testimony I noted that I failed to bring out the following point, which, however, is supported by my previous testimony and by documentary evidence.

"In connection with the alleged telephone conversation with me on 5 December to which Colonel Sadtler testified and which I did not recall in that form:

"On 5 December there was received from Colonel Thorpe in Batavia addressed to General Miles in the War Department. This message was transmitted by the *Naval Attaché* to *Navy Department* for delivery to General Miles. As I have already testified, the subject matter was under discussion between me and the War Department during that day. It is very probable that I would have called Colonel Sadtler and notified him of the fact that this message had been received and was being delivered to the War Department for General Miles on account of its importance. Since discussion took place between me and the War Department during that day on the subject matter of this message and the War Department recommended that we should make no change in our original translation of the set-up of the Winds Code (see previous testimony), it would appear that any possible authentic or false execute of the winds message would have also been discussed and settled during that day." Committee record, pp. 14101, 14102.

[22] See discussion, *infra*.

[23] Committee record, pp. 12605–12620.

8. The "Rochefort Message."

On December 5, 1941, a dispatch signed "Miles" was sent by the War Department to the assistant chief of staff headquarters G-2, Hawaiian Department, as follows:[24]

> Contact Commander Rochefort immediately thru Commandant Fourteen Naval District regarding broadcasts from Tokyo reference weather.

At first blush, the foregoing dispatch would suggest, inferentially at least, the possibility of an execute message having been received. Colonel Bratton, upon whose recommendation the dispatch was sent, testified, however:[25]

> I had a discussion with Commander McCollum, now Captain McCollum, as to the amount of knowledge that the Navy had in Hawaii. He assured me his man Rochefort there at that time knew practically everything that there was to be known about the U.S.-Japanese relations through one means or another. I knew that suitable warning messages had been sent out to Hawaii and elsewhere. I had not read the messages and did not know their exact contents. I wanted to make sure that our G–2 in Hawaii got in touch with the ONI man in Hawaii, to get from him all the intelligence that he had in his possession, and I knew that if they got together on the subject of this winds message—I did not know, but I felt that they were going from there, and that there would be a complete exchange of intelligence and that the Army G–2 would then be in possession of just as much intelligence as Rochefort, the ONI man, had.

Colonel Bratton's testimony is to the effect that the dispatch of the message to G–2 to contact Rochefort had nothing whatever to do with receipt of a message in execution of the winds code. In this regard Captain McCollum stated:[26]

> I understood that G–2 was very anxious for their G–2 in Hawaii to have direct access with Commander Rochefort, who had the only agency capable of intercepting the winds message in Hawaii, sir. The Army, as I understand it, had no parallel set-up in Hawaii at that time.

[24] Committee exhibit No. 32, p. 20.
[25] Committee record, p. 12120, 12121.
[26] Id., at pp. 9271, 9272.

Considerations Militating Against Likelihood of "Winds Code" Execute Message Having Been Received Prior to December 7, 1941

1. Examination of Circular 2353 (to which Captain Safford admits the alleged winds execute was responsive) reflects that an execute warning would be added in the middle and at the end of the daily Japanese language short wave news broadcast "in case of emergency (danger of cutting off our diplomatic relations), and *the cutting off of international communications.*" When the execute was heard "all code papers, etc." were to be destoyed.

A reasonable construction of this circular would indicate that the winds code was an emergency arrangement designed to be employed in the event ordinary commercial means of international communications were no longer available to the Japanese Government. Contemplating that such commercial means conceivably might not be available to her, it would appear natural that Japan should devise a means such as the winds code to direct her diplomatic establishments to destroy their codes and secret papers. Manifestly and quite naturally the winds code should provide for destruction of *all* code papers inasmuch as the necessity for having any codes whatever of the type outstanding would be precluded by the cutting-off of international communications.

Ordinary commercial means of communications were available to Japan up to the December 7 attack on Pearl Harbor and in fact committee exhibit 1 is replete wih instructions to Japanese diplomatic establishments with respect to destruction of codes.[27] Accordingly, it can fairly be concluded that recourse to the emergency system provided by the winds code was not necessitated and in consequence was not resorted to prior to December 7 inasmuch as the contingency contemplating its use (cutting off of international communications) did not materialize prior to the Pearl Harbor attack.

2. It is admitted and of course definitely known that a winds execute message (*Nishi No Kaze Hare*—west wind, clear) applying to England was transmitted from Tokyo stations JLG4 and JZJ between 0002 and 0035 GMT, December 8, 1941.[28] Such a message was of course reasonable inasmuch as Japan could very well contemplate that ordinary commercial means of communications would no longer be available after the Pearl Harbor attack.

Inasmuch as a genuine winds execute message applying to England was transmitted after the Pearl Harbor attack, it would appear anomalous that such a message should also have been sent prior to December 7.[29]

---

[27] See sections relating to destruction of codes, pts. III and IV, this report.
[28] See committee exhibit No. 142.
[29] Admiral Noyes suggested that Japan's sending an execute on December 7 was probably occasioned by reason of the fact that some Japanese diplomatic establishment had failed to

3. The investigation conducted in Japan by headquarters of the supreme allied commander reflected that a signal implementing Circulars 2353 and 2354 was probably not transmitted prior to December 8, Tokyo time, but was transmitted by radio voice broadcast at some hour after 0230, December 8, Tokyo time.[30] No evidence could be obtained that an implementing signal was transmitted by radio telegraph. Significantly, those who conducted the interrogation in Japan had no knowledge prior to the interrogation that the United States had information that the winds code was used on December 8, Tokyo time.[31]

Mr. Shinroku Tanomogi was head of the overseas department of the Japan Radio Broadcasting Corporation in December 1941, and as such was in charge of programs, including news programs, beamed to foreign countries. Upon interview he stated he had no recollection at all of any "east wind rain" report or any similar phrase being broadcast prior to December 8.[32]

4. Inquiry made through the State Department reflects that no winds execute message was intercepted prior to the Pearl Harbor attack by the British, Dutch, or Australians.[33]

5. In his statement submitted for the committee's consideration, Captain Safford definitely states that the alleged implementing winds message was part of a Japanese overseas "news" broadcast from station JAP (Tokyo) on 11980 kilocycles beginning at 1330 Greenwich civil time on Thursday, December 4, 1941, this time corresponding to 10:30 p.m., Tokyo time, and 8:30 a.m., Washington time, December 4, 1941; that the winds message broadcast was forwarded by teletype from Cheltenham to the Navy Department shortly before 9 a.m. on December 4, 1941. Further, that when he first saw the message it had already been translated by Kramer; that Kramer had underscored all three "code phrases" on the original incoming teletype sheet; and that he had written in pencil or colored crayon the following free translations:

War with England (including NEI, etc.)
War with the U.S.
Peace with Russia.

Kramer has testified that had he seen such a message, as alleged by Safford, he would in no case have interpreted a winds execute to mean war.[34]

---

respond to instructions to destroy their codes which had been dispatched through ordinary channels of communication.
[30] December 7, Washington time.
[31] See committee exhibit No. 142.
[32] Id., sec. 4B.
[33] Committee exhibit No. 142, secs. 4c, 4d, 4e. See also committee record, p. 11564.
[34] See Navy Court of Inquiry (top secret) record, pp. 968, 969, 975, 987; committee record, p. 10492.

In this regard, the Thorpe and Foote messages, which interpreted the winds code as meaning war, were not available to the Navy Department until after the time Safford alleges the winds execute came in and was interpreted by Kramer to mean war. The Thorpe dispatch, while intended for General Miles of the War Department, was sent by Naval Communications and was received at the Navy Department at 1:21 a.m., December 4, 1941.[35] It was not decoded until 1:45 a.m., December 5, 1941, the delay being occasioned by the fact that the dispatch was sent "deferred," the lowest priority in handling. [36] The Foote dispatch, it is to be noted, was not received in the State Department until 9:19 a.m., December 4. Consequently, as indicated, no information was available in the Navy Department on the morning of December 4 as alleged by Safford serving as basis for interpreting a winds execute message to mean war. Even conceding the availability of the Thorpe and Foote dispatches, it would scarcely appear likely that the Navy Department would disregard its own translation of the winds code and be guided solely by the dispatches from outside sources.

6. The winds execute message Safford alleges he saw on the morning of December 4, bore the "negative form for war with Russia" and mixed up the plain language broadcast with the Morse broadcast.[37] It is thus clear that the alleged winds execute of December 4 was not responsive to the establishing winds code.

Captain Kramer, it should be noted, testified before the joint committee that had the "negative form" been employed with respect to Russia, he would have regarded such fact as nullifying any credence to be placed in a broadcast purporting to be a winds execute message. It would appear agreed that the implementation of an establishing code must conform in meticulous detail to the code as originally established.

7. Referring to Captain Safford's statement, the following matters appear to be subject to serious question:

> **A.** Safford relies on Cincaf 281430[38] as basis for evaluation of a winds execute message to mean war, pointing out that this dispatch contained the statement "Nishi nishi England *including occupation of Thai or Invasion of Malay and N. E. I.*"
>
> It should be noted, however, that Cincaf 281430 indicates the winds code would be employed "if diplomatic relations are on verge of being severed." In any event the interpretation of Cincaf 281430 as relied upon by Safford while possibly indicating war with England does not by any reasonable construction indicate war with the United States.[38a]

---

[35] Committee record, p. 10135.
[36] Id., at pp. 11255, 11256.
[37] That is, Circular 2353 with Circular 2354.
[38] Set forth; supra.
[38a] See committee record, p. 9670.

B. Safford's reliance in his statement on Cincaf 281430 as providing basis for evaluating a winds execute as meaning war is in contradiction of his testimony before the Navy Court of Inquiry where reliance was placed on the Thorpe and Foote dispatches.[39]

While denied by Safford, the suggestion was made by counsel before the committee that Safford may have shifted reliance on the Thorpe and Foote dispatches to Cincaf 281430 by reason of the fact that he had learned that both the Thorpe and Foote dispatches were not available to the Navy Department until after the morning of December 4.[40]

C. Safford seeks to bring out that the alleged winds execute was intended for the Japanese London Embassy inasmuch as the latter had destroyed its codes 3 days previously and a winds message was the only way that Tokyo could get news to its London Ambassador secretly.[41]

This statement is not true insofar as it implies that no other means of communication between Tokyo and London was available. By Circular 2409 of November 27, 1941,[42] the Japanese established the "hidden word" code and by Circular 2461[43] instructed that this code be kept until the last moment. This code system of communication was clearly available to the Japanese in communicating with their London Ambassador and was in fact employed on December 7 in Circular 2494.[44] Safford admitted in his testimony before the joint committee the availability in the London Embassy of the hidden word code.

Furthermore, in Circular 2443, dated December 1,[45] to London instructions were issued to discontinue use of the code machine and to dispose of it immediately. Ostensibly other code systems were still available after destruction of the code machine and it is known that coded traffic in the system referred to as PA-K2 passed from the Japanese London Embassy to Tokyo December 6, 1941.[46]

D. By way of lending credence to his assertion that a winds execute was received, Safford has testified that McCollum's dispatch of December 4 (not sent) was predicated on such a winds execute and mentioned the execute in the last portion.[47]

McCollum definitely contradicted this in testifying before the committee, asserting that his dispatch was based on a memorandum he,

---

[39] Navy Court of Inquiry (top secret) record, p. 748; see also committee record, p. 9667.
[40] Committee record, pp. 9667, 9668.
[41] Id., at p. 9639.
[42] Committee exhibit No. 1, p. 186
[43] Id., at p. 226.
[44] Id., at p. 251.
[45] Id., at p. 209.
[46] Committee record, p. 9740.
[47] See pt. IV, this report, for discussion of so-called McCollum dispatch.

McCollum, had prepared under date of December 1[48] and bore no relationship to a winds execute message; that he neither saw nor received knowledge of a true winds execute prior to December 7.[49]

E. In further substantiation of his allegation that a winds execute was received on the morning of December 4, Safford has referred to the fact that the dispatches from OpNav to our own establishments to destroy their codes was based on a winds execute.

This assertion is diametrically contrary to testimony of Noyes[50] and Kramer[51] who declared that OpNav instructions to our establishments to destroy their codes was based on instructions sent out by the Japanese[52] to their diplomatic establishments to destroy codes, and bore no relationship to a winds execute. The testimony of McCollum and Ingersoll tends to confirm the foregoing.

F. Safford points out that the individual smooth translations of the alleged winds execute for authorized Navy Department officials and the White House were distributed at noon on December 4, 1941, in accordance with standard operating procedure.[53]

Kramer, in testifying before the joint committee, categorically denied that any copies of a winds execute message were prepared for distribution by his section, it being noted that it was the responsibility of Kramer to prepare and distribute the smooth translations.[54]

G. Captain Safford has pointed out that a winds execute was dispatched in Morse code. Captain Rochefort, who was in charge of the Communications Intelligence Unit at Pearl Harbor in December of 1941, testified that all of the broadcast schedules giving the various frequencies furnished by Washington were all voice frequencies; that to him the very setting up of the winds code implied "voice"; that if an execute message were sent in Morse code it would have meant that every Japanese Embassy (and consulate) in every Japanese location throughout the world for whom the message was intended by the Japanese Government would "have had to maintain Morse code operators, people capable of receiving Morse code. I do not think so."[55]

Rochefort further testified that they were monitoring for a winds execute message at Honolulu and continued to do so until after the attack; that four of his best language officers were on a 24-hour watch

---

[48] Committee exhibit No. 81.
[49] Committee record, pp. 9124–9134.
[50] Id., at p. 12623.
[51] Id., at p. 10504.
[52] Committee exhibit No. 1.
[53] Committee record, pp. 9763 et seq.
[54] Committee record, p. 10496.
[55] Id., at p. 12548.

for an execute; that no winds implementing message was intercepted.[56]

H. Admiral Noyes testified that he would not have regarded the message which Safford alleges was received as an authentic execute message inasmuch as (1) Morse code was allegedly used and in consequence not responsive to Circular 2353; (2) no provision was made in the winds code for a "negative form" with respect to Russia; (3) an execute message would not have been interpreted to mean war; and (4) no reference is made in Circular 2353 to N. E. I., although the alleged execute was responsive to Circular 2353 and Safford indicates reference was made to N. E. I.[57]

8. Safford, in testifying before the joint committee, placed emphasis on the fact that the winds code provided for destruction of *all* codes (Circular 2353) and by reason thereof a winds execute message would have more significance than the itercepts contained in committee exhibit 1 which gave instructions with respect to destruction of particular codes.[58]

If a winds execute message was dispatched for the Japanese London Embassy on December 4, as alleged by Safford, it would necessarily mean that *all* codes were to be destroyed by Japan's London Ambassador. It is definitely known, as earlier indicated, that London sent a dispatch to Tokyo in the system known as PA-K2 on December 6, 1941. Such fact would indicate strongly that no winds execute was dispatched on December 4 with consequent destruction of *all* codes.[59]

9. It appears clear that both the Navy and Army were still looking for a

---

[56] Id., at pp. 12532–12534.

[57] Id., at pp. 12614, 12615.

[58] When asked what there was in the winds execute message alleged by him to have been received which indicated *war*, Captain Safford testified: "For one thing there is instruction to destroy all code papers. If that is regarded as synonymous with the outbreak of war, as I have heard testified in this room, that by itself means something more than the wording of these three paragraphs above * * *. Tokyo had sent out instructions to various people telling them to burn their most important codes but to leave two codes open. One was the so-called PA–K2 code and the other was the LA code. Now, with those two exceptions all codes had been burnt, but this said, '*Please destroy all code papers,*' and so forth. In other words, there was no exceptions in this one." Committee record, p. 9778.

In marked contradiction of the foregoing testimony is the explanation of Captain Safford as to the reason for Japan's London Embassy having the PA–K2 code system after the alleged winds execute message was received. He stated: "There were two systems that were exempt from destruction. One was PA–K2, and the other was LA, neither of which were considered by ourselves as secret, and we presumed the Japanese did not consider them secret." Committee record, p. 9741.

It is to be noted, however, that the Honolulu consulate, as well as Tokyo, used the PA–K2 system for some of the most vital messages shortly before December 7 (see committee exhibit No. 2). While this was virtually the only system left after the messages ordering the destruction of various codes, the PA–K2 system was employed for the sending of messages which would probably have tipped off the attack on Pearl Harbor, had it not been for the fact they were not translated until after the attack.

[59] Committee record, p. 9740.

winds execute message after the morning of December 4, based on records of the Federal Communications Commission.[60]

In this connection at 7:50 p.m. on December 5, 1941, the watch officer of FCC phoned Colonel Bratton of the Army with respect to a false winds message received from the FCC Portland monitoring station. The FCC watch officer submitted the following memorandum for his superior with respect to Bratton's remarks:

> Remarks by Col. Bratton:
> Results still negative but am pleased to receive the negative results as it means we have that much more time. The information desired will occur in the middle of a program and possibly will be repeated at frequent intervals. (Asked Col. Bratton if I should communicate the information to Portland—concerning the fact that the desired data will be in the middle of a program.) No, I will have a conference with Lt. Col. Dusenberg in the morning and will contact Mr. Sterling in that regard.

The foregoing would indicate that the Army had received no genuine winds execute message by 7:50 p.m., December 5.

The FCC night watch log for December 4, 1941,[61] contains the notation that at 9:32 p.m. "Lt. Brotherhood called to inquire if any other reference to weather was made previously in program intercepted by Portland. Informed him that no other reference was made." There is manifested here an interest by the Navy in the nature of a winds message on the evening of December 4 which is hardly likely if a true execute was received on the morning of December 4.

Further, it would appear logical that had a true winds execute been received on the morning of December 4 the FCC would have been requested to discontinue its monitoring activities. This, however, was not done and the FCC was still monitoring for a winds execute and actually intercepted such an execute (with respect to England) after the Pearl Harbor attack.[62]

10. Collateral considerations tending to minimize likelihood that implementing winds message was dispatched from Tokyo.

A. Referring to the message telephoned by the FCC to Brotherhood at 9:05 p.m. on December 4,[63] Safford testified before Admiral Hewitt[64] that this was the "false" message which appeared on this surface to use the "winds" code relating to Russia but which was a genuine weather

---

[60] Committee exhibit No. 142–A.
[61] Id.
[62] See also testimony of Colonel Bratton, committee record, p. 12074.
[63] Committee exhibit No. 142, sec. 3.
[64] Hewitt inquiry record, p. 113.

broadcast. This message, Safford said, Brotherhood telephoned to Admiral Noyes and later *Kramer took one look at it and said it was not what was wanted and threw it into the waste basket.* He testified that this message was received * * * 12 hours or more after what he referred to as the "true winds message."

Query: Why would Kramer be "wanting" a winds execute message 12 hours after Safford alleges Kramer had an execute message and had noted thereon "War with England, War with U.S., peace with Russia"?

B. In testifying before the committee, Justice Roberts stated he had no knowledge of the winds matter and no access to Magic. This would appear to be partially at least in contradiction of Safford's testimony that he last saw the winds execute among material assembled for the Roberts Commission.

Further, Admiral Noyes testified that he was directed to prepare a folder for the Roberts Commission, but it did not include a winds execute message and the folder was in fact supposed to contain no magic nor any reference to it.[65]

C. Safford's detailed recollection of the winds matter, as set forth in his statement, is in sharp conflict with his indefinite and somewhat nebulous memory as reflected by his testimony and the letters directed to Kramer during December 1943, and January 1944.

It should be noted in this connection that Safford testified before Admiral Hart[66] that the winds implementing message came in on the evening of December 3 and Kramer went down to get it. From all of the testimony it appears that Safford's position before the committee was assumed after a process of elimination of possibilities and reconstruction of a situation concerning which he had only a partially independent recollection.

D. Considering the tight reign maintained by the military in Japan and particularly the desire to clothe the movement against Pearl Harbor with utmost secrecy, it would seem highly improbable that the Japanese would tip off her war decision in a news broadcast by advising her London Ambassador of such decision 3 days before Pearl Harbor.

E. If a true winds execute was received and distributed on December 4 it would appear reasonable to assume that some record of the message could be found in the War or Navy Departments. Yet despite repeated searches there is no record whatever in either department of such a message. In this connection Safford has suggested that intercept No. JD–7001, marked "cancelled" in the Navy file of intercepts, may have been the missing winds execute. Such a premise, of course, presupposes a

---

[65] Committee record, p. 12620.
[66] Hart inquiry record, p. 361.

deliberate abstraction by someone of an official record from the Navy Department.

In evaluation of Safford's suggestion with respect to No. JD–7001, it should be noted that the file of JD intercepts was maintained by Kramer who has emphatically testified that no winds execute came into his section or was distributed by him. Further, Kramer has pointed out that there are several examples of canceled JD numbers in the file[67] and presented several reasons in testifying before the committee why a JD number might be canceled.

Significantly, a check of the Army file of intercepts for the period December 3–5, 1941, reflected that the Navy file contains all intercepts that are in the Army file.[68]

Conceding for purposes of discussion that a winds execute message was received in the form alleged by Safford, it will be noted that such message would not indicate *where* or *when* Japan would strike but merely her possible purpose to go to war. Bearing in mind the rather frank admission by Army and Navy officials that they knew war was imminent in the days before December 7, credence could scarcely be placed in the theory that the message was deliberately destroyed when it contained no information that was not admittedly already possessed.

Admiral Ingersoll, for example, testified before the committee that had a true winds execute message been received it would have been regarded as merely confirmatory of the implications contained in Japanese instructions to destroy codes contained in committee exhibit 1, inasmuch as instructions to destroy codes, particularly in the consulates, meant war. The testimony of several other witnesses, including Admiral Noyes and Colonel Bratton, is to the same effect.

11. The testimony of Col. Robert E. Schukraft, assigned to the office of the chief signal officer at the time of the Pearl Harbor attack, before the committee on February 19, 1946, is of particular pertinence to the testimony of Captain Kramer, set forth under section 3, *supra*. Schukraft testified that 2 or 3 days prior to Pearl Harbor Col. Rex Minckler brought to Schukraft's office a piece of yellow teletype paper (the carbon copy) which contained what appeared to be a winds execute message but that the message upon examination was obviously not a true winds execute. Further, Schukraft testified Colonel Minckler had indicated that the Navy had thought the message a true winds execute, Captain Kramer having seen the message and so thinking. He stated that he concluded very positively that the message was not a true execute of the Winds Code.[69]

---

[67] This appears to be borne out by the record. See committee exhibit No. 142, sec. 6.
[68] See Army liaison memorandum dated January 26, 1946. Committee record, pp. 8965, 8966.
[69] Committee record, pp. 13093–13096.

12. The following officers have stated they have no knowledge of a message in execution of the Winds code prior to December 7, 1941:

Navy

Admiral Harold R. Stark, Chief of Naval Operations.[70]
Admiral Leigh Noyes, Director of Naval Communications.[71]
Admiral T. S. Wilkinson, Director of Naval Intelligence.[72]

Capt. Arthur N. McCollum, in charge, Far Eastern Section of Naval Intelligence.[73]

Admiral Joseph R. Redman, Assistant Director of Naval Communications.[74]

Lt. Comdr. George W. Linn, GY watch officer.[75]
Lt. Comdr. Alfred V. Pering, GY watch officer.[76]
Lt. Comdr. Allan A. Murray, GY watch officer.[77]

Lt. Frederick L. Freeman, assigned to section disseminating to ONI intelligence received from radio intelligence units.[78]

Capt. Redfield Mason, fleet intelligence officer, Asiatic Fleet.[79]
Commander Rudolph J. Fabian, Radio Intelligence Unit at Corregidor.[80]
Capt. Edwin T. Layton, Pacific Fleet intelligence officer.[81]

Capt. Joseph John Rochefort, in charge, Communications Intelligence Unit, Pearl Harbor.[82]

Army

Gen. George C. Marshall, Chief of Staff.[83]
Maj. Gen. Leonard T. Gerow, Chief of War Plans.[84]

---

[70] See Navy Court of Inquiry record, pp. 783, 872. Confirmed in testimony before the committee.
[71] Committee record, pp. 12605–12620.
[72] Hewitt inquiry record, pp. 398–401.
[73] Committee record, pp. 9124–9134.
[74] Navy Court of Inquiry record, p. 1103.
[75] Hewitt inquiry record, pp. 140–42.
[76] Id., at p. 148.
[77] Id., at pp. 433–441.
[78] Id., at pp. 149, 150.
[79] Id., at pp. 73, 78.
[80] Id., at pp. 73, 78.
[81] Id., at pp. 269–271.
[82] Id., at pp. 46, 48.
[83] See Army Pearl Harbor Board (Top Secret) record, pp. 35–39. Confirmed in testimony before the committee.
[84] Committee record, p. 4302.

Maj. Gen. Sherman Miles, Chief of G–2.[85]

Col. Rufus W. Bratton, Chief, Far Eastern Section of G–2.[86]

Col. Robert E. Schukraft, Chief, Radio Interception for SIS.[87]

Col. Rex W. Minckler, Chief, SIS.[88]

Brig. Gen. Thomas J. Betts, executive assistant to the Chief of Intelligence Branch MID.[89]

Lt. Col. Frank B. Rowlett, prior to Pearl Harbor attack a civilian technical assistant to the officer of the Cryptoanalytic unit, SIS.[90]

William F. Friedman, a cryptanalyst of War Department.[91]

Over-all observations with respect to Captain Safford's testimony:

13. As previously indicated Captain Safford has rather consistently testified that a true winds execute message was received prior to December 7. However, there are certain discrepancies in his testimony tending to show particularly that his recollection of the incident attending receipt of such an execute has not been definite and has been developed through a process of elimination.

A. The following testimony, in relation to a winds execute, of Captain Safford before Admiral Hewitt reflects rather clearly his indefinite recollection of the winds matter and his efforts to reconstruct a "vague memory":[92]

> Captain SAFFORD. In the fall of 1943 it appeared that there was going to be a trial or court martial of Admiral Kimmel. It was hinted in the newspapers and various people in the Navy Department were getting testimony ready for it. I realized I would be one of the important witnesses, that my memory was very vague, and I began looking around to get everything that I could to prepare a written statement which I could follow as testimony. That was the time when I studied the Robert's Report carefully for the first time and noted no reference to the winds message or to the message which McCollum had written and which I had seen and I thought had been sent. And then I began talking to everybody who had been around at the time and who I knew had been mixed up in it to see what they could remember to straighten me out on the thing and give me leads to follow down to where I could put my hands on official messages and things so that it would be a matter of fact

---

[85] See Clausen investigation record, pp. 214, 215. Confirmed in testimony before the committee.

[86] Committee record, pp. 12068–12077.

[87] Id., at pp. 13093–13096.

[88] Clausen investigation record, p. 217.

[89] Id., at p. 194.

[90] Id., at pp. 225, 226.

[91] Hewitt inquiry record, pp. 515–520.

[92] Id., at pp. 112, 113.

and not a matter of memory. I also talked the thing over with whatever Army people were still around at the time and had anything in this thing, and bit by bit these facts appeared to come together. The investigation was conducted, if you call it that, for the purpose of preparing myself to take the stand as a witness in a prospective court martial of Admiral Kimmel.

B. The letters directed to Captain Kramer by Safford and incorporated in the committee transcript also indicate an indefinite recollection of events prior to the attack on Pearl Harbor.[93]

C. In testifying before Admiral Hart, Safford stated:[94]

> The "Winds Message" was actually broadcast during the evening of December 3, 1941 (Washington time), which was December 4 by Greenwich time and Tokyo time. The combination of frequency, time of day, and radio propagation was such that the "Winds Message" was heard only on the East Coast of the United States, and even then by only one or two of the Navy stations that were listening for it. The other nations and other Navy C. I. Units, not hearing the "Winds Message" themselves and not receivng any word from the Navy Department, naturally presumed that the "Winds Message" had not yet been sent, and that the Japanese Government was still deferring the initiation of hostilities. When the Japanese attacked Pearl Harbor, the British at Singapore, the Dutch at Java, and the Americans at Manila were just as surprised and astonished as the Pacific Fleet and Army posts in Hawaii. It is apparent that the War Department, like the Navy Department failed to send out information that the "Winds Message" had been sent by Tokyo. The "Winds Message" was received in the Navy Department during the evening of December 3, 1941, while Lieutenant (j. g.) Francis M. Brotherhood, U. S. N. R., was on watch. There was some question in Brotherhood's mind as to what this message really meant because it came in a different form from what had been anticipated. Brotherhood called in Lieutenant Commander Kramer, who came down that evening and identified that message as the "Winds Message" we had been looking for.

Yet in his statement and in testifying before the committee Safford has the message coming in on the morning of December 4, 1941, it being brought to him by Lt. A. A. Murray.

[93] See testimony of Captains Kramer and Safford before the committee.
[94] Hart inquiry record, p. 361.

D. In testifying before the Navy Court of Inquiry Safford said:[95]

22. Q. Captain, in a previous answer you stated that the copy of the intercept using the winds code which you saw on the morning of 4 December 1941 indicated a break in diplomatic relations between the United States and Japan and Japan and Great Britain, and war between these nations. Was there anything in the establishment of the code originally which would indicate that a use of that code would indicate war as contrasted with a mere break in diplomatic relations?

A. The Dutch translation said "war." The Japanese language is very vague and you can put a number of constructions or interpretations or translations on the same message. In very important documents it was customary for the Army and Navy to make independent translations and the differences were sometimes surprising; that is, a difference in degree. The general facts would be alike. However, the people in Communication Intelligence and the people in Signal Intelligence Service and the people in the Far Eastern Section of Naval Intelligence, as well as the Director of Naval Intelligence, considered that meant war and it was a signal of execute for the Japanse war plans.

23. Q. Captain, I call your attention again to Document 3 in Exhibit 64 which is an English-language translation of the Dutch intercept. Was this your only source of information that the use of this code would indicate "a war decision" which is the wording used by the attaché in Batavia?

A. Mr. Foote's message to the State Department was even more specific. It said, "When crises leading to worst arises following will be broadcast at end of weather reports. 1. *East wind rain*—war with United States. 2. *North wind cloudy*—war with Russia. 3. *West wind clear*—war with Britain, including an attack on Thailand or Malaya and Dutch East Indies." This was apparently a verbatim quotation from the Dutch translation.

Significantly, in testifying before the committee Safford relies on Cincaf 281430 as the dispatch serving as basis for interpreting a winds execute message to mean war. It has now been conclusively shown that neither the Foote nor Thorpe dispatches were available in the Navy Department at the time Safford alleges an execute was received and interpreted to mean war; i. e. the morning of December 4, 1941.[96]

E. The testimony of Captain Safford taken in its entirety reflects substantial discrepancies as to where the alleged execute message was received. It was only at the time of submitting his statement to the committee that Safford stated definitely the message came in at the Navy's Cheltenham station.

---

[95] Navy Court of Inquiry record, p. 748.
[96] See in this connection, committee record, pp. 9667, 9668.

14. Because of substantial discrepancies in testimony given in prior proceedings with respect to the question of whether a winds execute message was received in the War or Navy Department, the inquiry conducted by Admiral Hewitt went fully into the matter, among others, of determining if such a message was intercepted prior to December 7, 1941. Admiral Hewitt found:[97]

> The interception of a "winds" message relating to the United States during the first week of December 1941, would not have conveyed any information of significance which the Chief of Naval Operations and the commander in chief, Pacific Fleet, did not already have.
> No message in the "winds" code relating to the United States was received by any of the watch officers in the Navy Department to whom such a message would have come had it been received in the Navy Department. No such message was intercepted by the radio intelligence units at Pearl Harbor or in the Philippines, although intensive efforts were made by those organizations to intercept such a message. The evidence indicates further that no such message was intercepted by the British or the Dutch, despite their efforts to intercept such a message. Neither the Fleet Intelligence Officer of the Asiatic Fleet nor the Fleet Intelligence Officer of the Pacific Fleet nor the Intelligence Officer of the Far Eastern Section of the Office of Naval Intelligence, recalled any such message. The Chief of Naval Operations; the Director of Naval Communications, and the Director of Naval Intelligence recalled no such message. Testimony to the effect that a "winds" code message was received prior to the attack was given by Captain Safford, in charge of Op–20–G, a communications security section at the Navy Department, who stated that such a message was received on December 3rd or 4th, that it related to the United States, and that no copy could be found in the Navy or Army files. In his testimony before Admiral Hart, Captain Safford named, in addition to himself, three other officers who, he stated, recalled having seen and read the "winds" message. Each of those officers testified that he had never seen such a message. The only other testimony to the effect that a "winds" message was received was by Captain Kramer, an intelligence officer assigned to Op–20–G, who said that he recalled that there was a message but that he could not recall whether or not it related to the United States or England or Russia. It may be noted that until he testified in this investigation, Captain Kramer erroneously thought that a "hidden

[97] For Hewitt Inquiry report, see committee exhibit No. 157.

word'' message intercepted on the morning of December 7th had been a ''winds'' message.

CONCLUSION: From consideration of all evidence relating to the winds code, it is concluded that no genuine message, in execution of the code and applying to the United States, was received in the War or Navy Department prior to December 7, 1941. It appears, however, that messages were received which were initially thought possibly to be in execution of the code but were determined not to be execute messages. In view of the preponderate weight of evidence to the contrary, it is believed that Captain Safford is honestly mistaken when he insists that an execute message was received prior to December 7, 1941. Considering the period of time that has elapsed, this mistaken impression is understandable.

Granting for purposes of discussion that a genuine execute message applying to the winds code was intercepted before December 7, it is concluded that such fact would have added nothing to what was already known concerning the critical character of our relations with the Empire of Japan.

‖ INDEX